The Mammoth Book of
EYEWITNESS
ANCIENT EGYPT

The Mammoth Book of
EYEWITNESS
ANCIENT EGYPT

Edited by

JON E. LEWIS

CARROLL & GRAF PUBLISHERS
New York

Carroll and Graf Publishers
An imprint of Avalon Publishing Group, Inc.
245W. 17th Street
NY 10011
www.carrollandgraf.com

First published in the UK by Robinson,
an imprint of Constable & Robinson Ltd 2003

First Carroll & Graf edition 2003

Reprinted 2004

ISBN 0-7867-1270-8

Printed and bound in the EU

For Penny, the other sort of Mummy. And Tris and Freda.

CONTENTS

Part Three: Empire
The Second Intermediate Period and
the New Kingdom, Egypt 1782–1070 BC   91

Part Four: Decline
The Third Intermediate Period, the Late Period
and the Ptolemaic Period, Egypt 1069–30 BC   271

CHRONOLOGY

Early dates are approximate. Aside from the lack of physical evidence, absolute dates also have to be calculated by complicated reference to the 1460 year astronomical cycle of Sothis (the dog star), the basis of the Egyptian calendar. Only from 664 BC and the beginning of the 26th Dynasty is Egyptian chronology truly accurate.

DATE	DYNASTY/ RULER	POLITICS, WAR	RELIGION, SOCIAL LIFE, ART
c. 3150 BC	Dynasty "0"		
	Scorpion		
3100	Narmer	Unification of Egypt	
3050	Dynasty 1		Introduction of 365-day calendar
	Hor-Aha	Foundation of Memphis	
	Djer		
	Djet		
	Den		
	Anedjib		
	Semerket		
	Qa'a		
2890	Dynasty 2		
	Hotepsekhemy		
	Raneb		
	Nynetjer		
	Seth-Peribsen		
	Khasekhemwy		

DATE	DYNASTY/ RULER	POLITICS, WAR	RELIGION, SOCIAL LIFE, ART
2686	*Dynasty 3* Sanakhte 2686–2668		
	Djoser		Building of the Step Pyramid of Saqqara
	2668–2649 Sekhemkhet 2649–2643 Khaba 2643–2637 Huni 2637–		
2613	*Dynasty 4* Snefru –2589		
	Kufu/Cheops		Building of the Great Pyramid, Giza
	2589–2566 Djedefre 2566–2558		
	Khafre 2558–2532		Building of the Great Sphinx
	Menkaure 2532–2504 Shepseskaf 2504–2500		
2498	*Dynasty 5*		First libraries, first use of papyrus; first mummifications
	Userkaf –2345 Sahure 2491–2477 Neferirkare 2477–2467 Shepseskare 2467–2460 Neferefre 2460–2453		

DATE	DYNASTY/ RULER	POLITICS, WAR	RELIGION, SOCIAL LIFE, ART
	Niuserre 2453–2422		
	Menkauhor 2422–2414		
	Djedkare 2414–2375		
	Unas 2375–		
2345	*Dynasty 6* Teti –2333		
	Pepi I 2332–2283		
	Merenre 2283–2278		
	Pepi II 2278–2184		
	Merenre II [?] 2184–		
2181	*Dynasties 7 & 8*	Rival dynasties at Herakleopolis and Thebes	
	Wadjkare Qakare Iby		
2610	*Dynasties 9 & 10* Meryibre Khety		
	Merykare		
	Kaneferre		
	Nebkaure Akhtoy		
2134	Dynasty 11 Intef I –2117		
	Intef II 2117–2069		
	Intef III 2069–2060		
	Mentuhotep I 2060–2010	Reunification of Egypt	
	Mentuhotep II 2010–1998		

DATE	DYNASTY/ RULER	POLITICS, WAR	RELIGION, SOCIAL LIFE, ART
	Mentuhotep III 1997–		
1991	Dynasty 12		Egyptians use 24-sign alphabet; "Book of the Dead";
	Amenemhet I –1961		"Story of Sinuhe"; contraceptives in use
	Senusret I 1971–1926		
	Amenemhet II 1929–1895		
	Senusret II 1897–1878		
	Senusret III 1878–1841		
	Amenemhet III 1842–1797		
	Amenemhet IV/ Queen Sebeknefru 1797–		
1782	Dynasty 13		
	Wegaf –1778		
	Ameny Intef IV [?]–1760		
	Hor 1760		
	Sobekhotep II 1750		
	Khendjer 1747		
	Sobekhotep III 1745		
	Neferhotep I 1741–1730		
	Sobekhotep IV 1730–1720		

DATE	DYNASTY/ RULER	POLITICS, WAR	RELIGION, SOCIAL LIFE, ART
	Ay		
1720	Neferhotep II	Hyskos sack Memphis	
	Dynasty 14		
	Nehesy		
1663	*Dynasty 15*	Hyskos rule in N./Thebans in S.	
	(Hyskos)		
	Sheshi		
	Yakubher		
	Khyan		
	Apepi I		
	Dynasty 16		
	(Hyskos vassals)		
	Anather		
	Yakobaam		
	Dynasty 17		
	(Theban)		
	Sobekemsaf I		
	Sobekemsaf II		
	Intef VII		
	Tao I		
	Apepi II		
	Tao II		
	Kamose		
1570	*Dynasty 18*		
	Ahmose −1546	Expulsion of Hyskos from Egypt	
	Amenhotep I 1551–1524		
	Tuthmosis I 1524–1518		
	Tuthmosis II 1518–1504		
	Tuthmosis III 1504–1450	Battle of Megiddo (1481), Syria.	

DATE	DYNASTY/ RULER	POLITICS, WAR	RELIGION, SOCIAL LIFE, ART
	Queen Hatshepsut 1498–1483	Naval expedition to Punt (prob. Somaliland)	
	Amenhotep II 1453–1419		Water clocks in use
	Tuthmosis IV 1419–1386		
	Amenhotep IV [aka Akhenaten] 1350–1334		Monotheistic Aten cult established
	Smenkhkare 1334		
	Tutankhamun 1334–1325		Polytheism reestablished
	Ay 1325–1321		
	Horemheb 1321–		
1293	Dynasty 19 Ramses I –1291		
	Seti 1291–1278		
	Ramses II 1279–1212	Battle of Kadesh, c. 1275; possible Exodus of the Jews	
	Merneptah 1212–1202		
	Amenmesses 1202–1199		
	Seti II 1199–1193		
	Siptah 1193–1187		
	Queen Tworset 1187–		
1185	Dynasty 20 Setnakhte –1182		

DATE	DYNASTY/ RULER	POLITICS, WAR	RELIGION, SOCIAL LIFE, ART
	Ramses III 1182–1151		
	Ramses IV 1151–1145		
	Ramses V 1145–1141		
	Ramses VI 1141–1133		
	Ramses VII 1133–1126		
	Ramses VIII ?–1126		
	Ramses IX 1126–1108		
	Ramses X 1108–1098		
	Ramses XI 1098–1070		Ascendancy of priesthood of Amun at Thebes
1069	Dynasty 21 Smendes –1043	Pharaonic capital moved to Tanis in Delta	
	Amenemnsiu 1043–1039		
	Psusennes I 1039–991		
	Amenemope 993–984		
	Osorkon the Elder 984–978		
	Siamun 978–959		
	Psusennes II 959–		
945	Dynasty 22 [Libyan dynasty]		

DATE	DYNASTY/ RULER	POLITICS, WAR	RELIGION, SOCIAL LIFE, ART
	Sheshonq I –924	Factions of Thebes and Tanis united; Invasion of Palestine	
	Osorkon I 924–889		
	Sheshonq II 889		
	Takelot I 889–874		
	Osorkon II 874–850		
	Takelot II 850–825		
818	Sheshonq III 825–773		
	Pami 773–767		
747	Sheshonq V 767–730		
	Osorkon IV 730–715		
	Dynasty 23 [at Leontopolis]		
	Pedibastet		
	Sheshonq IV		
	Osorkon III		
	Takelot III		
	Rudamon		
	Iuput		
	Peftjauabastet		
727	Dynasty 24		
	Tefnakht –720		
	Bakenrenef [Bocchoris] 720–715		
	Dynasty 25 [Nubian: 747–656]		

DATE	DYNASTY/ RULER	POLITICS, WAR	RELIGION, SOCIAL LIFE, ART
	Piankhi		
	Shabaka		
	Shebitku		
	Taharqa		
	Tatutamun		
664	*Dynasty 26*		
	Psamtik I	Capital moved to Sais.	
	–610	Assyrians overthrown	
	Necho		
	610–595		
	Psamtik II		
	595–589		
	Wahibre [Apries]		
	589–570		
	Amhose II		
	570–526		
	Psamtik III		
	526–		
525	*Dynasty 27* [Persian]	Persian invasion and victory at Pelusium	
	Cambyses II		
	–522		
	Darius I		
	521–486		
	Xerxes		
	485–465		
	Artaxerxes		
	465–424		
	Darius II		
	423–405		
	Artaxerxes II		
	405–359		
	Dynasty 28		
	Amyrtaeus		
	404–399		
	Dynasty 29		
	Nepherites I		
	399–393		

DATE	DYNASTY/ RULER	POLITICS, WAR	RELIGION, SOCIAL LIFE, ART
	Achoris 393–380		
	Dynasty 30		
	Nakhtnebef 380–362		
	Djedhor 362–360		
	Nakhthoreb [Nactanebo II] 360–343		
343	*Dynasty 31*	Second Persian conquest	
	Artaxerxes III –332		
	Arses 338–336		
	Darius III 336–		
332	*Macedonian Kings*		
	Alexander the Great –323		
	Philip Arrhidaeus 323–317		
	Alexander IV 317–		
305	*Ptolemaic Dynasty*		
	Ptolemy I 305–282		
	Ptolemy II 285–246		
	Ptolemy III 246–222		
	Ptolemy IV 225–205		
	Ptolemy V 205–180		
	Ptolemy VI 180–145		

DATE	DYNASTY/ RULER	POLITICS, WAR	RELIGION, SOCIAL LIFE, ART
	Ptolemy VII		
	145		
	Ptolemy VIII		
	170–163/145–116		
	Ptolemy IX		
	116–110/		
	109–107/88–80		
	Ptolemy X		
	110–109/107–88		
	Ptolemy XI		
	80		
	Ptolemy XIII		
	80–58/55–51		
	Queen Berenice		
	58–55		
	Queen Cleopatra VII		
	51–30		
	Ptolemy XV		
	[Caesarion]		
30	36–30	Egypt part of Roman empire	

PART ONE

The Age of the Pyramids

The Old Kingdom,
Egypt 2686–2181 BC

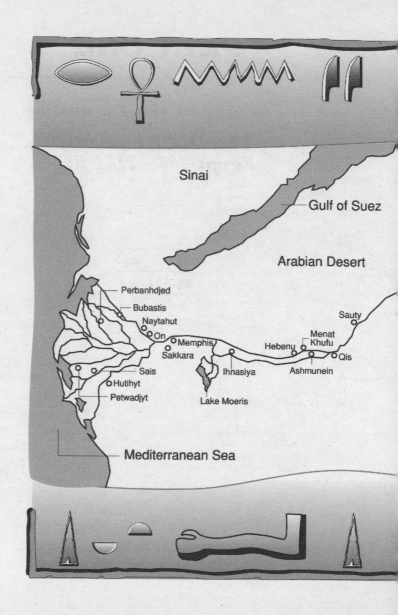

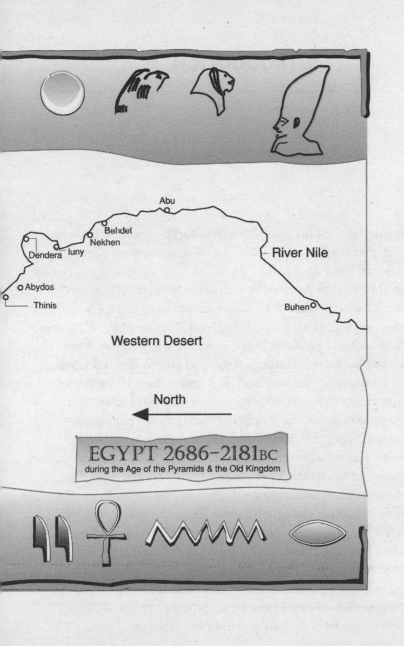

Abu

Behdet
Nekhen
Dendera Iuny

Abydos
Thinis

River Nile

Buhen

Western Desert

North

EGYPT 2686–2181BC
during the Age of the Pyramids & the Old Kingdom

INTRODUCTION

It was during the Old Kingdom that Egypt reached its first apex of civilization. Literally so, if one brings Khufu's pyramid at Giza to mind.

The ability of the Ancient Egyptians to build this Wonder of the World was predicated on advances in technology and architecture, but more so on the peculiar nature of the Egyptian monarchy. The semi-divine status of the king, who was believed to be the incarnation of the god Horus (from the 5th Dynasty onwards, the sun god Re) made him the envy of absolute rulers throughout antiquity. Only pharaonic absolutism could demand the manpower and resources to quarry, fashion and arrange 2,300,000 blocks of stone – some brought 500 miles – at an average weight of 2.5 tons into a pyramid. Only tens of thousands of people persuaded by religious duty would enslave themselves to do it, because the Great Pyramid of Khufu – like all the other pyramids of the 3rd to the 6th Dynasties – was a mausoleum from which the king would ascend to heaven. (Indeed, the Egyptian for pyramid is *mer*, "Place of Ascension".) In the Old Kingdom only the king was assured of eternal existence. Everybody else had to vicariously share his. And his heavenly journeyings in the "celestial barge" were only assured *if* he had a proper mausoleum.

To translate the pharaoh's commands into a pyramid required the other wonder of Ancient Egypt. The Egyptian bureaucracy. Based at Memphis, the bureaucracy oversaw public works, revenue-gathering, granaries and the armoury. It too was pyramidal in shape. At its peak was the vizier, at its base thousands of bustling scribes. Almost as centralized as the bureaucracy was the priesthood, which efficiently rationalized the numerous local deities and places of worship of pre-dynastic Egypt into three main religious centres, at Memphis, Heliopolis and Hermopolis.

In other words, the Egypt of the Old Kingdom was a highly centralized and absolutist theocracy. It was also relatively rich and populous, due to the agricultural surplus which came from the Nile's diluvian fertility and the extensive irrigation system in the floodplain. Over the millennium preceding 2000 BC, the population of Egypt rose from approximately 850,000 to two million. Most of these two million – perhaps 80 per cent of them – were peasants. Throughout the Old Kingdom – in fact, over the whole length of the pharaonic era – Egypt remained an overwhelmingly rural nation, with few urban centres outside the cities already noted.

The peasantry not only tilled the land but held arms, since the Old Kingdom pharaohs had no standing army. There was little need for one. Most of Egypt's "foreign affairs" in the Old Kingdom era were concerned with trade expeditions to bring back luxury goods for the king and his court. With Nubia, her immediate neighbour to the south, below the first Cataract of the Nile, Egypt had a love-hate affair. In peaceful times, the Egyptians traded their grain and honey for Nubia's gold and hard stone; in times of war, the pharaohs "hacked up the land of the Negro" and brought captives back as slaves (but almost incidentally

so; the Egyptians, unlike the other "civilizations" of antiquity, never made slavery the core of their economic
system). The most problematic of Egypt's neighbours in
the Old Kingdom era were to be found on the north-
eastern border, the "Asiatic Sand-Dwellers" of Sinai. As
the courtier and general Weni recorded in his tomb inscription, the peasant army of Pepi I bested the "Sand-
Dwellers" in c. 2399 BC but this was less proof of the efficacy
of Pepi's army than its overwhelming numbers. The Old
Kingdom Egyptians were poor at war.

The Sand-Dwellers came back to have a hand in the fall of
the Old Kingdom, though by the end of the 91-year reign of
Pepi II they were pushing at an already tottering structure.
From Dynasty 4 onwards, the power of the pharaoh was
weakened by the systematic granting of land, wealth and
titles – particularly the hereditary governorships of nomes –
to the nobility. The nomarchs eventually became rulers of
their own fiefdoms. Meanwhile the *regal-lite* pharaohs, beginning with Unas, resorted to magic spells to ensure their
greeting as an equal by the gods in heaven. Hieroglyphic
inscriptions – the Pyramid Texts – by the hundred were
carved on the inside of their pyramids' walls. Religion,
though, proved little salvation on earth when the priesthood,
in return for political support, required their temples to be tax
exempted – which only reduced the anyway dwindling royal
income. Even the climate turned against the Old Kingdom
pharaohs. Around 2200 BC a dry phase caused desertification
and a consequent reduction in agricultural output.

With the Sand-Dwellers beating at the door, even breaking into the Delta, centralized pharaonic Egypt fragmented
into the anarchy of the so-called First Intermediate Period,
when the Beloved Land became a kaleidoscope of petty
states ruled over by warring princelets.

THE LIFE OF METHEN, c. 2669–2610 BC

Anonymous

Methen rose from humble scribe to high-flying governor of towns in the Delta and part of the Seventeenth nome of Upper Egypt. His achievements – and their lavish material reward – were inscribed on the wall of his mastaba *(tomb) adjacent to the step pyramid of Djoser at Saqqara.*

He was made chief scribe of the provision magazine, and overseer of the things of the provision magazine. He was made [?] becoming local governor of Xois (Ox-nome), and inferior field-judge of Xois. He was appointed judge, he was made overseer of all flax of the king, he was made ruler of Southern Perked, and deputy, he was made local governor of the people of Dep, palace-ruler of Miper and Persepa, and local governor of the Saitic nome, ruler of the stronghold of Sent, deputy of nomes, ruler of Pershesthet, ruler of the towns of the palace, of the Southern lake. Sheret-Methen was founded, and the domain which his father Anubisemonekh presented to him.

Administrator, nomarch, and overseer of commissions in the Anubis nome, overseer of [?] of the Mendesian nome, [?] stat of land, with people and everything . . . There were founded for him the 12 towns of Shet-Methen in the saitic nome, in the Xoite nome, and the Sekhemite nome . . . There were conveyed to him as a reward 200 stat of lands by numerous royal [?], a mortuary offering of 100 loaves every day from the mortuary temple of the mother of the king's children, Nemathhap; a house 200 cubits long and 200 cubits wide, built and equipped; fine trees were set out, a very large lake was made therein, figs and vines were set out. It was recorded therein according to the king's writings; their names were according to the decree of the king's writings. Very plentiful trees and vines were set out, a great quantity of wine was made therein. A vineyard was made for him: 200 stat of land within the wall, trees were set out, in Imeres, Sheret-Methen, Yat-Sebek, Shet-Methen.

THE EXPEDITIONS OF SNEFRU TO NUBIA AND THE LEBANON, c. 2613–2589 BC

Anonymous

As recorded on the Palermo Stone, Snefru was the founder of the 4th Dynasty. Raiding negro Nubia, south of Aswan, was almost a ritual pharaonic occupation, until the region was eventually colonized; slaves were not the least by-product of these sorties. The cedar wood mentioned, to be used for temple doors, came from the Lebanon. According to the scribe, all the events below happened in one busy year of Snefru's reign.

Building of 100-cubit dewatowe-ships of meru wood, and of 60 sixteen barges of the king.

Hacking up the land of the Negro.

Bringing of 7,000 living prisoners, and 200,000 large and small cattle.

Building of the wall of the Southland and Northland called "Houses-of-Snefru".

Bringing of 40 ships filled (with) cedar wood.

TOMB DEDICATION, c. 2580 BC

Hotep

Inscribed by Hotep in the mastaba *of his father. Such pious (and not entirely altruistic) dedications by sons were standard in nobles' tombs.*

Sole companion of love, leader of the palace-hall, overseer of the baths of the palace, overseer of the bounty of the king's field of offerings, revered by his lord every day, governor of the Cow stronghold, Kam. (This tomb is) what his eldest son, his revered, the judge and inferior scribe Hotep, made for him, that he (the son) might be revered by him (the father) when he (the son) journeyed to his (own) *ka* (viz., died).

PHARAOH MENKAURE INSPECTS THE PYRAMIDS AT GIZA AND ORDERS A TOMB FOR DEBHEN, c. 2520 BC

Debhen

For so lengthy a reign – 28 years – Menkaure built a conspicuously small pyramid at Giza, possibly because his father and grandfather's grandiose projects had emptied the royal coffers. Menkaure's pyramid at 228 ft is less than half the height of Khufu's Great Pyramid (481 ft). Menkaure was famously benevolent, a quality caught in his assigning 50 workmen from his pyramid to build a tomb for his official Debhen. The following inscription is from Debhen's tomb at Giza.

As for this tomb, it was the king of Upper and Lower Egypt, Menkaure, living forever, who caused that it be made when his majesty was upon the road beside the pyramid Hir*, in order to inspect the work on the pyramid: "Divine-in-Menkaure" . . . there came the naval commander and the two high priests of Memphis, and the workmen, standing upon the pyramid Hir, to inspect the work on the pyramid, "Divine-in-Menkaure" . . . 50 workmen were assigned to do the work on it [Debhen's tomb] every day . . . His majesty commanded that no man should be taken for any forced labour . . . His majesty commanded to clear the place of rubbish . . . that there be brought stone from

* Which belonged to Menkaure's family.

Troja . . . together with two false doors, and a front for this tomb . . .

THE SADNESS OF THE PHARAOH NEFERIRKARE AT THE DEATH OF WESHPTAH, c. 2470 BC

Mernuterseteni

Neferirkare reigned c. 2477–2467. Weshptah was the royal architect. Mernuter-seteni, Weshptah's son, inscribed the following incident on his father's tomb at Abusir, adjacent to the pyramid of the 5th Dynasty regent Sahure (Neferirkare's own tomb, along with that of Niuserre, is in the same complex of rubble and mud-bricks pyramids).

Neferirkere came to see the beauty of Weshptah's last building . . . and they wondered very greatly . . . Then, lo, his majesty praised him because of it.

His majesty saw him however that he heard not . . . When the royal children and companions, who were of the court, heard, great fear was in their hearts.

He was conveyed to the court and his majesty had the royal children, companions, ritual priests and chief physicians come . . . His majesty had brought for him a case of writings (medical). They said before his majesty that he was lost. The heart of his majesty was exceedingly sad beyond everything; his majesty said that he would do everything according to his heart's desire, and returned to the privy chamber [. . .] His majesty commanded that there be made for him [Weshptah] a coffin of ebony wood sealed. Never was it done to one like him before . . . His majesty had him anointed by the side of his majesty.

"I WILL COMMEND THEM TO THE GOD FOR IT VERY GREATLY": THE DEAD PRIEST HOTEPHIRYAKHET INDUCES MORTUARY OFFERINGS, c. 2450 BC

Hotephiryakhet

Hotephiryakhet was a priest of pharaoahs Neferirkare and Niuserre. By an inscription on his tomb he requests visitors to make offerings to him – in return for his commending the donors to god.

I have made this tomb as a just possession, and never have I taken a thing belonging to any person. Whosoever shall make offering to me therein, I will do (it) for them; I will commend them to the god for it very greatly; I will do this for them, for bread, for beer, for clothing, for ointment, and for grain, in great quantity. Never have I done aught of violence toward any person. As the god loves a true matter. I was in honour with the king.

I have made this my tomb upon the western arm in a pure place. There was no tomb of any person therein, in order that the possessions of him, who has gone to his *ka*, might be protected. As for any people who shall enter into this tomb as their mortuary property or shall do an evil thing to it, judgment shall be had with them for it, by the great god. I have made this tomb as my shelter; I was honoured by the king, who brought for me a sarcophagus.

THE MAXIMS OF PTAH-HOTEP, c. 2380 BC

Ptah-hotep

A manual of polite conduct. Such instructional literature was greatly popular in Ancient Egypt.

Precepts of the prefect, the lord Ptah-hotep, under the Majesty of the King of the South and North, Assa*, living eternally forever
The prefect, the feudal lord Ptah-hotep, says: O Ptah with the two crocodiles, my lord, the progress of age changes into senility. Decay falls upon man and decline takes the place of youth. A vexation weighs upon him every day; sight fails, the ear becomes deaf; his strength dissolves without ceasing. The mouth is silent, speech fails him; the mind decays, remembering not the day before. The whole body suffers. That which is good becomes evil; taste completely disappears. Old age makes a man altogether miserable; the nose is stopped up, breathing no more from exhaustion. Standing or sitting there is here a condition of . . . Who will cause me to have authority to speak, that I may declare to him the words of those who have heard the counsels of former days? And the counsels heard of the gods, who will give me authority to declare them? Cause that it be so and that evil be removed from those that are enlightened; send the double . . . The majesty of this god says: Instruct him in the sayings of former days. It is this which constitutes the merit of the children of the great. All that which makes the soul equal penetrates him who hears it, and that which it says produces no satiety.

* aka Isesi, aka Djedkare, the penultimate pharaoh of the 5th Dynasty. A heap of rubble is all that nowadays stands of his pyramid at Saqqara.

Beginning of the arrangement of the good sayings, spoken by the noble lord, the divine father, beloved of Ptah, the son of the king, the first-born of his race, the prefect and feudal lord Ptah-hotep, so as to instruct the ignorant in the knowledge of the arguments of the good sayings. It is profitable for him who hears them, it is a loss to him who shall transgress them. He says to his son:

Be not arrogant because of that which you know; deal with the ignorant as with the learned; for the barriers of art are not closed, no artist being in possession of the perfection to which he should aspire. But good words are more difficult to find than the emerald, for it is by slaves that that is discovered among the rocks of pegmatite.

If you find a disputant while he is hot, and if he is superior to you in ability, lower the hands, bend the back, do not get into a passion with him. As he will not let you destroy his words, it is utterly wrong to interrupt him; that proclaims that you are incapable of keeping yourself calm, when you are contradicted. If then you have to do with a disputant while he is hot, imitate one who does not stir. You have the advantage over him if you keep silence when he is uttering evil words. "The better of the two is he who is impassive," say the bystanders, and you are right in the opinion of the great.

If you find a disputant while he is hot, do not despise him because you are not of the same opinion. Be not angry against him when he is wrong; away with such a thing. He fights against himself; require him not further to flatter your feelings. Do not amuse yourself with the spectacle which you have before you; it is odious, it is mean, it is the part of a despicable soul so to do. As soon as you let yourself be moved by your feelings, combat this desire as a thing that is reproved by the great.

If you have, as leader, to decide on the conduct of a great number of men, seek the most perfect manner of doing so that your own conduct may be without reproach. Justice is great, invariable, and assured; it has not been disturbed since the age of Ptah. To throw obstacles in the way of the laws is to open the way before violence. Shall that which is below gain the upper hand, if the unjust does not attain to the place of justice? Even he who says: I take for myself, of my own free-will; but says not: I take by virtue of my authority. The limitations of justice are invariable; such is the instruction which every man receives from his father.

Inspire not men with fear, else Ptah will fight against you in the same manner. If any one asserts that he lives by such means, Ptah will take away the bread from his mouth; if any one asserts that he enriches himself thereby, Ptah says: I may take those riches to myself. If any one asserts that he beats others, Ptah will end by reducing him to impotence. Let no one inspire men with fear; this is the will of Ptah. Let one provide sustenance for them in the lap of peace; it will then be that they will freely give what has been torn from them by terror.

If you are among the persons seated at meat in the house of a greater man than yourself, take that which he gives you, bowing to the ground. Regard that which is placed before you, but point not at it; regard it not frequently; he is a blameworthy person who departs from this rule. Speak not to the great man more than he requires, for one knows not what may be displeasing to him. Speak when he invites you and your worth will be pleasing. As for the great man who has plenty of means of existence, his conduct is as he himself wishes. He does that which pleases him; if he desires to repose, he realizes his intention. The great man stretching forth his hand does that to which other men do not attain. But as the means of existence are under the will of Ptah, one can not rebel against it.

If you are one of those who bring the messages of one great man to another, conform yourself exactly to that wherewith he has charged you; perform for him the commission as he has enjoined you. Beware of altering in speaking the offensive words which one great person addresses to another; he who perverts the trustfulness of his way, in order to repeat only what produces pleasure in the words of every man, great or small, is a detestable person.

If you are a farmer, gather the crops in the field which the great Ptah has given you, do not boast in the house of your neighbours; it is better to make oneself dreaded by one's deeds. As for him who, master of his own way of acting, being all-powerful, seizes the goods of others like a crocodile in the midst even of watchment, his children are an object of malediction, of scorn, and of hatred on account of it, while his father is grievously distressed, and as for the mother who has borne him, happy is another rather than herself. But a man becomes a god when he is chief of a tribe which has confidence in following him.

If you abase yourself in obeying a superior, your conduct is entirely good before Ptah. Knowing who you ought to obey and who you ought to command, do not lift up your heart against him. As you know that in him is authority, be respectful toward him as belonging to him. Wealth comes only at Ptah's own good-will, and his caprice only is the law; as for him who . . . Ptah, who has created his superiority, turns himself from him and he is overthrown.

Be active during the time of your existence, do no more than is commanded. Do not spoil the time of your activity; he is a blameworthy person who makes a bad use of his moments. Do not lose the daily opportunity of increasing that which your house possesses. Activity produces riches, and riches do not endure when it slackens.

If you are a wise man, bring up a son who shall be pleasing to Ptah. If he conforms his conduct to your way and occupies himself with your affairs as is right, do to him all the good you can; he is your son, a person attached to you whom your own self has begotten. Separate not your heart from him . . . But if he conducts himself ill and transgresses your wish, if he rejects all counsel, if his mouth goes according to the evil word, strike him on the mouth in return. Give orders without hesitation to those who do wrong, to him whose temper is turbulent; and he will not deviate from the straight path, and there will be no obstacle to interrupt the way.

If you are employed in the larit, stand or sit rather than walk about. Lay down rules for yourself from the first: not to absent yourself even when weariness overtakes you. Keep an eye on him who enters announcing that what he asks is secret; what is entrusted to you is above appreciation, and all contrary argument is a matter to be rejected. He is a god who penetrates into a place where no relaxation of the rules is made for the privileged.

If you are with people who display for you an extreme affection, saying: "Aspiration of my heart, aspiration of my heart, where there is no remedy! That which is said in your heart, let it be realized by springing up spontaneously. Sovereign master, I give myself to your opinion. Your name is approved without speaking. Your body is full of vigour, your face is above your neighbours." If then you are accustomed to this excess of flattery, and there be an obstacle to you in your desires, then your impulse is to obey your passion. But he who . . . according to his caprice, his soul is . . . his body is . . . While the man who is master of his soul is superior to those whom Ptah has loaded with his gifts; the man who obeys his passion is under the power of his wife.

Declare your line of conduct without reticence; give your opinion in the council of your lord; while there are people who turn back upon their own words when they speak, so as not to offend him who has put forward a statement, and answer not in this fashion: "He is the great man who will recognize the error of another; and when he shall raise his voice to oppose the other about it he will keep silence after what I have said."

If you are a leader, setting forward your plans according to that which you decide, perform perfect actions which posterity may remember, without letting the words prevail with you which multiply flattery, which excite pride and produce vanity.

If you are a leader of peace, listen to the discourse of the petitioner. Be not abrupt with him; that would trouble him. Say not to him: "You have already recounted this." Indulgence will encourage him to accomplish the object of his coming. As for being abrupt with the complainant because he described what passed when the injury was done, instead of complaining of the injury itself, let it not be! The way to obtain a clear explanation is to listen with kindness.

If you desire to excite respect within the house you enter, for example the house of a superior, a friend, or any person of consideration, in short everywhere where you enter, keep yourself from making advances to a woman, for there is nothing good in so doing. There is no prudence in taking part in it, and thousands of men destroy themselves in order to enjoy a moment, brief as a dream, while they gain death, so as to know it. It is a villainous intention, that of a man who thus excites himself; if he goes on to carry it out, his mind abandons him. For as for him who is without repugnance for such an act, there is no good sense at all in him.

If you desire that your conduct should be good and preserved from all evil, keep yourself from every attack of bad humour. It is a fatal malady which leads to discord, and there is no longer any existence for him who gives way to it. For it introduces discord between fathers and mothers, as well as between brothers and sisters; it causes the wife and the husband to hate each other; it contains all kinds of wickedness, it embodies all kinds of wrong. When a man has established his just equilibrium and walks in this path, there where he makes his dwelling, there is no room for bad humor.

Be not of an irritable temper as regards that which happens at your side; grumble not over your own affairs. Be not of an irritable temper in regard to your neighbours; better is a compliment to that which displeases than rudeness. It is wrong to get into a passion with one's neighbours, to be no longer master of one's words. When there is only a little irritation, one creates for oneself an affliction for the time when one will again be cool.

If you are wise, look after your house; love your wife without alloy. Fill her stomach, clothe her back; these are the cares to be bestowed on her person. Caress her, fulfil her desires during the time of her existence; it is a kindness which does honour to its possessor. Be not brutal; tact will influence her better than violence; her . . . behold to what she aspires, at what she aims, what she regards. It is that which fixes her in your house; if you repel her, it is an abyss. Open your arms for her, respond to her arms; call her, display to her your love.

Treat your dependents well, in so far as it belongs to you to do so; and it belongs to those whom Ptah has favored. If any one fails in treating his dependents well it is said: "He is a person . . ." As we do not know the events which may happen tomorrow, he is a wise person by whom one is well treated. When there comes the necessity of showing zeal, it will then be the dependents themselves who say: "Come on, come on," if good treatment has not quitted the place; if it has quitted it, the dependents are defaulters.

Do not repeat any extravagance of language; do not listen to it; it is a thing which has escaped from a hasty mouth. If it is repeated, look, without hearing it, toward the earth; say nothing in regard to it. Cause him who speaks to you to know what is just, even him who provokes to injustice; cause that which is just to be done, cause it to triumph. As for that which is hateful according to the law, condemn it by unveiling it.

If you are a wise man, sitting in the council of your lord, direct your thought toward that which is wise. Be silent rather than scatter your words. When you speak, know that which can be brought against you. To speak in the council is an art, and speech is criticized more than any other labor; it is contradiction which puts it to the proof.

If you are powerful, respect knowledge and calmness of language. Command only to direct; to be absolute is to run into evil. Let not your heart be haughty, neither let it be mean. Do not let your orders remain unsaid and cause your answers to penetrate; but speak without heat, assume a serious countenance. As for the vivacity of an ardent heart,

temper it; the gentle man penetrates all obstacles. He who
agitates himself all the day long has not a good moment;
and he who amuses himself all the day long keeps not his
fortune. Aim at fullness like pilots; once one is seated
another works, and seeks to obey one's orders.

Disturb not a great man; weaken not the attention of him
who is occupied. His care is to embrace his task, and he
strips his person through the love which he puts into it.
That transports men to Ptah, even the love for the work
which they accomplish. Compose then your face even in
trouble, that peace may be with you, when agitation is with
. . . These are the people who succeed in what they desire.

Teach others to render homage to a great man. If you
gather the crop for him among men, cause it to return fully
to its owner, at whose hands is your subsistence. But the gift
of affection is worth more than the provisions with which
your back is covered. For that which the great man receives
from you will enable your house to live, without speaking of
the maintenance you enjoy, which you desire to preserve; it
is thereby that he extends a beneficent hand, and that in
your home good things are added to good things. Let your
love pass into the heart of those who love you; cause those
about you to be loving and obedient.

If you are a son of the guardians deputed to watch over
the public tranquillity, execute your commission without
knowing its meaning, and speak with firmness. Substitute
not for that which the instructor has said what you believe
to be his intention; the great use words as it suits them.
Your part is to transmit rather than to comment upon.

If you are annoyed at a thing, if you are tormented by
someone who is acting within his right, get out of his sight,
and remember him no more when he has ceased to address
you.

If you have become great after having been little, if you have become rich after having been poor, when you are at the head of the city, know how not to take advantage of the fact that you have reached the first rank, harden not your heart because of your elevation; you are become only the administrator, the prefect, of the provisions which belong to Ptah. Put not behind you the neighbour who is like you; be unto him as a companion.

Bend your back before your superior. You are attached to the palace of the king; your house is established in its fortune, and your profits are as is fitting. Yet a man is annoyed at having an authority above himself, and passes the period of life in being vexed thereat. Although that hurts not your . . . Do not plunder the house of your neighbours, seize not by force the goods which are beside you. Exclaim not then against that which you hear, and do not feel humiliated. It is necessary to reflect when one is hindered by it that the pressure of authority is felt also by one's neighbour.

Do not make . . . you know that there are obstacles to the water which comes to its hinder part, and that there is no trickling of that which is in its bosom. Let it not . . . after having corrupted his heart.

If you aim at polished manners, call not him whom you accost. Converse with him especially in such a way as not to annoy him. Enter on a discussion with him only after having left him time to saturate his mind with the subject of the conversation. If he lets his ignorance display itself, and if he gives you all opportunity to disgrace him, treat him with courtesy rather; proceed not to drive him into a corner; do not . . . the word to him; answer not in a crushing manner; crush him not; worry him not; in order that in his turn he may not return to the subject, but depart to the profit of your conversation.

Let your countenance be cheerful during the time of your existence. When we see one departing from the storehouse who has entered in order to bring his share of provision, with his face contracted, it shows that his stomach is empty and that authority is offensive to him. Let not that happen to you; it is . . .

Know those who are faithful to you when you are in low estate. Your merit then is worth more than those who did you honour. His . . . behold that which a man possesses completely. That is of more importance than his high rank; for this is a matter which passes from one to another. The merit of one's son is advantageous to the father, and that which he really is, is worth more than the remembrance of his father's rank.

Distinguish the superintendent who directs from the workman, for manual labour is little elevated; the inaction of the hands is honourable. If a man is not in the evil way, that which places him there is the want of subordination to authority.

If you take a wife, do not . . . Let her be more contented than any of her fellow-citizens. She will be attached to you doubly, if her chain is pleasant. Do not repel her; grant that which pleases her; it is to her contentment that she appreciates your work.

If you hear those things which I have said to you, your wisdom will be fully advanced. Although they are the means which are suitable for arriving at the maat, and it is that which makes them precious, their memory would recede from the mouth of men. But thanks to the beauty of their arrangement in rhythm all their words will now be carried without alteration over this earth eternally. That will create a canvas to be embellished, whereof the great will speak, in order to instruct men in its sayings. After having listened to them the pupil will become a master, even he who shall have properly listened to the sayings because he shall have heard them. Let him win success by placing himself in the first rank; that is for him a position perfect and durable, and he has nothing further to desire forever. By knowledge his path is assured, and he is made happy by it on the earth. The wise man is satiated by knowledge; he is a great man through his own merits. His tongue is in accord with his mind; just are his lips when he speaks, his eyes when he gazes, his ears when he hears. The advantage of his son is to do that which is just without deceiving himself.

To attend therefore profits the son of him who has attended. To attend is the result of the fact that one has attended. A teachable auditor is formed, because I have attended. Good when he has attended, good when he speaks, he who has attended has profited, and it is profitable to attend to him who has attended. To attend is worth more than anything else, for it produces love, the good thing that is twice good. The son who accepts the instruction of his father will grow old on that account. What Ptah loves is that one should attend; if one attends not, it is abhorrent to Ptah. The heart makes itself its own master when it attends and when it does not attend; but if it attends, then his heart is a beneficent master to a man. In attending to instruction, a man loves what he attends to, and to do that which is prescribed is pleasant. When a son attends to his father, it is a twofold joy for both; when wise things are prescribed to him, the son is gentle toward his master. Attending to him who has attended when such things have been prescribed to him, he engraves upon his heart that which is approved by his father; and the recollection of it is preserved in the mouth of the living who exist upon this earth.

When a son receives the instruction of his father there is no error in all his plans. Train your son to be a teachable man whose wisdom is agreeable to the great. Let him direct his mouth according to that which has been said to him; in the docility of a son is discovered his wisdom. His conduct is perfect while error carries away the unteachable. Tomorrow knowledge will support him, while the ignorant will be destroyed.

As for the man without experience who listens not, he effects nothing whatsoever. He sees knowledge in ignorance, profit in loss; he commits all kinds of error, always accordingly choosing the contrary of what is praiseworthy. He lives on that which is mortal, in this fashion. His food is evil words, whereat he is filled with astonishment. That which the great know to be mortal he lives upon every day, flying from that which would be profitable to him, because of the multitude of errors which present themselves before him every day.

A son who attends is like a follower of Horus; he is happy after having attended. He becomes great, he arrives at dignity, he gives the same lesson to his children. Let none innovate upon the precepts of his father; let the same precepts form his lessons to his children. "Verily," will his children say to him, "to accomplish what you say works marvels." Cause therefore that to flourish which is just, in order to nourish your children with it. If the teachers allow themselves to be led toward evil principles, verily the people who understand them not will speak accordingly, and that being said to those who are docile they will act accordingly. Then all the world considers them as masters and they inspire confidence in the public; but their glory endures not so long as would please them. Take not away then a word from the ancient teaching, and add not one;

put not one thing in place of another; beware of uncovering the rebellious ideas which arise in you; but teach according to the words of the wise. Attend if you wish to dwell in the mouth of those who shall attend to your words, when you have entered upon the office of master, that your words may be upon our lips . . . and that there may be a chair from which to deliver your arguments.

Let your thoughts be abundant, but let your mouth be under restraint, and you shall argue with the great. Put yourself in unison with the ways of your master; cause him to say: "He is my son," so that those who shall hear it shall say "Praise be to her who has borne him to him!" Apply yourself while you speak; speak only of perfect things; and let the great who shall hear you say: "Twice good is that which issues from his mouth!"

Do that which your master bids you. Twice good is the precept of his father, from whom he has issued, from his flesh. What he tells us, let it be fixed in our heart; to satisfy him greatly let us do for him more than he has prescribed. Verily a good son is one of the gifts of Ptah, a son who does even better than he has been told to do. For his master he does what is satisfactory, putting himself with all his heart on the part of right. So I shall bring it about that your body shall be healthful, that the Pharaoh shall be satisfied with you in all circumstances and that you shall obtain years of life without default. It has caused me on earth to obtain one hundred and ten years of life, along with the gift of the favor of the Pharaoh among the first of those whom their works have ennobled, satisfying the Pharaoh in a place of dignity.

It is finished, from its beginning to its end, according to that which is found in writing.

"I GAVE BREAD TO THE HUNGRY, I SATISFIED THE WOLVES OF THE MOUNTAIN AND THE FOWL OF HEAVEN WITH SMALL CATTLE": THE BENEFICENCE OF THE NOMARCH HENKU, c. 2390 BC

Henku

Henku was nomarch – local ruler – of twelfth nome in Upper Egypt. This record of his beneficence is from his cliff-tomb at der el-Gebrawi; the kindess to wolves and hawks ("fowl of heaven") was not sentiment, but religious duty. They were sacred animals in Henku's locality.

I gave bread to all the hungry of the Cerastes-Mountain; I clothed him who was naked therein. I filled its shores with large cattle, and its lowlands with small cattle. I satisfied the wolves of the mountain and the fowl of heaven with flesh of small cattle . . . I was lord and overseer of southern grain in this nome . . . I settled the feeble towns in this nome with the people of other nomes; those who had been peasant-serfs therein, I made their offices as officials.

I never oppressed one in possession of his property, so that he complained of me because of it to the god of my city; (but) I spake, and told that which was good; never was there one fearing because of one stronger than he, so that he complained because of it to the god.

I arose then to be ruler in the Cerastes-Mountain, together with my brother, the revered, the sole companion, ritual priest, Re-am, I was a benefactor to it (the nome) in the folds of the cattle, in the settlements of the fowlers. I settled its every district with men and cattle – small cattle indeed. I speak no lie, for I was one beloved of his father, praised of his mother, excellent in character to his brother, and amiable to [his sister] . . .

THE DEAD PHARAOH ASCENDS TO HEAVEN AND OTHER PYRAMID SPELLS, c. 2375–2300 BC

Anonymous

When the Egyptologist Gaston Maspero entered the Pyramid of Unas at Saqqara in 1881, he found long hieroglyphic inscriptions on the walls. These "Pyramid Texts" were spells to help the deceased pharaoh on his voyage to his celestial abode. Many of them were recited during the burial service itself. Unas was the first pharaoh to decorate his pyramid with the texts, but they became de rigeur for his 5th Dynasty successors. Over 750 have been collected.

Spell 309
King Unas goes to the sky, king Unas goes to the sky! On the wind! On the wind!

Spell 217
O Re-Atum! This king Unas comes to thee, an imperishable glorious son, lord of the affairs of the place of the four pillars (the sky). Thy son comes to thee. This king Unas comes to thee.

Spell 476
"How beautiful to see, how satisfying to behold", says the gods, when this god (i.e. the king) ascends to the sky. His fearfulness is on his head, his terror is at his side, his magical charms are before him.

Spell 220
"The doors of the horizon are opened, its bolts are drawn back."
    Speech by the priest: "He* has come to you, O crown of Lower Egypt; he has come to you, O Fiery Serpent; he has

* i.e., the king

come to you, O Great One; he has come to you, O Great of Magic, being pure for you and fearing you. May you be pleased with him, may you be pleased with his purity, and may you be pleased with his speech which he says to you. How kindly is your face, for you are content, renewed, and rejuvenated, even as the father of the gods fashioned you. He has come to you, O Great of Magic, for he is Horus encircled with the protection of his Eye, O Great of Magic."

Spell 222

The officiating priest addresses the king: "Stand upon it, this earth which issued from Atum, this spittle which issued from Kheprer; come into being upon it, be exalted upon it, so that your father may see you, so that Re may see you."

The king speaks: "I have come to you, my father, I have come to you, O Re. I have come to you, my father, I have come to you, O Ndi. I have come to you, my father, I have come to you, O Pndn. I have come to you, my father, I have come to you, O Dndn. I have come to you, my father, I have come to you, O Great Float-user. I have come to you, my father, I have come to you, O Sopdu. I have come to you, my father, I have come to you, O Sharp of Teeth. Grant that I may seize the sky and take possession of the horizon. Grant that I may rule the Nine and provide for the Ennead. Place the crook in my hand, that the head of Lower and Upper Egypt may be bowed. I charge my opponent and stand up, the great headman in my great waters. Nephthys has favored me, and I have captured my opponent."

The priest speaks: "Provide yourself with the Great of Magic, (even) Seth dwelling in Nubet, Lord of Upper Egypt; nothing is lost to you, nothing has ceased(?) for you; behold, you are more renowned and more powerful than the gods of Upper Egypt and their spirits. O you whom the Pregnant One ejected, you have terminated(?) the night, being equipped as Seth who broke forth violently, (even) you whom Isis has favoured.

"Equip yourself as Horus, being young; indeed nothing is lost to you, nothing has ceased(?) for you; behold, you are more renowned and more powerful than the northern gods and their spirits. Cast off your impurity for Atum in Heliopolis and go down with him; assign the needs(?) of the Lower Sky and succeed to the thrones of the Abyss(?). May you come into being with your father Atum, may you go up on high with your father Atum, may you rise with your father Atum, may (your) needs(?) be loosed from you, your head being under the care of(?) the Lady of Heliopolis. Go up, open your way by means of the bones of Shu, the embrace of your mother Nut will enfold you. Be pure in the horizon and get rid of your impurity in the Lakes of Shu.

"Ascend and descend; descend with Re, sink into darkness with Ndi. Ascend and descend; ascend with Re, rise with the Great Float-user. Ascend and descend; descend with Nephthys, sink into darkness with the Night-bark. Ascend and descend; ascend with Isis, rise with the Day-bark.

"May you have power in your body, for you have no hindrance; you are born for Horus, you are conceived for Seth. Be pure in the Western Nome, receive your purification in the Heliopolitan Nome with your father, with Atum. Come into being, go up on high, and it will be well with you, it will be pleasant for you in the embrace of your father, in the embrace of Atum. O Atum, raise this King up to you, enclose him within your embrace, for he is your son of your body forever."

A PALACE CONSPIRACY, C. 2300 BC

Weni

Weni was a high-court judge and royal official. He was chosen by Pepi I to be the sole arbiter in a conspiracy case involving Queen Weret-Imtes and the King's Harem. The account below is extracted from the autobiography of Weni inscribed on the walls of his tomb at Abydos.

When legal procedure was instituted in private in the harem against the queen, Imtes, his majesty caused me to enter, in order to hear (the case) alone. No chief judge and vizier at all, no prince at all was there, but only I alone, because I was excellent, because I was pleasant to the heart of his majesty; because his majesty loved me. I alone was the one who put (it) in writing, together with a single judge attached to Nekhen; while my office was (only) that of superior custodian of the domain of Pharaoh. Never before had one like me heard the secret of the royal harem, except that the king caused me to hear (it), because I was more excellent to the heart of his majesty than any official of his, than any noble of his, than any servant of his.

Weni does not elucidate the outcome of the case, but presumably the Queen was executed.

WENI BESEECHES THE KING FOR A LIMESTONE SARCOPHAGUS, c. 2300 BC

Then I [be]sought – the majesty of the king that there be brought for me a limestone sarcophagus from Troja. The king had the treasurer of the god ferry over, together with a troop of sailors under his hand, in order to bring for me this sarcophagus from Troja; and he arrived with it, in a large ship belonging to the court, together with [its] lid, the false door; the setting, two [–], and one offering-tablet. Never was the like done for any servant, for I was excellent to the heart of his majesty, for I was pleasant to the heart of his majesty, for his majesty loved me.

THE WAR AGAINST THE SAND-DWELLERS, c. 2300 BC

Weni

Having distinguished himself in the conspiracy case against Queen Weret-Imtes, Weni was chosen by Pepi I to lead the Egyptian campaign against the "Asiatics" of northern Sinai. Subsequently, Weni's troops reached into southern Palestine, the first recorded Egyptian invasion of that country.

His majesty made war on the Asiatic Sand-dwellers and his majesty made an army of many ten thousands: in the entire South, southward to Elephantine, and northward to Aphroditopolis; in the Northland on both sides entire in the stronghold, and in the midst of the strongholds, among the Irthet negroes, the Mazoi negroes, the Yam negroes, among the Wawat negroes, among the Kau negroes, and in the land of Temeh.

His majesty sent me at the head of this army while the counts, while the wearers of the royal seal, while the sole companions of the palace, while the nomarchs and commanders of strongholds belonging to the South and the Northland; the companions, the caravan-conductors, the superior prophets belonging to the South and the Northland, the overseers of the crown-possessions, were (each) at the head of a troop of the South or the Northland, of the strongholds and cities which they commanded, and of the negroes of these countries. I was the one who made for them the plan while my office was (only) that of superior custodian of the domain of Pharaoh of [–] not one thereof [–] with his neighbour; not one thereof plundered dough (or) sandals from the wayfarer; not one thereof took bread from any city; not one thereof took any goat from any people. I despatched them from the Northern Isle, the Gate of Ihotep, the bend of Horus, Nibmat. While I was of this rank— everything, I inspected the number of these troops, (although) never had any servant inspected.

This army returned in safety, (after) it had hacked up the land of the Sand-dwellers; this army returned in safety, (after) it had destroyed the land of the Sand-dwellers; this army returned in safety, (after) it had overturned its strongholds; this army returned in safety, (after) it had cut down its figs and its vines; this army returned in safety, (after) it had thrown fire in all its troops; this army returned in safety, (after) it had slain troops therein, in many ten thousands; this army returned in safety (after) it had carried away, therefrom a great multitude as living captives. His majesty praised me on account of it above everything.

His majesty sent me to despatch [this army] five times, in order to traverse the land of the Sand-dwellers at each of their rebellions, with these troops. I did so that [his] majesty praised me on account of it.

When it was said there were revolters because of a matter among these barbarians in the land of Gazelle-nose, I crossed over in troop-ships with these troops, and I voyaged to the back of the height of the ridge on the north of the Sand-dwellers.* When this army had been brought in the highway, I came and smote them all and every revolter among them was slain.

* i.e. southern Palestine

THE BUILDING OF A PYRAMID: AN EXPEDITION TO THE SOUTHERN QUARRIES, c. 2283 BC

Weni

Under Pepi I's successor, Merenre [Mernere], Weni was appointed to the exalted position of Governor of the South and accordingly entrusted with securing black granite for the royal pyramid at Saqqara. To transport the granite, which was probably quarried near Aswan, Weni was obliged to cut canals through the first cataract of the Nile.

His Majesty sent me to Elephantine to bring a false door of granite, together with its offering-tablet, doors and settings of granite; to bring doorways and offering-tablets of granite, belonging to the upper chamber of the pyramid called "Mernere-Shines-and-is Beautiful", of the queen. Then I sailed down-stream to the pyramid called "Mernere-Shines-and-is-Beautiful" with six cargo-boats, three tow-boats and three [?] boats to only one warship. Never had Ibhet and Elephantine been visited in the time of any kings with only one warship. Whatsoever his majesty commanded me I carried out completely according to all that his majesty commanded me . . . His majesty sent me [on a second expedition] to dig five canals in the South and to make three cargo-boats and four tow-boats of acacia wood of Wawat. Then the negro chiefs of Irthet, Wawat, Yam and Mazoi drew timber thereof, and I did the whole in only one year. They were launched and laden with very large granite blocks for the pyramid "Mernere-Shines-and-is-Beautiful". I then [?] for the palace in all these five canals, because I honoured, because I [?], because I praised the fame of the king of Upper and Lower Egypt, Mernere, who lives forever, more than all gods and because I carried out

everything according to the mandate which his *ka* commanded me.

THE JOURNEYS OF A CARAVAN-CONDUCTOR, c. 2283–2278 BC

Harkhuf

Harkhuf was an eminent official – indeed, governor of the South – and was also a major trader with the Negroes of the extreme south. During the reign of Merenre, Harkhuf led three commercial expeditions to the Nubian country of Yam and beyond.

First Journey
The majesty of Mernere my lord, sent me, together with my father, the sole companion, and ritual priest, Iri, to Yam, in order to explore a road to this country. I did it in only seven months, and brought all (kinds of) gifts from it [—]. I was very greatly praised for it.

Second Journey
His majesty sent me a second time alone; I went forth upon the Elephantine road, and I descended from Irthet, Mekher, Tereres, Irtheth, being an affair of eight months. When I descended I brought gifts from this country in very great quantity. Never before was the like brought to this land. I descended from the dwelling of the chief of Sethu and Irthet, after I had explored these countries. Never had any companion or caravan-conductor who went forth to Yam before this, done (it).

Third Journey
His majesty now sent me a third time to Yam; I went forth from [—] upon the Uhet road, and I found the chief of

Yam going to the land of Temeh to smite Temeh as far as the western corner of heaven. I went forth after him to the land of Temeh, and I pacified him, until he praised all the gods for the king's sake. [. . .]

Now when I had pacified that chief of Yam – below Irthet and above Sethu, I found the chief of Irthet, Sethu, and Wawat.

I descended with 300 asses laden with incense, ebony, heknu, grain, panthers, ivory, throw-sticks, and every good product. Now when the chief of Irthet, Sethu, and Wawat saw how strong and numerous was the troop of Yam, which descended with me to the court, and the soldiers who had been sent with me, (then) this [chief] brought and gave to me bulls and small cattle, and conducted me to the roads of the highlands of Irthet, because I was more excellent, vigilant, and – than any count, companion or caravan-conductor, who had been sent to Yam before. Now, when the servant there was descending to the court, one sent the –, sole companion, the master of the bath, Khuni, up-stream with a vessel laden with date-wine, cakes, bread, and beer. The count, wearer of the royal seal, sole companion, ritual priest, treasurer of the god, privy councillor of decrees, the revered, Harkhuf.

PEPI II DEMANDS TO SEE THE DANCING DWARF, c. 2276 BC

Pepi II

On a fourth expedition to Yam, the caravan-leader Harkhuf returned with a dancing dwarf. When Harkhuf sent word of the dwarf to Pepi II (reigned c. 2278–2184), the boy pharaoh demanded in a letter that the curiosity be hurried to court. The letter was later engraved on the facade of Harkhuf's tomb.

I have noted the matter of this thy letter, which thou hast sent to the king, to the palace, in order that one might know that thou hast descended in safety from Yam with the army which was with thee. Thou hast said [in] this thy letter, that thou hast brought all great and beautiful gifts, which Hathor, mistress of Imu hath given to the *ka* of the king of Upper and Lower Egypt Neferkere, who liveth forever and ever. Thou hast said in this thy letter, that thou hast brought a dancing dwarf of the god from the land of spirits, like the dwarf which the treasurer of the god Burded brought from Punt in the time of Isesi. Thou hast said to my majesty: "Never before has one like him been brought by any other who has visited Yam."

Come northward to the court immediately; [–] thou shalt bring this dwarf with thee, which thou bringest living, prosperous and healthy from the land of spirits, for the dances of the god, to rejoice and gladden the heart of the king of Upper and Lower Egypt, Neferkere, who lives forever. When he goes down with thee into the vessel, appoint excellent people, who shall be beside him on each side of the vessel; take care lest he fall into the water. When [he] sleeps at night appoint excellent people, who shall sleep beside him in his tent; inspect ten times a night. My majesty desires to see this dwarf more than the gifts of Sinai and of Punt. If thou arrivest at court this dwarf being with thee alive, prosperous and healthy, my majesty will do for thee a greater thing than that which was done for the treasurer of the god, Burded in the time of Isesi, according to the heart's desire of my majesty to see this dwarf.

Commands have been sent to the chief of the New Towns, the companion, and superior prophet, to command that sustenance be taken from him in every store-city and every temple, without stinting therein.

THE RECOVERY OF A FATHER'S BODY FROM THE NEGROES, c. 2250 BC

Sebni

Sebni's father, Mekhu, met his death on an expedition to Nubia; when news of the tragedy reached Sebni, he set out to rescue the corpse for embalming and proper burial – for without ritual the father could not be assured of an afterlife.

Then came the ship captain, Intef . . . to give information that . . . Mekhu was dead . . . Then I took a troop of my estate, and 100 asses with me, bearing ointment, honey, clothing, oil, and [—] of every sack, in order to make presents [in] these countries . . . I pacified these countries . . . I loaded the body of this sole companion upon an ass, and I had him carried by the troop of my estate. I made for him a coffin . . . I sent the royal attendant Iri, with two people of my estate . . . bearing incense, clothing . . . one tusk in order to give information . . . and that I had brought this my father and all kinds of gifts from these countries . . . When I descended . . . behold, Iri came from the court. . . . He brought . . . embalmers, the chief ritual priest . . . the mourners, and all offerings of the White House. He brought festival oil from the Double White House and secret things . . . and all the burial equipment which is issued from the Court . . . I buried this my father in his tomb of the necropolis.

ZAU BUILDS A TOMB FOR HIS BELOVED FATHER AND HIMSELF, c. 2200 BC

Zau

Zau was a nomarch of the 12th nome. His desire to be buried with his father so that he might see him "every day . . . be with him in one place" is poignant 4000 years on.

His eldest son, his beloved, of his body; – his favourite, his darling, prince of the palace, wearer of the royal seal, commander of a stronghold, real sole companion, great lord of the nome of Cerastes-Mountain, Zau. I say: "I was one beloved of his father, praised of his mother, whom his brothers and sisters loved.

Father's Burial

I buried my father the count, Zau, beyond the splendour, beyond the godliness of any equal of his who was in this South. I requested as an honour from the majesty of my lord, the king of Upper and Lower Egypt, Neferkere (Pepi II), who lives forever, that there be taken a coffin, clothing, and festival perfume for this Zau. His majesty caused that the custodian of the royal domain should bring a coffin of wood, festival perfume, oil, clothing, 200 (pieces) of prime linen, and of fine southern linen of [—], taken from the double White House of the court for this Zau. Never had it been done to another of his rank.

Son's Burial

Now, I caused that I should be buried in the same tomb with this Zau, in order that I might be with him in one place; not, however, because I was not in a position to make a second tomb; but I did this in order that "I might see this Zau every day, in order that I might be with him in one place."

PART TWO

Chaos and Resurrection

The First Intermediate Period and The Middle Kingdom, Egypt 2181–1782 BC

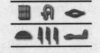

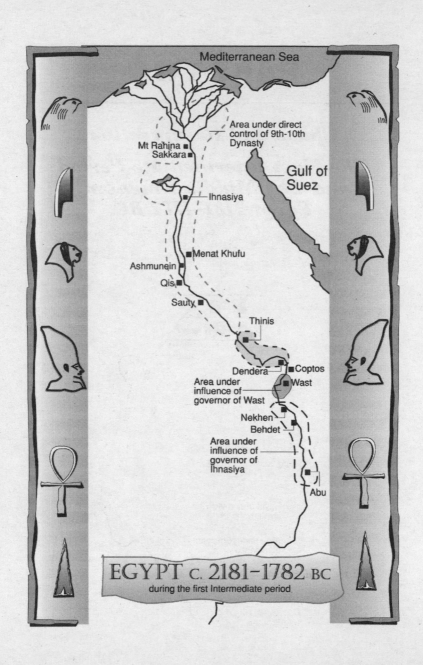

Mediterranean Sea

Area under direct
control of 9th-10th
Dynasty

Gulf of
Suez

Mt Rahina
Sakkara

Ihnasiya

Menat Khufu

Ashmunein
Qis
Sauty

Thinis

Dendera
Coptos

Area under
influence of
governor of Wast

Wast

Nekhen
Behdet

Area under
influence of
governor of
Ihnasiya

Abu

EGYPT c. 2181–1782 BC
during the first Intermediate period

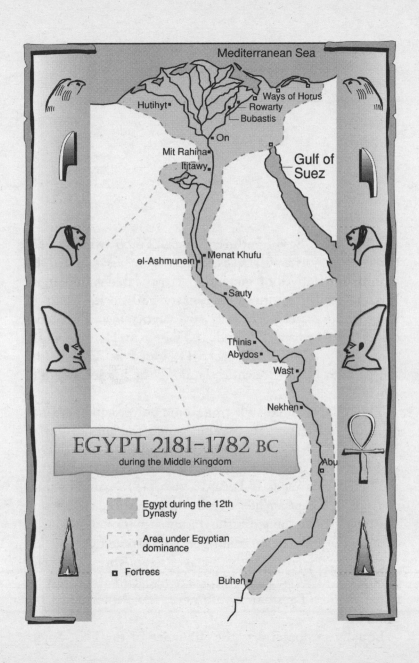

Mediterranean Sea

Hutihyt■

Ways of Horus
Rowarty
Bubastis

■On

Mit Rahina■
Itjtawy■

Gulf of
Suez

el-Ashmunein■ ■Menat Khufu

■Sauty

Thinis■
Abydos ■

Wast■

Nekhen■

EGYPT 2181–1782 BC
during the Middle Kingdom

■Abu

Egypt during the 12th
Dynasty

Area under Egyptian
dominance

■ Fortress

Buhen■

INTRODUCTION

For 140 years Egypt endured chaos. Tombs were looted, there were riots and strikes, rulers were assassinated by ambitious relatives or generals. A truncated kingdom at Memphis ruled by the 8th Dynasty had no less than 17 kings in 20 years. Eventually sovereignty over Egypt became split: Dynasties 9 and 10, based at Herakleopolis, controlled the north; Dynasty 11, based at Thebes, the south. They clashed relentlessly along the border, north of Abydos.

The collapse of old-style pharaonic power had enormous effect on the Egyptian psyche. Since the unification of Egypt in 3100 BC the Blacklanders had lived an ordered and peaceful existence in their Nile oasis. With the onset of the "First Intermediate Period", *Maat* – the fundamental concept of Egyptian life: equilibrium, justice, rightness – shattered. Something of the ensuing national gloom is captured in the religious dialogue "A Dispute over Suicide (pp 48–51). Eventually the speaker's soul (presented as a separate entity) persuades him against self-killing, but an Old Kingdom Egyptian would never have entertained the thought.

Equally profound was the influence of the First Intermediate Period on the nature of kingship itself. It was discredited. If the pharaoh was an all powerful god, why hadn't he maintained *Maat*. Individuals began to seek their own eternity. Magic spells, previously reserved for the pharaoh as "Pyramid Texts" began to be inscribed on the coffins of commoners (the so-called "Coffin Texts").

It took an exceptional man to pull Egypt out of the maelstrom of the First Intermediate Period. This was Mentuhotep I of the 11th Dynasty at Thebes which by Year 39 of his reign (c. 2021 BC) had managed to reunite the Two Lands.

The Middle Kingdom reached its apogee under the succeeding Dynasty 12 of the Amenemhets and Senusrets. Amenemhet I moved the royal capital to Itjawy in the Fayum, to more easily supervise both halves of the kingdom. He also introduced the astute practice of co-regency, as a sort of hands-on training period for the designated heir, and heavily promoted the religious cult of Re-Amun. Militarily he subdued Lower Nubia. Of all Amenemhet's successors, the martially minded Senusret III most actively pursued the conquest of Nubia, subjugating that land to the 2nd Cataract, where he built a series of immense mudbrick forts. (These were maintained by that Middle Kingdom innovation, the standing army.) Egyptian influence was also extended northwards, as far as Byblos, which became a vassal state. Inside Egypt Senusret III instigated a new system of government which bypassed the nomarchs, and he continued the reclamation of the marshes of the Nile begun by his immediate predecessors. Senusret III reigned for 37 years and was buried in a pyramid at Dashur. Senusret III was arguably the greatest of the Middle Kingdom pharaohs, yet his pyramid – which was the largest of the 12th Dynasty pyramids – says something about the reduced status of kingship in the Middle Kingdom. The pharaoh was still a god on earth, but a lesser god on earth. Accordingly, Senusret III's pyramid was half the size of Khufu's Great Pyramid and was made not of solid stone but mud-brick cased with limestone. Similarly, royal portraiture in the Middle Kingdom abandons the standardized "godlike" representations of the pharaoh for a more recognizably realistic and individual likeness.

Senusret III was succeeded by his son, Amenhemet III, another able and long-lived ruler. Yet neither pharaoh was able to prevent the Middle Kingdom falling into decay. After Amenhemet III the only known 12th Dynasty ruler is the queen regnant Sobeknefru. Quite why or how the Middle Kingdom disappeared into "The Second Intermediate Period" with its parallel competing dynasties is uncertain. What is known, is that out of this darkness emerged Egypt's golden empire: the New Kingdom.

THE INSTRUCTION FOR KING MERYKARE, c. 2169 BC

Meryibre Khety

Meryibre Khety of Herakleopolis was the founder of the 9th Dynasty. The troubled mood of the First Intermediate Period is caught accurately in this instruction to his son. No longer was it supposed that spells alone would secure the afterlife; it had to be earned by good works on earth. Not that good should be extended to all. Doubtless pricked by his own experience, Meryibre Khety enjoins his son to have no mercy on rebels.

Do justice so long as thou abidest on earth. Calm the weeper and oppress not the widow. Do not oust a man from the property of his father. Do not harm officials in respect of their posts. Beware of punishing wrongfully. Do not kill: it shall not profit thee. Punish with caution by beatings – so shall this country be peaceful – except (for) the rebel when his plans have been discovered, for God knows the treacherous of heart, and God requiteth his sins in blood. It is the mild man who . . . a lifetime. Do not slay a man whose good qualities thou knowest, one with whom thou didst chant the writings and read in the inventory . . . God, bold of thy step in difficult places. The soul cometh to the place it knoweth: it cannot stray from the paths of yesterday and no magic can oppose it. It cometh to those that give it water.

The judges who judge the deficient, thou knowest that they are not lenient on that day of judging the miserable, in the hour of performing (their) duty. It is hard when the accuser is possessed of knowledge. Put not thy trust in length of years: they regard a lifetime as an hour. A man surviveth after death and his deeds are placed beside him in heaps. Eternal is the existence yonder. He who makes light of it is a fool. As for him who reaches it without doing wrong, he shall exist yonder like a god, striding forth like the Lords of Eternity.

COFFIN TEXTS, C. 2134–1782 BC

Anonymous

During the Middle Kingdom it became funerary fashion for spells to be be carved on coffins and sarcophagi. Unlike the earlier "Pyramid Texts", these "Coffin Texts" were not the exclusive right of the pharaoh but were enjoyed by nobility as well. The Texts' purpose was to guide the individual soul on its perilous journey to the land of eternal life. They are frequently deeply fearful and morbid (see spell 33). The chaos of the First Intermediate Period is impressed within them.

Spell 33

O Lord of the gods, save me from those who inflict wounds, those whose fingers are painful, those who stand guard against the enemy and those who instil terror in the mutilators. They who do not relax their vigil, their knives shall not slice into me. I shall not go into their abattoir, I shall not sit in their vats, and nothing which the god detests shall be done to me.

Spell 74

Ah Helpless One!
Ah Helpless One Asleep!
Ah Helpless One in this place
which you know not – yet I know it!
Behold, I have found you [lying] on your side
the great Listless One.
"Ah, Sister!" says Iris to Nephthys,
"This is our brother,
Come, let us lift up his head,
Come, let us [rejoin] his bones,
Come, let us reassemble his limbs,
Come, let us put an end to all his woe,

that, as far as we can help, he will weary no more.
May the moisture begin to mount for this spirit!
May the canals be filled through you!
May the names of the rivers be created through you!
Osiris, live!
Osiris, let the great Listless One arise!
I am Isis."
"I am Nephthys.
It shall be that Horus will avenge you,
It shall be that Thoth will protect you,
– your two sons of the Great White Crown –
It shall be that you will act against him who acted – against
you,
It shall be that Geb will see,
It shall be that the Company will hear.
Then will your power be visible in the sky
And you will cause havoc among the [hostile] gods,
for Horus, your son, has seized the Great White Crown,
seizing it from him who acted against you.
Then will your father Atum call 'Come!' Osiris, live!
Osiris, let the great Listless One arise!"

Spell 330
Whether I live or die I am Osiris,
I enter in and reappear through you,
I decay in you, I grow in you,
I fall down in you, I fall upon my side.
The gods are living in me for I live and grow in the corn
that sustains the Honoured Ones.
I cover the earth,
whether I live or die I am Barley.
I am not destroyed.
I have entered the Order,

I rely upon the Order,
I become Master of the Order,
I emerge in the Order,
I make my form distinct,
I am the Lord – of the Chennet (Granary of Memphis?)
I have entered into the Order,
I have reached its limits . . .

Spell 404

He will arrive at another doorway. He will find the sisterly companions standing there and they will say to him, "Come, we wish to kiss you." And they will cut off the nose and lips of whoever does not know their names.

Spell 714

I was (the spirit in?) The Primeval Waters,
he who had no companion when my name came into existence.
The most ancient form in which I came into existence was as a drowned one.
I was (also) he who came into existence as a circle,
he who was the dweller in his egg.
I was the one who began (everything), the dweller in the Primeval Waters.
First Hahu* emerged from me
and then I began to move.
I created my limbs in my "glory"
I was the maker of myself, in that I formed myself according to my desire and in accord with my heart.

---

* the wind which separated the waters

ARISTOCRATIC CHILDHOOD, c. 2130 BC

Kheti

Kheti was nomarch of the Lycopolite nome.

I was a favourite of the king, a confidant of his princes, his exalted ones before Middle Egypt. He caused that I should rule as a child of a cubit (in height); he advanced my seat as a youth.

He had me instructed in swimming along with the royal children. I was one correct of speech, free from opposition to his lord, who brought him up as a child. Siut was satisfied with my administration; Heracleopolis praised god for me. Middle Egypt and the Northland (Delta) said: "It is the instruction of a king."

A DISPUTE OVER SUICIDE, c. 2100 BC

Anonymous

"The Dispute over Suicide" is a religious dialogue in which a man argues in favour of suicide – while his soul argues for life. Like "The Instruction for King Merykare", it is a pessimistic product of its time.

My soul opened its mouth to me that it might answer what I had said. If thou recallest burial, it is a sad matter. It is the bringing of tears, making a man sad. It is dragging a man from his house and casting him on the hillside. Thou shalt never go up that thou mayest see the sun. Those who built in granite and who hewed chambers in fine pyramid(s) with good work, when the builders became gods their offering stelæ were destroyed like (those of) the weary ones that died on the dyke, through lack of a survivor, the water having taken its toll, and the sun likewise to whom the fishes of the river banks talk. Listen to me. Behold it is good for men to listen. Follow pleasure and forget care . . .

I opened my mouth to my soul that I might answer what it had said.

Behold my name stinks
    Behold more than the stench of fish
    On a summer's day when the sky is hot . . .
Behold my name stinks
    Behold more than a woman,
    About whom a lie has been told to a man.
Behold my name stinks
    Behold more than a sturdy lad
    About whom it is said "He belongs to his rival."

To whom shall I speak today?
    Brothers are evil,
    The companions of yesterday do not love.
To whom shall I speak today?
    Hearts are rapacious,
    Every man seizes the goods of his neighbour . . .
To whom shall I speak today?
    Men are contented with evil,
    Goodness is neglected everywhere.
To whom shall I speak today?
    One who should make a man enraged by his evil behaviour
    Makes everyone laugh, though his iniquity is grievous . . .

To whom shall I speak today?
    The wrongdoer is an intimate,
    The brother with whom one should act is become an enemy.

To whom shall I speak today?
  Yesterday is not remembered,
  No one now helps him that hath done (good).
To whom shall I speak today?
  Faces are averted,
  Every man has (his) face downcast towards his
brethren.
To whom shall I speak today?
  Hearts are rapacious,
  No man has a heart upon which one can rely.
To whom shall I speak today?
  There are no righteous men.
  The land is left over to workers of iniquity . . .
To whom shall I speak today?
  I am laden with misery
  Through lack of an intimate.
To whom shall I speak today?
  The sin that roams the land,
  It has no end.
Death is in my sight today
  (Like) the recovery of a sick man,
  Like going abroad after detention.
Death is in my sight today
  Like the smell of myrrh,
  Like sitting under an awning on a windy day.
Death is in my sight today
  Like the scent of lotus flowers,
  Like sitting on the bank of drunkenness.
Death is in my sight today
  Like a well trodden way,
  As when a man returns home from an expedition.
Death is in my sight today
  Like the clearing of the sky,

Like a man attracted thereby to what he knows not.
Death is in my sight today
Like the longing of a man to see home,
When he has spent many years held in captivity.
Surely he who is yonder shall
Be a living god,
Punishing the sin of him who commits it.
Surely he who is yonder shall
Stand in the barque of the sun,
Causing the choicest things to be given therefrom to
the temples.
Surely he who is yonder shall
Be a man of knowledge,
Who cannot be prevented from petitioning Re
when he speaks.

What my soul said to me. Put care aside, my comrade and brother. Make an offering on the brazier and cling to life, according as I (?) have said. Desire me here and reject the West, but desire to reach the West when thy body goes into the earth, that I may alight after thou hast grown weary. Then let us make an abode together.

It is finished from its beginning to its end, as it was found in writing.

HYMN TO THE NILE, c. 2100 BC

Anonymous

To the Ancient Egyptians, the Nile was simply the River. Their dependence upon it was obvious: if the annual inundation was too low, not enough black silt was spread for an abundant harvest; if the inundation was too much, the floods damaged the permanent orchards and water-logged the fields. Accordingly, the Blacklanders prayed and hymned to the River for a "good" flood.

Hail to thee, O Nile! Who manifests thyself over this land, and comes to give life to Egypt! Mysterious is thy issuing forth from the darkness, on this day whereon it is celebrated! Watering the orchards created by Re, to cause all the cattle to live, you give the earth to drink, inexhaustible one! Path that descends from the sky, loving the bread of Seb and the first-fruits of Nepera, You cause the workshops of Ptah to prosper!

Lord of the fish, during the inundation, no bird alights on the crops. You create the grain, you bring forth the barley, assuring perpetuity to the temples. If you cease your toil and your work, then all that exists is in anguish. If the gods suffer in heaven, then the faces of men waste away.

Then He torments the flocks of Egypt, and great and small are in agony. But all is changed for mankind when He comes; He is endowed with the qualities of Nun. If He shines, the earth is joyous, every stomach is full of rejoicing, every spine is happy, every jaw-bone crushes (its food).

He brings the offerings, as chief of provisioning; He is the creator of all good things, as master of energy, full of sweetness in his choice. If offerings are made it is thanks to Him. He brings forth the herbage for the flocks, and sees that each god receives his sacrifices. All that depends on Him is a precious incense. He spreads himself over Egypt, filling the granaries, renewing the marts, watching over the goods of the unhappy.

He is prosperous to the height of all desires, without fatiguing Himself therefore. He brings again his lordly bark; He is not sculptured in stone, in the statutes crowned with the uraeus serpent, He cannot be contemplated. No servitors has He, no bearers of offerings! He is not enticed by incantations! None knows the place where He dwells, none discovers his retreat by the power of a written spell.

No dwelling (is there) which may contain you! None penetrates within your heart! Your young men, your children applaud you and render unto you royal homage. Stable are your decrees for Egypt before your servants of the North! He stanches the water from all eyes and watches over the increase of his good things.

Where misery existed, joy manifests itself; all beasts rejoice. The children of Sobek, the sons of Neith, the cycle of the gods which dwells in him, are prosperous. No more reservoirs for watering the fields! He makes mankind valiant, enriching some, bestowing his love on others. None commands at the same time as himself. He creates the offerings without the aid of Neith, making mankind for himself with multiform care.

He shines when He issues forth from the darkness, to cause his flocks to prosper. It is his force that gives existence to all things; nothing remains hidden for him. Let men clothe themselves to fill his gardens. He watches over his works, producing the inundation during the night. The associate of Ptah . . . He causes all his servants to exist, all writings and divine words, and that which He needs in the North.

It is with the words that He penetrates into his dwelling; He issues forth at his pleasure through the magic spells. Your unkindness brings destruction to the fish; it is then that prayer is made for the (annual) water of the season; Southern Egypt is seen in the same state as the North. Each one is with his instruments of labour. None remains behind his companions. None clothes himself with garments. The children of the noble put aside their ornaments.

He night remains silent, but all is changed by the inundation; it is a healing-balm for all mankind. Establisher of justice! Mankind desires you, supplicating you to

answer their prayers; You answer them by the inundation!
Men offer the first-fruits of corn; all the gods adore you!
The birds descend not on the soil. It is believed that with
your hand of gold you make bricks of silver! But we are not
nourished on lapis-lazuli; wheat alone gives vigour.

A festal song is raised for you on the harp, with the
accompaniment of the hand. Your young men and your
children acclaim you and prepare their (long) exercises.
You are the august ornament of the earth, letting your bark
advance before men, lifting up the heart of women in labor,
and loving the multitude of the flocks.

When you shine in the royal city, the rich man is sated
with good things, the poor man even disdains the lotus; all
that is produced is of the choicest; all the plants exist for
your children. If you have refused (to grant) nourishment,
the dwelling is silent, devoid of all that is good, the country
falls exhausted.

O inundation of the Nile, offerings are made unto you,
men are immolated to you, great festivals are instituted for
you. Birds are sacrificed to you, gazelles are taken for you in
the mountain, pure flames are prepared for you. Sacrifice is
metle to every god as it is made to the Nile. The Nile has
made its retreats in Southern Egypt, its name is not known
beyond the Tuau. The god manifests not his forms, He
baffles all conception.

Men exalt him like the cycle of the gods, they dread him
who creates the heat, even him who has made his son the
universal master in order to give prosperity to Egypt. Come
(and) prosper! Come (and) prosper! O Nile, come (and)
prosper! O you who make men to live through his flocks
and his flocks through his orchards! Come (and) prosper,
come, O Nile, come (and) prosper!

THE TALE OF THE ELOQUENT PEASANT, c. 2050 BC

Anonymous

The reverence of the Ancient Egyptians for "The Tale of the Eloquent Peasant" was seemingly predicated on its fine prose style. En passant, it shows the workings of civil justice in the age of the pharaohs.

There was a man, Hunanup by name, a peasant of Sechet-hemat, and he had a wife, . . . by name. Then said this peasant to his wife: "Behold, I am going down to Egypt to bring back bread for my children. Go in and measure the grain that we still have in our storehouse, . . . bushel." Then he measured for her eight bushels of grain. Then this peasant said to his wife: "Behold, two bushels of grain shall be left for bread for you and the children. But make for me the six bushels into bread and beer for each of the days that I shall be on the road." Then this peasant went down to Egypt after he had loaded his asses with all the good produce of Sechet-hemat.

This peasant set out and journeyed southward to Ehnas. He came to a point opposite Per-fefi, north of Medenit, and found there a man standing on the bank, Dehuti-necht by name, who was the son of a man named Iseri, who was one of the serfs of the chief steward, Meruitensi.

Then said this Dehuti-necht, when he saw the asses of this peasant which appealed to his covetousness: "Oh, that some good god would help me to rob this peasant of his goods!"

The house of Dehuti-necht stood close to the side of the path, which was narrow, not wide. It was about the width of a . . . cloth, and upon one side of it was the water and upon the other side was growing grain. Then said Dehuti-necht to his servant: "Hasten and bring me a shawl from the house!" And it was brought at once. Then he spread this shawl upon the middle of the road, and it extended, one edge to the water, and the other to the grain.

The peasant came along the path which was the common highway. Then said Dehuti-necht: "Look out, peasant, do not trample on my clothes!" The peasant answered: "I will do as you wish; I will go in the right way!" As he was turning to the upper side, Dehuti-necht said: "Does my grain serve you as a road?" Then said the peasant: "I am going in the right way. The bank is steep and the path lies near the grain and you have stopped up the road ahead with your clothes. Will you, then, not let me go by?" Upon that one of the asses took a mouthful of grain. Then said Dehuti-necht: "See, I will take away your ass because it has eaten my grain."

Then the peasant said: "I am going in the right way. As one side was made impassable I have led my ass along the other, and will you seize it because it has taken a mouthful of grain? But I know the lord of this property; it belongs to the chief steward, Meruitensi. It is he who punishes every robber in this whole land. Shall I, then, be robbed in his domain?"

Then said Dehuti-necht: "Is it not a proverb which the people employ: 'The name of the poor is only known on account of his lord?' It is I who speak to you, but the chief steward of whom you think." Then he took a rod from a green tamarisk and beat all his limbs with it, and seized his asses and drove them into his compound.

Thereupon the peasant wept loudly on account of the pain of what had been done to him. Dehuti-necht said to him: "Don't cry so loud, peasant, or you shall go to the city of the dead." The peasant said: "You beat me and steal my goods, and will you also take the wail away from my mouth? O Silence-maker! Give me my goods again! May I never cease to cry out, if you fear!"

The peasant consumed four days, during which he besought Dehuti-necht, but he did not grant him his rights. Then this peasant went to the south, to Ehnas to implore the chief steward, Meruitensi. He met him as he was coming out of the canal-door of his compound to embark in his boat. Thereupon the peasant said: "Oh, let me lay before you this affair. Permit one of your trusted servants to come to me, that I may send him to you concerning it." Then the steward Meruitensi sent one of his servants to him, and he sent back by him an account of the whole affair. Then the chief steward, Meruitensi, laid the case of Dehuti-necht before his attendant officials, and they said to him: "Lord, it is presumably a case of one of your peasants who has gone against another peasant near him. Behold, it is customary with peasants to so conduct themselves toward others who are near them. Shall we beat Dehuti-necht for a little natron and a little salt? Command him to restore it and he will restore it."

The chief steward, Meruitensi, remained silent – he answered neither the officials nor the peasant. The peasant then came to entreat the chief steward Meruitensi, for the first time, and said: "Chief steward, my lord, you are greatest of the great, you are guide of all that which is not and which is. When you embark on the sea of truth, that you may go sailing upon it, then shall not the . . . strip away your sail, then your ship shall not remain fast, then shall no misfortune happen to your mast, then shall your spars not be broken, then shall you not be stranded – if you run fast aground, the waves shall not break upon you, then you shall not taste the impurities of the river, then you shall not behold the face of fear, the shy fish shall come to you, and you shall capture the fat birds. For you are the father of the orphan, the husband of the widow, the brother of the desolate, the garment of the motherless. Let me place your name in this land higher than all good laws: you guide without avarice, you great one free from meanness, who destroys deceit, who creates truthfulness. Throw the evil to the ground. I will speak; hear me. Do justice, O you praised one, whom the praised ones praise. Remove my oppression: behold, I have a heavy weight to carry; behold, I am troubled of soul; examine me, I am in sorrow."

The peasant addresses Meruitensi again and again, with ever greater eloquence until:

This peasant came to implore him for the eighth time, and said:

"Chief steward, my lord, man falls on account of . . . Greed is absent from a good merchant. His good commerce is . . . Your heart is greedy, it does not become you. You despoil: this is not praiseworthy for you . . . Your daily rations are in your house; your body is well filled. The officers, who are set as a protection against injustice, – a curse to the shameless are these officers, who are set as a bulwark against lies. Fear of you has not deterred me from supplicating you; if you think so, you have not known my heart. The Silent one, who turns to report to you his difficulties, is not afraid to present them to you. Your real estate is in the country, your bread is on your estate, your food is in the storehouse. Your officials give to you and you take it. Are you, then, not a robber? They plough for you . . . for you to the plots of arable land. Do the truth for the sake of the Lord of Truth. You reed of a scribe, you roll of a book, you palette, you god Thoth, you ought to keep yourself far removed from injustice. You virtuous one, you should be virtuous, you virtuous one, you should be really virtuous. Further, truth is true to eternity. She goes with those who perform her to the region of the dead. He will be laid in the coffin and committed to the earth; – his name will not perish from the earth, but men will remember him on account of his property: so runs the right interpretation of the divine word.

"Does it then happen that the scales stand aslant? Or is it thinkable that the scales incline to one side? Behold, if I come not, if another comes, then you host opportunity to speak as one who answers, as one who addresses the silent, as one who responds to him who has not spoken to you. You have not been . . . ; You have not been sick. You have not fled, you have not departed. But you have not yet granted me any reply to this beautiful word which comes from the mouth of the sun-god himself: 'Speak the truth; do the truth: for it is great, it is mighty, it is everlasting. It will obtain for you merit, and will lead you to veneration.' For does the scale stand aslant? It is their scale-pans that bear the objects, and in just scales there is no . . . wanting."

After the peasant's ninth speech, the story concludes:

Then the chief steward, Meruitensi, sent two servants to bring him back. Thereupon the peasant feared that he would suffer thirst, as a punishment imposed upon him for what he had said. Then the peasant said . . .

Then said the chief steward, Meruitensi: "Fear not, peasant! See, you shall remain with me."

Then said the peasant: "I live because I eat of your bread and drink your beer forever."

Then said the chief steward, Meruitensi: "Come out here . . ." Then he caused them to bring, written on a new roll, all the addresses of these days. The chief steward sent them to his majesty, the king of Upper and Lower Egypt, Neb-kau-re, the blessed, and they were more agreeable to the heart of his majesty than all that was in his land. His majesty said, "Pass sentence yourself, my beloved son!" Then the chief steward, Meruitensi, caused two servants to go and bring a list of the household of Dehuti-necht from the government office, and his possessions were six persons, with a selection from his . . . from his barley, from his spelt, from his asses, from his swine, from his . . .

Few words from the remainder of the story are intelligible, but the gist is that the goods from the estate of Dehuti-necht were given to the peasant, who returned home rejoicing.

MYRRH, SOLDIERS, WELLS: EXPEDITION TO PUNT, c. 2002 BC

Henu

The steward of Mentuhotep II, Henu was dispatched to Punt (probably modern-day Somalia or Tigre) to secure myrrh for the regent. As Henu records in his inscription at the Wadi Hammamat, the expedition required force of arms and the sinking of wells for water.

My lord, life, prosperity, health sent me to despatch a ship to Punt to bring for him fresh myrrh from the sheiks over the Red Land, by reason of the fear of him in the highlands.

Then I went forth from Koptos (Kuft) upon the road,

which his majesty commanded me. There was with me an army of the South from [—] of the Oxyrrhincus Nome, the beginning thereof as far as Gebelen (*sic*), the end thereof as far as [—], every officer of the king's house, those who were in town and field, united, came after me.

The army cleared the way before, overthrowing those hostile to the king, the hunters and the children of the highlands were posted as the protection of my limbs. Every official body was placed under my authority. They reported messengers to me, as one alone commanding to whom many hearken.

I went forth with an army of 3,000 men. I made the road a river and the Red Land a stretch of field, for I gave a leathern bottle, a carrying pole, jars of water, and twenty loaves to each one among them every day. The asses were laden with sandals . . .

Now I made twelve wells in the bush and two wells in Idehet 20 square cubits in one, and 31 square cubits in another in Iheteb 20 by 20 cubits on each side . . .

Then I reached the (Red) Sea; then I made this ship, and I despatched it with everything, when I had made for it a great oblation of cattle, bulls and ibexes.

Now, after my return from the (Red) Sea, I executed the command of his majesty, and I brought for him all the gifts, which I had found in the regions of God's-Land. I returned through the valley of Hammamat, I brought for him august blocks for statues belonging to the temple. Never was brought down the like thereof for the king's court; never was done the like of this by any king's-confidant sent out since the time of the god. I did this for the majesty of my lord because he so much loved me . . .

THE TRADES IN EGYPT, c. 2000 BC

Dua-Khety

"The Instruction of Dua-Khety" is satirical warning by a father to his son on the dangers of not working hard at school. Education leads to the revered position of scribe. Illiteracy means a future as a tradesman of some sort. To underline his point, Dua-Khety itemises the trades of Egypt and their awful drawbacks.

1. The beginning of the teaching which the man of Tjel* named Dua-Khety made for his son named Pepy, while he sailed southwards to the Residence to place him in the school of writings among the children of the magistrates, the most eminent men of the Residence.

2. So he spoke to him: Since I have seen those who have been beaten, it is to writings that you must set your mind. Observe the man who has been carried off to a work force. Behold, there is nothing that surpasses writings! They are a boat upon the water. Read then at the end of the Book of Kemyet this statement in it saying: As for a scribe in any office in the Residence, he will not suffer want in it.

3. When he fulfils the bidding of another, he does not come forth satisfied. I do not see an office to be compared with it, to which this maxim could relate. I shall make you love books more than your mother, and I shall place their excellence before you. It [the office of scribe] is greater than any office. There is nothing like it on earth. When he began to become sturdy but was still a child, he was greeted (respectfully). When he was sent to carry out a task, before he returned he was dressed in adult garments.

* Tjel is Sile in the northeast Delta on the borders of Egypt.

4. I do not see a stoneworker on an (important) errand or a goldsmith in a place to which he has been sent, but I have seen a coppersmith at his work at the door of his furnace. His fingers were like the claws of the crocodile, and he stank more than fish excrement.

5. Every carpenter who bears the adze is wearier than a field-hand. His field is his wood, his hoe is the axe. There is no end to his work, and he must labour excessively in (his) activity. At nighttime he (still) must light (his lamp).

6. The jeweller pierces (stone) in stringing beads in all kinds of hard stone. When he has completed the inlaying of the eye-amulets, his strength vanishes and he is tired out. He sits until the arrival of the sun, his knees and his back bent at (the place called) Aku-Re.

7. The barber shaves until the end of the evening. But he must be up early, crying out, his bowl upon his arm. He takes himself from street to street to seek out someone to shave. He wears out his arms to fill his belly, like bees who eat (only) according to their work.

8. The reed-cutter goes downstream to the Delta to fetch himself arrows. He must work excessively in (his) activity. When the gnats sting him and the sand fleas bite him as well, then he is judged.

9. The potter is covered with earth, although his lifetime is still among the living. He burrows in the field more than swine to bake his cooking vessels. His clothes being stiff with mud, his headcloth consists (only) of rags, so that the air which comes forth from his burning furnace enters his nose. He operates a pestle with his feet, with which he himself is pounded, penetrating the courtyard of every house and driving (earth) into (every) open place.

10. I shall also describe to you the bricklayer. His kidneys are painful. When he must be outside in the wind, he lays

bricks without a garment. His belt is a cord for his back, a string for his buttocks. His strength has vanished through fatigue and stiffness, kneading all his excrement. He eats bread with his fingers, although he washes himself but once a day.

11. It is miserable for the carpenter when he planes the roofbeam. It is the roof of a chamber 10 by 6 cubits. A month goes by in laying the beams and spreading the matting. All the work is accomplished. But as for the food which is to be given to his household (while he is away), there is no one who provides for his children.

12. The vintner carries his shoulder-yoke. Each of his shoulders is burdened with age. A swelling is on his neck, and it festers. He spends the morning in watering leeks and the evening (with) corianders, after he has spent the mid-day in the palm grove. So it happens that he sinks down (at last) and dies through his deliveries, more than one of any (other) profession.

13. The fieldhand cries out more than the guinea fowl. His voice is louder than the raven's. His fingers have become ulcerous with an excess of stench. When he is taken away to be enrolled in Delta labour, he is in tatters. He suffers when he proceeds to the island, and sickness is his payment. The forced labour then is tripled. If he comes back from the marshes there, he reaches his house worn out, for the forced labour has ruined him.

14. The weaver inside the weaving house is more wretched than a woman. His knees are drawn up against his belly. He cannot breathe the air. If he wastes a (single) day without weaving, he is beaten with 50 whip lashes. He has to give food to the doorkeeper to allow him to come out to the daylight.

15. The arrow maker, completely wretched, goes into the

desert. Greater (than his own pay) is what he has to spend for his she-ass for its work afterwards. Great is also what he has to give to the fieldhand to set him on the (right) road (to the flint source). When he reaches his house in the evening, the journey has ruined him.

16. The courier goes abroad after handing over his property to his children, being fearful of the lions and the Asiatics. He only knows himself (again) when he is (back) in Egypt. But his household (by then) is only a tent. There is no happy homecoming.

17. The furnace-tender, his fingers are foul, the smell thereof is as corpses. His eyes are inflamed because of the heaviness of the smoke. He cannot get rid of his dirt, although he spends the day at the reed pond. Clothes are an abomination to him.

18. The sandalmaker is utterly wretched carrying his tubs of oil. His stores are provided with carcasses, and what he bites is hides.

19. The washerman launders at the riverbank in the vicinity of the crocodile. I shall go away, father, from the flowing water, said his son and his daughter, to a more satisfactory profession, one more distinguished than any (other) profession. His food is mixed with filth, and there is no part of him which is clean. He cleans the clothes of a woman in menstruation. He weeps when he spends all day with a beating stick and a stone there. One says to him, dirty laundry, come to me, the brim overflows.

20. The fowler is utterly weak while searching out for the denizens of the sky. If the flock passes by above him, then he says: would that I might have nets. But God will not let this come to pass for him, for He is opposed to his activity.

21. I mention to you also the fisherman. He is more miserable than (one of) any (other) profession, one who is

at his work in a river infested with crocodiles. When the totalling of his account is made for him, then he will lament. One did not tell him that a crocodile was standing there, and fear has (now) blinded him. When he comes to the flowing water, so he falls (as) through the might of God. See, there is no office free from supervisors, except the scribe's. He is the supervisor!

22. But if you understand writings, then it will be better for you than the professions which I have set before you. Behold the official and the dependent pertaining to him. The tenant farmer of a man cannot say to him: Do not keep watching (me). What I have done in journeying southward to the Residence is what I have done through love of you. A day at school is advantageous to you. Seek out its work early, while the workmen I have caused you to know hurry on and cause the recalcitrant to hasten.

Hereafter, Dua-Kehty continues with the general advice typical of instructional literature.

THE WONDERS IN THE WADI HAMMAMAT, c. 1995 BC

Anonymous

The two wonders recorded below occurred during an expedition to retrieve stone for the lid of the sarcophagus of Mentuhotep III [Nibtowere]. The commander of the expedition was the vizier Amenemhet; he seems to have later overthrown his lord and become the founder of the 12th Dynasty.

This wonder which happened to his majesty: that the beasts of the highlands came down to him; there came a gazelle great with young, going with her face toward the people before her, while her eyes looked backward; (but) she did not turn back, until she arrived at this august mountain, at this block, it being still in its place, (intended) for this lid of this sarcophagus. She dropped her young upon it while this army of the king was looking. Then they cut off her neck before it (the block) and brought fire. It descended in safety.

Eight days after the first wonder, a second wonder occurred, which was immediately committed to record on the rocks.

One set to work on this mountain on the lid block of the sarcophagus. The wonder was repeated, rain was made, the forms of this god appeared, his fame was shown to men, the highland was made a lake, the water went to the margin of the stone, a well was found in the midst of the valley, 10 cubits by 10 cubits on its every side, filled with fresh water, to its edge, undefiled, kept pure and cleansed from gazelles, concealed from Troglodyte barbarians. Soldiers of old, and kings who had lived aforetime, went out and returned by its side, no eye had seen it, the face of man had not fallen upon it, (but) to his majesty himself it was revealed . . . Those who were in Egypt heard it, the people who were in Egypt, South and Northland (Delta), they bowed their heads to the ground, they praised the goodness of his majesty forever and ever.

THE PROPHECIES OF NERFERTI, c. 1991 BC

Anonymous

Amenemhet I came to the throne in a coup d'état. *To consolidate his new Dynasty 12, he encouraged a deal of justifying political propoganda. "The Prophecies of Neferti" is one such literary political support. Set in the time of the Old Kingdom it tells of King Snefru asking for entertainment, at which the soothsayer Neferti is brought forth. He "foretells" that in the future Egypt will be struck by calamities but a new king called "Ameny" (i.e. Amenemhet) restores order and prosperity.*

Now it so happened that when the late King Snefru was potent king in this entire land, one of these days it happened that the Council of the Residence entered into the Great House to give greeting,[1] and when they had given greeting, they went out in accordance with their daily custom. Then said His Majesty to the seal-bearer who was at his side: Go and fetch for me the Council of the Residence which has gone out from here after having given greeting today. They were ushered in to him/immediately, and again they prostrated themselves before His Majesty. And His Majesty said to them: Comrades, see, I have caused you to be summoned in order that you may seek out for me a son of yours who is wise, a brother of yours who is trustworthy, or a friend of yours who has achieved some noble deed, someone who shall say some fine words to me, choice phrases at the hearing of which My Majesty will be entertained. They prostrated themselves again before His Majesty: There is a Great Lector of Bastet,[2] O Sovereign our lord,/whose name is Neferti; he is a commoner valiant with his arm, he is a scribe skilled with his fingers, and he is a wealthy man who has more possessions than any of his equals. Let him be [permitted] to see Your Majesty. His Majesty said: Go and fetch him to me. And he was ushered in to him immediately.

He prostrated himself before His Majesty, and His Majesty said: Come, Neferti my friend, say some fine words to me, choice phrases at hearing which My Majesty will be entertained. The Lector Neferti said: Of what has happened or of what shall happen, O Sovereign, [my]

1 To the king.
2 A cat-goddess.

lord?/His Majesty said: Of what shall happen; today has come into being and one has passed it by. Thereupon he[3] stretched out his hand to a box of writing materials and took out a papyrus-roll and a palette, and he put into writing what the Lector Neferti said; he was a sage of the East[4] who belonged to Bastet when she rises and he was a native of the Heliopolitan nome.

He brooded over what should happen in the land and considered the condition of the east, when the Asiatics raid[5] and terrorize those at the harvest, taking away their teams engaged in ploughing./He said: stir yourself, my heart, weep for this land in which you began, for he who is silent is a wrongdoer. See, that (now) exists which was spoken of as something dreadful. See, the great one is overthrown in the land in which you began. Do not become weary; see, they[6] are before your eyes; rise up against what is before you. See, there are great men in the governance of the land, yet what has been done is as though it had never been done. Re must begin by refounding the land, which is utterly ruined, and nothing remains; not even did a fingernail profit from what had been ordained. This land is destroyed and there are none who care for it; there are none who speak and there are none who act. Weeper, how fares this land? The sun is veiled,/and will not shine when the people would see; none will live when [the sun] is veiled [by] cloud, and everyone is dulled by the lack of it.

I will speak of what is before my eyes, I will never foretell what is not to come. The river of Egypt is dry and men cross the water on foot; men will seek water for ships in order to navigate it,[7] for their course has become the riverbank, and

3 The king.
4 i.e. the eastern Delta.
5 Lit. "travel in their power".
6 The facts of the case.
7 The river.

the bank (serves) for water; the place of water [has become] a riverbank, the south wind will oppose the north wind, and the sky will not be with one single wind. A strange bird[8] will be born in the marshes of the Delta, and a nest shall be made for it on account of the neighbours,/for men have caused it to approach through want. Perished are those erstwhile good things, the fish ponds of those who carry slit fish, teeming with fish and fowl. All good things have passed away, the land being cast away through trouble by means of that food of the Asiatics who pervade the land. Enemies have come into being in the east; Asiatics have come down into Egypt, for a fortress lacks another beside it,[9] and no guard will hear. Men will hold back and look out by night,[10] the fortress will be entered, and sleep will be banished from my eyes,/so that I spend the night wakeful. Wild game will drink from the river of Egypt, taking their ease on their riverbanks through lack of anyone to fear. This land is in commotion, and no one knows what the result may be, for it is hidden from speech, sight, and hearing because of dullness, silence being to the fore.

I show you the land in calamity, for what had never happened has now happened. Men will take weapons of war and the land will live in/confusion. Men will make arrows of bronze, men will beg for the bread of blood, men will laugh aloud[11] at pain; none will weep at death, none will lie down hungry at death,[12] and a man's heart will think of himself alone. None will dress hair today; hearts are entirely astray because of it, and a man sits quiet, turning his back, while one man kills another.

8 A bird of ill-omen.
9 To support it so as to keep the barbarians out.
10 i.e. will not venture out, but stare apprehensively into the darkness.
11 Lit. "laugh with a laughing".
12 Meaning that men will not fast after a death.

I show you a son as an enemy, a brother as a foe, a man/ killing his father. Every mouth is full of "Love me"; all good things have passed away; a law is decreed for the ruin of the land. Men wreak destruction on what has been made and make a desolation of what has been found; what has been made is as though it had never been made; a man's possessions are taken from him and are given to an outsider.

I show you the owner of (but) a little, while the outsider is content. He who did not fill for himself now goes empty;[13] men give (something) unwillingly, so as to silence a talking mouth. A sentence is answered and a hand goes out with a stick; [men say]: "Do not kill him," but the discourse of speech is like fire to the heart,/and none can endure utterance. The land is diminished, though its controllers are many; he who was rich in servants is despoiled and corn is trifling, even though the corn-measure is great and it is measured to overflowing.[14] Re separates himself from men; he shines, that the hour may be told,[15] but no one knows when noon occurs,[16] for no one can discern his shadow, no one is dazzled when [he] is seen; there are none whose eyes stream with water, for he is like the moon in the sky, (though) his accustomed times do [not] go astray, and his rays are in (men's) sight as on former occasions.[17]

I show you the land in calamity; the weak-armed now possesses an arm, and men/salute one who used to do the saluting. I show you [the lowermost] uppermost, men pursuing him who flees away;[18] men are living in the necropolis. The poor man will achieve wealth, while the

13 The result of improvidence.
14 i.e. those who should issue the corn keep it in store.
15 Lit. "that the hour may exist", referring to dawn.
16 The sun is too weak to cast the necessary shadow.
17 The sun performs its normal motions but sheds no more light than the moon.
18 Lit. "men turn round after him who turns his body round" in order to run away.

great lady will [beg] to exist; it is the poor who will eat bread, while servants are . . .; there will be no Heliopolitan nome to be the birth-land of every god.

A king of the South will come, Ameny by name,[19] the son of a woman of Zety-land,[20] a child of Khenkhen.[21] He will assume the White Crown, he will wear the Red Crown,/he will join together the Double Crown, he will propitiate the Two Lords[22] with what they desire; the land will be enclosed in [his] grasp, the oars swinging;[23] the people of his reign will rejoice, the well-born man will make his name forever and ever. Those who have fallen into evil and have planned rebellion have stultified[24] their utterances through fear of him; the Asiatics will fall at the dread of him; the Libyans will fall at his flaming, the rebels at his wrath, the disaffected at/ the awe of him, while the uraeus[25] which is on his forehead will pacify the disaffected. Men will build "Walls of the Ruler",[26] and there will be no letting the Asiatics go down into Egypt that they may beg water after their accustomed fashion to let their herds drink. Right will come to its place (again) and Wrong will be thrust outside; joyful will be [he] who will see (it) and he who will serve the king. The learned man shall pour [a libation to me when he sees that what I have said] has come to pass.

It has come happily to an end.

19 Here the real purpose of this work begins to show; it is propaganda in favour of Ammenemes I, the saviour who will set right the miseries of the preceding period of chaos. Ameny is a shortened form of his name.
20 This geographical term embraced the territory both north and south of the First Cataract; here the northern portion, the first nome of Upper Egypt, is probably what is intended.
21 A name for Upper Egypt.
22 Horus and Seth.
23 When he is rowed on his royal progresses through the land.
24 Lit. "have caused to fall".
25 The royal cobra.
26 The frontier fortifications in the Wadi Tumilat, built by Ammenemes I.

THE INSTRUCTION OF PHARAOH
AMENEMHET, c. 1971 BC

Akhtoy

The Instruction purports to be the advice of the dead Amenemhet to his son and successor, Senusret I; actually, the injunctions were written by the scribe Akhtoy. Akhtoy's tone of vicarious misanthropism was justified though: Amenemhet was assassinated in a coup. His reign was notable for both founding the institution of co-regency (Amenemhet shared the throne with Senusret for ten years before his murder) and a new capital, Itj-tawy. The site of this fortified city has never been found.

Be thou in splendour like the god, my son . . .
Hearken and hear my words, if thou wouldst reign
In Egypt and be ruler of the world,
Excelling in thy greatness . . . Live apart
In stern seclusion, for the people heed
The man who makes them tremble; mingle not
Alone among them; have no bosom friend,
Nor intimate, nor favourite in thy train –
These serve no goodly purpose.

  Ere to sleep
Thou liest down, prepare to guard thy life –
A man is friendless in the hour of trial . . .
I to the needy gave, the orphan nourished,
Esteemed alike the lowly and the great;
But he who ate my bread made insurrection,
And those my hands raised up, occasion seized
Rebellion to create . . . They went about
All uniformed in garments that I gave
And deemed me but a shadow . . . Those who shared

My perfumes for anointment, rose betimes
And broke into my harem.

   Through the land
Beholden are my statues, and men laud
The deeds I have accomplished . . . yet I made
A tale heroic that hath ne'er been told,
And triumphed in a conflict no man saw . . .

Surely these yearned for bondage when they smote
The king who set them free . . . Methinks, my son,
Of no avail is liberty to men
Grown blind to their good fortune.

   I had dined
At eve and darkness fell. I sought to rest
For I was weary. On my bed I lay
And gave my thoughts release, and so I slept . . .
The rebels 'gan to whisper and take arms
With treacherous intent . . . I woke and heard
And like the desert serpent waited there
All motionless but watchful.

   Then I sprang
To fight and I alone . . . A warrior fell,
And lo! he was the captain of my guard.
Ah! had I but his weapons in that hour
I should have scattered all the rebel band –
Mighty my blows and swift! . . . but he, alas!
Was like a coward there . . . Nor in the dark,
And unprepared, could I achieve renown.

Hateful their purpose! . . . I was put to shame.
Thou wert not nigh to save . . . Announced I then
That thou didst reign, and I had left the throne.
And gave commands according to thy will . . .
Ah! as they feared me not, 't was well to speak
With courtesy before them . . . Would I could
Forget the weakness of my underlings!

My son, Senusert, say – Are women wont
To plot against their lords? Lo! mine have reared
A brood of traitors, and assembled round
A rebel band forsworn. They did deceive
My servants with command to pierce the ground
For speedy entry.

   Yet to me from birth
Misfortune hath a stranger been. I ne'er
Have met mine equal among valiant men . . .
Lo! I have set in order all the land.
From Elephantine adown the Nile
I swept in triumph: so my feet have trod
The outposts of my kingdom . . . Mighty deeds
Must now be measured by the deeds I've done.

I loved the corn god . . . I have grown the grain
In every golden valley where the Nile
Entreated me; none hungered in my day,
None thirsted, and all men were well content –
They praised me, saying: "Wise are his commands."

I fought the lion and the crocodile,
I smote the dusky Nubians, and put
The Asian dogs to flight.

Mine house I built.
Gold-decked with azure ceilings, and its walls
Have deep foundations; doors of copper are,
The bolts of bronze . . . It shall endure all time.
Eternity regards it with dismay!
I know each measurement, O Lord of All!

Men came to see its beauties, and I heard
In silence while they praised it. No man knew
The treasure that it lacked . . . I wanted thee,
My son, Senusert . . . Health and strength be thine!
I lean upon thee, O my heart's delight;
For thee I look on all things . . . Spirits sang
In that glad hour when thou wert born to me.

All things I've done, now know, were done for thee;
For thee must I complete what I began
Until the end draws nigh . . . O be my heart
The isle of thy desire . . . The white crown now
Is given thee, O wise son of the god —
I'll hymn thy praises in the bark of Ra . . .
Thy kingdom at Creation was. 'T is thine
As it was mine — how mighty were my deeds!
Rear thou thy statues and adorn thy tomb . . .
I struck thy rival down . . . 'T would not be wise
To leave him nigh thee . . . Health and strength be
thine!

THE FLIGHT OF THE COURTIER SINUHE,
c. 1971 BC

Sinuhe

"The Story of Sinuhe" is a semi-factual account of the adventures of the eponymous courtier, who fled to Palestine and Syria for fear of implication in the assassination of Amenemhet I. The story was a favourite of Ancient Egypt and used as school text.

In year 30, second month of the first season, on the
7th day,
Departed the god into his horizon,
The king of Upper and Lower Egypt, Sehetepibre [i.e.
Amenemhet I].
He ascended [to] heaven, joined with the sun;
The divine limbs were mingled with him that begat
him.
In the court, silence.
The great double doors were closed,
The court sat (in mourning),
The people [bowed down in] silence.
  Behold, his majesty had sent out
A numerous army to the land of the Libyans;
The eldest son was commander thereof,
The Good God Sesostris [Senusret].
Now, just as he was returning, having taken
Living captives of the Libyans,
And all cattle, without limit;
The companions of the court,
They sent to the west side,
In order to inform the king
Of their plan, conceived in the cabinet chamber.

The messengers found him on the way,
They reached him at the time of evening.

The hawk, he flew, together with his following,
Without letting his army know it.
Then sent the royal children,
Who followed this army;
No one had called to one of them.
Behold, I stood; I heard his voice
  As he spoke,
My heart cleaved, my arms opened,
While trembling fell on all my members.
I stole away
To seek for myself a place of concealment.
I placed myself between two bushes,
To avoid the way which they went.
I proceeded up-stream,
  Not intending (however) to reach the court;
I thought there was fighting (there).

  I reached [–] in the region of Sycomore,
I arrived at the Isle of Snefru.
I tarried in a stretch of field.
It grew light, I went on, when it was day.
I came upon a man, standing in the way;
He saluted me, and was afraid.
  When the time of the evening meal drew on,
I reached the city of the Ox.
I ferried over, in a vessel without a rudder,
By means of a wind of the west.
I passed by on the east of the quarry,
  Past the highland goddess, mistress of the Red
Mountain.

As I gave the way to my feet, going northward,
I came to the Walls of the Ruler,
Made to repulse the Bedwin,
    And to smite the sand-rangers.
I bowed down in the bushes,
For fear the sentinels on the fort,
Who belonged to its day (-watch), should see me.
I went on at time of evening,
As the earth brightened, I arrived at Peten.
    When I had reached the lake of Kemwer
I fell down for thirst, fast came my breath,
My throat was hot,
    I said: This is the taste of death.
I upheld my heart, I drew my limbs together,
As I heard the sound of the lowing of cattle,
I beheld the Bedwin.
    That chief among them, who had been in Egypt,
recognized me.
    He gave me water, he cooked for me milk.
I went with him to his tribe,
Good was that which they did (for me).
One land sent me on to another,
I loosed for Suan
I arrived at Kedem;
I spent a year and a half there.
    Emuienshi, that sheik of Upper Tenu, brought me
forth
Saying to me: "Happy art thou with me,
(For) thou hearest the speech of Egypt."
He said this, (for) he knew my character,
He had heard of my wisdom;
The Egyptians who were there with him, bear witness
of me.

[. . . Emuisenshi questions Sinuhe about the reason for his flight, and when Sinuhe prevaricates the sheikh replies:]

"Behold, thou shalt now abide with me;
Good is that which I shall do for thee."
He put me at the head of his children,
He married me to his eldest daughter,
He made me select for myself of his land,
     Of the choicest of that which he had,
On his boundary with another land.
It was a goodly land, named Yaa;
There were figs in it and vines,
More plentiful than water was its wine,
Copious was its honey, plenteous its oil;
All fruits were upon its trees.
     Barley was there, and spelt,
Without end all cattle.
Moreover, great was that which came to me,
Which came for love of me,
When he appointed me sheik of the tribe,
From the choicest of his land.
I portioned the daily bread,
And wine for every day,
Cooked flesh, and fowl in roast;
Besides the wild goats of the hills,
Which were trapped for me, and brought to me;
Besides that which my dogs captured for me.
     There was much – made for me,
And milk in every sort of cooked dish.
I spent many years,
My children became strong,
Each the mighty man of his tribe.

The messenger going north,
Or passing southward to the court,
    He turned in to me.
For I had all men turn in (to me).

THE RETURN OF SINUHE TO EGYPT, c. 1941 BC

Sinuhe

After many years exile in Palestine, Sinuhe is pardoned by Senusret I and permitted to return to Egypt.

I tarried at the Ways of Horus.* The commander in charge of the patrol there sent a message to the capital to give them notice. His Majesty had them send a capable overseer of field labourers of the royal estate and with him ships laden with presents of the royal bounty for the Asiatics who had come with me to lead me to the Ways of Horus. I called each one of them by name. I started out and raised sail. Each servant was at his task. Dough was kneaded and strained (for beer) beside me until I reached the wharf of Itjtowy.**

When dawn came and it was morning, I was summoned. Ten men came and ten men went to usher me to the palace. I touched my forehead to the ground between the sphinxes. The royal children waited in the gateway to meet me. The Companions who showed me into the pillared court set me on the way to the reception hall. I found His Majesty upon the Great Throne set in a recess (panelled) with fine gold. As I was stretched out on my belly, I lost consciousness in

* A town of the Egyptian frontier
** The then capital

his presence. This God addressed me in a friendly way, and I was like a man caught by nightfall. My soul fled and my body shook. My heart was not in my body: I could not tell life from death.

His Majesty said to one of these Companions: Lift him up and let him speak to me. And His Majesty said: See, you have returned, now that you have roamed the foreign lands. Exile has ravaged you; you have grown old. Old age has caught up with you. The burial of your body is no small matter, for now you will not be escorted by the bowmen. Do not creep any more. You did not speak when your name was called out. I feared punishment, and I answered with a timorous answer: What has my lord said to me? If I try to answer, there is no shortcoming on my part toward God. Fear is in my body, like that which brought to pass the fated flight. I am in your presence. Life belongs to you. May Your Majesty do as he wishes.

The royal children were then brought in, and His Majesty said to the queen: Here is Sinuhe, who has returned as an Asiatic whom the bedouin have raised. She let out a cry, and the royal children shouted all together. They said before His Majesty: It is not really he, O Sovereign, my lord. His Majesty said: It is he indeed. Then they brought their *menyat*-necklaces, their rattles, and their *sistra* with them, and they offered them to His Majesty. May your arms reach out to something nice, O enduring king, to the ornaments of the Lady of Heaven. May the Golden One give life to your nostrils, and may the Lady of the Stars be joined to you. The crown of Upper Egypt will go northward, and the crown of Lower Egypt will go southward that they may unite and come together at the word of Your Majesty, and the cobra goddess Wadjet will be placed on your forehead. As you have kept your subjects from evil, so may Re, Lord of the Lands, be compassionate toward you. Hail to you. And also to the Lady of All. Turn aside your horn, set down your arrow. Give breath to the breathless. Give us this happy reward, this bedouin chief Simehyet, the bowman born in Egypt. It was through fear of you that he took flight and through dread of you that he left the land. Yet there is no one whose face turns white at the sight of your face. The eye which looks at you will not be afraid. His Majesty said: He shall not fear, he shall not be afraid. He shall be a Companion among the nobles and he shall be placed in the midst of the courtiers. Proceed to the audience hall to wait upon him.

When I came from the audience hall, the royal children gave me their hands, and we went to the Great Double Gate. I was assigned to the house of a king's son. Fine things were in it, a cooling room in it, and representations of the horizon. Valuables of the treasury were in it, vestments of royal linen were in every apartment, and first-grade myrrh of the king and the courtiers whom he loves. Every domestic servant was about his prescribed task. Years were caused to pass from my body. I was depilated, and my hair was combed out. A load was given to the desert, and clothes to the sand-dwellers. I was outfitted with fine linen and rubbed with the finest oil. I passed the night on a bed. I gave the sand to those who live on it and wood oil to those who rub themselves with it. A house of a plantation owner, which had belonged to a Companion, was given to me. Many craftsmen had built it, and all its trees were planted anew. Meals were brought from the palace three and four times a day, in addition to what the royal children gave. There was not a moment of interruption. A pyramid of stone was built for me in the midst of the pyramids. The overseer of stonecutters of the pyramids marked out its ground plan. The master draftsman sketched in it, and the master sculptors carved in it. The overseers of works who were in the necropolis gave it their attention. Care was taken to supply all the equipment which is placed in a tomb chamber. Ka-servants were assigned to me, and an endowed estate was settled on me with fields attached, at my mooring place, as is done for a Companion of the first order. My statue was overlaid with gold leaf, its apron in electrum. His Majesty ordered it to be done. There was no commoner for whom the like had ever been done. So I remained in the favour of the king until the day of mooring came.

Its beginning has come to its end, as it has been found in writing.

FAMINE, c. 1900 BC

Heqanakhte

Heqanakhte was a ka-priest sent on a mission to the north of Egypt. He writes to his family in Thebes.

I arrived here and collected as much food for you as possible. The Nile, is it not in fact very low? And the food we have collected is proportionate to the flood . . . Here, one has begun to eat people. Nowhere is there someone to whom nourishment is given. You must hold out until my return: I intend to spend the season of *shemu* (March to July) here.

MISTREATMENT OF A STEPMOTHER, c. 1900 BC

Heqanakhte

Here the ka-priest writes to his sons.

Make sure that the housemaid Senen is thrown out of my
house at once. Be sure to do this on the very day that Sa-
Hathor arrives with this letter. If she spends one more day
in my house be sure I shall hold you responsible for any evil
she does to my new wife. I should not have to tell you this.
Are you afraid of her? What can she possibly do to five
strapping lads like you?

HORUS AND THE PIG, c. 1900 BC

Anonymous

*A Coffin Text which seemingly explains the Ancient Egyptian prohibition on pork
at religious festivals. Otherwise, pig meat was widely enjoyed.*

O Batit of the evening, you swamp-dwellers, you of
Mendes, ye of Buto, you of the shade of Re which knows
not praise, you who brew stoppered beer – do you know
why Rekhyt [Lower Egypt] was given to Horus? It was Re
who gave it to him in recompense for the injury in his eye.
It was Re – he said to Horus: "Pray, let me see your eye
since this has happened to it" [injured in the fight with
Seth]. Then Re saw it. Re said: "Pray, look at that injury in
your eye, while your hand is a covering over the good eye
which is there." Then Horus looked at that injury. It
assumed the form of a black pig. Thereupon Horus
shrieked because of the state of his eye, which was stormy
[inflamed]. Horus said: "Behold, my eye is as at that first
blow which Seth made against my eye!" Thereupon Horus

swallowed his heart before him [lost consciousness]. Then Re said: "Put him upon his bed until he has recovered." It was Seth – he has assumed form against him as a black pig; thereupon he shot a blow into his eye. Then Re said: "The pig is an abomination to Horus." "Would that he might recover," said the gods. That is how the pig became an abomination to the gods, as well as men, for Horus' sake . . .

SENUSRET III CONQUERS NUBIA, c. 1862 BC

Anonymous

Inside Egypt, Senusret III (Sesostris III) was conspicuously successful in curtailing the power of the local nomarchs; outside Egypt he was no less successful in subjugating the Nubians. He initiated three expeditions against his uppity southern neighbours, at the commencement of them re-cutting the canal of Weni (see pp 32-33) at the first cataract of the Nile to enable the ready deployment of the fleet. On later occasions Senusret erected stone stelae to be set up as boundary pillars. The great stele at Semna records the glory of Senusret's offensive against Nubia:

Year 16, third month of the second season occurred his majesty's making the southern boundary as far as Heh. I have made my boundary beyond that of my fathers: I have increased that which was bequeathed to me. I am a king who speaks and executes; that which my heart conceives is that which comes to pass by my hand . . . eager to possess . . . not allowing a matter to sleep in his heart . . . attacking him who attacks, silent in a matter, or answering a matter according to that which is in it, since if one is silent after attack, it strengthens the heart of the enemy. Valiance is eagerness, cowardice is to slink back; he is truly a craven who is repelled upon his border; since the Negro hearkens to the [—] of the mouth; it is answering him which drives him back; when one is eager against him, he turns his back;

when one slinks back he begins to be eager. But they are not a people of might, they are poor and broken in heart. My majesty has seen them, it is not an untruth.

I captured their women, I carried off their subjects, went forth to their wells, smote their bulls; I reaped their grain, and set fire thereto. As my father lives for me, I speak in truth, without a lie therein coming out of my mouth. Now as for every son of mine who shall maintain this boundary which my majesty has made, he is my son, he is born to my majesty, the likeness of a son who is the champion of his father, who maintains the boundary of him that begat him. Now as for him who shall relax it, and shall not fight for it; he is not my son, he is not born to me.

TRANSPORT OF A GIANT STATUE, c. 1847 BC

Thuthotep

Thuthotep was nomarch of the Hare nome, the main city of which was Hermopolis. It took 172 of his subjects, pulling on four ropes, to haul the block of alabaster he desired for a statue. The Egyptologist JH Breasted calculated that the block weighed "toward 60 tons" and was 22 feet in length.

Following* is a statue of 13 cubits, of stone of Hatnub. Lo, the way upon which it came, was very difficult, beyond anything. Lo, the dragging of the great things was difficult for the heart of the people, because of the difficult stone of the ground, being hard stone.

I caused the youth, the young men of the recruits to come, in order to make for it a road, together with shifts of necropolis miners and of quarrymen, the foremen and the wise. The people of strength said, "We come to bring it";

* The original inscription heads a scene in Thuthotep's tomb of the statue being pulled

while my heart was glad; the city was gathered together rejoicing; very good it was to see beyond anything. The old man among them, he leaned upon the child, the strong-armed together with the tremblers, their courage rose. Their arms grew strong; one of them put forth the strength of a thousand men. . . . Behold, this statue, being a squared block on coming forth from the great mountain, was more valuable than anything. Vessels were equipped, filled with supplies, in advance of my army of recruits . . . My nome shouted praise. I arrived in the district of this city, the people were gathered together, praising; very good it was to see, beyond anything . . .

MINING IN SINAI, c. 1820 BC

Harrure

The Sinai peninsula was ruthlessly quarried by Amenemhet III for its precious supplies of turquoise and malachite. Conditions in the mines, as the treasurer Harrure relates in a stele erected in warning to future generations, were harsh:

The majesty of this god (Amenemhet) despatched the treasurer of the god, master of the double cabinet – Harurre to this Mineland; I arrived in this land in the third month of the second season although it was not the season for going to this Mineland. This treasurer of the god saith to the officials who shall come to this Mineland at this season: "Let not your face flinch on that account; behold, Hathor will turn it to profit." I looked to myself and I dealt with myself; when I came from Egypt my face flinched and it was hard for me . . . The highlands are hot in summer, and the mountains brand the skin. When morning dawns a man is [—], I addressed the workmen concerning it: "How favoured is he who is in this Mineland!" They said, "There is malachite in this eternal mountain; it is [—] to seek [it] at this season. One like us hears the like of [such] marvels coming at this season. It is [—] to [—] for it in this evil summer season.

I succeeded in mining the good sort, and I finished in the first month of the third season. I brought genuine costly stone for the luxuries, more than anyone . . . It was better than the accustomed seasons thereof. Offer ye, offer ye to the mistress of Heaven, appease ye Hathor; if ye do it, it will be profitable for you . . . I led my army very kindly, and I was not loud-voiced toward the workmen. I acted before all the army and the recruits they rejoiced in me! . . .

HOW TO TREAT A BROKEN NOSE, 1800 BC

Anonymous

From the "Edwin Smith Medical Papyrus", which relates 48 case studies for trainee physicians. It is the oldest medical treatise in the world. Although the Edwin Smith Papyrus was scribed around 1800 BC, the original treatise itself may date back to the 30th century BC.

Instructions concerning a break in the column of the nose: If you examine a man having a break in the column of his nose, his nose being disfigured and having a depression in it while the swelling that is in it protrudes and he has lost blood from both nostrils, you may say concerning him: "He has a broken nose, this is an ailment I can treat." You should cleanse it with plugs of linen then place two more plugs of linen saturated with grease inside his nostrils. . . . You should apply a stiff roll of linen by which his nose is held fast.

PART THREE

Empire

*The Second Intermediate Period
and the New Kingdom,
Egypt 1782–1070 BC*

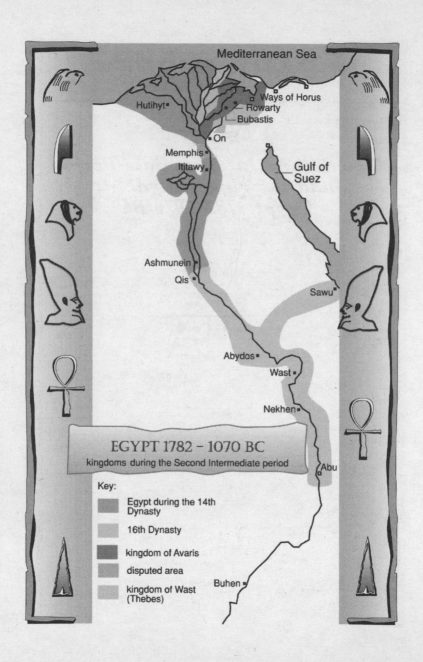

Mediterranean Sea

Ways of Horus

Hutihyt▪ Rowarty

Bubastis

▪On

Memphis▪

Ititawy▪ Gulf of
Suez

Ashmunein▪

Qis▪

Sawu▪

Abydos▪

Wast▪

Nekhen▪

Abu▪

EGYPT 1782 – 1070 BC
kingdoms during the Second Intermediate period

Buhen▪

Key:

Egypt during the 14th
Dynasty

16th Dynasty

kingdom of Avaris

disputed area

kingdom of Wast
(Thebes)

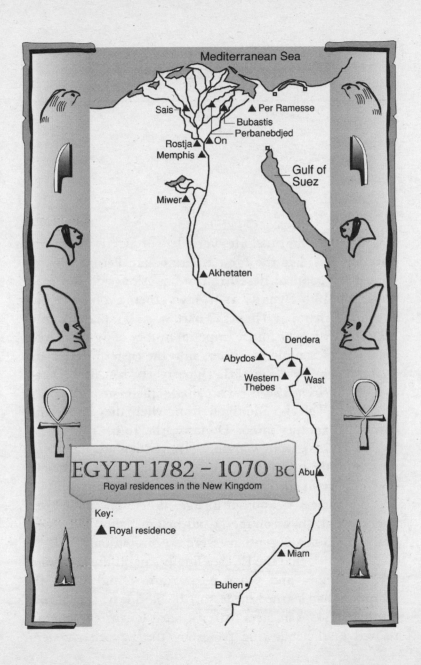

Mediterranean Sea

Sais

Per Ramesse
Bubastis
Perbanebdjed
Rostja
On
Memphis

Gulf of Suez

Miwer

Akhetaten

Dendera
Abydos
Western Thebes
Wast

EGYPT 1782 – 1070 BC
Royal residences in the New Kingdom

Abu

Key:
▲ Royal residence

Miam
Buhen

INTRODUCTION

The Second Intermediate Period of some two centuries duration was, like the First Intermediate Period, characterized by political decentralization. Alongside the main house, the 13th Dynasty at Itj-tawy, there evolved Dynasties in the Delta, at Thebes. There was also, perhaps most importantly for the future imperial history of Egypt, a mass incursion of Semitic foreigners into the eastern desert and Delta. These were the 15th Dynasty Hyksos, the "Desert Princes" (*Hikau-khoset*), who made their strongholds at Avaris and Tell el-Yahudiyeh, from where they apparently controlled another minor Dynasty, the 16th.

The Hyksos were warriors. In particular, they were masters of the iron-fitted chariot. It is difficult to overstate how important the chariot was to warfare in antiquity. It was the nuclear weapon of its age. Wheresoever the charioteers went, they conquered all before them. The essentially unmilitary Egyptians were no opposition at all.

The irony is that the Hyksos finally taught the Egyptians the techniques and ethos of warfare – and when the Egyptians had learned the lesson the hard way, they turned on their Hyksos masters. After a hard fought campaign – related in the following pages by the Egyptian general

Ahmose, son of Ebana – the Theban princes of the 17th Dynasty ejected the Hyksos from Egypt. The *coup de grâce* fell to Ahmose I, who thus inaugurated the 18th Dynasty and the New Kingdom.

This was a golden age for Egypt. There was a renaissance of the religious arts, there was a revival of royal authority. The immense building works of the New Kingdom pharaohs, such as the temple at Karnak, still stand, still have the power to awe.

There was also a tremendous expansion in Egyptian geopolitical influence. Above all else, the New Kingdom was an Empire. Tuthmosis III (1504–1450 BC) set out, in his own words, to "extend the boundaries of Egypt in accordance with the command of his [divine] father Amun-Re" and did so northwards – on his chariot – to the Euphrates River. Small wonder that Tuthmosis III has been dubbed "the Napoleon of Ancient Egypt". To the south, Tuthmosis sent punitive expeditions in Nubia, before it was eventually colonized. These territorial extensions of *Maat* only strengthed the pharaonic mystique.

One result is that the New Kingdom monarchy was strong enough to survive the occasional pharaonic aberration. Queen Hatshepsut was the first female monarch of Egypt, although she confused matters mightily by wearing in public the official regalia of a male king, down to the false beard. Later Egyptians found her an embarrassment and tried to crase memorials of her reign; in her lifetime, however, she was tolerated because she oversaw a series of trading expeditions (including one to fabled Punt) which garnered great wealth.

A more serious challenge to New Kingdom *Maat* was posed by the religious revolution of Amenhotep IV, who succeeded to the throne in 1350 BC. He sought a religious revolution, the substitution of the monotheistic cult of the sun-disc Aten for the old style polytheism. He changed his name to Akenaten and moved the capital to a new site in middle Egypt, el-Amarna, and closed down the priesthood of the then pre-eminent cult of Amun. Such, however, was the godlike prestige of the New Kingdom monarchy that this revolution from above was passively accepted by the people. The all-important bureaucracy, notably, carried on business as usual and the country ran like clockwork.

The efficiency of Egyptian government extended to filing the king's mail in the "House of Correspondence of Pharaoh". Some of these papyri were discovered in the late 19th century AD, and from them we learn that the Egyptian empire in Syria was under sustained attack from the Hittites. Akenhaten was too preoccupied with his new religion to care, but turmoils of the Near East would cast an ever lengthening shadow over the New Kingdom.

Akenhaten's religious reformation did not survive him. As soon as the boy pharaoh Tutankhaten was installed the court moved back to Thebes and the old worship of Amun. Accordingly, Tutankhaten had his name changed to the famous Tutankhamun. Not long afterwards he was buried in the Valley of the Kings, in a splendour which suggests gratitude for his restoration of the old religious ways.

When Tutankhamun died in 1325 BC the New Kingdom had two and a half centuries left to it. The reigns of the soldier-builders Ramses II (the original of Percy Shelley's "Ozymandias, King of Kings" and the pharaoh which caused the Hebrew Exodus; see appendix IV) and Ramses III were still to come, but after them the curve of imperial power and influence was unmistakably downwards. The signs were evident for all to see. There were strikes, riots, conspiracies and attempted coups. In unprecedented acts of sacrilege, the tombs of the pharaohs at Thebes were robbed of their gilt and goodies. The priesthood of Amun aggrandized remorselessly and set up an alternative power base in the south. Some of the later Ramses were little more than prisoners in a pretty palace. And by the reign of the last New Kingdom pharaoh Ramses XII, the country was bankrupt.

Meanwhile, the Mediterranean was turmoiled by waves of emigration by Aegean and Asiatic peoples. It was not merely the New Kingdom which was eroded away at the end of the second millennium. So was the whole Ancient World in which the New Kingdom sat.

THE EXPULSION OF THE HYKSOS, c. 1560–50 BC

Ahmose, Son of Ebana

The writer served as an officer in many campaigns against the Hyksos, notably those undertaken by his royal namesake Ahmose I. After besieging Avaris, the Hyksos stronghold in Egypt, the two Ahmoses pursued the remnant of the "Asiatics" into Palestine. The below is taken from the inscription on the walls of the tomb of Ahmose, son of Ebana, at el-Kab.

Campaign against the Hyksos; Siege of Avaris

One besieged the city of Avaris; I showed valour on foot before his majesty; then I was appointed to (the ship) "Shining-in-Memphis".

Second Battle of Avaris

One fought on the water in the canal: Pezedku of Avaris. Then I fought hand to hand, I brought away a hand. It was reported to the royal herald. One gave to me the gold of valour.

Third Battle of Avaris

Then there was again fighting in this place; I again fought hand to hand there; I brought away a hand. One gave to me the gold of bravery in the second place.

Capture of Avaris

One captured Avaris; I took captive there one man and three women, total four heads, his majesty gave them to me for slaves.

Siege of Sharuhen [in Palestine]

One besieged Sharuhen for six years, (and) his majesty took it. Then I took captive there two women and one hand. One gave me the gold of bravery, besides giving me the captives for slaves.

SPELLS FOR THE AFTERLIFE: THE BOOK OF THE DEAD, c 1550–200 BC

Anonymous

The funerary spells collected in the "Book of the Dead" were a New Kingdom innovation. They accorded primacy to Osiris as the judge of the dead, dropped many of the terrors of the Coffin Texts and promised the "True of Voice" a free and easy afterlife. The spells were written on a papyrus roll, illustrated with "vignettes", which was then usually inserted into the bandages of the mummy between the legs or inside a wooden statuette of the funerary god Ptah-Sokaris-Osiris. Every Egyptian who could afford a copy of "The Book of the Dead" was buried with one (a "democratic progress" from the exclusivity of the Pyramid and Coffin Texts). The "Book of the Dead" may have been a New Kingdom novelty, but it was added to until the Hellensitic invasion a thousand years later.

Hymn to Osiris

"Homage to thee, Osiris, Lord of eternity, King of the Gods, whose names are manifold, whose forms are holy, thou being of hidden form in the temples, whose Ka is holy. Thou art the governor of Tattu (Busiris), and also the mighty one in Sekhem (Letopolis). Thou art the Lord to whom praises are ascribed in the nome of Ati, thou art the Prince of divine food in Anu. Thou art the Lord who is commemorated in Maati, the Hidden Soul, the Lord of Qerrt (Elephantine), the Ruler supreme in White Wall (Memphis). Thou art the Soul of Ra, his own body, and hast thy place of rest in Henensu (Herakleopolis). Thou art the beneficent one, and art praised in Nart. Thou makest thy soul to be raised up. Thou art the Lord of the Great House in Khemenu (Hermopolis). Thou art the mighty one of victories in Shas-hetep, the Lord of eternity, the Governor of Abydos. The path of his throne is in Ta-tcheser (a part of Abydos). Thy name is established in the mouths of men. Thou art the substance of Two Lands. Thou art Tem, the feeder of Kau (Doubles), the Governor of the Companies of the gods. Thou art the beneficent Spirit among the spirits. The god of the Celestial Ocean (Nu) draweth from thee his waters. Thou sendest forth the north wind at eventide, and breath from thy nostrils to the satisfaction of thy heart. Thy heart reneweth its youth, thou producest the . . . The stars in the celestial heights are obedient unto thee, and the great doors of the sky open themselves before thee. Thou art he to whom praises are ascribed in the southern heaven, and thanks are given for thee in the northern heaven. The imperishable stars are under thy supervision, and the stars which never set are thy thrones. Offerings appear before thee at the decree of Keb. The Companies of the Gods praise thee, and the gods of the Tuat (Other World) smell the earth in paying homage to thee. The uttermost parts of the earth bow before thee, and the limits of the skies entreat thee with supplications when they see thee. The holy ones are overcome before thee, and all Egypt offereth thanksgiving unto thee when it meeteth Thy Majesty. Thou art a shining Spirit-Body, the governor of Spirit-Bodies; permanent is thy rank, established is thy rule. Thou art the well-doing Sekhem (Power) of the Company of the Gods, gracious is thy face, and beloved by him that seeth it. Thy fear is set in all the lands by reason of thy perfect love, and they cry out to thy name making it the first of names, and all people make offerings to thee. Thou art the lord who art commemorated in heaven and upon earth. Many are the cries which are made to thee at the Uak festival, and with one heart and voice Egypt raiseth cries of joy to thee.

"Thou art the Great Chief, the first among thy brethren, the Prince of the Company of the Gods, the establisher of Right and Truth throughout the World, the Son who was set on the great throne of his father Keb. Thou art the beloved of thy mother Nut, the mighty one of valour, who overthrew the Sebau-fiend. Thou didst stand up and smite thine enemy, and set thy fear in thine adversary. Thou dost bring the boundaries of the mountains. Thy heart is fixed, thy legs are set firm. Thou art the heir of Keb and of the sovereignty of the Two Lands (Egypt). He (Keb) hath seen his splendours, he hath decreed for him the guidance of the world by thy hand as long as times endure. Thou hast made this earth with thy hand, and the waters, and the winds, and the vegetation, and all the cattle, and all the feathered fowl, and all the fish, and all the creeping things, and all the wild animals therof. The desert is the lawful possession of the son of Nut. The Two Lands (Egypt) are content to crown thee upon the throne of thy father, like Ra.

"Thou rollest up into the horizon, thou hast set light over the darkness, thou sendest forth air from thy plumes, and thou floodest the Two Lands like the Disk at daybreak. Thy crown penetrateth the height of heaven, thou art the companion of the stars, and the guide of every god. Thou art beneficent in decree and speech, the favoured one of the Great Company of the Gods, and the beloved of the Little Company of the Gods.

"His sister [Isis] hath protected him, and hath repulsed the fiends, and turned aside calamities (of evil). She uttered the spell with the magical power of her mouth. Her tongue was perfect, and it never halted at a word. Beneficent in command and word was Isis, the woman of magical spells, the advocate of her brother. She sought him untiringly, she wandered round and round about this earth in sorrow, and she alighted not without finding him. She made light with her feathers, she created air with her wings, and she uttered the death wail for her brother. She raised up the inactive members of whose heart was still, she drew from him his essence, she made an heir, she reared the child in loneliness, and the place where he was not known, and he grew in strength and stature, and his hand was mighty in the House of Keb. The Company of the Gods rejoiced, rejoiced, at the coming of Horus, the son of Osiris, whose heart was firm, the triumphant, the son of Isis, the heir of Osiris."

Spell 125: The Declaration of Innocence [The Negative Confession]

Hail, Usekh-nemmt, who comest forth from Anu, I have not committed sin.

Hail, Hept-khet, who comest forth from Kher-aha, I have not committed robbery with violence.

Hail, Fenti, who comest forth from Khemenu, I have not stolen.

Hail, Am-khaibit, who comest forth from Qernet, I have not slain men and women.

Hail, Neha-her, who comest forth from Rasta, I have not stolen grain.

Hail, Ruruti, who comest forth from heaven, I have not purloined offerings.

Hail, Arfi-em-khet, who comest forth from Suat, I have not stolen the property of God.

Hail, Neba, who comest and goest, I have not uttered lies.

Hail, Set-qesu, who comest forth from Hensu, I have not carried away food.

Hail, Utu-nesert, who comest forth from Het-ka-Ptah, I have not uttered curses.

Hail, Qerrti, who comest forth from Amentet, I have not committed adultery, I have not lain with men.

Hail, Her-f-ha-f, who comest forth from thy cavern, I have made none to weep.

Hail, Basti, who comest forth from Bast, I have not eaten the heart.

Hail, Ta-retiu, who comest forth from the night, I have not attacked any man.

Hail, Unem-snef, who comest forth from the execution chamber, I am not a man of deceit.

Hail, Unem-besek, who comest forth from Mabit, I have not stolen cultivated land.

Hail, Neb-Maat, who comest forth from Maati, I have not been an eavesdropper.

Hail, Tenemiu, who comest forth from Bast, I have not slandered [no man].

Hail, Sertiu, who comest forth from Anu, I have not been angry without just cause.

Hail, Tutu, who comest forth from Ati (the Busirite Nome), I have not debauched the wife of any man.

Hail, Uamenti, who comest forth from the Khebt chamber, I have not debauched the wife of [any] man.

Hail, Maa-antuf, who comest forth from Per-Menu, I have not polluted myself.

Hail, Her-uru, who comest forth from Nehatu, I have terrorized none.

Hail, Khemiu, who comest forth from Kaui, I have not transgressed [the law].

Hail, Shet-kheru, who comest forth from Urit, I have not been wroth.

Hail, Nekhenu, who comest forth from Heqat, I have not shut my ears to the words of truth.

Hail, Kenemti, who comest forth from Kenmet, I have not blasphemed.

Hail, An-hetep-f, who comest forth from Sau, I am not a man of violence.

Hail, Sera-kheru, who comest forth from Unaset, I have not been a stirrer up of strife.

Hail, Neb-heru, who comest forth from Netchfet, I have not acted with undue haste.

Hail, Sekhriu, who comest forth from Uten, I have not pried into matters.

Hail, Neb-abui, who comest forth from Sauti, I have not multiplied my words in speaking.

Hail, Nefer-Tem, who comest forth from Het-ka-Ptah, I have wronged none, I have done no evil.

Hail, Tem-Sepu, who comest forth from Tetu, I have not worked witchcraft against the king.

Hail, Ari-em-ab-f, who comest forth from Tebu, I have never stopped [the flow of] water.

Hail, Ahi, who comest forth from Nu, I have never raised my voice.

Hail, Uatch-rekhit, who comest forth from Sau, I have not cursed God.

Hail, Neheb-ka, who comest forth from thy cavern, I have not acted with arrogance.

Hail, Neheb-nefert, who comest forth from thy cavern, I have not stolen the bread of the gods.

Hail, Tcheser-tep, who comest forth from the shrine, I have not carried away the khenfu cakes from the Spirits of the dead.

Hail, An-af, who comest forth from Maati, I have not snatched away the bread of the child, nor treated with contempt the god of my city.

Hail, Hetch-abhu, who comest forth from Ta-she (the Fayyum), I have not slain the cattle belonging to the god.

Spell 30B: The Judgement of the Dead
The Heart of the Dead Man is Weighed in the Scales of the Balance Against the Feather of Righteousness.

O my heart which I had from my mother! O my heart which I had from my mother! O my heart of my different ages! Do not stand up as a witness against me, do not be opposed to me in the tribunal, do not be hostile to me in the presence of the Keeper of the Balance, for you are my *ka* which was in my body, the protector who made my members hale. Go forth to the happy place whereto we speed; do not make my name stink to the Entourage who make men. Do not tell lies about me in the presence of the god; it is indeed well that you should hear!

Thus says Thoth, judge of truth, to the Great Ennead which is in the presence of Osiris: Hear this word of very truth. I have judged the heart of the deceased, and his soul stands as a witness for him. His deeds are righteous in the great balance, and no sin has been found in him. He did not diminish the offerings in the temples, he did not destroy what had been made, he did not go about with deceitful speech while he was on earth.

Thus says the Great Ennead to Thoth who is in Hermopolis: This utterance of yours is true. The vindicated Osiris N is straightforward, he has no sin, there is no accusation against him before us, Ammit shall not be permitted to have power over him. Let there be given to him the offerings which are issued in the presence of Osiris, and may a grant of land be established in the Field of Offerings as for the Followers of Horus.

Thus says Horus son of Isis: I have come to you, O Wennefer, and I bring N to you. His heart is true, having gone forth from the balance, and he has not sinned against any god or any goddess. Thoth has judged him in writing which has been told to the Ennead, and Maat the great has witnessed. Let there be given to him bread and beer which have been issued in the presence of Osiris, and he will be for ever like the Followers of Horus.

Thus says N: Here I am in your presence, O Lord of the West. There is no wrong-doing in my body, I have not wittingly told lies, there has been no second fault. Grant that I may be like the favoured ones who are in your suite, O Osiris, one greatly favoured by the good god, one loved of the Lord of the Two Lands, N, vindicated before Osiris.

Spell IB: For Permitting the Noble Dead to Descend to the Netherworld

Hail to you who are in the sacred desert of the West! N knows you and knows your name; may you save him from those snakes which are in Rosetjau, which live on the flesh of men and gulp down their blood, because N knows you and knows your names.

The First One, Osiris, Lord of All, mysterious of body, gives command, and he puts breath into those frightened ones who are in the midst of the West; what has been commanded for him is the governance of those who exist. May his place within the darkness be opened up for him, may a spirit-shape be given to him in Rosetjau, even to the Lord of gloom who goes down as the swallower of snakes in the West; his voice is heard but he is not seen. The Great God within Busiris, those who are among the languid ones fear him, they having gone forth under report to the shambles of the god.

I have come, even I the vindicated Osiris N, on business of the Lord of All, while Horus has taken possession of his throne and his father has given to him all those honours which are within his father's sacred bark. Horus has come with a report; he goes in that he may tell what he has seen in Heliopolis. Their great ones on earth wait on him, the scribes who are on their mats magnify him, and there has been given to him the mottled snake in Heliopolis. He has taken possession of the sky, he has inherited the earth, and who shall take this sky and earth from him? He is Re, the eldest of the gods; his mother has suckled him, she has given to him a nurse who is in the horizon.

This spell is to be recited after going to rest in the West, the Tjenenet-shrine being made content with its lord Osiris when going to and fro to the Sacred Bark of Re; his body on his bier shall be reckoned up, and shall be enduring in the Netherworld, namely that of N.

Spell 27: For Not Permitting a Man's Heart to be Taken from Him in the Realm of the Dead

O you who take away hearts and accuse hearts, who recreate a man's heart (in respect of) what he has done, he is forgetful of himself through what you have done. Hail to you, lords of eternity, founders of everlasting! Do not take N's heart with your fingers wherever his heart may be. You shall not raise any matter harmful to him, because as for this heart of N, this heart belongs to one whose names are great, whose words are mighty, who possesses his members. He sends out his heart which controls his body, his heart is announced to the gods, for N's heart is his own, he has power over it, and he will not say what he has done. He himself has power over his members, his heart obeys him, for he is your lord and you are in his body, you shall not turn aside. I command you to obey me in the realm of the dead, even I, N, who am vindicated in peace and vindicated in the beautiful West in the domain of eternity.

Spell 32: For Repelling a Crocodile Which Comes to Take Away a Spirit's Magic in the Realm of the Dead
The Great One has fallen on his side, but the Ennead have pulled him together. I come, my soul speaks with my father, and I have this Great One from those eight crocodiles. I know them by their names and their lives, and I save my father from them.

Get back, you crocodile of the West, who lives on the Unwearying Stars! Detestation of you is in my belly, for I have absorbed the power of Osiris, and I am Seth.

Get back, you crocodile of the West! The nau-snake is in my belly, and I have not given myself to you; your flame will not be on me.

Get back, you crocodile of the East, who lives on those who are mutilated! Detestation of you is in my belly, and I have gone away, for I am Osiris.

Get back, you crocodile in the East! The nau-snake is in my belly, and I have not given myself to you; your flame will not be on me.

Get back, you crocodile of the South, living on faeces, smoke and want! Detestation of you is in my belly, and my blood is not in your hand, for I am Sopd.

Get back, you crocodile in the South! I will erase you, for I become a bebet-herb, and I have not given myself to you.

Get back, you crocodile of the North, living on the . . . which is in the midst of the stars! Detestation of you is in my belly, your poison is in my head; I am Atum.

Get back, you crocodile in the North! A scorpion is in my belly, but I will not give it birth.

Spell 44: For Not Dying Again in the Realm of the Dead
My cavern is opened, the spirits fall within the darkness.

The Eye of Horus makes me holy, Wepwawet has caressed me; O Imperishable Stars, hide me among you.

My neck is Re, my vision is cleared, my heart is in its proper place, my speech is known.

The god Re speaks: I am Re who himself protects himself; I do not know you, I do not look after you, your father the son of Nut lives for you.

The deceased replies: I am your eldest son who sees your secrets, I have appeared as King of the Gods, and I will not die again in the realm of the dead.

Spell 130: For Making a Spirit Worthy on the Birthday of Osiris and For Making a Soul Live Forever
May the sky be opened, may the earth be opened, may the West be opened, may the East be opened, may the chapel of Upper Egypt be opened, may the chapel of Lower Egypt be opened, may the doors be opened, may the eastern portals be thrown open for Re when he ascends from the horizon. May the doors of the Night-bark be opened for him, may the portals of the Day-bark be thrown open for him, may he breathe Shu, may he create Tefnut, may those who are in the suite serve him, may they serve me like Re daily.

I am a follower of Re, who receives his firmament; the god occupies his shrine, Horus having approached his lord, whose seats are secret, whose shrine is pure, messenger of the god to him whom he loved. I am one who takes hold of Maat, having presented her before him; I am he who knots the cord and lashes his shrine together. What I detest is storm, and there will be no heaping up of waters in my presence, I will not be turned back because of Re, I will not be driven off by whoever acts with his hands, I will not go into the Valley of Darkness, I will not enter into the Lake of Criminals, I will not be in the weakening of striking-power, I will not fall as plunder, I will go in among those who are taken before him, behind the slaughter-block of the shambles of Sopd.

Hail to you, you squatting gods! The seclusion of the god is in the secrecy of the arms of Geb at dawn; who is he who will guide the Great One? He will number the children in his good time, while Thoth is in the secret places; he will make purity for Him who counts the myriads who are to be counted, who opens up the firmament and dispels all cloudiness. I have reached him in his place, I grasp the staff, I receive the head-cloth for Re, whose fair movements are great. Horus flames up around his eye, and his two Enneads are about his throne; if they remove the sore pain which he suffers, then will I remove the pain, that I may be made comfortable thereby. I will open up the horizon for Re, and I have built his ship "She who proceeds happily"; the face of Thoth will be made bright for me, and I will worship Re, he will hearken to me, for he has implanted an obstacle on my behalf against my enemies. I will not be left boatless, I will not be turned back from the horizon, for I am Re. I will not be left boatless in the great crossing by Him whose face is on his knee and whose hand is bent down, because the name of Re is in my body, his dignity is in my mouth. So he has told me, and I hear his word.

Praise to you, Re, Lord of the Horizon; hail to you for whom the sun-folk are pure, for whom the sky is controlled in the great moment when the hostile oarsmen pass by. See, I have come among those who make truth known, because I am far away in the West; I have broken up the storm of *Apep*, O Double Lion, as I promised you. See, I have come; O you who are before the Great Throne, hearken to me. I go down into your tribunal, I rescue Re from *Apep* every day, and there is no-one who can attack him, for those who are about him are awake. I lay hold of the writings, I receive offerings, I equip

Thoth with what was made for him, I cause truth to circulate over the Great Bark, I go down vindicated into the tribunal, I establish the Chaos-gods, I lead the Entourage, I grant to them a voyage in utter joy, when the crew of Re goes round about following his beauty. Maat is exalted so that she may reach her lord, and praise is given to the Lord of All.

I take the staff, I sweep the sky with it, and the sunfolk give me praise as to Him who stands and does not tire. I extol Re in what he has made, I dispel cloudiness, I see his beauty, I display the terror of him, I make his oarsmen firm when his Bark travels over the sky at dawn. I am the Great One within his Eye, who kneels at the head of the Great Bark of Khepri. I come into being and what I have said comes into being, I am this one who traverses the sky towards the West, and those who heap up the air stand up in joy; they have taken the bow-warp of Re from his crew, and Re traverses the sky happily in peace by my command; I will not be driven away, the fiery breath of your power will not carry me off, the power of repulsion in your mouth will not go forth against me, I will not walk on the paths of pestilence, for to fall into it is the detestation of my soul; what I detest is the flood, and it shall not attack me. I go aboard your Bark, I occupy your seat, I receive my dignity, I control the paths of Re and the stars, I am he who drives off the Destructive One who comes at the flame of your Bark upon the great plateau. I know them by their names, and they will not attack your Bark, for I am in it, and I am he who prepares the offerings.

To be said over a Bark of Re drawn in ochre on a clean place. *When you have placed a likeness of this spirit in front of it, you shall draw a Night-bark on its right side and a Day-bark on its left side. There shall be offered to them in their presence bread and beer and all good things on the birthday of Osiris. If this is done for him, his soul will live for ever and he will not die again.*

PRESCRIPTION FOR CONTRACEPTION, c. 1542 BC

Anonymous

From the Ebers medical papyrus, written in c. 1542 BC but possibly a copy of a much older medical textbook.

Prescription to make a woman cease to become pregnant for one, two or three years: Grind together finely a measure of acacia dates with some honey. Moisten seed-wool with the mixture and insert into the vagina.

CORONATION DECREE, c. 1524 BC

Tuthmosis I

A decree sent to Thure, viceroy of Nubia, informing him of the pharaoh's accession, the titulary and the royal names to be used on oblations and oaths. The decree was then cut on stelae and set up for public perusal.

Superscription
Royal command to the king's-son, the governor of the south countries, Thure triumphant.

Announcement of Accession
Behold, there is brought to thee this command of the king in order to inform thee that my majesty has appeared as King of Upper and Lower Egypt upon the Horus-throne of the living, without his like forever.

Titulary
Make my titulary as follows:
   Horus: "Mighty Bull, Beloved of Mat";
   Favourite of the Two Goddesses: "Shining in the Serpent-diadem, Great in Strength";

Golden Horus: "Goodly in Years, Making Hearts Live";
King of Upper and Lower Egypt: "Okheperkere";
Son of Re: "[Tuthmosis], Living forever, and ever."

Name to be Used in the Cults
Cause thou oblations to be offered to the gods of Elephantine of the South, as follows: "Performance of the pleasing
ceremonies on behalf of the King of Upper and Lower
Egypt, Okheperkere, who is given life."

Name to be Used in the Oath
Cause thou that the oath be established in the name of my
majesty, born of the king's-mother, Seniseneb, who is in health.

Conclusion
This is a communication to inform thee of it; and of the fact
that the royal house is well and prosperous –

Date
Year 1, third month of the second season (seventh month)
twenty-first day; the day of the feast of coronation.

THE NUBIAN WAR: TUTHMOSIS I CASTS THE FIRST LANCE, c. 1524 BC

Ahmose, son of Ebana

*Despite the brevity of his reign, Tuthmosis I (c. 1524–1518) achieved a major
expansion of Egypt's boarder in the south, conquering Nubia as far as the third
cataract. During this Nubian campaign, Ahmose was promoted to admiral.*

I sailed the King Okheperkere, [Tuthmosis I] triumphant,
when he ascended the river to Khenthennofer in order to
cast out violence in the highlands, in order to suppress the

raiding of the hill region. I showed bravery in his presence in the bad water, in the passage of the ship by the bend. One appointed me chief of the sailors. His majesty was—.

His majesty was furious thereat, like a panther; his majesty cast his first lance, which remained in the body of that fallen one. This was—powerless before his flaming uraeus* made so in an instant of destruction; their people were brought off as living prisoners. His majesty sailed down-river, with all countries in his grasp, that wretched Nubian Troglodyte being hanged head downward at the prow of the barge of his majesty, and landed at Karnak.

REBELLION IN KUSH, C. 1518 BC

Anonymous

The accession of Tuthmosis II (probably after a brief period of co-regency with his father) was met with uprising by the negoes of Kush. His crushing of the rebellion is recorded in an inscription at Aswan.

A messenger came to inform his majesty as follows: "The wretched Kush has begun to rebel, those who were under the dominion of the Lord of the Two Lands purpose hostility, beginning to smite him. The inhabitants of Egypt are about to bring away the cattle behind this fortress which thy father built in his campaigns, the King of Upper and Lower Egypt, Okheperkere (Tuthmosis I), living forever, in order to repulse the rebellious barbarians, the Nubian Troglodytes of Khenthennofer, for those who are there on the north of the wretched Kush—with the two Nubian Troglodytes among the children of the chief of the wretched Kush who—before the Lord of the Two Lands—." His majesty was furious threat, like a panther,

---

* The sacred serpent on the king's forehead.

when he heard it. Said his majesty, "I swear, as Re loves me, as my father, lord of gods, Amon, lord of Thebes, favours me, I will not let live anyone among their males—among them."

Then his majesty dispatched a numerous army into Nubia on his first occasion of a campaign, in order to overthrow all those who were rebellious against his majesty or hostile to the Lord of the Two Lands. Then this army of his majesty arrived at wretched Kush—. This army of his majesty overthrew those barbarians; they did [not] let live anyone among their males, according to all the command of his majesty, except one of those children of the chief of wretched Kush, who was taken away alive as a living prisoner with their people to his majesty. They were placed under the feet of the Good God; for his majesty had appeared upon his throne when the living prisoners were brought in, which this army of his majesty had captured. This land was made a subject of his majesty as formerly, the people rejoiced, the chiefs were joyful; they gave praise to the Lord of the Two Lands, they lauded this god, excellent in examples of his divinity. It came to pass on account of the fame of his majesty, because his father Amon loved him so much more than any king who has been since the beginning. The King of Upper and Lower Egypt: Okheper-nere, Son of Re: Tuthmosis (II), Beautiful in Diadems, given life, stability, satisfaction, like Re, forever.

QUEEN HATSHEPSUT'S EXPEDITION TO PUNT: THE VESSELS ARE LOADED AND RETURNED TO EGYPT, c. 1490–1489 BC

Anonymous

Wife (and half-sister) of Tuthmosis II, Hatshepsut usurped her infant stepson Tuthmosis III to become "King" of Egypt for fifteen years. At her death, when

Tuthmosis III reassumed power, her name and image were widely erased as being too gender-aberrant to remember. This "chiselling out" of history was not altogether successful; the relief recording the Punt expedition in Hatshepsut's mortuary temple at Deir el-Bahri still retains traces of her name as instigator. The purpose of the expedition was the importation of incense and incense trees for the Deir el-Bahri temple. (See pp. 60–61) for Henu's expedition to Punt, half a millennium before).

*The loading of the ships very heavily with marvels of the country of Punt; all goodly fragrant woods of God's-Land, heaps of myrrh-resin, with fresh myrrh trees, with ebony and pure ivory, with green gold of Emu, with cinnamon wood, khesyt wood, with ihmut-incense, sonter-incense, eye-cosmetic, with apes, monkeys, dogs, and with skins of the southern panther, with natives and their children. Never was brought the like of this for any king who has been since the beginning.

Sailing, arriving in peace, journeying to Thebes with joy of heart, by the army of the Lord of the Two Lands, with the chiefs of this country behind them. They have brought that, the like of which was not brought for other kings, being marvels of Punt, because of the greatness of the fame of this revered god, Amon-Re, Lord of Thebes.

MEGIDDO, c. 1481 BC

Thanuny

During the reign of Hatshepsut, Egyptian influence over the Near East waned with a number of vassals transferring allegiance to the kingdom of Mitanni. On becoming sole regent, Tuthmosis III immediately reasserted Egyptian control in a devastating campaign which marched from Thebes to the Lebanon, built a fort, fought three decisive battles, and marched home for a victory celebration – in less than five months. The key engagement was the battle and siege of Megiddo, which

* Inscription accompanies scene of vessels being loaded in Punt and then sailed home to Egypt

broke the Syrian coalition against Egypt. Thanuny, a scribe and army officer,
recorded the campaign, at Tuthmosis's order, in the great temple of Karnak.

Year 22*, fourth month of the second season, on the twenty-fifth day his majesty was in Tharu on the first victorious expedition to extend the boundaries of Egypt with might.

Now, at that period the Asiatics had fallen into disagreement, each man fighting against his neighbour. Now, it happened that the tribes – the people, who were there in the city of Sharuhen; behold, from Yeraza to the marshes of the earth, they had begun to revolt against his majesty.

Year 23, first month of the third season, on the fourth day, the day of the feast of the king's coronation, he arrived at the city, the possession of the ruler, Gaza.

Year 23, first month of the third season, on the fifth day; departure from this place in might, – in power, and in triumph, to overthrow that wretched foe, to extend the boundaries of Egypt, according as his father, Amon-Re, had commanded that he seize.

Year 23, first month of the third season, on the sixteenth day, he arrived at the city of Yehem.

His majesty ordered a consultation with his valiant troops, saying as follows: "That wretched enemy, the chief of Kadesh, has come and entered into Megiddo; he is there at this moment. He has gathered to himself the chiefs of all the countries which are on the water of Egypt, and as far as Naharin, consisting of the countries of the Kharu, the Kodc, their horses, their troops. Thus he speaks, 'I have arisen to fight against his majesty in Megiddo.'"

They spoke in the presence of his majesty, "How is it, that we should go upon this road, which threatens to be narrow? While they come and say that the enemy is there

* i.e. Year 22 of his reign, including the co-regency with Hatshepsut; it was Year 1 of
his independent reign.

waiting, holding the way against a multitude. Will not horse come behind horse and man behind man likewise? Shall our advance-guard be fighting while our rear-guard is yet standing yonder in Aruna not having fought? There are yet two other roads: one road, behold, it will carry us, for it comes forth at Taanach, the other, behold, it will bring us upon the way north of Zefti, so that we shall come out to the north of Megiddo. Let our victorious lord proceed upon the road he desires; but cause us not to go by a difficult road."

Then went messengers concerning this design which they had uttered, in view of what had been said by the majesty of the Court: "I swear, as Re loves me, as my father Amon, favours me, as my nostrils are rejuvenated with satisfying life, my majesty will proceed upon this road of Aruna. Let him who will among you, go upon those roads ye have mentioned, and let him who will among you, come in the following of my majesty. Shall they think among those enemies whom Re detests: 'Does his majesty proceed upon another road? He begins to be fearful of us,' so will they think."

They spoke before his majesty: "May thy father Amon, lord of Thebes, presider over Karnak, grant thee life. Behold, we are the following of thy majesty in every place, whither thy majesty proceedeth; as the servant is behind his master."

Then his majesty commanded the entire army to march upon that road which threatened to be narrow. His majesty swore, saying: "None shall go forth in the way before my majesty." He went forth at the head of his army himself, showing the way by his own footsteps; horse behind horse, his majesty being at the head of his army.

Year 23, first month of the third season, on the nine-teenth day; the watch in safety in the royal tent was at the city of Aruna. "My majesty proceeded northward under the protection of my father, Amon-Re, lord of Thebes, who went before me, while Harakhte strengthened my arms."

The enemy went forth in numerous battle array. The southern wing was in Taanach the northern wing was on the ground south of Megiddo. His majesty cried out to them before they fell; behold, that wretched foe of the city Aruna.

Now, the rear of the victorious army of his majesty was at the city of Aruna, the front was going forth to the valley; they filled the opening of this valley. Then they said in the presence of his majesty: "Behold, his majesty goeth forth with his victorious army, and it has filled the hollow of the valley; let our victorious lord hearken to us this time and let our lord protect for us the rear of his army and his people. Let the rear of this army come forth to us behind; then shall they also fight against these barbarians; then we shall not need to take thought for the rear of our army." His majesty halted outside and waited there, protecting the rear of his victorious army.

Behold, when the front had reached the exit upon this road, the shadow had turned, and when his majesty arrived at the south of Megiddo on the bank of the brook of Kina, the seventh hour was turning, measured by the sun.

Then was set up the camp of his majesty, and command was given to the whole army, saying: "Equip yourselves! Prepare your weapons! for we shall advance to fight with that wretched foe in the morning." Therefore the king rested in the royal tent, the affairs of the chiefs were arranged, and the provisions of the attendants. The watch of the army went about, saying, "Steady of heart! Steady of heart! Watchful! Watchful! Watch for life at the tent of the king." One came to say to his majesty, "The land is well, and the infantry of the South and North likewise."

Year 23, first month of the third season, on the twenty-first day, the day of the feast of the new moon, corresponding to the royal coronation, early in the morning, behold, command was given to the entire army to move. His majesty went forth in a chariot of electrum, arrayed in his weapons of war, like Horus, the Smiter, lord of power; like Montu of Thebes, while his father, Amon, strengthened his arms. The southern wing of this army of his majesty was on a hill south of the brook of Kina, the northern wing was at the northwest of Megiddo, while his majesty was in their centre, with Amon as the protection of his members, the valour of his limbs. Then his majesty prevailed against them at the head of his army, and when they saw his majesty prevailing against them they fled headlong to Megiddo in fear, abandoning their horses and their chariots of gold and silver. The people hauled them up, pulling them by their clothing, into this city; the people of this city having closed it against them and lowered clothing to pull them up into this city. Now, if only the army of his majesty had not given their heart to plundering the things of the enemy, they would have captured Megiddo at this moment, when the wretched foe of Kadesh and the wretched foe of this city were hauled up in haste to bring them into this city. The fear of his majesty had entered their hearts, their arms were powerless, his serpent diadem was victorious among them.

Then were captured their horses, their chariots of gold and silver were made spoil, their champions lay stretched out like fishes on the ground. The victorious army of his majesty went around counting their portions. Behold, there was captured the tent of that wretched foe in which was his son. The whole army made jubilee, giving praise to Amon for the victory which he had granted to his son on this day, giving praise to his majesty, exalting his victories. They brought up the booty which they had taken, consisting of hands, of living prisoners, of horses, chariots of gold and silver . . .

Then spake his majesty on hearing the words of his army, saying: "Had ye captured this city afterward, behold, I would have given Re this day; because every chief of every country that has revolted is within it; and because it is the capture of a thousand cities, this capture of Megiddo. Capture ye mightily, mightily."

His majesty commanded the officers of the troops to go, assigning to each his place. They measured this city, surrounding it with an inclosure, walled about with green timber of all their pleasant trees. His majesty himself was upon the fortification east of this city, inspecting.

It was walled about with its thick wall. Its name was made: "Menkheperre Thutmose III-is-the-Surrounder-of-the-Asiatics". People were stationed to watch over the tent of his majesty; to whom it was said: "Steady of heart! Watch." His majesty commanded, saying: "Let not one among them come forth outside, beyond this wall, except to come out in order to knock at the other door of their fortification."

Now, all that his majesty did to this city, to that wretched foe and his wretched army, was recorded on each day by its the day's name. Then it was recorded upon a roll of leather in the temple of Amon this day.

Behold, the chiefs of this country came to render their portions, to do obeisance to the fame of his majesty, to crave breath for their nostrils, because of the greatness of his power, because of the might of the fame of his majesty the country came to his fame, bearing their gifts, consisting of silver, gold, lapis lazuli, malachite; bringing clean grain, wine, large cattle, and small cattle for the army of his majesty. Each of the Kode among them bore the tribute southward. Behold, his majesty appointed the chiefs anew.

340 living prisoners; 83 hands; 2,041 mares; 191 foals; 6 stallions; a chariot, wrought with gold, its pole of gold,

belonging to that foe; a beautiful chariot, wrought with gold, belonging to the chief of Megiddo; 892 chariots of his wretched army; total, 924 chariots; a beautiful suit of bronze armour, belonging to that foe; a beautiful suit of bronze armour, belonging to the chief of Megiddo; 200 suits of armour, belonging to his wretched army; 502 bows; 7 poles of mry wood, wrought with silver, belonging to the tent of that foe. Behold, the army of his majesty took 1,929 large cattle, 2,000 small cattle, 20,500 white small cattle.

List of that which was afterward taken by the king, of the household goods of that foe who was in the city of Yenoam, in Nuges, and in Herenkeru, together with all the goods of those cities which submitted themselves, which were brought to his majesty: 38 lords of theirs, 87 children of that foe and of the chiefs who were with him, 5 lords of theirs, 1,796 male and female slaves with their children, non-combatants who surrendered because of famine with that foe, 103 men; total 2,503. Besides flat dishes of costly stone and gold, various vessels, a large two-handled vase of the work of Kharu, vases, flat dishes, dishes, various drinking-vessels, 3 large kettles, 87 knives, amounting to 784 deben. Gold in rings found in the hands of the artificers, and silver in many rings, 966 deben and 1 kidet. A silver statue in beaten work, the head of gold, the staff with human faces; 6 chairs of that foe, of ivory, ebony and carob wood, wrought with gold; 6 footstools belonging to them; 6 large tables of ivory and carob wood, a staff of carob wood, wrought with gold and all costly stones in the fashion of a scepter, belonging to that foe, all of it wrought with gold; a statue of that foe, of ebony wrought with gold, the head of which was inlaid with lapis lazuli; vessels of bronze, much clothing of that foe.

TUTHMOSIS III HUNTS ELEPHANTS, c. 1471 BC

Amenemhab

The author was an officer in the army of Tuthmosis III. At the time of the hunt the pharaoh was approximately 60.

Again I beheld another excellent deed which the Lord of the Two Lands did in Niy [in Syria]. He hunted 120 elephants, for the sake of their tusks and—. I engaged the largest which was among them, which fought against his majesty; I cut off his hand [i.e. trunk] while he was alive before his majesty, while I stood in the water between two rocks. Then my lord rewarded me with gold; he gave – and 3 changes of clothing.

THE SYRIAN WARS: AMENEMHAB BREACHES THE WALL OF KADESH, c. 1462 BC

Amenemhab

Megiddo was only the beginning of Tuthmosis III's military accomplishments. He undertook sixteen more campaigns into the Near East and western Asia, their culmination coming in c. 1462 when he definitively subdued the Asiatic (Hyksos) capital of Kadesh.

The prince of Kadesh sent forth a mare* before the army; in order to—them, she entered among the army. I pursued after her on foot, with my sword, and I ripped open her belly; I cut off her tail, I set it before the king; while there was thanksgiving to god for it! He gave (me) joy, it filled my body, with rejoicing, he endued my limbs.

---

* to sexually excite – and so militarily negate – the stallions of the Egyptian chariotry

His majesty sent forth every valiant man of his army, in order to pierce the wall for the first time, which Kadesh had made. I was the one who pierced it, being the first of all the valiant; no other before me did (it). I went forth, I brought off 2 men, lords, as living prisoners. Again my lord rewarded me because of it, with every good thing for satisfying the heart, of the king's presence.

HYMN OF VICTORY, c. 1460 BC

Anonymous

By the end of his reign, Tuthmosis III ruled an empire that stretched from the Euphrates to far into Sudan. To celebrate the victories of the most militarily able of the pharaohs, a stele was set up in the temple at Amun-Re at Karnak.

Utterance of Amon-Re, lord of Thebes:
Thou comest to me, thou exultest, seeing my beauty,
O my son, my avenger, Menkheperre [Tuthmosis III],
    living forever.
I shine for love of thee,
My heart is glad at thy beautiful comings into my temple;
(My) two hands furnish thy limbs with protection and life.
How pleasing is thy pleasantness toward my body.
I have established thee in my dwelling,
I have worked a marvel for thee;
I have given to thee might and victory against all countries,
I have set thy fame (even) the fear of thee in all lands.
Thy terror as far as the four pillars of heaven;
I have magnified the dread of thee in all bodies,
I have put the roaring of thy majesty among the Nine Bows.
The chiefs of all countries are gathered in thy grasp,
I myself have stretched out my two hands,
I have bound them for thee.

I have bound together the Nubian Troglodytes by tens of
 thousands and thousands,
The Northerners by hundreds of thousands as captives.
I have felled thine enemies beneath thy sandals,
Thou hast smitten the hordes of rebels according as I
 commanded thee.
The earth in its length and breadth, Westerners and
 Easterners are subject to thee,
Thou tramplest all countries, thy heart glad;
None presents himself before thy majesty,
While I am thy leader, so that thou mayest reach them.
Thou hast crossed the water of the Great Bend[1] of Naharin
 with victory, with might.
I have decreed for thee that they hear thy roarings and
 enter into caves;
I have deprived their nostrils of the breath of life.
I have set the terrors of thy majesty in their hearts,
My serpent-diadem upon thy brow, it consumes them,
It makes captive by the hair the Kode-folk,
 It devours those who are in their marshes with its flame.
Cut down are the heads of the Asiatics, there is not a
 remnant of them;
Fallen are the children of their mighty ones.
 I have caused thy victories to circulate among all lands,
My serpent-diadem gives light to thy dominion.
There is no rebel of thine as far as the circuit of heaven;
They come, bearing tribute upon their backs,
 Bowing down to thy majesty according to my command.
I have made powerless the invaders who came before thee;
Their hearts burned, their limbs trembling.
 I have come, causing thee to smite the princes of Zahi[2];

---

[1] Euphrates
[2] Palestine and part of Phoenicia

I have hurled them beneath thy feet among their
   highlands.
I have caused them to see thy majesty as lord of radiance,
So that thou hast shone in their faces like my image.
   I have come, causing thee to smite the Asiatics,
Thou hast made captive the heads of the Asiatics of
   Retenu.
I have caused them to see thy majesty equipped with thy
   adornment,
When thou takest the weapons of war in the chariot.
   I have come, causing thee to smite the eastern land,
Thou hast trampled those who are in the districts of
   God's-Land.
I have caused them to see thy majesty like a circling star,
When it scatters its flame in fire, and gives forth its dew.
   I have come, causing thee to smite the western land,
Keftyew[3] and Cyprus are in terror.
I have caused them to see thy majesty as a young bull,
Firm of heart, ready-horned, irresistible.
   I have come, causing thee to smite those who are in their
   marshes,
The lands of Mitanni tremble under fear of thee.
I have caused them to see thy majesty as a crocodile,
Lord of fear in the water, unapproachable.
   I have come, causing thee to smite those who are in the
   isles;
Those who are in the midst of the Great Green (Sea) hear
   thy roarings.
I have caused them to see thy majesty as an avenger
Who rises upon the back of his slain victim.
   I have come, causing thee to smite the Tehenu
   (Libyans),

[3] Crete

The isles of the Utentyew[4] are subject to the might of thy
   prowess.
I have caused them to see thy majesty as a fierce-eyed lion,
Thou makest them corpses in their valleys.
   I have come, causing thee to smite the uttermost ends of
   the lands,
The circuit of the Great Circle (Okeanos) is inclosed in thy
   grasp.
I have caused them to see thy majesty as a lord of the wing,
Who seizeth upon that which he seeth, as much as he
   desires.
   I have come, causing thee to smite those who are in front
   of their land.
Thou hast smitten the Sand-dwellers as living captives.
I have caused them to see thy majesty as a southern jackal,
Lord of running, stealthy-going, who roves the Two Lands.
   I have come, causing thee to smite the Nubian
   Troglodytes,
As far as they are in thy grasp.
I have caused them to see thy majesty as thy two brothers,
I have united their two arms for thee in victory.
   Thy two sisters, I have set them as protection behind
   thee,
The arms of my majesty are above, warding off evil.
I have caused thee to reign, my beloved son,
Horus, Mighty Bull, Shining in Thebes, whom I have
   begotten, in uprightness of heart.
Tuthmosis, living forever, who hast done for me all that my
   ka desired;
Thou hast erected my dwelling as an everlasting work,
Enlarging and extending (it) more than the past which had
   been.

4 unknown

The great doorway—.

Thou hast fêted the beauty of Amon-Re,

Thy monuments are greater than those of any king who has
been.

When I commanded thee to do it, I was satisfied therewith;

I established thee upon the Horus-throne of millions of
years;

Thou shalt continue life.

AMENHOTEP II SACRIFICES CAPTIVES TO AMUN, c. 1451 BC

Anonymous

With the death of Tuthmosis III, the Syrians saw an opportunity to break away from the Egyptian empire, but the dead regent's son and successor had something of the same military vigour about him. In Year Two of his reign, Amenhotep II marched overland into northern Syria, subduing all before him. Tikhsi seems to have been the focal point of the rebellion, and from that locality Amenhotep took seven princes captive. On return to Egypt, Amenhotep himself sacrificed the captives before the god Amun. The event was recorded in stelae at temples on Elephantine island and at Amada.

When his majesty returned with joy of heart to his father, Amon, he slew with his own weapon the seven princes, who had been in the district of Tikhsi and had been placed head downward at the prow of his majesty's barge, the name of which was: "Okheprure (Amenhotep II) is-the-Establish-er-of-the-Two-Lands". One hanged the six men of those fallen ones, before the wall of Thebes; those hands likewise. Then the other fallen one was taken up-river to Nubia and hanged on the wall of Napata, in order to cause to be manifest the victories of his majesty, forever and ever in all lands and countries of the land of the Negro; since he had taken the Southerners and bound the Northerners, the back-lands of the whole earth, upon which Re shines; that he might make his boundary as far as he desired, none opposing his hands, according to the command of his father Re, Amon-Re, lord of Thebes; in order that the Son of Re, of his body, his beloved, Amenhotep (II), divine ruler of Heliopolis, might be given life, stability, satisfaction, joy of heart, through him, like Re, forever and ever.

DUTIES OF THE VIZIER, c. 1440 BC

Rekmire

The vizier was the "prime minister" of pharaonic government. In the time of the Old Kingdom, the vizier was a member of the royal family; by the New Kingdom he was invariably selected on merit. The expansion of empire and trade under the 18th Dynasty caused the office of vizier to be split into two, with a vizier in the north and a vizier in the south. Rekmire was southern vizier to Tuthmosis III and Amenhotep II. He recorded his vast and eclectic duties on his tomb at Shekh Abd el-Kurna.

The Sitting of the Vizier in his Hall

. . . The vizier shall sit upon a chair, with a rug upon the floor, and a dais upon it, a cushion under his back, a cushion under his feet, a—upon it, and a baton at his hand; the 40 skins shall be open before him. Then the magnates of the South (shall stand) in the two aisles before him, while the master of the privy chamber is on his right, the receiver of income on his left, the scribes of the vizier at his (either) hand; one corresponding to another, with each man at his proper place. One shall be heard after another, without allowing one who is behind to be heard before one who is in front. If one in front says: "There is none being heard at my hand," then he shall be taken by the messenger of the vizier.

Intercourse of Palace with Outside World
There shall be reported to him the sealing of the sealed chambers up to that hour and the opening of them up to that hour. There shall be reported to him the affairs of the fortresses of the South and North. The going out of all that goes out of the king's-house shall be reported to him; and the coming in of all that comes into the king's-house shall be reported to him. Now, as for everything going in and everything going out on the floor of the court, they shall go out and they shall go in through his messenger, who shall cause them to go in (and) go out.

Reports of Overseers
The overseers of hundreds and the overseers of—shall report to him their affairs.

Daily Report to Pharaoh
Furthermore, he shall go in to take counsel on the affairs of the king, L. P. H., and there shall be reported to him the affairs of the Two Lands in his house every day. He shall go in to Pharaoh, before the chief treasurer; he shall wait at the northern flagstaff. Then the vizier shall come, proceeding from the gate of the great double façade.

Report of Treasurer and Vizier to Each Other
Then the chief treasurer, he shall come to meet him the vizier and shall report to him, saying: "All thy affairs are sound and prosperous; every responsible incumbent has reported to me, saying: 'All thy affairs are sound and prosperous, the king's-house is sound and prosperous.'"

Then the vizier, he shall report to the chief treasurer, saying: "All thy affairs are sound and prosperous; every seat of the court is sound and prosperous. There have been reported to me the sealing of the sealed chambers to this hour and the opening of them to this hour, by every responsible incumbent."

Daily Opening of the King's-House
Now, after each has reported to the other, of the two officials, then the vizier shall send to open every gate of the king's-house, to cause to go in all that goes in, and to go out all that goes out likewise, by his messenger, who shall cause it to be put in writing.

Irregularities among the Princes
Let not any official be empowered to judge against a superior in his hall. If there be any assailant against any of these officials in his hall, then he shall cause that he be brought to the judgment-hall. It is the vizier who shall punish him, in order to expiate his fault. Let not any official have power to punish in his hall. There shall be reported to him every judgment which is against the hall, when he repairs thereto.

Criminals
Now, as for every act of the vizier, while hearing in his hall; he shall record everything concerning which he hears. He who has not disproved the charge at his hearing, which takes place—, then it shall be entered in the criminal docket. He who is in the great prison, not able to disprove the charge of his messenger, likewise; when their case comes on another time, then one shall report and determine whether it is in the criminal docket, and there shall be

executed the things concerning which entry was made, in order to expiate their offence.

Loan of Vizier's Records

As for any writing sent by the vizier to any hall, being those which are not confidential, it shall be taken to him together with the documents of the keepers thereof under seal of the officers, and the scribes thereof after them; then he shall open it; then after he has seen it, it shall return to its place, sealed with the seal of the vizier. But if he furthermore ask for a confidential writing, then let it not be taken by the keepers thereof.

Summons of Petitioner

Now, as for every messenger whom the vizier sends on account of any petitioner, he shall cause that he go to him.

Real Estate Cases

Now, as for every petitioner to the vizier concerning lands, he shall dispatch him (the messenger) to him, in addition to a hearing of the land-overseer and the local council of the district. He shall decree a stay for him of two months for his lands in the South or North. As for his lands, however, which are near to the Southern City and to the court, he shall decree a stay for him of three days, being that which is according to law; (for) he shall hear every petitioner according to this law which is in his hand.

Reports of District Officials

It is he who brings in the officials of the district; it is he who sends them out; they report to him the affairs of their districts.

Wills, Etc.
Every property-list is brought to him; it is he who seals it.

Settlement of Registered Boundaries
It is he who administers the gift-lands in all regions. As for every petitioner who shall say: "Our boundary is unsettled"; one shall examine whether it is under the seal of the official thereof; then he shall seize the seizures of the local council who unsettled it.

Manner of Petition
One shall put every petition in writing, not permitting that he petition orally. Every petitioner to the king shall be reported to him, after he puts it in writing.

Intercourse between Court and Local Authorities
It is he who dispatches every messenger of the king's-house, L. P. H., who is sent to the mayors and village sheiks. It is he who dispatches every circuit messenger, every expedition of the king's-house. It is he who acts as the one who—in the South and North, the Southern Frontier and Abydos. They shall report to him all that happens among them, on the first day of every four-month season; they shall bring to him the writing thereof, in their hands, together with their local council.

Mustering King's Escort
It is he who gathers the troops, moving in attendance upon the king, in journeying northward or southward.

Garrison of Residence City
It is he who stations the rest who remain in the Southern City, and in the court, according to the decision in the king's-house, L. P. H.

General Army Orders

The commandant of the ruler's table is brought to him, to his hall, together with the council of the army, in order to give to them the regulation of the army.

Advisory Functions

Let every office, from first to last, proceed to the hall of the vizier, to take counsel with him.

Felling Timber

It is he who dispatches to cut down trees according to the decision in the king's-house.

Water-Supply

It is he who dispatches the official staff, to attend to the water-supply in the whole land.

Annual Ploughing

It is he who dispatches the mayors and village sheiks to plough for harvest time.

Overseers of Labour?

It is he who appoints the overseers of hundreds in the hall of the king's-house.

Audience for Town Authorities

It is he who arranges the hearing of the mayors and village sheiks who go forth in his name, of South and North.

Administration of Fortresses

Every matter is reported to him; there are reported to him the affairs of the southern fortress; and every arrest which is for seizing

Nome Administration, Boundaries, Etc.
It is he who makes the—of every nome; it is he who "hears"
it. It is he who dispatches the district soldiers and scribes to
carry out the administration of the king. The records of the
nome are in his hall. It is he who hears concerning all lands.
It is he who makes the boundary of every nome, the field—,
all divine offerings and every contract.

Record of Depositions, Etc.
It is he who takes every deposition; it is he who hears the
rejoinder when a man comes for argument with his opponent.

Appointment of Courts for Special Cases, Etc.
It is he who appoints every appointee to the hall of
judgment, when any litigant comes to him from the
king's-house. It is he who hears every edict.

Sacred and Royal Revenues in Residence City and Court
It is he who hears concerning the "Great Beauty" of every
divine offering. It is he who levies all taxes of the income,
and who gives it to him—every—in the Southern City, and
in the court. It is he who seals it under his seal. It is he who
hears every matter; it is he who makes the distribution of
the tribute to the crown possessions. The great council shall
report to him their dues . . . It is he who opens the gold-
house, together with the chief treasurer. It is he who
inspects the tribute of all, lands—chief steward, together
with the great council. It is he who makes the lists of all
bulls, of which a list is made.

Canal Inspection in Residence City
It is he who inspects the water-supply on the first of every
ten-day period.

Revenues from Local Authorities

The mayors, village sheiks, and every man shall report to him, all their tribute. Every district supervisor, and every overseer of hundreds, they shall report to him every litigation – they shall report to him furthermore, monthly, in order to control the tribute.

Observation of Sirius and High Nile

—the rising of Sirius, and the—of the Nile. There shall be reported to him the high (Nile).

Administration of Navy

It is he who exacts the ships for every requisition made upon him. It is he who dispatches every messenger of the king's-house to—. When the king is with the army, it is he who makes report . . .

Report is made to him by all the officials of the head of the navy, from the highest to the lowest. It is he who seals the edicts.

Method of Reporting to Vizier

Every report shall be reported to him by the doorkeeper of the judgment-hall, who reports on his part all that he (the vizier) does while hearing in the hall of the vizier.

THE TEACHING OF AMENEMOPE, c. 1400 BC

Anonymous

"The Teaching of Amenemope" is one of the most famous instructional texts of Ancient Egypt, differing from the materialism of most by stressing religious piety and moral rectitude. Indeed, its sheer "spirituality" is a precursor to Akhenaten's cult of Aten (see pp 146–147) "The Teaching" also has some close parallels with

the Bible's book of Proverbs, especially Proverbs 22:17 and 24:22, leading to conjecture that the Hebrew borrowed directly from the Egyptian; at the very least there was cultural intercourse between the nations of North Africa and the Near East.

Preface

The beginning of instruction on how to live,
Guidance for well-being;
Every direction for consorting with elders,
Rules for a courtier;
Ability to refute him who uttereth an accusation,
And to bring back a report to one who hath sent him.
To direct him to the path of life,
To make him prosper upon the earth;
To let his heart go into its shrine,
Steering him clear of evil;
To save him from the mouth of strangers,
Praised in the mouth of men.

First Chapter

Give thine ears, hear what is said,
Give thy mind to interpret them.
To put them in thy heart is beneficial;
It is detrimental for him who neglecteth them.
Let them rest in the casket of thy belly,
That they may be a *pnat* in thy heart.
Even when there is a whirlwind of words,
They shall be a mooring-stake for thy tongue.
If thou spendest thy lifetime while this is in thy heart,
Thou wilt find it a success,
Thou wilt find my words a treasury of life;
Thy body will prosper upon earth.

Second Chapter
Guard thyself against robbing the wretched
And against being puissant over the man of broken arm.
Stretch not forth thy hand to repel an old man,
Nor anticipate the aged.
Let not thyself be sent on a wicked mission,
Nor love him who hath performed it.
Cry not out against him whom thou hast injured,
Nor answer him back to justify thyself.
He who hath done evil, the river-bank abandons him,
And his flooded land carries him away.
The north wind cometh down that it may end his hour;
It is united to the tempest;
The thunder is loud, and the crocodiles are evil.
O hot-head, what is thy condition?
He is crying out, his voice to heaven.
O Moon, arraign his crime!
Steer that we may ferry the wicked man across,
For we shall not act like him –
Lift him up, give him thy hand;
Leave him (in) the hands of the god;
Fill his belly with bread that thou hast,
So that he may be sated and may cast down his eye.

Fourth Chapter
As for the hot-headed man in a temple,
He is like a tree growing in an enclosed space.
A moment completeth its loss of foliage.
Its end is reached in the *makherma*.
It is sunk far from its place;
The flame is its burial shroud.
The truly silent man, he withdraweth himself apart.
He is like a tree growing in a plot.

It groweth green and doubleth its yield;
It is before its lord.
Its fruit is sweet; its shade is pleasant.
Its end is reached in the grove.

Sixth Chapter
Remove not the landmark at the boundaries of the arable land,
Nor disturb the position of the measuring-cord;
Covet not a cubit of land,
Nor throw down the boundaries of a widow . . .
Beware of throwing down the boundaries of the fields,
Lest a terror carry thee off . . .
Better is poverty in the hand of the god
Than riches in a storehouse;
Better is bread, when the heart is happy,
Than riches with vexation.

Seventh Chapter
Cast not thy heart after riches;
There is no ignoring Shay and Renent.
Place not thy heart upon externals;
Every man belongeth to his hour.
Labour not to seek for increase;
Thy needs are safe for thee.
If riches are brought to thee by robbery,
They will not spend the night with thee;
At daybreak they are not in thy house:
Their places may be seen, but they are not.
The ground has opened its mouth – "Let him enter that it
may swallow",
They sink into the underworld.
They have made for themselves a great breach suitable to
their size

And are sunken down in the storehouse.
They have made themselves wings like geese
And are flown away to heaven.
Rejoice not thyself (over) riches (gained) by robbery,
Nor groan because of poverty.

Ninth Chapter
Associate not with the hot-head,
Nor become intimate with him in conversation . . .
Leap not to cleave to such a one,
Lest a terror carry thee off.

Tenth Chapter
Salute not thy hot-headed (opponent) perforce,
And hurt thine own heart (thereby).
Say not to him: "Hail to thee!" falsely,
While there is dread in thy belly.

Eleventh Chapter
Covet not the property of an inferior person,
Nor hunger for his bread.
As for the property of an inferior person, it is an obstruction
to the throat,
It maketh a vomiting in the gullet.
By false oaths he hath produced it,
His heart being perverted in his body . . .

Thirteenth Chapter
Injure not a man, [with] pen upon papyrus —
O abomination of the god!
Bear not witness with lying words,
Nor seek another's reverse with thy tongue.
Make not a reckoning with him who hath nothing,

Nor falsify thy pen.
If thou hast found a large debt against a poor man,
Make it into three parts,
Forgive two, and let one remain,
In order that thou shalt find thereby the ways of life.
Thou wilt lie down – the night hasteneth away –
(lo !) thou art in the morning;
Thou hast found it like good news.
Better is praise for one who loves men
Than riches in a storehouse;
Better is bread, when the heart is happy,
Than riches with contention.

Sixteenth Chapter
Tamper not with the scales nor falsify the weights,
Nor damage the fractions of the measure.
Desire not the agricultural measure,
And neglect those of the Treasury . . .

Eighteenth Chapter
Lie not down at night being fearful of the morrow.
When the day breaks, what is the morrow like?
Man knoweth not what the morrow is like.
God is (ever) in his success,
Whereas man is in his failure;
One thing are the words which men have said,
Another is that which the god doeth . . .

Twenty-First Chapter
Empty not thine inmost self to everybody,
And so damage thine influence.
Spread not thine utterances to the common people,
Nor associate with thyself the over-communicative.

Better is a man who concealeth his report in his inmost self
Than he who speaketh it out injuriously.

Twenty-Third Chapter
Eat not bread in the presence of a noble,
Nor apply thy mouth at the beginning.
If thou art satisfied — false chewings
Be a diversion for thy saliva!
Look at the cup which is in thy presence
And let it serve thy needs.

Twenty-Fifth Chapter
Laugh not at a blind man nor tease a dwarf,
Nor injure the plans of the lame.
Tease not a man who is in the hand of the god,
Nor be furious against him when he hath erred.
As for man, clay and straw,
The god is his builder.
He teareth down and buildeth up every day.
He maketh a thousand poor men at his will,
(Or) he maketh a thousand men as overseers,
When he is in his hour of life.
How joyful is he who hath reached the West,
Being safe in the hand of the god.

Thirtieth Chapter
See for thyself these thirty chapters:
They give pleasure; they instruct;
They are the foremost of all books;
They instruct the ignorant.
If they are read out in the presence of the ignorant,
Then he will be cleansed by reason of them.
Fill thyself with them; put them in thy heart,

And be a man who can explain them,
Interpreting them as a teacher.
As for the scribe who is experienced in his office,
He shall find himself worthy to be a courtier.

Colophon
It has come to its end
In the writing of Senu, son of the God's Father Pa-miu.

AMENHOTEP III BUILDS HIS MORTUARY TEMPLE IN SPLENDOUR, c. 1386–70 BC

Anonymous

Today all that stands of Amenhotep III's mortuary temple at Deir el Bahri (the west bank of Luxor) are the two 60-feet statues known as the "Colossi of Menon". The temple's original spendour, however, was recorded by an official scribe on a giant granite stele recovered by the Victorian Egyptologist Flinders Petrie.

Behold, the heart of his majesty was satisfied with making a very great monument; never has happened the like since the beginning.

He made (it) as his monument for his father, Amon, lord of Thebes, making for him an august temple on the west of Thebes, an eternal, ever-lasting fortress of fine white sandstone, wrought with gold throughout; its floor is adorned with silver, all its portals with electrum; it is made very wide and large, and established forever; and adorned with this very great monument. It is numerous in royal statues, of Elephantine granite, of costly gritstone, of every splendid costly stone, established as everlasting works. Their stature shines more than the heavens, their rays are in the faces (of men) like the sun, when he shines early in the morning. It is supplied with a "Station of the King", wrought with gold and many costly stones. Flagstaves are set up before it, wrought with electrum; it resembles the horizon in heaven when Re rises therein. Its lake is filled with the great Nile, lord of fish and fowl, pure in—

Its storehouse is filled with male and female slaves, with children of the princes of all the countries of the captivity of his majesty.

Its storehouses contain all good things, whose number is not known. It is surrounded with settlements of Syrians, colonized with children of princes, its cattle are like the sand of the shore, they make up millions.

The bow-rope of the Southland in it and the stern-rope of the Northland, even his majesty revealed himself like Ptah, was skilful-minded like Him-South-of-His-Wall (Ptah), searching out excellent things for his father, Amon-Re, King of Gods, making for him a very great pylon [i.e. giant doorway] over against Amon. Its beautiful name which his majesty made was: "Amon-Has-Received-His-Divine-Barque", a place of rest for the lord of the gods at his "Feast of the Valley" on the western voyage of Amon to behold the western gods, in order that he may endow his majesty with satisfying life.

Amenhotep III was an inveterate constructor of temples. In addition to his mortuary temple, he built temples at Thebes, Luxor and at Soleb in Nubia. He also enlarged the temple to Amun at Karnak.

WILD CATTLE HUNT, c. 1384 BC

Anonymous

In which the hunt-loving Amenhotep III killed, with a bow-and-arrow, more than 76 wild cattle in two days' sport. From a commemorative scarab.

Marvel which happened to his majesty. One came to say to his majesty: "There are wild cattle upon the highlands, as far as the region of Sheta."* His majesty sailed down-stream in the royal barge, Khammat at the time of evening, beginning the goodly way, and arriving in safety at the region of Sheta at the time of morning.

His majesty appeared upon a horse, his whole army being behind him. The commanders and the citizens of all the army in its entirety and the children with them were commanded to keep watch over the wild cattle. Behold, his majesty commanded to cause that these wild cattle be surrounded by a wall with an inclosure. His majesty commanded to count all these wild cattle. Statement thereof: 170 wild cattle. Statement of that which his majesty captured in the hunt on this day: 56 wild cattle.

His majesty tarried four days – to give fire to his horses. His majesty appeared upon a horse a second time. Statement of these wild cattle, which he captured in the [second] hunt: 20 (+ x) wild cattle.

MASSACRE AT IBHET, c. 1381 BC

Anonymous

The reign of Amenhotep III was amongst the most stable in pharaonic history; only the Nubians had any taste for rebellion and this was brutally put down by Amenhotep III's son, the viceroy of Kush. According to a stele at Semneh, it took the the viceroy's troops but a single hour to kill and capture more than a thousand Nubians:

* unknown, but probably in the Delta

List of the captivity which his majesty took in the land of Ibbet, the wretched:

Living negroes	150 heads
Archers	110 heads
Negresses	250 heads
Servants of the negroes	55 heads
Their children	175 heads
Total	740 living heads
Hands thereof*	312
United with the living heads	1,052

AN ORDER FOR BEAUTIFUL CONCUBINES, c. 1376 BC

Amenhotep III

The order was placed by the pharaoh with Milkilu, prince of Gezer.

Behold, I have sent you Hanya, the commissioner of the archers, with merchandise in order to have beautiful concubines, i.e. weavers. Silver, gold, garments, all sort of precious stones, chairs of ebony, as well as all good things, worth 160 deben. In total: forty concubines – the price of every concubine is forty of silver. Therefore, send very beautiful concubines without blemish.

AMENHOTEP III CONSTRUCTS A PLEASURE LAKE FOR QUEEN TIY, c. 1375 BC

Anonymous

Most of the wealth of early 18th Dynasty came from the spoils of war; during the reign of Amenhotep III the proceeds of trade and gold-mining filled the pharaonic

---

* i.e. the severed right hands of the slain

coffers. It was a time of unprecedented luxury for the royal circle, not the least proof of which was the pleasure lake dug for Queen Tiy to sail on at "Zerukha" (almost certainly adjacent the palace of Amenhotep III, on the west bank of Thebes).

His majesty commanded to make a lake for the Great King's-Wife, Tiy, in her city of Zerukha. Its length is 3,700 cubits*, its width, 700 cubits. His majesty celebrated the feast of the opening of the lake, in the third month of the first season, day 16, when his majesty sailed thereon in the royal barge: "Aton-Gleams".

THE AKHENATEN REVOLUTION: THE HYMN TO ATEN, c. 1345 BC

Akhenaten

Under the 18th Dynasty Egypt became the world's greatest power. Under the 18th Dynasty, thanks to a a revolutionary religious doctrine, Egypt lost her empire. The iconolast responsible was Amenhotep IV, son of Amenhotep III and Queen Tiy, who in Year 5 of his reign began the zealous promotion of a monotheistic cult which worshipped the physical orb of the sun – the Aten. In mark, Amenhotep IV changed his name to Akhenaten ("Servant of the Aten" and the seat of government to a virgin site in middle Egypt, Akhenaten ("The Horizon of the Aten": now el-Amarna). Undoubtedly, Akhenaten was driven by idealism, although his reformation of Egyptian religion had two potential political positives for the monarchy: it reduced the power of the priesthood at Thebes; it elevated the power of the pharaoh because only the pharaoh had access to the god Aten. That said, Akhenaten's preoccupation with the new theology meant major neglect of his Asiatic domains. With fatal result.

"The Hymn to Aten", ostensibly written by Akhenaten himself, was a central document of the new faith, as well as an outstanding piece of ancient poetry.

* i.e. over one mile

Thou dost appear beautiful on the horizon of heaven,
  O living Aten, thou who wast the first to live.
When thou hast risen on the eastern horizon,
  Thou hast filled every land with thy beauty.
Thou art fair, great, dazzling, high above every land;
  Thy rays encompass the lands to the very limit of all thou
    hast made.
Being Re, thou dost reach to their limit
  And curb them [for] thy beloved son;
Though thou art distant, thy rays are upon the earth;
  Thou art in their faces, yet thy movements are unknown (?).

When thou dost set on the western horizon,
  The earth is in darkness, resembling death.
Men sleep in the bed-chamber with their heads covered,
  Nor does one eye behold the other.
Were all their goods stolen which are beneath their heads,
  They would not be aware of it.
Every lion has come forth from his den,
  All the snakes bite.
Darkness prevails, and the earth is in silence,
  Since he who made them is resting in his horizon.

At daybreak, when thou dost rise on the horizon,
  Dost shine as Aten by day,
Thou dost dispel the darkness
  And shed thy rays.
The Two Lands are in festive mood,
  Awake, and standing on (their) feet,
For thou hast raised them up;
  They cleanse their bodies and take (their) garments;
Their arms are (lifted) in adoration at thine appearing;
  The whole land performs its labour.

All beasts are satisfied with their pasture;
   Trees and plants are verdant.
The birds which fly from their nests, their wings are
      (spread) in adoration to thy soul;
   All flocks skip with (their) feet;
All that fly up and alight
   Live when thou hast risen [for] them.
Ships sail upstream and downstream alike,
   For every route is open at thine appearing.
The fish in the river leap before thee,
   For thy rays are in the midst of the sea.

Thou creator of issue in woman, who makest semen into
      mankind,
   And dost sustain the son in his mother's womb,
Who dost soothe him with that which stills his tears,
   Thou nurse in the very womb, giving breath to sustain
      all thou dost make!
When he issues from the womb to breathe on the day of his
      birth,
   Thou dost open his mouth completely and supply his
      needs.
When the chick in the egg cheeps inside the shell,
   Thou givest it breath within it to sustain it.
Thou hast set it its appointed time in the egg to break
      it,
   That it may emerge from the egg to cheep at its ap-
pointed time;
   That it may walk with its feet when it emerges from it.

How manifold is that which thou hast made, hidden from
      view!
   Thou sole god, there is no other like thee!

Thou didst create the earth according to thy will, being
    alone:
  Mankind, cattle, all flocks,
Everything on earth which walks with (its) feet,
  And what are on high, flying with their wings.

The foreign lands of Hurru and Nubia, the land of Egypt –
  Thou dost set each man in his place and supply his
      needs;
  Each one has his food, and his lifetime is reckoned.
Their tongues are diverse in speech and their natures
      likewise;
  Their skins are varied, for thou dost vary the foreigners.
Thou dost make the Nile in the underworld,
  And bringest it forth as thou desirest to sustain the
      people,
As thou dost make them for thyself,
  Lord of them all, who dost weary thyself with them,
Lord of every land, who dost rise for them,
  Thou Aten of the day, great in majesty.

As for all distant foreign lands, thou makest their life,
  For thou hast set a Nile in the sky,
That it may descend for them,
  That it may make waves on the mountains like the sea,
  To water their fields amongst their towns.
How excellent are thy plans, thou lord of eternity!
  The Nile in the sky is for the foreign peoples,
For the flocks of every foreign land that walk with (their)
      feet,
  While the (true) Nile comes forth from the underworld
for Egypt.

Thy rays suckle every field;
  When thou dost rise, they live and thrive for thee.
Thou makest the seasons to nourish all that thou hast made:
    The winter to cool them; the heat that they(?) may taste
      thee.
Thou didst make the distant sky to rise in it,
  To see all that thou hast made.
Being alone, and risen in thy form as the living Aten,
    Whether appearing, shining, distant, or near,
Thou makest millions of forms from thyself alone:
    Cities, towns, fields, road, and river.

Every eye perceives thee level with them,
    When thou art the Aten of the day above the earth (?)
When thou didst go away because all men existed,
    Thou didst create their faces that thou mightest not see
      [thy]self [alone],
    . . . one . . . which thou didst make.
Thou art in my heart;
    There is no other that knows thee,
Save thy son Akhenaten,
    For thou hast made him skilled in thy plans and thy
      might.
The earth came into being by thy hand,
    Just as thou didst make them (i.e. mankind).

When thou hast risen, they live;
  When thou dost set, they die.
For thou art lifetime thyself; one lives through thee;
    Eyes are upon (thy) beauty until thou dost set.
All labour is put aside when thou dost set in the west;
    When [thou] risest [thou] makest . . . flourish for the
      king.

As for all who hasten on foot,
    Ever since thou didst fashion the earth,
Thou dost raise them up for thy son who came forth from
    thyself,
    The King of Upper and Lower Egypt, Akhenaten.

COLLAPSE OF EMPIRE: LETTERS FROM THE SYRIAN FRONTIER, c. 1340–1334 BC

Various

It was not only Akhenaten's otherwordliness which ill-suited him as an imperial ruler, he seems to have suffered from a debilitating physical condition. Some have guessed at a tumour of the pituitary gland, for artistic representations of the pharaoh show him with the skull malformation and female-like body-fat indicative of Frohlich's Syndrome. Certainly Akhenaten was no soldier. When the northern reaches of the empire were overrun by movement of the Hittites south, local governors and officers sent desperate appeals and complaints to the monarch at el-Amarna, all carefully filed in the "House of Correspondence of the Pharaoh" but not acted upon.[1]

The officials of the City of Dunip

In which they warn the pharaoh that Aziru of Amurru had become a traitor and joined with the Hittites.

"My lord, Dunip, your servant, speaks, saying – Who formerly could have plundered Dunip, without being plundered by Manahbiria (i.e. Tuthmosis III). And now for twenty years we have been sending to the king, our lord, but our messengers remain with the king, our lord. And now Aziru, your servant . . . in the land of Hatat has captured them (probably dependents of Dunip) by force. If

---

[1] the correspondence was discovered at el-Amarna in AD 1887 by an Egyptian peasant on an unofficial dig.

his (the king's) soldiers and chariots come too late, Aziru will make us like the city of Ni (i.e. desolate) . . .

"If however we have to mourn, the king of Egypt will mourn over those things which Aziru has done . . . And when Aziru enters Simyra, Aziru will do to us as he pleases, in the territory of our lord the king, and on account of these things, our lord will have to lament. And now Dunip, your city, weeps, and her tears are running, and there is no help for us. For twenty years we have been sending to our lord the king, the king of Egypt, but there has not come to us a word from our lord, not one.

Rib-Addi of Byblos

Rib-addi was a faithful vassal of Egypt. After years of holding out against the various Hittite, Phoenician and Syrian enemies of the pharoah, Rib-Addi was forced to flee Byblos (also Gubla or Gebal) by his brother's conspiracy in favour of Aziru of Amurru. Rib-Addi took sanctuary in Beirut where (see his last letter) he continued to petition the pharaoh for aid.

. . . And moreover if the king should march forth, though all the lands were in rebellion against him what could they do to us? In this case they would altogether do good, but I am very greatly afraid that there is no man to rescue me out of their hands; like a bird which is caught in a net, so shall I be in Gebal. Why will you neglect your land? Behold I wrote thus to the king's palace, but they paid no attention to my message. Verily Amanappa is with you; ask him, he knows about it, and has seen the distress, which has come upon me . . . Verily I am thus mindful day and night.

. . . Behold, I remain shut up in my city, I am not strong enough to go out of its gate. (Letter 64.) Their sons, their daughters, and the timbers of their houses are no more,

having been given to Jarimuta for their sustenance. Verily
three times three years have passed over me, and for two
years my grain has grown. (Now however in the third year)
there is no grain for us to eat. Who should have sown it?

Behold Tyre has acted rebelliously . . . I have deposited my
property in Tyre, in order that it might be at my disposi-
tion. Verily they (of Tyre) killed their commander, and
also my sister and her sons. I had sent my sister's daughters
to Tyre from fear of Abdasirta.

As long as I am in the city I guard it for my lord. But . . .
my brother has incited the city, so as to deliver it to Abd-
asirta's[2] sons. O may not my lord, the king, neglect the city!
For there is a very great deal of silver and gold in it; in its
temples there is much property if they capture it! . . .
Behold I have sent your servant, my son, to my lord,
the king, and may the king send him immediately, with
men for the occupation of the city . . .
. . . Why did my lord, the king, write to me, saying
"Defend yourself, and then you will be protected"? Wherewith shall I defend it against my enemies? . . . If the king
does not protect his servant.

The ships and people of Simyra, Beirut and Sidon, all of
them that are in Amurru are pressing me hard, and behold
now Japa-addi and Aziru have attacked me, and verily he
has seized my ship. And behold they have thus sailed forth
into the ocean, in order to capture my ships . . . my subjects
are intending to desert – a messenger whom I had sent . . .
was not able to enter Simyra, for all the roads were cut off.

[2] Aziru was son of Abd-asirta

. . . And you, do not abandon (me); if there are no troops there now, send ships to bring me alive, with the gods to my lord.

Rib-addi [speaks] to the king, his Lord, the sun of all countries; I have prostrated myself seven times and seven times at the feet of the king, my Lord.[3] I have written repeatedly in order to obtain, troops but have not received them, and the king, my Lord, has not listened to the words of his servant. I have sent my messenger to the palace, and he has returned with empty hands: there were troops for him. When the people of my house saw that no money had been given, they reproached me, the governors, my brothers, and they despised me. On the other hand, I set out for Hammuniri and in the meantime a brother of mine, younger than me, conspired against me at Gubla[4] to deliver the city to the sons of Abdi-Ashirta. When my brother saw that my messenger had returned empty handed and that there were no occupation troops with him, he despised me and thus he committed a crime, and he expelled me from the city. May the king, my Lord, not hold back before the actions of this dog.

Now I cannot enter the land of Mitsru[5]; I am old and I (suffer of) a serious disease in my own flesh. May the king, my Lord, know, that the Gods of Gubla are angered and the disease has become chronic, although I have confessed my sin to the Gods. Therefore I have not appeared before the king, my Lord. Now then, I have sent my son, servant of the king, my Lord, to the king, my Lord. May the king, my Lord, listen to the words of his servant and may the

[3] A standard act of obeisance, here undertaken metaphorically.
[4] i.e. Byblos
[5] i.e. Egypt

king, my Lord, give troops of archers to conquer the city of Gubla in order that enemy troops not enter her, nor the sons of Abdi-Ashirta, and it become necessary that the troops of archers of the king, my Lord, reconquer it. See, (there are) many men who love me in the city and few are my enemies. When the troops of archers will be leaving and the day of their arrival be known, the city will return to the king, my Lord. And may my Lord know (that) I am willing to die for him.

When I was in the city, I made an effort to keep it for my Lord and my heart was firm in the support of the king, my Lord. It would not have delivered the city to the sons of Abdi-Ashirta.

Therefore my brother has caused enmity between me and the city, to deliver it to the sons of Abdi-Ashirta. May the king, my Lord, hold back with respect to the city. Certainly there is inside her walls much gold and silver, and in her temples there is much of everything. If they conquer her, may the king, my Lord, do with his servant as he wants, but may he give me the city of Buruzilim as residence.

Now I am with Hammuniri, since Buruzilim has made the (other) cities hostile (to me). They have become enemies for fear of the sons of Abdi-Ashirta. When I came to Hammuniri because of the sons of Abdi-Ashirta, when they were stronger than I and there was no encouragement for me from the mouth of the king, I said to the king, my Lord: See, the city of Gubla (is) his. In her (there are) many things of the king, the possessions of our ancestors. If the king holds back, he will not have left any city of Kinahnu. May the king not hold back his action. Now I have sent to the king, my Lord, your servant, my son. May the king send him quickly with troops to take the city. If the king, my Lord, feels compassion for me and returns me to the city, then I will keep it for the king, my Lord, like previously . . .

May [the king, my Lord], listen to [the words] of his servant and send immediately troops to take the city. May the king, my Lord, not hold back with regard to this evil deed, that was committed against the countries of the king, [my Lord], and may the king, my Lord, quickly send troops of archers to take the city immediately. When they say in front of the king about the city: "the city is strong", it is not strong before the troops of the king, my Lord.

Yapahu of Gezer

Gezer (also Gazru) was a city in Judea

To the king, my lord, my god, my sun, the sun in the sky. Thus says Yapahu, the amelu [ruler] of Gazru, your servant, the dust of your two feet, the stable-man of your horse: At the two feet of the king, my lord, the sun in the sky, seven times and seven times I prostrate myself both upon the belly and back. And to all that the king, my lord, has told me I have paid close attention. I am the king's servant and the dust of your two feet.

Let the king, my lord, be aware that my younger brother, has rebelled against me and has entered Muh-hazu, and he has given over his two hands to the leader of the Apiru[6] And since [Ti?] is at war with me, take care of your land. May my lord write to his rabisu[7] *about this matter.*

---

[6] Habiru, nomadic invaders infiltrating Palestine from the north.
[7] pharaonic representative

Abdiheba

The governor of Jerusalem.

To the king, my lord . . . Thus says Abdiheba, thy servant. At the feet of my lord seven times and seven times I fall. I have heard all the words the king, my lord, has sent in to me concerning (?) . . . Behold, the deed which the Habiru(?) have done . . . of bronze . . . the word . . . . . . brought in to [Keila]h(?). Let the king know that all the lands are at peace,[8] but there is hostility against me; so let the king take thought about his land. Behold, the land of Gezer, the land of Ashkelon and Lachish (?) have given them food, oil and all their needs; so let the king take thought about archers; let him send archers against the men who are committing a crime against the king, my lord. If this year there are archers, then the lands and the regent will belong to the king, my lord, but if there are no archers, the lands and the regents will not belong to the king. Behold, this land of Jerusalem, neither my father nor my mother gave it to me; the mighty arm of the king gave it to me. Behold, this deed is the deed of Milkilu and the deed of the sons of Labaya who have given the land of the king to the Habiru. Behold, O king, my lord, I am in the right. As for the Cushites, let the king ask the commissioners if the house is really very strong; for they attempted a grave and serious crime; they took their implements and broke through the . . . of the roof . . . sent into the land . . . came up (?) with . . . (40) servants. Let the king take thought about them . . . gone forth (?) . . . the lands into their hand, so let the king demand (satisfaction) from them – abundance of food, abundance of oil and abundance of clothing, until Pauru, the commissioner of the king, comes

[8] i.e. have made peace with the pharaoh's enemies

up to the land of Jerusalem. Addaya has left with the men
of the warden's garrison which the king gave me. Let the
king know. Addaya said to me: "Behold, I am leaving, but
thou shalt not abandon it." This year send me a garrison
and send me a commissioner of the king. Even as we are (?),
I sent [gift]s (?) to the king, my lord . . . captives, five
thousand [shekels of silver (?) and (?)] eight (?) bearers in
caravans for the king, but they were captured in the open
country at Aijalon. Let the king, my lord, know. I am not
able to send a caravan to the king, my lord – that thou
mayest know. Behold, the king has set his name in the land
of Jerusalem for ever, so he cannot abandon the lands of
Jerusalem.

To the scribe of the king, my lord, say: Thus says
Abdiheba, thy servant. At the feet I fall; thy servant am
I. Take in clear words to the king, my lord. I am a warden
of the king. I am subordinate to thee.

But they did a wicked deed against me, the Cushites. I
was almost killed by the hand of the Cushites in the midst of
my house. Let the king demand satisfaction from them.
Seven times and seven times I fall at the feet of the king, my
lord. I am in the right.

To the king, my lord, my Sun-god, say: Thus says Abdiheba, thy servant. At the feet of the king, my lord, seven
times and seven times I fall. Behold, the king, my lord, has
set his name at the rising of the sun and at the setting of the
sun. It is outrageous what they have committed against me.
Behold, I am not a regent, but I am a warden to the king,
my lord. Behold, I am a shepherd of the king, and a tribute-
bringer of the king am I. Neither my father nor my mother
but the mighty arm of the king set me in the house of my
father . . . [Behold,] . . . came to me . . . I gave ten servants

[into his h] and. Shuta, the commissioner of the king, came to me. Twenty-one maidens and eighty male captives I gave into the hand of Shuta as a gift to the king, my lord. Let the king take counsel for his land. The land of the king is lost; all of it is taken away from me. There is hostility against me as far as the lands of Seir and as far as Gath-carmel. There is peace to all the regents, but there is hostility against me. I am treated like a Habiru, and I do not see the eyes of the king, my lord, for there is hostility against me. I am made like a ship in the midst of the sea. The mighty arm of the king may take Naharaim and Cush, but now the Habiru have taken the cities of the king. No regent is left to the king, my lord; all are lost. Behold, Turbazu has been killed in the city-gate of Zilu, yet the king holds back. Behold, Zimrida at Lachish – his servants have smitten him and have made themselves over to the Habiru. Yaptihadda has been killed in the city-gate of Zilu, yet the king holds back and does not demand (satisfaction) from them. So let the king take thought [about his land and] let the king give his attention to (sending) archers for his (?) land. For if there are no archers this year all the lands of the king, my lord, will be lost. They are not reporting in the presence of the king, my lord, that the land of the king, my lord, is lost and that all the regents are lost. If there are no archers this year, let the king send a commissioner, and let him take me to himself with my brothers, and we shall die beside the king, our lord.

Abi Milku of Tyre

To the king, my lord, my god, my Sun: Message of Abi-Milku, your servant. I fall at the feet of the king, my lord, seven times and seven times. I am the dirt under the sandals of the king, my lord. My lord is the Sun who comes forth over all lands day by day, according to the way (of being) the sun, his gracious father, who gives life by his sweet breath and returns with his north wind; who establishes the entire land in peace, by the power of his arm: ha-ap-si; *who gives forth his cry in the sky like Baal, and all the land is frightened at his cry.*

The servant herewith writes to his lord that he heard the gracious messenger of the kind who came to his servant, and the sweet breath that came forth from the mouth of the king, my lord, to his servant – his breath came back! Before the arrival of the messenger of the king, my lord, breath had not come back; my nose was blocked. Now the breath of the king has come forth to me, I am very happy and: a-ru-u *(he is satisfied)* day by day. Because I am happy, does the earth not pr[osp]er? When I heard that the gracious me [sse]nger from my lord, all the land was in fear of my lord, when I heard the sweet breath and the gracious messenger who came to me. When the king, my lord, said ku-na *"(Prepare) before the arrival of a large army," then the servant said to his lord:* ia-a-ia-ia *("Yes, yes, yes!")* On my front and on su-ri-ia *(my back)* I carry the word of the king, my lord. Whoever gives heed to the king, his lord, and serves him in his place, the sun com[e]s forth over him, and the sweet breath comes back from the mouth of his lord. If he does not heed the word of the king, his lord, his city is destroyed, never (again) does his name exist in all the land. (But) look at the servant who gives heed to his lord. His city prospers, his house prospers, his name exists forever.

You are the Sun who comes forth over me, and a brazen wall set up for him, and because of the powerful arm: nu-uh-ti *(I am at rest):* ba-ti-i-ti *(I am confident).* I indeed said to the Sun, the father of the king, my lord, "When shall I see the face of the king, my lord?" I am indeed guarding

Tyre, the principal city, for the king, my lord, until the powerful arm of the king comes forth over me, to give me water to drink and wood to warm myself.

Moreover, Zimredda, the king of Sidon, writes daily to the rebel Arizu, the son of Abdi-Asratu, about every word he has heard from Egypt. I herewith write to my lord, and it is good that he knows.

HOREMHEB DELIVERS THE POOR FROM OPPRESSION, c. 1315 BC

Horemheb

Regarded by the 19th Dynasty as their founder, Horemheb was an army general who seized power on the death of the last of Amarnas (i.e. descendants of Akhenaten), the decrepit Ay. To curry favour from the populace Horemheb reopened the temples of Amun – although he wisely appointed priests from the army, not the old self-aggrandizing priesthood – and legislated against corruption by judges, tax officials and soldiers.

Behold, his majesty spent the whole time seeking the welfare of Egypt and searching out instances of oppression in the land . . . came the scribe of his majesty. Then he seized palette and roll; he put it into writing according to all that his majesty, the king himself said. He spoke as follows: "My majesty commands concerning all instances of oppression in the land."

Enactment Against Robbing the Poor of Dues for the Royal Breweries and Kitchens
If the poor man made for himself a craft with its sail, in order to be able to serve the Pharaoh, L. P. H., loading it with the dues for the breweries and kitchens of the Pharaoh, and he was robbed of the craft and the dues, the poor man

stood reft of his goods and stripped of his many labours. This is wrong, and the Pharaoh will suppress it by his excellent measures. If there be a poor man who pays the dues of the breweries and kitchens of the Pharaoh, L. P. H., to the two deputies, and he be robbed of his goods and his craft, my majesty commands: that every officer who seizeth the dues and taketh the craft of any citizen of the army or of any person who is in the whole land, the law shall be executed against him, in that his nose shall be cut off, and he shall be sent to Tharu.

Against Robbing the Poor of Wood Due the Pharaoh
Furthermore, concerning the impost of wood, my majesty commands that if any officer find a poor man without a craft, then let him bring to him a craft for his impost from another, and let him send him to bring for him the wood; thus he shall serve the [Pharaoh].

Against Exacting Dues from a Poor Man Thus Robbed
Furthermore, my majesty commands that if any poor man be oppressed by robbery, his cargo be emptied by theft of them, and the poor man stand reft of his goods, no further exactions for dues shall be made from him when he has nothing. For it is not good, this report of very great injustice.

Against Robbing the Poor of Dues for the Harem or the Gods by the Soldiers
. . . my majesty commands that if any officer is guilty of extortions or thefts, the law shall be [executed] against him, in that his nose shall be cut off, and (he) shall be sent to Tharu likewise.

Against Unlawful Appropriation of Slave Service

When the officers of the Pharaoh's house of offerings have gone about tax-collecting in the towns . . . they have seized the slaves of the people, and kept them at work for 6 days or 7 days, without one's being able to depart from them afar so that it was an excessive detention indeed. It shall be done likewise against them. If there be any place where the stewards shall be tax-collecting, and any one shall hear, saying: "They are tax-collecting, to take katha-plant for themselves," and another shall come to report, saying: "My man slave (or) my female slave has been taken away and detained many days at work by the stewards"; it shall be done likewise against them.

Against Stealing of Hides by the Soldiers

The two divisions of troops which are in the field, one in the southern region, the other in the northern region, stole hides in the whole land, not passing a year, without applying the brand of the royal house to cattle which were not due to them, thereby increasing their number, and stealing that which was stamped from them. They went out from house to house, beating and plundering without leaving a hide for the people—. Then the officer of Pharaoh went about to each one, to collect the hides charged against him, and came to the people demanding them, but the hides were not found with them although the amount charged against them could be established. They satisfied them, saying: "They have been stolen from us." A wretched case is this, therefore it shall be [done] likewise.

When the overseer of the cattle of Pharaoh, L. P. H., goes about to attend to the loan-herds in the whole land, and there be not brought to him the hides of the—which are on the lists, he shall not hold the people responsible for the hides if they have them not, but they shall be released by command of his majesty, according to his just purposes. As for any citizen of the army, (concerning) whom one shall hear, saying: "He goeth about stealing hides," beginning with this day, the law shall be executed against him, by beating him a hundred blows, opening five wounds, and taking from him by force the hides which he took.

Enactment Against Corrupt Judges

I have improved this entire land—I have sailed it, as far as south of the wall . . . I have learned its whole interior, I have travelled it entirely in its midst, I have searched in— and I have sought two officials perfect in speech, excellent in good qualities, knowing how to judge the innermost heart, hearing the words of the palace, the laws of the judgment-hall. I have appointed them to judge the Two Lands, to satisfy those who are in—. I have given to each one his seat; I have set them in the two great cities of the South and the North; every land among them cometh to him without exception; I have put before them regulations in the daily register of the palace . . . I have directed them to the way of life, I lead them to the truth, I teach them, saying: "Do not associate with others of the people; do not receive the reward of another, not hearing—" How, then, shall those like you judge others, while there is one among you committing a crime against justice.

Now, as to the obligation of silver and gold—[my] majesty remits it, in order that there be not collected an obligation of anything from the official staff of the South and North.

Punishment of Bribery

Now, as for any official or any priest (concerning whom) it shall be heard, saying: "He sits, to execute judgment among the official staff appointed for judgment, and he commits a crime against justice therein"; it shall be against him a capital crime. Behold, my majesty has done this, to improve the laws of Egypt

BEATINGS, IMPALINGS AND THE CUTTING OFF OF EARS: PHARAONIC PUNISHMENTS FOR STEALING FROM THE GODS, c. 1280 BC

Seti I

From a decree of Seti I exempting his Nubian estate from tax assessment, so that all income might go to his cenotaph temple at Abydos. Effectively therefore, the Nubian estate belonged to the gods and pilfering from it was punished heavily. The decree was carved high in the cliff face at Nauri in stark warning to any prospective thieves.

His Majesty has commanded that ordinance be made for the House of Millions of Years of Menmaatre "The Heart is at Ease in Abydos" on water and on land throughout the provinces of Upper and Lower Egypt: to prevent interference with any person belonging to the House in the whole land, whether man or woman; to prevent interference with any goods belonging to this estate in the whole land; to prevent the taking of any people belonging to this estate by capture from one district for another district . . .

As to any Viceroy of Kush, any foreign chief, any mayor, any inspector or any person who shall take any person belonging to the House . . . punishment shall be done to him by beating him with two hundred blows and five open wounds, together with exacting the work of the person belonging to the Residence from him for every day that he shall spend with him, to be given to the House . . .

Now as to any high officer, any superintendent of the land belonging to this estate, any keeper of plough-oxen, any inspector who shall interfere with the boundary of lands belonging to the House . . . punishment shall be done to him by the cutting off of his ears, he being put to be a cultivator in the Residence . . .

As to any keeper of cattle, any keeper of hounds, any herdsman . . . who shall give any head of animals belonging to the House by defalcation to another . . . punishment shall be done to him by casting him down and impaling him on a stake, forfeiting his wife and children and all his property to the House and extracting the herd of animals from him to whom he shall have given it at the rate of a hundred to one.

RAMSES II FINDS THE NECROPOLIS BUILDINGS IN RUINS, c. 1279 BC

Anonymous

Not without reason is Ramses II popularly called "Ramses the Great". Aside from the sheer longevity of his reign (1279–1212), he sired 120 plus children and built and restored more temples than any other pharaoh, beginning in Year One of his reign when, as related in the inscription at Abydos extracted below Ramses voyaged there from Thebes to find Seti I's mortuary unfinished and other royal cemetery buildings in ruins. Naturally, as a good son of the god Osiris and his earthly father Seti I, Ramses II promptly set about their restoration.

He began the way, to make the voyage, while the royal barges illuminated the flood, turning down-stream to the seat of might, "House of Ramses Meriamon-Great-in-Victory." His majesty entered, to see his father, the voyage of the waters of the canal of Abydos, in order to found offerings for Wennofer, consisting of every good thing, that which his *ka* loves, in order to praise—for his brother, Onouris, son of Re in truth, like himself.

He found the buildings of the cemetery belonging to former kings, their tombs in Abydos, beginning to be in ruin. The half of them were in process of construction, their walls lying incomplete, not one brick touching another. That which was only begun had become mere rubbish. There was no one building—who was carrying out according to his plans, since their lord had flown to heaven. There was no other son, who renewed the monuments of his father, which were in the cemetery.

Lo, the house of Menmare (Seti I), its front and its rear were in process of construction, when he entered into heaven. Its monuments were not finished, its columns were not set up on its platform, its statue was upon the ground, it was not fashioned after the regulation for it, of the gold-house. Its divine offerings had ceased, the lay priesthood likewise. That which was brought from its fields was taken away, their boundaries were not fixed in the land.

Said his majesty to the wearer of the royal seal who was at his side: "Speak thou, call the court, the king's-grandees, all the commanders of the army, all the chiefs of works, and the keepers of the house of rolls (books)." They were brought before his majesty, their noses were bowed in the dust, their knees were on the earth in adoration, smelling the earth; their hands were uplifted to his majesty, they praised this Good God, magnifying his beauty in the presence. They told the story according to that which he had done, they likened his brave deeds, as they were; every word which came out of their mouths, was that which the Lord of the Two Lands had actually done. They were upon their bellies, wallowing upon the earth before his majesty, saying:

"We come to thee, lord of heaven, lord of earth, Re, life of the whole earth, lord of duration, of fruitful revolution, Atum for the people, lord of destiny, creator of Renenet, Khnum who fashioned the people, giver of breath into the nostrils of all, making all the gods live, pillar of heaven, support of earth,—adjusting the Two Lands, lord of food, plentiful in grain, in whose footsteps is the harvest goddess, maker of the great, fashioner of the lowly, whose word produces food, the lord vigilant when all men sleep, whose might defends Egypt, valiant in foreign lands, who returns when he has triumphed, whose sword protects the Egyptians, beloved of truth, in which he lives by his laws, defender of the Two Lands, rich in years, great in victory, the fear of whom expels foreign lands, our king, our lord, our Sun, by the words of whose mouth Atum lives. Lo, we are now before thy majesty, that thou mayest decree to us the life that thou givest, Pharaoh, L. P. H., breath of life, who makes all men live when he has shone on them."

Said his majesty to them: "Behold, I have caused that they call you, because of a plan that is before me. I have seen that the buildings of the cemetery, the tombs that are in Abydos, and the works therein, are in an unfinished state, since the time of their lord until this day. When a son arose in the place of his father, the monuments of him that begat him were not restored. Then I conversed with my own heart: 'It is a happy example, to provide for them that have passed away, excellent to behold good—Horus who shaped the thought of the son, that he should incline the heart after his father. My heart leads me in doing excellent things for Merneptah (Seti I). I will cause it to be said forever and ever: "It was his son, who made his name live."' May my father, Osiris, favour me with the long life of his son, Horus, according as I do that which he did; I do excellent things, as he did excellent things, for him who begat me."

"I came forth from Re, although ye say, from Menmare (Seti I), who brought me up. The All-Lord himself made me great, while I was a child, until I reigned. He gave to me the land while I was in the egg; the great smelled the earth before me, when I was installed as eldest son, as hereditary prince upon the throne of Keb. I reported as lord of infantry and chariotry. When my father appeared to the public, I being a child between his arms. He said concerning me: "Crown him as king, that I may see his beauty while I live with him.' Thereupon approached the courtiers, to set the double diadem upon my head. 'Place for him the crown upon his head,' so spake he concerning me, while he was upon earth. 'Let him organize this land, let him administer, let him show his face to the people,' so spake he because the love of me was so great in his bowels. He equipped me with household women, a royal harem, like the beauties of the palace, he chose for me wives . . . As for the monuments, I will not neglect his seat, after the manner of those children who forgot their father . . . My mighty deeds for my father as a child, I will now complete, being Lord of the Two Lands; I will construct them in the proper way . . . I will lay the walls in the temple of him that begat me. I will charge the man of my choice, to conduct this work therein. I will mason up therein the breaches in its walls, in its pylon towers. I will cover its house, I will erect its columns, I will set stones in the places of the lower foundation, making monument upon monuments, two excellent things at one time, bearing my name and the name of my father, for the son is like him that begat him."

Then spake the royal companions, and they answered the Good God: "Thou art Re, thy body is his body. There has been no ruler like thee, (for) thou art unique, like the son of Osiris, thou hast achieved the like of his designs. Isis hath not loved a king since Re, except thee and her son; greater is that which thou hast done than that which he did when he ruled after Osiris. The laws of the land proceed according to his position. The son is compassionate to him that made him, the divine seed . . . None hath done that which Horus did for his father to this day, except thy majesty. Thou who doest it; thou art the one who repeatest monument on monument for the gods, according as thy father, Re, commanded that thy name should be known in every land, from Khenthennofer of the South, northward, from the shores of the sea to the countries of Retenu, and among the settlements and strongholds of the king, the towns colonized and supplied with people—every city should know that thou art the god of all people, that they may awake, to give to thee incense at the command of thy father, Atum; that Egypt as well as the Red Land may adore thee."

Now, after these utterances which these nobles [had spoken] in the presence of their lord, his majesty commanded to commission the chiefs of works; he set apart soldiers, workmen, carvers with the chisel, draughtsmen, all ranks of artificers, to build the holy place of his father, to erect that which was in ruins in the cemetery, the mortuary house of his father. Lo, he began to fashion his statue in the year 1; while the offerings were doubled before his *ka*, his temple was properly victualled, and he supplied his necessities.

"THE WATER IN THE NETHERWORLD HEARKENS TO HIM": RAMSES II DIVINES WATER IN THE DESERT, c. 1277 BC

Anonymous

Payment for Ramses II's multifarious building projects required the extraction of ever increasing amounts of gold from Egyptian mines. Exploitation of gold in the Wadi Alaki was hampered by the lack of water on the desert road there from Kubban, which caused many miners and hauliers to die of thirst. Undeterred by his father's inability to find water in the region, Ramses II ordered the viceroy of Kush to dig a successful well. From a stele at Kubban.

Now, when his majesty was in Memphis, performing the pleasing ceremonies of his fathers, all the gods of South and North, according as they gave to him might and victory, and long life of myriads of years; on one of these days it came to pass that, lo, his majesty was sitting upon a great throne of electrum, diademed with the double-feathered crown, recounting the countries, from which gold is brought, and devising plans for digging wells on a road lacking in water, after hearing said that there was much gold in the country of Akita, whereas the road thereof was very lacking in water. If a few of the caravaneers of the gold-washing went thither, it was only half of them that arrived there, (for) they died of thirst on the road, together with the asses which they drove before them. There was not found for them their necessary supply of drink, in ascending and descending, from the water of the skins. Hence no gold was brought from this country for lack of water.

Court is Summoned

Said his majesty to the wearer of the royal seal, who was at his side: "Call the princes of the court, his majesty would counsel with them concerning this country, (how) I may take the necessary measures." They were immediately brought before the Good God, their hands uplifted to his *ka*, acclaiming and smelling the earth before his beautiful face. One (= the king) told them the character of this country, counselling with them concerning the plan of opening a well upon the road thereof.

Address of the Court

They said before his majesty: "Thou art like Re in all that thou doest; that which thy heart wishes comes to pass. If thou desirest a matter in the night, in the morning it quickly comes to pass. We have been beholding a multitude of thy marvels, since thy appearance as king of the Two Lands; we have not heard, neither have our eyes seen, (yet) do they come to pass as they are. As for everything that comes out of thy mouth, it is like the words of Harakhte. Thy tongue is a pair of balances, more accurate are thy two lips than the correct weight of Thoth. What is that which thou knowest not? Who is the finisher of it like thee? Where is the place, which thou hast not seen? There is no country which thou hast not trodden. All matters pass through thy ears, since thou hast exercised authority over this land. Thou didst make plans while thou wast (still) in the egg, in thy office of child of a prince. The affairs of the Two Lands were told thee, while thou wert a child wearing the curl; no monument was executed, which was not under thy authority; there was no commission without thy knowledge. Thou wast chief of the army while thou wast a boy of the tenth year. Every work that was carried out, it was thy hand which made the foundation thereof. If thou sayest to the water: 'Come upon the mountain,' the flood comes forth quickly after thy word, for thou art Re in limbs, and

Khepri with his true form. Thou art the living image on earth of thy father, Atum of Heliopolis. Taste is in thy mouth, intelligence in thy heart; the seat of thy tongue is the shrine of truth, the god sits upon thy two lips. Thy words come to pass every day, thy heart is made into the likeness of (that of) Ptah, the creator of handicrafts. Thou art forever, it shall be done by thy plans, all that thou sayest is heard, O Sovereign, our lord."

Statement of the Viceroy of Kush

"As for the country of Akita, this is said concerning it," said the king's-son of Kush the wretched, concerning it before his majesty, "that it has been in this manner lacking in water, since the time of the god. They die therein of thirst, and every earlier king desired to open a well therein, but did not succeed. King Menmare (Seti I) did the like, and caused to be dug a well of 120 cubits depth in his time. It is (however), forsaken on the road, (for) no water came out of it. (But) if thou thyself say to thy father Hapi, the father of the gods: 'Let water be brought upon the mountain,' he will do according to all that thou hast said, like all thy designs, which come to pass before us, (although) they have not been heard in conversation; because thy fathers, all the gods love thee, more than any king, who has been since Re."

Ramses Determines to Dig a Well in Akita

Said his majesty to these princes: "How true is all that which ye have said —, that no water has been dug in this country since the time of the god, as ye say. But I will open a well there, furnishing water every day as in the valley of the Nile, at command of my father, Amon-Re, lord of Thebes, and all the gods of Nubia, according as their heart is satisfied with the things desired."

Then these princes praised their lord, smelling the ground, throwing themselves upon their bellies in the presence, exulting to the height of heaven . . .

Lo, the king's son of Kush mustered the people for digging the well. But they said: "What then is it which the king's son shall do? Shall the water which is in the nether world hearken to him?" Then they dug the well on the road to the country of Akita . . .

A Letter Announcing Success from the Viceroy of Kush

One came, bearing a letter from the king's-son of Kush the wretched, saying: "The well is finished; that which thy majesty spake with his own mouth has come to pass; the water has come forth from it at 12 cubits, being 4 cubits therein in depth.

[. . .]

"Never was done . . . the like since the time of the god— Akita rejoices with great joy, those who are far away from the ruler. The water which is in the nether world hearkens to him, when he digs water upon the mountain."

KADESH: THE POET'S VIEW, c. 1275 BC

Anonymous

There was certain inevitability about Ramses II's war with the Hittites. There was his own ambition to emulate the imperial conquests of the 18th Dynasty. There was the Hittite revival under Suppilliumas and Mutwatallish which pushed ever southwards into "Egyptian" Syria. Both sides wanted a military engagement to once-and-forever settle control of the region.

Thus it was that the Egytians and Hittites met for battle at the north Syrian city of Kadesh (also Qadesh) on the Orontes River in May 1275 BC. Behind Ramses II, having marched over a thousand miles, were 20,000 troops of the Amun, Re,

Ptah and Seth divisions. The Hittites and their 18 vassals possessed an ever bigger army, numbering perhaps 35,000 soldiers, including 3,000 charioteers. The course of the first part of the battle, which was only saved for the Egyptians by the personal bravery of Ramses II, is related in the "Poem of Pentaur", seemingly written by a participant or court scribe with access to the mouth of one.

Beginning of the victory of King Usermare-Setepnere Ramses II, who is given life, forever, which he achieved in the land of Kheta and Naharin, in the land of Arvad, in Pedes, in the Derden, in the land of Mesa, in the land of Kelekesh, Carchemish, Kode, the land of Kadesh, in the land of Ekereth, and Mesheneth.

Behold, his majesty prepared his infantry and his chariotry, the Sherden of the captivity of his majesty from the victories of his word – they gave the plan of battle. His majesty proceeded northward, his infantry and his chariotry being with him. He began the goodly way to march. Year 5, the second month of the third season tenth month, on the ninth day, his majesty passed the fortress of Tharu, like Montu when he goes forth. Every country trembled before him, fear was in their hearts; all the rebels came bowing down for fear of the fame of his majesty, when his army came upon the narrow road, being like one who is upon the highway.

Now, after many days after this, behold, his majesty was in Usermare-Meriamon, the city of cedar. His majesty proceeded northward, and he then arrived at the highland of Kadesh. Then his majesty marched before, like his father, Montu lord of Thebes, and crossed over the channel of the Orontes, there being with him the first division of Amon named: "Victory-of-King-Usermare-Setepnere".

When his majesty reached the city, behold, the wretched, vanquished chief of Kheta* had come, having

* the king of the Hittites

gathered together all countries from the ends of the sea to the land of Kheta, which came entire: the Naharin likewise, and Arvad, Mesa, Keshkesh, Kelekesh, Luka, Kezweden, Carchemish, Ekereth, Kode, the entire land of Nuges, Mesheneth, and Kadesh. He left not a country which was not brought together with their chiefs who were with him, every man bringing his chariotry, an exceeding great multitude, without its like. They covered the mountains and the valleys; they were like grasshoppers with their multitudes. He left not silver nor gold in his land but he plundered it of all its possessions and gave to every country, in order to bring them with him to battle.

Behold, the wretched, vanquished chief of Kheta, together with numerous allied countries, were stationed in battle array, concealed on the northwest of the city of Kadesh, while his majesty was alone by himself, with his bodyguard, and the division of Amon was marching behind him. The division of Re crossed over the river-bed on the south side of the town of Shabtuna, at the distance of an iter from the division of Amon; the division of Ptah was on the south of the city of Aranami; and the division of Sutekh was marching upon the road. His majesty had formed the first rank of all the leaders of his army, while they were on the shore in the land of the Amor. Behold, the wretched vanquished chief of Kheta was stationed in the midst of the infantry which was with him, and he came not out to fight, for fear of his majesty. Then he made to go the people of the chariotry, an exceedingly numerous multitude like the sand, being three people to each span. Now, they had made their combinations thus: among every three youths was one man of the vanquished of Kheta, equipped with all the weapons of battle. Lo, they had stationed them in battle array, concealed on the northwest the city of Kadesh.

They came forth from the southern side of Kadesh, and they cut through the division of Re in its middle, while they were marching without knowing and without being drawn up for battle. The infantry and chariotry of his majesty retreated before them. Now, his majesty had halted on the north of the city of Kadesh, on the western side of the Orontes. Then came one to tell it to his majesty.

His majesty shone like his father Montu, when he took the adornments of war; as he seized his coat of mail, he was like Baal in his hour. The great span which bore his majesty called: "Victory-in-Thebes", from the great stables of Ramses II, was in the midst of the leaders. His majesty halted in the rout; then he charged into the foe, the vanquished of Kheta, being alone by himself and none other with him. When his majesty went to look behind him, he found 2,500 chariotry surrounding him, in his way out, being all the youth of the wretched Kheta, together with its numerous allied countries: from Arvad, from Mesa, from Pedes, from Keshkesh, from Erwenet, from Kezweden, from Aleppo, Eketeri, Kadesh, and Luka, being three men to a span, acting in unison.

KADESH: THE OFFICIAL REPORT, c. 1275 BC

Anonymous

As inscribed on the walls of temples at Luxor, Karnak, the Ramseseum, Abydos, Derr and Abu Simbel.

Year 5, third month of the third season, day 9; under the majesty of Horus: Mighty Bull, Beloved of Truth; King of Upper and Lower Egypt: Usermare-Setepnere; Son of Re; Ramses-Meriamon, given life forever.

Lo, his majesty was in Zahi on his second victorious

campaign. The goodly watch in life, prosperity and health, in the tent of his majesty, was on the highland south of Kadesh.

When his majesty appeared like the rising of Re, he assumed the adornments of his father, Montu. When the king proceeded northward, and his majesty had arrived at the locality south of the town of Shabtuna, there came two Shasu, to speak to his majesty as follows: "Our brethren, who belong to the greatest of the families with the vanquished chief of Kheta, have made us come to his majesty, to say: 'We will be subjects of Pharaoh and we will flee from the vanquished chief of Kheta; for the vanquished chief of Kheta sits in the land of Aleppo, on the north of Tunip. He fears because of Pharaoh to come southward.'" Now, these Shasu spake these words, which they spake to his majesty, falsely, for the vanquished chief of Kheta made them come to spy where his majesty was, in order to cause the army of his majesty not to draw up for fighting him, to battle with the vanquished chief of Kheta.

Lo, the vanquished chief of Kheta came with every chief of every country, their infantry and their chariotry, which he had brought with him by force, and stood, equipped, drawn up in line of battle behind Kadesh the Deceitful, while his majesty knew it not. Then his majesty proceeded northward and arrived on the northwest of Kadesh; and the army of his majesty made camp there.

Then, as his majesty sat upon a throne of gold, there arrived a scout who was in the following of his majesty, and he brought two scouts of the vanquished chief of Kheta. They were conducted into the presence, and his majesty said to them: "What are ye?" They said: "As for us, the vanquished chief of the Kheta has caused that we should come to spy out where his majesty is." Said his majesty to

them: "He! Where is he, the vanquished chief of Kheta?
Behold, I have heard, saying: 'He is in the land of Aleppo.'" Said they: "See, the vanquished chief of Kheta is
stationed, together with many countries, which he has
brought with him by force, being every country which is
in the districts of the land of Kheta, the land of Naharin,
and all Kode. They are equipped with infantry and chariotry, bearing their weapons; more numerous are they than
the sand of the shore. See, they are standing, drawn up for
battle, behind Kadesh the Deceitful."

Then his majesty had the princes called into the presence, and had them hear every word which the two scouts
of the vanquished chief of Kheta, who were in the presence,
had spoken. Said his majesty to them: "See ye the manner
wherewith the chiefs of the peasantry and the officials
under whom is the land of Pharaoh have stood, daily,
saying to the Pharaoh: 'The vanquished chief of Kheta is in
the land of Aleppo; he has fled before his majesty, since
hearing that, behold, he came.' So spake they to his majesty
daily. But see, I have held a hearing in this very hour, with
the two scouts of the vanquished chief of Kheta, to the effect
that the vanquished chief of Kheta is coming, together with
the numerous countries that are with him, being people
and horses, like the multitudes of the sand. They are
stationed behind Kadesh the Deceitful. But the governors
of the countries and the officials under whose authority is
the land of Pharaoh were not able to tell it to us."

Said the princes who were in the presence of his majesty:
"It is a great fault, which the governors of the countries and
the officials of Pharaoh have committed in not informing
that the vanquished chief of Kheta was near the king; and
in that they told his report to his majesty daily."

Then the vizier was ordered to hasten the army of his

majesty, while they were marching on the south of Shabtuna, in order to bring them to the place where his majesty
was.

Lo, while his majesty sat talking with the princes, the
vanquished chief of Kheta came, and the numerous countries, which were with him. They crossed over the channel
on the south of Kadesh, and charged into the army of his
majesty while they were marching, and not expecting it.
Then the infantry and chariotry of his majesty retreated
before them, northward to the place where his majesty was.
Lo, the foes of the vanquished chief of Kheta surrounded
the bodyguard of his majesty, who were by his side.

When his majesty saw them, he was enraged against
them, like his father, Montu, lord of Thebes. He seized the
adornments of battle, and arrayed himself in his coat of
mail. He was like Baal in his hour. Then he betook himself
to his horses, and led quickly on, being alone by himself. He
charged into the foes of the vanquished chief of Kheta, and
the numerous countries which were with him. His majesty
was like Sutekh, the great in strength, smiting and slaying
among them; his majesty hurled them headlong, one upon
another into the water of the Orontes.

"I charged all countries, while I was alone, my infantry
and my chariotry having forsaken me. Not one among
them stood to turn about. I swear, as Re loves me, as my
father, Atum, favours me, that, as for every matter which
his majesty has stated, I did it in truth, in the presence of
my infantry and my chariotry."

*The battle of Kadesh was not quite the overwhelming victory suggested by the
official recorder. Muwatallis sued for a cease-fire and the weary, over-stretched
Ramses II was obliged to agree. Over the next decade hostilities flared periodically,
but Ramses II was unable to conquer northern Syria just as the Hittites were unable*

to eject Egypt from the south of the country. Eventually, in 1259 BC, the Hittites, menaced by Assyria, proposed a binding peace and mutual non-aggression pact with the pharaoh. The most important clauses (as inscribed at Karnak) state:

Now, at the beginning, since eternity, the relations of the great ruler of Egypt with the great chief of Kheta were such that the god prevented hostilities between them, by treaty. Whereas, in the time of Metella [Muwatallis], the great chief of Kheta, my brother, he fought w[ith] Ramses II the great ruler of Egypt, yet afterward, beginning with this day, behold, Khetasar, the great chief of Kheta, is [in] a treaty-relation for establishing the relations which the Re made, and which Sutekh made, for the land of Egypt, with the land of Kheta, in order not to permit hostilities to arise between them, forever.

Behold then, Khetasar, the great chief of Kheta, is in treaty relation with Usermare-Setepnere (Ramses II), the great ruler of Egypt, beginning with this day, in order to bring about good peace and good brotherhood between us forever, while he is in brotherhood with me, he is in peace with me; and I am in brotherhood with him, and I am in peace with him, forever. Since Metella the great chief of Kheta, my brother, succumbed to his fate, and Khetasar sat as great chief of Kheta upon the throne of his father, behold, I am together with Ramses-Meriamon, the great ruler of Egypt, and he is with me in our peace and our brotherhood. It is better than the former peace and brotherhood which were in the land. Behold, I, even the great chief of Kheta, am with Ramses II the great ruler of Egypt, in good peace and in good brotherhood. The children of the children of the great chief of Kheta shall be in brotherhood and peace with the children of the children of Ramses-Meriamon, the great ruler of Egypt, being in our relations of brotherhood and our relations of peace, that the land of [Egypt] may be with the land of Kheta in peace and brotherhood like ourselves, forever.

There shall be no hostilities between them, forever. The great chief of Kheta shall not pass over into the land of Egypt, forever, to take anything therefrom. Ramses-Meriamon, the great ruler of Egypt, shall not pass over into the land of Kheta, to take anything therefrom, forever . . .

If another enemy come against the lands of Usermare-Setepnere (Ramses II), the great ruler of Egypt, and he shall send to the great chief of Kheta, saying: "Come with me as reinforcement against him," the great chief of Kheta shall come, and the great chief of Kheta shall slay his enemy. But if it be not the desire of the great chief of Kheta to come, he shall send his infantry and his chariotry, and shall slay his enemy.

If another en[emy come] against the great chief of Kheta, [and he shall send] to the great chief (sic!) [of Egypt], Usermare-Setepnere for reinforcements then he shall come to him as reinforcement, to slay his enemy. But if it be not the desire of Ramses-Meriamon, the great ruler of Egypt, to come, he shall send his infantry and his chariotry and shall slay his enemy.

If a man or two men who are unknown flee, and if they escape from the country of Egypt and if they don't want to serve him, then Hattusili, the great king, the king of the country of Hatti, has to deliver them into his brother's hands and he shall not allow them to inhabit the country of Hatti.

"BEWARE OF A WOMAN WHO IS A STRANGER . . .": ADVICE TO A YOUNG MAN CONCERNING WOMEN, c. 1270 BC

Any

Any was a scribe at the court of Nefertari, one of the principal wives of Ramses II.

Beware of the woman who is a stranger, who is not known in her town. Do not stare at her as she passes by and do not have intercourse with her. A woman who is away from her husband is a deep water whose course is unknown.

> Take a wife while you're young,
> That she make a son for you;
> She should bear for you while you're youthful.
> It is proper to make people.
> Happy the man whose people are many.
> He is saluted on account of his progeny.

> Do not control your wife in her house,
> When you know she is efficient;
> Don't say to her: "Where is it? Get it!"
> When she has put it in the right place.
> Let your eye observe in silence,
> Then you will recognize her skill;
> It is a joy when your hand is with her,
> There are many who don't know this.

A PRAYER OF GRATITUDE FOR THE RECOVERY OF A SON FROM ILLNESS, c. 1270 BC

Nebre

Inscribed by Nebre, a Theban draughtsman, on a stele erected in gratitude to the gods for his son's recovery from serious illness. As is clear from the prayer, Nebre believed the illness to have been a divine punishment for some unspecified offence involving a cow belonging to the temple herd of Amon-Re.

Giving praises to Amun:
I compose hymns to him in his name,
   I render him praises to the height of heaven
     And to the breadth of earth;
   I recount his might to him who sails downstream
     And to him who sails upstream.

Beware of him!
   Proclaim him to son and daughter,
     To great and small;
   Tell of him to generations of generations
     Which have not yet come into being.

   Tell of him to the fish in the deep,
     To the birds in the sky;
   Proclaim him as the one who knows him not
     And to the one who knows him.
Beware of him!

Thou art Amun, the Lord of the silent man,
   One who comes at the cry of a poor man.

Were I to call upon thee when I am ill,
    Thou comest, that thou mightest rescue me,
That thou mightest give breath [to] him who is weak
    And rescue the one who is shut in.

Thou art Amon-Re, Lord of Thebes,
    Rescuer of him who is in the underworld;
Because thou art [merciful (?)],
    When one calls upon thee,
Thou art the one who comes from afar . . .

Hymns were composed to him in his name,
    Because of the greatness of his might;
Supplications were made to him in his presence,
    Before the whole land,
On behalf of the outline draughtsman Nakhtamun*,
      justified
    While he was lying ill in a state of death,
Being [under] the power of Amun
    Because of his cow . . .

The servant was bent on doing wrong,
    Yet the Lord is bent on being merciful.
The Lord of Thebes does not spend a whole day angry;
    As for his anger, in the completion of a moment
      nothing is left.
The wind is turned back to us in mercy;
    Amun has returned with his breezes.
As thy soul endures, thou wilt be merciful,
    We shall not repeat what has been averted . . .

---

* Nebre's son. An outline draughtsman was one who drew on tomb walls the red outlines of pictures for the sculptors to carve.

I will make this stele in thy name,
   And establish these hymns for thee in writing
     upon it,
Since thou didst rescue the outline draughtsman
   Nakhtamun for me.
Thus I spoke to thee, and thou didst hear me;
   See! I am doing what I said.
Thou art the Lord of him who calls upon thee,
   Contented with justice, the Lord of Thebes.

BROTHER-SISTER INCEST, c. 1210 BC

Princess Ahura

The veracity of this tale from "The Magic Book" is uncertain. Ahura may or may not have been a daughter of the 19th Dynasty pharaoh, Merneptah. Certainly, the incest which she recounts so happily was rife in New Kingdom royal families. The reasons had nothing to do with psychology and everything to do with politics. Incestuous marriage maintained the exclusivity of the royal family; it even mirrored the practice of of those other gods, Osiris and Isis. Incestuous marriage also negated the problem of princesses marrying non-royal husbands who might be tempted to grab the throne on their spouse's behalf.

   Egyptian princesses, incidentally, were banned from marrying foreigners.

We were the two children of the King Merneptah, and he loved us very much, for he had no others; and Naneferkaptah was in his palace as heir over all the land. And when we were grown, the king said to the queen, "I will marry Naneferkaptah to the daughter of a general, and Ahura to the son of another general." And the queen said, "No, he is the heir, let him marry his sister, like the heir of a king, none other is fit for him." And the king said, "That is not fair; they had better be married to the children of the general." And the queen said, "It is you who are not dealing rightly with me." And the king answered, "If I have no more than these two children, is it right that they should marry one another? I will marry Naneferkaptah to the daughter of an officer, and Ahura to the son of another officer. It has often been done so in our family."

And at a time when there was a great feast before the king, they came to fetch me to the feast. And I was very troubled, and did not behave as I used to do. And the king said to me, "Ahura, have you sent some one to me about this sorry matter, saying, 'Let me be married to my elder brother?'" I said to him, "Well, let me marry the son of an officer, and he marry the daughter of another officer, as it often happens so in our family." I laughed, and the king laughed. And the king told the steward of the palace, "Let them take Ahura to the house of Naneferkaptah tonight, and all kinds of good things with her." So they brought me as a wife to the house of Naneferkaptah; and the king ordered them to give me presents of silver and gold, and things from the palace.

And Naneferkaptah passed a happy time with me*, and received all the presents from the palace; and we loved one another. And when I expected a child, they told the king, and he was most heartily glad; and he sent me many things, and a present of the best silver and gold and linen. And when the time came, I bore this little child that is before you. And they gave him the name of Merab, and registered him in the book of the "House of Life".

And when my brother Naneferkaptah went to the cemetery of Memphis, he did nothing on earth but read the writings that are in the catacombs of the kings and on the tablets of the "House of Life", and the inscriptions that are

---

* a euphemism for sexual intercourse

seen on the monuments, and he worked hard on the
writings. And there was a priest there called Nesiptah;
and as Naneferkaptah went into a temple to pray, it
happened that he went behind this priest, and was reading
the inscriptions that were on the chapels of the gods. And
the priest mocked him and laughed. So Naneferkaptah said
to him, "Why are you laughing at me?" And he replied, "I
was not laughing at you, or if I happened to do so, it was at
your reading writings that are worthless. If you wish so
much to read writings, come to me, and I will bring you to
the place where the book is that Thoth himself wrote with
his own hand, and which will bring you to the gods. When
you read but two pages in this, you will enchant the
heaven, the earth, the abyss, the mountains, and the sea;
you shall know what the birds of the sky and the crawling
things are saying; you shall see the fishes of the deep, for a
divine power is there to bring them up out of the depth.
And when you read the second page, if you are in the world
of ghosts, you will become again in the shape you were in
on earth. You will see the sun shining in the sky, with all the
gods, and the full moon."

And Naneferkaptah said, "By the life of the king! Tell me
of anything you want done, and I'll do it for you, if you will
only send me where this book is." And the priest answered
Naneferkaptah, "If you want to go to the place where the
book is, you must give me a hundred pieces of silver for my
funeral, and provide that they shall bury me as a rich
priest." So Naneferkaptah called his lad and told him to
give the priest a hundred pieces of silver; and he made them
do as he wished, even everything that he asked for. Then
the priest said to Naneferkaptah, "This book is in the
middle of the river at Koptos, in an iron box; in the iron
box is a bronze box; in the bronze box is a sycamore box; in

the sycamore box is an ivory and ebony box; in the ivory and ebony box is a silver box; in the silver box is a golden box; and in that is the book. It is twisted all round with snakes and scorpions and all the other crawling things around the box in which the book is; and there is a deathless snake by the box." And when the priest told Naneferkaptah, he did not know where on earth he was, he was so much delighted.

And when he came from the temple, he told me all that had happened to him. And he said, "I shall go to Koptos, for I must fetch this book; I will not stay any longer in the north." And I said, "Let me dissuade you, for you prepare sorrow and you will bring me into trouble in the Thebaid." And I laid my hand on Naneferkaptah, to keep him from going to Koptos, but he would not listen to me; and he went to the king, and told the king all that the priest had said. The king asked him, "What is it that you want?" And he replied, "Let them give me the royal boat with its belongings, for I will go to the south with Ahura and her little boy Merab, and fetch this book without delay." So they gave him the royal boat with its belongings, and we went with him to the haven, and sailed from there up to Koptos.

Then the priests of Isis of Koptos, and the high priest of Isis, came down to us without waiting, to meet Naneferkaptah, and their wives also came to me. We went into the temple of Isis and Harpokrates; and Naneferkaptah brought an ox, a goose, and some wine, and made a burnt offering and a drink offering before Isis of Koptos and Harpokrates. They brought us to a very fine house, with all good things; and Naneferkaptah spent four days there and feasted with the priests of Isis of Koptos, and the wives of the priests of Isis also made holiday with me.

And the morning of the fifth day came; and Nanefer-

kaptah called a priest to him, and made a magic cabin that
was full of men and tackle. He put the spell upon it and put
life into it, and gave them breath, and sank it in the water.
He filled the royal boat with sand, and took leave of me,
and sailed from the haven: and I sat by the river at Koptos
that I might see what would become of him. And he said,
"Workmen, work for me, even at the place where the book
is." And they toiled by night and by day; and when they
had reached it in three days, he threw the sand out and
made a shoal in the river. And then he found on it entwined
serpents and scorpions, and all kinds of crawling things
around the box in which the book was; and by it he found a
deathless snake around the box. And he laid the spell upon
the entwined serpents and scorpions and all kinds of
crawling things which were around the box, that they
would not come out. And he went to the deathless snake,
and fought with him, and killed him; but he came to life
again, and took a new form. He then fought again with him
a second time; but he came to life again, and took a third
form. He then cut him in two parts, and put sand between
the parts, that he should not appear again.

Naneferkaptah then went to the place where he found
the box. He uncovered a box of iron, and opened it; he
found then a box of bronze, and opened that; then he found
a box of sycamore wood, and opened that; again he found a
box of ivory and ebony, and opened that; yet, he found a
box of silver, and opened that; and then he found a box of
gold; he opened that, and found the book in it. He took the
book from the golden box, and read a page of spells from it.
He enchanted the heaven and the earth, the abyss, the
mountains, and the sea; he knew what the birds of the sky,
the fish of the deep, and the beasts of the hills all said. He
read another page of the spells, and saw the sun shining in

the sky, with all the gods, the full moon, and the stars in their shapes; he saw the fishes of the deep, for a divine power was present that brought them up from the water. He then read the spell upon the workmen that he had made, and taken from the haven, and said to them, "Work for me, back to the place from which I came." And they toiled night and day, and so he came back to the place where I sat by the river of Koptos; I had not drunk nor eaten anything, and had done nothing on earth, but sat like one who is gone to the grave.

I then told Naneferkaptah that I wished to see this book, for which we had taken so much trouble. He gave the book into my hands; and when I read a page of the spells in it, I also enchanted heaven and earth, the abyss, the mountains, and the sea; I also knew what the birds of the sky, the fishes of the deep, and the beasts of the hills all said. I read another page of the spells, and I saw the sun shining in the sky with all the gods, the full moon, and the stars in their shapes; I saw the fishes of the deep, for a divine power was present that brought them up from the water. As I could not write, I asked Naneferkaptah, who was a good writer and a very learned one; he called for a new piece of papyrus, and wrote on it all that was in the book before him. He dipped it in beer, and washed it off in the liquid; for he knew that if it were washed off, and he drank it, he would know all that there was in the writing.

We went back to Koptos the same day, and made a feast before Isis of Koptos and Harpokrates. We then went to the haven and sailed, and went northward of Koptos. And as we went on, Thoth discovered all that Naneferkaptah had done with the book; and Thoth hastened to tell Ra, and said, "Now, know that my book and my revelation are with Naneferkaptah, son of the King Merneptah. He has forced himself into my place, and robbed it, and seized my box with the writings, and killed my guards who protected it." And Ra replied to him, "He is before you, take him and all his kin." He sent a power from heaven with the command, "Do not let Naneferkaptah return safe to Memphis with all his kin." And after this hour, the little boy Merab, going out from the awning of the royal boat, fell into the river: he called on Ra, and everybody who was on the bank raised a cry. Naneferkaptah went out of the cabin, and read the spell over him; he brought the body up because a divine power brought him to the surface. He read another spell over him, and made him tell of all that happened to him, and of what Thoth had said before Ra. We turned back with him to Koptos. We brought him to the Good House, we fetched the people to him, and made one embalm him; and we buried him in his coffin in the cemetery of Koptos like a great and noble person.

And Naneferkaptah, my brother, said, "Let us go down, let us not delay, for the king has not yet heard of what has happened to him, and his heart will be sad about it." So we went to the haven, we sailed, and did not stay to the north of Koptos. When we were come to the place where the little boy Merab had fallen into the water, I went out from the awning of the royal boat, and I fell into the river. They called Naneferkaptah, and he came out from the cabin of the royal boat. He read a spell over me, and brought my body up, because a divine power brought me to the surface. He drew me out, and read the spell over me, and made me tell him of all that had happened to me, and of what Thoth had said before Ra. Then he turned back with me to Koptos, he brought me to the Good House, he fetched the people to me, and made one embalm me, as great and noble people are buried, and laid me in the tomb where Merab my young child was.

He turned to the haven, and sailed down, and delayed not in the north of Koptos. When he was come to the place where we fell into the river, he said to his heart, "Shall I not better turn back again to Koptos, that I may lie by them? For if not, when I go down to Memphis, and the king asks after his children, what shall I say to him? Can I tell him, 'I have taken your children to the Thebaid and killed them, while I remained alive, and I have come to Memphis still alive?'" Then he made them bring him a linen cloth of striped byssus; he made a band, and bound the book firmly, and tied it upon him. Naneferkaptah then went out of the awning of the royal boat and fell into the river. He cried on Ra; and all those who were on the bank made an outcry, saying, "Great woe! Sad woe! Is he lost, that good scribe and able man that has no equal?"

The royal boat went on without any one on earth knowing where Naneferkaptah was. It went on to Memphis, and they told all this to the king. Then the king went down to the royal boat in mourning, and all the soldiers and high priests and priests of Ptah were in mourning, and all the officials and courtiers. And when he saw Naneferkaptah, who was in the inner cabin of the royal boat – from his rank of high scribe – he lifted him up. And they saw the book by him; and the king said, "Let one hide this book that is with him." And the officers of the king, the priests of Ptah, and the high priest of Ptah, said to the king, "Our Lord, may the king live as long as the sun! Naneferkaptah was a good scribe and a very skilful man." And the king had him laid in his Good House to the sixteenth day, and then had him wrapped to the thirty-fifth day, and laid him out to the seventieth day, and then had him put in his grave in his resting-place.

I have now told you the sorrow which has come upon us because of this book.

TEN DAYS IN THE LIFE OF AN EGYPTIAN FRONTIER OFFICIAL, c. 1209 BC

Anonymous

The official was stationed on the frontier of Palestine (an Egyptian possession), where he recorded the human traffic into and out of Syria.

Year 3, first month of the third season (ninth month), fifteenth day:

There went up the servant of Baal, Roy, son of Zeper of Gaza, who had with him for Syria two different letters, to wit: (for) the captain of infantry, Khay one letter; (for) the chief of Tyre, Baalat-Remeg, one letter.

Year 3, first month of the third season (ninth month), seventeenth day:

There arrived the captains of the archers of the Well of Merneptah-Hotephirma, L. P. H., which is (on) the highland, to report in the fortress which is in Tharu.

Year 3, first month of the third season (ninth month), day:

There returned the attendant, Thutiy, son of Thekerem of Geket; Methdet, son of Shem-Baal (of) the same (town); Sutekhmose, son of Eperdegel (of) the same (town), who had with him, for the place where the king was, (for) the captain of infantry, Khay, gifts and a letter.

There went up the attendant, Nakhtamon, son of Thara of the Stronghold of Merneptah-Hotephirma, L. P. H., who journeyed (to) Upper Tyre, who had with him for Syria, two different letters, to wit: (for) the captain of infantry, Penamon, one letter; (for) the steward, Ramses-nakht, of this town, one letter.

There returned the chief of the stable, Pemerkhetem, son

of Ani, of the Town of Merneptah-Hotephirma, which is in
the district of the Aram, who had with him (for) the place
where the king was, two letters, to wit: (for) the captain of
infantry, Peremhab, one letter; for the deputy, Peremhab,
one letter.

Year 3, first month of the third season (ninth month),
twenty-fifth day:
   There went up the charioteer, Enwau, of the great stable
of the court of Binre-Meriamon, (Merneptah), L. P. H.

"GREAT REJOICING HAS ARISEN IN EGYPT": MERNEPTAH STEMS THE LIBYAN INVASION, APRIL 1207 BC

Anonymous

*When Merneptah succeeded his nonagenarian father, Ramses II, the Libyans had
already trickled through the western border of Egypt. In Year 5 of Merneptah's
reign, Libyan infiltration turned into a full-scale invasion of the Delta, with the
aim of seizing it for settlement. Only Merneptah's lightning retaliation saved the
Delta for Egypt. At Perire in the western Delta, the Libyans were routed in a six-
hour battle that cost them 9,000 dead. The victorious Egyptian army left the
battlefield "laden with the uncircumcized phalli of Libya" as trophy. To celebrate
the victory Merneptah had inscribed a "hymn of victory" on a stele in his mortuary
temple at Thebes. The stele is further notable for containing the only reference to
Israel in the whole literature of Ancient Egypt.*

The sun, dispelling the cloud that was over Egypt,
   Letting To-meri see the rays of the sun disc;
Removing the copper mountain from the neck of the
      patricians,
   Giving breath to the plebeians who were shut in;

Slaking the desire of Memphis over their foes,
    Making Tjanen rejoice over his adversaries;
Opening the doors of Memphis which had been
        blocked up,
    And letting its temples receive their food
        (-offerings) . . .

The sole one, restoring the courage of hundreds of
        thousands,
    For breath enters their nostrils at the sight of him;
Breaking into the land of Temeh in his lifetime;
    Putting eternal terror into the hearts of the Meshwesh;
Making the Libyans, who had trampled Egypt,
        retreat
    With great dread in their hearts because of
        To-meri*;
Their advanced troops abandoned their rear,
    Their feet did not stand firm, but ran away;
Their archers cast away their bows,
    The hearts of their running men were faint from
travelling;
They loosened their water-skins, which were thrown
to the ground,
    Their packs were untied and cast away.

The wretched enemy prince of Libya
    Fled alone in the depth of night;
No feather was on his head, his feet were unshod,
    His wives were seized in his presence;
The grain(?) for his food was taken away,
    He had no water in the water-skin to sustain him.

*i.e. Egypt

His brothers' faces were fierce enough to slay him,
　　One fought the other amongst his leaders.
Their tents were burned and reduced to ashes;
　　All his belongings became food for the soldiers
When he reached his (own) country, in grief,
　　Every survivor in his land was discontented at
　　　receiving him . . .

Great rejoicing has risen in Egypt,
　　Jubilation has issued from the towns of To-meri;
They recount the victories
　　Which Merenptah wrought in Tehenu:
"How beloved he is, the victorious ruler!
　　How exalted is the king among the gods!
How fortunate he is, the master of command!
　　Ah, how pleasant it is to sit when one is engaged in
　　　chatter!"

One may walk freely on the road,
　　Without any fear in the hearts of men.
Fortresses are left to themselves;
　　Wells are open, accessible to messengers;
The ramparts of the encircling wall are secure in the
sunlight
　　Until their watchmen awake.
The Medjay are stretched out in sleep,
　　The Tjukten hunt in the fields as they wish . . .

The princes lie prostrate, saying, "Salaam"!
　　Not one lifts his head among the Nine Bows.
Destruction for Tehenu! Hatti is pacified;
　　Canaan is plundered with every evil;
Ashkelon is taken; Gezer is captured;

Yanoam is made non-existent;
Israel lies desolate; its seed is no more;
   Hurru has become a widow for To-meri;
All the lands in their entirety are at peace,
   Everyone who was a nomad has been curbed by
      King Merenptah.

LOVE SONGS, c. 1200 BC

Anonymous

1

If I am [not] with you, where will you set your heart?
If you do [not] embrace [me], [where will you go?]
If good fortune comes your way, [you still cannot find]
   happiness.
But if you try to touch my thighs and breasts,
[Then you'll be satisfied.]
Because you remember you are hungry
   would you then leave?
Are you a man
   thinking only of his stomach?
Would you [walk off from me
   concerned with] your stylish clothes
and leave me the sheet?
Because of hunger
   would you then leave me?
   [or because you are thirsty?]
Take then my breast:
   for you its gift overflows.
Better indeed is one day in your arms . . .
   than a hundred thousand [anywhere] on earth.

2

Distracting is the foliage of my pasture:
[the mouth] of my girl is a lotus bud,
her breasts are mandrake apples,
her arms are [vines],
[her eyes] are fixed like berries,
her brow a snare of willow,
and I the wild goose!
My [beak] snips [her hair] for bait,
as worms for bait in the trap.

3

I sail downstream in the ferry by the pull of the current,
my bundle of reeds in my arms.
I'll be at Ankh-towy*,
and say to Ptah, the lord of truth,
give me my girl tonight.

The sea is wine,
Ptah its reeds,
Sekhmet its kelp,
the Dew Goddess its buds,
Nefertum its lotus flower.

[The Golden Goddess] rejoices
and the land grows bright at her beauty.
For Memphis is a flask of mandrake wine
placed before the good-looking god.

4

The voice of the turtledove speaks out. It says:
day breaks, which way are you going?

* Memphis

Lay off, little bird,
must you so scold me?
I found my lover on his bed,
and my heart was sweet to excess.

We said:

I shall never be far away [from] you
while my hand is in your hand,
and I shall stroll with you
in every favourite place.

He set me as first of the girls
and he does not break my heart.

5

My heart remembers well your love,
one half of my temple was combed,
I came rushing to see you,
and I forgot my hair.

6

The kisses of my beloved are on the other bank of the river; a
branch of the stream floweth between us, a crocodile lurketh
on the sand-bank. But I step down into the water and plunge
into the flood. My courage is great in the waters, the waves
are as solid ground under my feet. Love of her lendeth me
strength. Ah! She hath given me a spell for the waters.

7

When I kiss her, and her lips are open, then need I not ale to
inspire me. When the time is come to make ready the couch,
oh servant! then say I unto thee: "Lay fine linen between her

limbs, a bed for her of royal linen; give heed to the white embroidered linen, besprinkled with the finest oil."

8

Oh! were I but her negress, following her footsteps. Ah! Then should I joy in seeing the forms of all her limbs.

9

Love to thee filleth my inmost being, as [wine] pervadeth water, as fragrance pervadeth resin, as sap mingleth itself [with liquid]. And thou, thou hastenest to see thy beloved as the steed rusheth to the field of battle. Heaven hath formed her love, as the flame taketh hold [on the straw] and [his longing] like unto the hawk as he swoopeth down (?)

10

Is not my heart well inclined unto thy love? Never shall I be severed from love even though one should beat me . . . to Syria with sticks and cudgels, to Nubia with rods of the palm tree, to the mountain land with whips, to the plain with switches. Never will I give ear unto their counsel that I should give up my heart's desire.

11

I will lay me down in my shelter, sick shall I be with grief. Oh! here come my neighbours to care for me. There cometh my beloved with them; she putteth the physicians to scorn, for she knoweth my malady.

12

Near the country house of my beloved, where the water tank lieth in the midst of her land, the door openeth, the bolt springeth open, my love is wroth. Oh! were I made her porter, I should cause her to be wrathful with me. Then, when I did but hear her voice, the voice of her anger, a child should I be for fear.

13
Thou beautiful one! My heart longeth to make ready the food for thee, as thy house mistress, my arm should rest on thy arm. If thou turnedst away thy caresses then would my heart say within me in my beseeching: "My dear (friend) is wanting to me this night, and thus am I like one sojourning in the grave." For art thou not to me health and life? Thy coming filleth with joy in thy prosperity the heart that hath sought thee.

"NO ONE CAN RIVAL HER": THE EGYPTIAN IDEAL OF FEMININE BEAUTY, c. 1200 BC

Anonymous

From the Chester Beatty Papyrus I.

My sister is unique – no one can rival her, for she is the most beautiful woman alive. Look, she is like Sirius, which marks the beginning of a good year. She radiates perfection and glows with health. The glance of her eye is gorgeous. Her lips speak sweetly, and not one word too many. Long-necked and milky breasted she is, her hair the colour of pure lapis. Gold is nothing compared to her arms, and her fingers are like lotus flowers. Her buttocks are full but her waist is narrow. As for her thighs – they only add to her beauty . . .

THE FATE OF AN UNFAITHFUL WIFE, c. 1200 BC

Anonymous

Although the Ancient Egyptians had a relaxed attitude to sex between single consenting adults (there was no particular stigma against illegitimate children), when a woman married she was expected to be faithful to her husband. Thus he could be certain that children of the union – his heirs and the inheritors of his property – were his. There was no official sanction against a woman engaging in extra-marital intercourse. The private punishments were divorce, beatings and sometimes, as illustrated in " The Tale of Two Brothers", death. The two brothers Anpu (Anubis) and Bata are of course gods.

There were once two brothers, and they were sons of the same father and of the same mother. Anpu was the name of the elder, and the younger was called Bata. Now Anpu had a house of his own, and he had a wife. His brother lived with him as if he were his son, and made garments for him. It was Bata who drove the oxen to the field, it was he who ploughed the land, and it was he who harvested the grain. He laboured continually upon his brother's farm, and his equal was not to be found in the land of Egypt; he was imbued with the spirit of a god.

In this manner the brothers lived together, and many days went past. Each morning the younger brother went forth with the oxen, and when evening came on he drove them again to the byre, carrying upon his back a heavy burden of fodder which he gave to the animals to eat, and he brought with him also milk and herbs for Anpu and his wife. While these two ate and drank together in the house, Bata rested in the byre with the cattle and he slept beside them.

When day dawned, and the land grew bright again, the younger brother was first to rise up, and he baked bread for

Anpu and carried his own portion to the field and ate it there. As he followed the oxen he heard and he understood their speech. They would say: "Yonder is sweet herbage," and he would drive them to the place of their choice, whereat they were well pleased. They were indeed noble animals, and they increased greatly.

The time of ploughing came on, and Anpu spake unto Bata, saying: "Now get ready the team of oxen, for the Nile flood is past and the land may be broken up. We shall begin to plough on the morrow; so carry seed to the field that we may sow it."

As Anpu desired, so did Bata do. When the next day dawned, and the land grew bright, the two brothers laboured in the field together, and they were well pleased with the work which they accomplished. Several days went past in this manner, and it chanced that on an afternoon the seed was finished ere they had completed their day's task.

Anpu thereupon spake to his younger brother saying: "Hasten to the granary and procure more seed."

Bata ran towards the house, and entered it. He beheld his brother's wife sitting upon a mat, languidly pleating her hair.

"Arise," he said, "and procure corn for me, so that I may hasten back to the field with it. Delay me not."

The woman sat still and said: "Go thou thyself and open the storeroom. Take whatsoever thou dost desire. If I were to rise for thee, my hair would fall in disorder."

Bata opened the storeroom and went within. He took a large basket and poured into it a great quantity of seed. Then he came forth carrying the basket through the house.

The woman looked up and said: "What is the weight of that great burden of thine?"

Bata answered: "There are two measures of barley and three of wheat. I carry in all upon my shoulders five measures of seed."

"Great indeed is thy strength," sighed the woman. "Ah, thee do I contemplate and admire each day!"

Her heart was moved towards him, and she stood up saying: "Tarry here with me. I will clothe thee in fine raiment."

The lad was made angry as the panther, and said: "I regard thee as a mother, and my brother is like a father unto me. Thou hast spoken evil words and I desire not to hear them again, nor will I repeat unto any man what thou hast just spoken."

He departed abruptly with his burden and hastened to the field, where he resumed his labour.

At eventide Anpu returned home and Bata prepared to follow after him. The elder brother entered his house and found his wife lying there, and it seemed as if she had suffered violence from an evildoer. She did not give him water to wash his hands, as was her custom. Nor did she light the lamp. The house was in darkness. She moaned where she lay, as if she were in sickness, and her garment was beside her.

"Who hath been here?" asked Anpu, her husband.

The woman answered him: "No one came nigh me save thy younger brother. He spoke evil words unto me, and I said: 'Am I not as a mother, and is not thine elder brother as a father unto thee?' Then was he angry, and he struck me until I promised that I would not inform thee . . . Oh! if thou wilt allow him to live now, I shall surely die."

The elder brother became like an angry panther. He sharpened his dagger and went out and stood behind the door of the byre with purpose to slay young Bata when he came nigh.

The sun had gone down when the lad drove the oxen into the byre, carrying on his back fodder and herbs, and in one hand a vessel of milk, as was his custom each evening.

The first ox entered the byre, and then it spoke to Bata, saying: "Beware! for thine elder brother is standing behind the door. In his hand is a dagger, and he desires to slay thee. Draw not nigh unto him."

The lad heard with understanding what the animal had said. Then the second ox entered and went to its stall, and spake likewise words of warning, saying: "Take speedy flight."

Bata peered below the byre door, and he saw the legs of his brother, who stood there with a dagger in his hand. He at once threw down his burden and made hurried escape. Anpu rushed after him furiously with the sharp dagger.

In his sore distress the younger brother cried unto the sun god Ra-Harmachis, saying: "O blessed lord! thou art he who distinguisheth between falsehood and truth."

The god heard his cry with compassion, and turned round. He caused a wide stream to flow between the two brothers, and, behold! it was full of crocodiles. Then it came that Anpu and Bata stood confronting one another, one upon the right bank and the other upon the left. The elder brother twice smote his hands with anguish because that he could not slay the youth.

Bata called out to Anpu, saying: "Tarry where thou art until the earth is made bright once again. Lo! when Ra, the sun god, riseth up, I shall reveal in his presence all that I know, and he shall judge between us, discerning what is false and what is true . . . Know thou that I may not dwell with thee any longer, for I must depart unto the fair region of the flowering acacia."

When day dawned, and the sun god Ra appeared in his glory, the two brothers stood gazing one upon the other across the stream of crocodiles. Then the lad spake to his elder brother, saying: "Why didst thou come against me, desiring to slay me with treachery ere yet I had spoken for myself? Am I not thy younger brother, and hast thou not been as a father and thy wife as a mother unto me? Hear and know now that when I hastened to procure seed thy wife spoke, saying: 'Tarry thou with me.' But this happening hath been related unto thee in another manner."

So spake Bata, and he told his brother what was true regarding the woman. Then he called to witness the sun god, and said: "Great was thy wickedness in desiring to murder me by treachery." As he spoke he cut off a piece of his flesh and flung it into the stream, where it was devoured by a fish.[1] He sank fainting upon the bank.

Anpu was stricken with anguish; tears ran from his eyes. He desired greatly to be beside his brother on the opposite bank of the stream of crocodiles.

Bata spake again, saying: "Verily, thou didst desire an evil thing, but if thy desire now is to do good, I shall instruct thee what thou shouldst do. Return unto thy home and tend thine oxen, for know now that I may not dwell with thee any longer, but must depart unto the fair region of the flowering acacia. What thou shalt do is to come to seek for me when I need thine aid, for my soul shall leave my body and have its dwelling in the highest blossom of the acacia. When the tree is cut down, my soul will fall upon the ground. There thou mayest seek it, even if thy quest be for seven years, for, verily, thou shalt find it if such is thy desire. Thou must then place it in a vessel of water, and I shall

---

[1] He was thus mutilated like Osiris, Attis, Adonis, and other gods.

come to life again and reveal all that hath befallen and what shall happen thereafter. When the hour cometh to set forth on the quest, behold! the beer given to thee will bubble, and the wine will have a foul smell. These shall be as signs unto thee."

Then Bata took his departure, and he went into the valley of the flowering acacia, which was across the ocean.[2] His elder brother returned home. He lamented, throwing dust upon his head. He slew his wife and cast her to the dogs, and abandoned himself to mourning for his younger brother.

Many days went past, and Bata reached at length the valley of the flowering acacia. He dwelt there alone and hunted wild beasts. At eventide he lay down to rest below the acacia, in whose highest blossom his soul was concealed. In time he built a dwelling place and he filled it with everything that he desired.

Now it chanced that on a day when he went forth he met the nine gods, who were surveying the whole land. They spoke one to another and then asked of Bata why he had forsaken his home because of his brother's wife, for she had since been slain. "Return again," they said, "for thou didst reveal unto thine elder brother the truth of what happened unto thee."

They took pity on the youth, and Ra spoke, saying: "Fashion now a bride for Bata, so that he may not be alone."

Then the god Khnumu[3] fashioned a wife whose body was more beautiful than any other woman's in the land, because that she was imbued with divinity.

Then came the seven Hathors[4] and gazed upon her. In one voice they spoke, saying: "She shall surely die a speedy death."

[2] Probably in Syria.
[3] A creative god who resembles Ptah.
[4] The seven Fates.

Bata loved her dearly. Each day she remained in his house while he hunted wild beasts, and he carried them home and laid them at her feet. He warned her each day, saying: "Walk not outside, lest the sea may come up and carry thee away. I could not rescue thee from the sea spirit,[5] against whom I am as weak as thou art, because my soul is concealed in the highest blossom of the flowering acacia. If another should find my soul I must needs fight for it."

Thus he opened unto her his whole heart and revealed its secrets.

Many days went past. Then on a morning when Bata had gone forth to hunt, as was his custom, his girl wife went out to walk below the acacia, which was nigh to the house.

Lo! the sea spirit beheld her in all her beauty and caused his billows to pursue her. Hastily she fled away and returned to the house, whereat the sea spirit sang to the acacia: "Oh, would she were mine!"

The acacia heard and cast to the sea spirit a lock of the girl wife's hair. The sea bore it away towards the land of Egypt and unto the place where the washers of the king cleansed the royal garments.

Sweet was the fragrance of the lock of hair, and it perfumed the linen of the king. There were disputes among the washers because that the royal garments smelt of ointment, nor could anyone discover the secret thereof. The king rebuked them.

Then was the heart of the chief washer in sore distress, because of the words which were spoken daily to him regarding this matter. He went down to the seashore; he stood at the place which was opposite the floating lock of hair, and he beheld it at length and caused it to be carried

[5] A non-Egyptian conception apparently.

unto him. Sweet was its fragrance, and he hastened with it to the king.

Then the king summoned before him his scribes, and they spake, saying: "Lo! this is a lock from the hair of the divine daughter of Ra, and it is gifted unto thee from a distant land. Command now that messengers be sent abroad to seek for her. Let many men go with the one who is sent to the valley of the flowering acacia so that they may bring the woman unto thee.

The king answered and said: "Wise are your words, and they are pleasant unto me."

So messengers were sent abroad unto all lands. But those who journeyed to the valley of the flowering acacia returned not, because that Bata slew them all; the king had no knowledge of what befell them.

Then the king sent forth more messengers and many soldiers also, so that the girl might be brought unto him. He sent also a woman, and she was laden with rare ornaments . . . and the wife of Bata came back with her.

Then was there great rejoicing in the land of Egypt. Dearly did the king love the divine girl, and he exalted her because of her beauty. He prevailed upon her to reveal the secrets of her husband, and the king then said: "Let the acacia be cut down and splintered in pieces."

Workmen and warriors were sent abroad, and they reached the acacia. They severed from it the highest blossom, in which the soul of Bata was concealed. The petals were scattered, and Bata dropped down dead.

A new day dawned, and the land grew bright. The acacia was then cut down.

Meanwhile Anpu, the elder brother of Bata, went into his house, and he sat down and washed his hands. He was given beer to drink, and it bubbled, and the wine had a foul smell.

He seized his staff, put on his shoes and his garment, and armed himself for his journey, and departed unto the valley of the flowering acacia.

When he reached the house of Bata he found the young man lying dead upon a mat. Bitterly he wept because of that. But he went out to search for the soul of his brother at the place where, below the flowering acacia, Bata was wont to lie down to rest at eventide. For three years he continued his search, and when the fourth year came his heart yearned greatly to return to the land of Egypt. At length he said: "I shall depart at dawn to-morrow."

A new day came, and the land grew bright. He looked over the ground again at the place of the acacia for his brother's soul. The time was spent thus. In the evening he continued his quest also, and he found a seed, which he carried to the house, and, lo! the soul of his brother was in it. He dropped the seed into a vessel filled with cold water, and sat down as was his custom at evening.

Night came on, and then the soul absorbed the water. The limbs of Bata quivered and his eyes opened and gazed upon his elder brother, but his heart was without feeling. Then Anpu raised the vessel which contained the soul to the lips of Bata, and he drank the water. Thus did his soul return to its place, and Bata was as he had been before.

The brothers embraced and spoke one to the other. Bata said: "Now I must become a mighty bull with every sacred mark. None will know my secret. Ride thou upon my back, and when the day breaks I shall be at the place where my wife is. Unto her must I speak. Lead me before the king, and thou shalt find favour in his eyes. The people will wonder when they behold me, and shout welcome. But thou must return unto thine own home."

A new day dawned, and the land grew bright. Bata was a

bull, and Anpu sat upon his back and they drew nigh to the royal dwelling. The king was made glad, and he said: "This is indeed a miracle." There was much rejoicing throughout the land. Silver and gold were given to the elder brother, and he went away to his own home and waited there.

In time the sacred bull stood in a holy place, and the beautiful girl wife was there. Bata spoke unto her, saying: "Look thou upon me where I stand, for, lo! I am still alive."

Then said the woman: "And who art thou?"

The bull made answer: "Verily, I am Bata. It was thou who didst cause the acacia to be cut down; it was thou who didst reveal unto Pharaoh that my soul had dwelling in the highest blossom, so that it might be destroyed and I might cease to be. But, lo! I live on, and I am become a sacred bull."

The woman trembled; fear possessed her heart when Bata spoke unto her in this manner. She at once went out of the holy place.

It chanced that the king sat by her side at the feast, and made merry, for he loved her dearly. She spoke, saying: "Promise before the god that thou wilt do what I ask of thee."

His Majesty took a vow to grant her the wish of her heart, and she said: "It is my desire to eat of the liver of the sacred bull, for he is naught to thee."[6]

Sorrowful was the king then, and his heart was troubled, because of the words which she spake . . .

A new day dawned, and the land grew bright. Then the king commanded that the bull should be offered in sacrifice.

One of the king's chief servants went out, and when the

___

[6] It was believed that the soul was in the liver.

bull was held high upon the shoulders of the people he smote its neck and it cast two drops of blood[7] towards the gate of the palace, and one drop fell upon the right side and one upon the left. There grew up in the night two stately Persea trees[8] from where the drops of blood fell down.

This great miracle was told unto the king, and the people rejoiced and made offerings of water and fruit to the sacred trees.

A day came when his majesty rode forth in his golden chariot. He wore his collar of lapis lazuli, and round his neck was a garland of flowers. The girl wife was with him, and he caused her to stand below one of the trees, and it whispered unto her:

"Thou false woman, I am still alive. Lo! I am even Bata, whom thou didst wrong. It was thou who didst cause the acacia to be cut down. It was thou who didst cause the sacred bull to be slain, so that I might cease to be."

Many days went past, and the woman sat with the king at the feast, and he loved her dearly. She spake, saying: "Promise now before the god that thou wilt do what I ask of thee."

His Majesty made a vow of promise, and she said: "It is my desire that the Persea trees be cut down so that two fair seats may be made of them."

As she desired, so was it done. The king commanded that the trees should be cut down by skilled workmen, and the fair woman went out to watch them. As she stood there, a small chip of wood entered her mouth, and she swallowed it.

After many days a son was born to her, and he was brought before the king, and one said: "Unto thee a son is given."

[7] The belief that the soul was in the blood.
[8] One tree for the spirit and one for the soul.

A nurse and servants were appointed to watch over the babe.

There was great rejoicing throughout the land when the time came to name the girl wife's son. The king made merry, and from that hour he loved the child, and he appointed him Prince of Ethiopia.

Many days went past, and then the king chose him to be heir to the kingdom.

In time His Majesty fulfilled his years, and he died, and his soul flew to the heavens.

The new king (Bata) then said: "Summon before me the great men of my Court, so that I may now reveal unto them all that hath befallen me and the truth concerning the queen."

His wife[9] was then brought before him. He revealed himself unto her, and she was judged before the great men, and they confirmed the sentence.[10]

Then Anpu was summoned before His Majesty, and he was chosen to be the royal heir.

When Bata had reigned for thirty years,[11] he came to his death, and on the day of his burial his elder brother stood in his place.

A SOLDIER'S LOT, c. 1190 BC

Anonymous

Possibly a set-text in schools, certainly an accurate recounting of the hardships of an Egyptian soldier's life.

---

[9] Who was also his mother. Bata was reborn as the son of his wife. The tale is based upon belief in the transmigration of souls.
[10] The sentence is not given, but is indicated by the prophecy of the seven Hathors, who said she would die "a speedy death" (a death by violence).
[11] This suggests that he was sacrificed at the Sed festival.

What is it that you say they relate, that the soldier's is more pleasant than the scribe's (profession)? Come, let me tell you the condition of the soldier, that much castigated one. He is brought while a child to be confined in the camp. A searing beating is given his body, an open wound inflicted on his eye-brows. His head is split open with a wound. He is laid down and he is beaten like papyrus. He is struck with torments. Come, (let me relate) to you his journey to Khor and his marching upon the hills. His rations and his water are upon his shoulder like the load of an ass, while his neck has been made a backbone like that of an ass. The vertebrae of his back are broken, while he drinks of foul water. He stops work (only) to keep watch. He reaches the battle, and he is like a plucked fowl. He proceeds to return to Egypt, and he is like a stick which the worm has devoured. He is sick, prostration overtakes him. He is brought back upon an ass, his clothes taken away by theft, his henchman fled. Scribe Inena, turn back from the saying that the soldier's is more pleasant than the scribe's (profession).

OUT OF ANARCHY: SETNAKHTE FOUNDS THE 20TH DYNASTY, c. 1190–5 BC

Anonymous

The 19th Dynasty collapsed in confusion and vying claims to the throne. Quite who Setnakhte (Setnakht) was is uncertain, but the Papyrus Harris enshrines him as the saviour of Egypt who quelled rebellions by the Asiatics, reopened the temples and founded a new Dynasty. Setnakhte was buried in the Valley of the Kings, in a tomb originally intended for the 19th Dynasty regnant queen Twosret.

The land of Egypt was overthrown from without, and every man was thrown out of his right; they had no chief mouth for many years formerly until other times. The land of

Egypt was in the hands of chiefs and of rulers of towns; one slew his neighbour, great and small. Other times having come after it, with empty years, Yarsu, a certain Syrian was with them as chief. He set the whole land tributary before him together; he united his companions and plundered their possessions. They made the gods like men, and no offerings were presented in the temples.

But when the gods inclined themselves to peace, to set the land in its right according to its accustomed manner, they established their son, who came forth from their limbs, to be Ruler, L. P. H., of every land, upon their great throne, Userkhare-Setepnere-Meriamon, L. P. H., Son of Re, Setnakht-Mererre-Meriamon, L. P. H. He was Khepri-Set, when he is enraged; he set in order the entire land, which had been rebellious; he slew the rebels who were in the land of Egypt; he cleansed he great throne of Egypt; he was Ruler, L. P. H., of the Two Lands, on the throne of Atum. He gave ready faces, which had been turned away. Every man knew his brother who had been walled in. He established the temples in possession of divine offerings, to offer to the gods according to their customary stipulations.

THE GIFTS OF RAMSES III TO THE GOD AMUN, c. 1182–1151 BC

Ramses IV

On his father's death, Ramses IV had listed on a papyrus all the late pharaoh's benefactions to the gods. It was intended that the papyrus be buried with Ramses III but for reasons unknown it ended up in a private tomb at Deir el-Medina, where it was discovered in AD 1855 and sold to one Mr A.C. Harris. "The Great Papyrus Harris" is the longest papyrus – it measures 133 feet – to have survived from Ancient Egypt. The main sections list Ramses' devotions from his 31-year reign;

below are merely the benefactions made to Amun at Thebes; of similar length are the sections detailing the benefactions made to Re at Heliopolis and Ptah at Memphis. Two smaller sections deal with the lesser temples. As is transparent from Ramses' gifts to Amun and the itemization of Amun's estate, religion in Ancient Egypt was big business; the temples owned perhaps 15 per cent of the land and 2 per cent of the population. The final, sixth, section of the "Great Papyrus Harris" is an historical summary of Ramses III's reign.

I was king upon earth, ruler of the living; thou settedst the crown upon my head, as thou didst; I was inducted in peace into the august palace; I sat upon thy throne with joy of heart. Thou it was, who didst establish me upon the throne of my father, as thou didst for Horus on the throne of Osiris. I did not oppress, I did not deprive another of his throne. I did not transgress thy command, which was before me. Thou gavest peace and contentment of heart among my people, and every land was in adoration before me. I know of the excellent things which thou didst as king, and I multiplied for thee many benefactions and mighty deeds.

Medinet Habu Temple
I made for thee an august house of millions of years, abiding upon the mountain of "Lord-of-Life", before thee, built of sandstone, gritstone, and black granite; the doors of electrum and copper in beaten work. Its towers were of stone, towering to heaven, adorned and carved with the graver's tool, in the great name of thy majesty. I built a wall around it, established with labour, having ramps and towers of sandstone. I dug a lake before it, flooded with Nun, planted with trees and vegetation like the Delta.

Temple Endowment and Equipment

I filled its treasury with the products of the lands of Egypt: gold, silver, every costly stone by the hundred-thousand. Its granary was overflowing with barley and wheat; (its) lands, its herds, their multitudes were like the sand of the shore. I taxed for it the Southland as well as the Northland. Nubia and Zahi [came] to it, bearing their impost. It was filled with captives, which thou gavest to me among the Nine Bows, (and with) classes which I trained by the ten-thousand. I fashioned thy great statue resting in its midst; "Amon-Endowed-with-Eternity" was its august name; it was adorned with real costly stone like the horizon. When it appeared, there was rejoicing to see it. I made for it table-vessels, of fine gold; others of silver and copper, without number. I multiplied the divine offerings presented before thee, of bread, wine, beer, and fat geese; numerous oxen, bullocks, calves, cows, white oryxes, and gazelles offered in his slaughter yard.

Accessory Monuments

I dragged great monuments like mountains of alabaster and hus stone, sculptured with labour, and resting on the right and the left of its portal, carved with the great name of thy majesty forever; other statues of granite and gritstone; scarabs of black granite, resting in its midst. I fashioned Ptah-Sokar, Nefertem and all the gods of heaven and earth, resting in its chapel, wrought with fine gold, and silver in beaten work, with inlay of real costly stones, beautified with labour.

Pavilion and Connected Buildings

I made for thee an august palace of the king in its midst, like the great house of Atum which is in heaven. The columns, door-posts, and doors were of electrum; the great balcony for the (royal) appearances was of fine gold.

Temple Ships

I made for it ships laden with barley and wheat for transport to its granary without cessation. I made for it great treasure-ships upon the river, laden with a multitude of things for its august treasury.

Temple Lands

It was surrounded with gardens and arbour-areas, filled with fruit and flowers for the two serpent-goddesses. I built their châteaux having windows; I dug a lake before them, supplied with lotus flowers.

Small Karnak Temple

I made for thee a mysterious horizon in thy city of Thebes over against thy forecourt, O lord of gods, (named): "House-of-Ramses-Ruler-of-Heliopolis,-L.-P.-H.,-in-the-House-of-Amon", abiding like the heavens bearing the sun. I built it, I laid it in sandstone, having great doors of fine gold. I filled its treasury with the things which my hands carried off, to bring them before thee every day.

Southern Karnak Temple

I adorned for thee Southern Opet with great monuments; I built for thee a house therein like the throne of the All-Lord (named): "Temple-of-Ramses-Ruler-of-Heliopolis,-L.-P.-H.,-Possessed-of-Joy-in-Karnak".

Works in Great Karnak Temple

I again established thy monuments in "Victorious Thebes", the place of thy heart's rest, beside thy face (named): "House-of-Usermare-Meriamon-in-the-House-of-Amon", like the shrine of the All-Lord; built of stone, like a marvel established as an eternal work; the doorways upon them were of granite, doors and doorposts of gold. I supplied it with classes which I trained, bearing offerings by the hundred-thousand.

Monolithic Shrine
I made for thee a mysterious shrine in one block of fine granite, the doors upon it were of copper in hammered work, engraved with thy divine name. Thy great image rested in it, like Re in his horizon, established upon his throne unto eternity in thy great and august court.

Cultus Utensils
I made for thee a great sacrificial tablet of silver in hammered work, mounted with fine gold, the inlay-figures being of Ketem-gold, bearing statues of the king, L. P. H., of gold in hammered work, an offering-tablet bearing thy divine offerings, offered before thee.

I made for thee a great vase-stand, for thy forecourt, mounted with fine gold, with inlay of stone; its vases were of gold, containing wine and beer, in order to present them before thee every morning.

Feast of the Appearance
I made for thee a storehouse for the "Feast of the Appearance", with male and female slaves. I supplied them with bread, beer, oxen, fowl, wine, incense, fruit, vegetables, flowers, pure offerings before thee every day, being an increase of the daily offering which was before.

Ornaments of Cultus Statue, Etc.

I made for thee a splendid amulet of gold, with inlay; great collars and tassels of Ketem-gold complete, to bind them to thy body, every time thou appearest in thy great and splendid seat in Karnak. I made for thee a statue of the king, of gold, in hammered work, resting in the place which he knows, in thy august shrine.

Record Tablets

I made for thee great tablets of gold, in beaten work, engraved with the great name of thy majesty, bearing my prayers. I made for thee other tablets of silver, in beaten work, engraved with the great name of thy majesty, with the decrees of the house. I made for thee great tablets of silver, in beaten work, engraved with the great name of thy majesty, carved with the graver's tool, bearing the decrees and the inventories of the houses and temples which I made in Egypt, during my reign on earth; in order to administer them in thy name forever and ever. Thou art their protector, answering for them. I made for thee other tablets of copper in beaten work, of a mixture of six parts, of the colour of gold, engraved and carved with the graver's tool with the great name of thy majesty, with the house-regulations of the temples; likewise the many praises and adorations which I made for thy name. Thy heart was glad at hearing them, O lord of gods.

Cultus Sieve

I made for thee a great vase of pure silver, its rim of gold, engraved with thy name. A sieve was upon it of beaten work, of pure silver, a great sifting-vessel of silver, having a sieve and feet.

Golden Statues

I wrought upon the portable images of Mut and Khonsu, fashioned and made anew in the gold-houses, made of fine gold in thick overlay, with inlay of every costly stone which Ptah made, having collars before and behind, and tassels of Ketem-gold. They rest with heart satisfied at the mighty deeds which I did for them.

I made for thee great stelæ for thy portal, overlaid with fine gold, with inlay-figures of Ketem-gold; large bases were under them, overlaid with silver, bearing inlay-figures in gold, to the pavement line.

Grain

I gave to thee ten ten-thousands of measures of grain, to provision thy divine offerings of every day, to convey them to Thebes every year, in order to multiply thy granaries with barley and wheat.

Foreign Revenues

I brought to thee the captives of the Nine Bows, the gifts of the lands and countries for thy court. I made the road to Thebes like a foot to lead before thee, bearing much provision.

Periodic Offerings

I founded for thee oblations at the feasts of the beginnings of the seasons, to make offering before thee at thy every appearance. They were supplied with bread, beer, oxen, fowl, wine, incense, and fruit without number. They were levied anew upon the princes and inspectors as an increase of all the benefactions which I did for thy *ka*.

Sacred Barge

I hewed for thee thy august ship "Userhet" of 130 cubits (length) upon the river, of great cedars of the (royal) domain, of remarkable size, overlaid with fine gold to the water line, like the barge of the Sun, when he comes from the east, and everyone lives at the sight of him. A great shrine was in the midst of it, of fine gold, with inlay of every costly stone like a palace; rams' heads of gold from front to rear, [fitted] with uraeus-serpents wearing etef-crowns.

Products of Punt

I led to thee Punt with myrrh, in order to encircle thy house every morning, I planted incense sycamores in thy court; they had not seen (it) before since the time of the god.

Mediterranean Fleet

I made for thee transports, galleys, and barges, with archers equipped with their arms, upon the sea. I gave to them captains of archers and captains of galleys, manned with numerous crews, without number, in order to transport the products of the land of Zahi and the countries of the ends of the earth to thy great treasuries in "Victorious Thebes".

Cattle and Fowl

I made for thee herds in the South and North containing large cattle, fowl, and small cattle by the hundred-thousand, having overseers of cattle, scribes, overseers of the horns, inspectors, and numerous shepherds in charge of them; having cattle-fodder; in order to offer them to thy *ka* at all thy feasts, that thy heart may be satisfied with them, O ruler of gods.

Vineyards, Trees, Etc.
I made for thee wine-gardens in the Southern Oasis, and the
Northern Oasis likewise without number; others in the South
with numerous lists; they were multiplied in the Northland
by the hundred-thousand. I manned them with gardeners
from the captives of the countries; having lakes of my digging,
supplied with lotus flowers, and with shedeh[1] and wine like
drawing water, in order to present them before thee in
"Victorious Thebes". I planted thy city, Thebes, with trees,
vegetation, isi-plants, and menhet flowers for thy nostrils.

Khonsu-Temple
I built a house for thy son, Khonsu in Thebes, of good
sandstone, red gritstone, and black stone (granite). I overlaid its doorposts and doors with gold, (with) inlay-figures
of electrum, like the horizon of heaven. I worked upon thy
statues in the gold-houses, with every splendid costly stone
which my hands brought.

Sanctuary in Residence City
I made for thee an august quarter in the city of the
Northland, established as thy property forever; "House-
of-Ramses-Ruler-of-Heliopolis,-L.-P.-H.,-Great-in-Victory",
it is called, forever. I conveyed to it Egypt with its tribute; the
people of every land were gathered in its midst. It was
furnished with large gardens and places for walking about,
with all sorts of date groves, bearing their fruits, and a sacred
avenue, brightened with the flowers of every land, isi-plants,
papyrus, and dedmet flowers, like sand.

Its Vineyard and Olive Garden
I made for it Kanekeme, inundated like the Two Lands,
in the great olive-lands; bearing vines; surrounded by a

---
[1] An intoxicating drink of uncertain character.

wall around them by the iter; planted with great trees in all their many paths, wherein was oil more than the sand of the shore; in order to bring them to thy *ka*, to "Victorious Thebes"; wine like drawing water without measure, to present them before thee as a daily offering. I built for thee thy temple in the midst of its ground, established with labour, excellent in stone of Ayan. Its door and its doorposts were of gold, mounted with copper; the inlay-figures were of every costly stone, like the double doors of the sky.

Cultus Image

I fashioned thy august image, wherewith the "Appearance" is made like Re when he brightens the earth with his beams; "Amon-of-Ramses-Ruler-of-Heliopolis" was its great and august name. I filled its house with male and female slaves, whom I carried off from the lands of the Bedwin. The lay priests of the temple were —— children of great men, whom I trained. Its treasury was overflowing with products of every land; its granaries approached heaven, its herds were multiplied more than the sand; cattle yards, offered to his *ka*, (as) divine offerings daily, full and pure before him; fattening-houses containing fat geese; poultry yards containing wild fowl; gardens with wine, provided with their fruit, vegetables and all kinds of flowers.

Temple in Nubia

I made for thee an august house in Nubia, engraved with thy august name, the likeness of the heavens (named): "House-of-Ramses-Ruler-of-Heliopolis,-L.-P.-H.,-Great-in-Victory", abiding, bearing thy name forever.

Temple in Zahi

I built for thee a mysterious house in the land of Zahi like the horizon of heaven which is in the sky, (named): "The-House-of-Ramses-Ruler-of-Heliopolis,-L.-P.-H.,-in-Peka-nan", as the property of thy name. I fashioned thy great statue resting in the midst of it (named): "Amon-of-Ramses-Ruler-of-Heliopolis,-L.-P.-H." The Asiatics of Retenu came to it, bearing their tribute before it, for it was divine.

Miscellaneous

I brought the earth, united for thee, bearing their imposts, to convey them to Thebes, thy mysterious city. I made for thee statues in the districts of Egypt; they were for thee and the gods who preserve this land. I built for them temples, gardens containing their groves, lands, small cattle, large cattle, many slaves; they are thine forever, thine eye is upon them, thou art their protector unto eternity. I wrought upon thy great and grand statues which are in their districts in the lands of Egypt. I restored their temples which were in ruin. I multiplied the divine offerings presented to their *ka*'s as an increase of the daily offerings which were formerly.

Lists

See, I have listed all that I did before thee, O my august, divine father, lord of gods, that men and gods may know of my benefactions, which I did for thee in might, while I was upon earth.

Amon's Estate

List of things, cattle, gardens, lands, galleys, workshops, and towns, which Pharaoh, L. P. H., gave to the house of his august father, Amon-Re, king of gods, Mut, Khonsu, and all the gods of Thebes, as property forever and ever[2]:

People Attached to Temples, Etc. Medinet Habu Temple
"The-House-of-King-Usermare-Meriamon,-L.-P.-H.,-in-the-House-of-Amon", in the South and North, under charge of the officials of the temples of this house, equipped with all its things: heads 62,626

Small Karnak Temple
"House-of-Usermare-Meriamon,-L.-P.-H.,-in-the-House-of-Amon", in the South and North, under charge of the officials, equipped with all its things: heads 970

Luxor Temple
"House-of-Ramses-Ruler-of-Heliopolis,-L.-P.-H.,-in-the-House-of-Amon", in the South and North, under charge of the officials, equipped with all its things: heads 2,623

Southern Karnak Temple
"The   House-of-Ramses-Ruler-of-Heliopolis,-L.-P.-H.,-Possessed-of-Joy-in-the-House-of-Amon", under charge of the High Priest; equipped with all its things: heads 49

Five Herds of the Theban Temples
Herd of "Usermare-Meriamon,-L.-P.-H.,-in-the-House-of-Amon", which is (called): "Usermare-Meriamon,-L.-P.-H.,-Captor-of-Rebels-is-a-Great-Nile":   heads[3] 113
Herd (called): "Usermare-Meriamon,-L.-P.-H.,-is-the-Conqueror-of-the-Meshwesh-at-the-Water-of-Re", under charge of the steward Pay; Meshwesh: heads 971

---

[2] The list now follows, and the first series of items is a statement of the numbers of people ("*heads*") attached to the various temples, to herds, etc.
[3] These are not "*heads*" of cattle, but the people in charge of the herd.

Herd (called): "Ramses-Ruler-of-Heliopolis,-L.-P.-H.,-in-the-House-of-Amon-is-a-Great-Nile:"   heads 1,867
Herd (called): "Usermare-Meriamon,-L.-P.-H.,-in-the-House-of-Amon",—under charge of the Vizier of the South: heads 34
Herd of "Ramses-Ruler-of-Heliopolis,-L.-P.-H.,-in-the-House-of-Amon", under charge of the cattle-overseer Key: heads 279

Royal Residence
"House-of-Ramses-Ruler-of-Heliopolis,-L.-P.-H.,-Great-in-Victory", the city which the Pharaoh, L. P. H., made for thee in the North, in the ownership of the house of Amon-Re, king of gods, saying: "As thou art mighty, thou shalt cause it to abide forever and ever":   heads 7,872

Khonsu-Temple
House-of-Ramses-Ruler-of-Heliopolis,-L.-P.-H.,-in-the-House-of-Khonsu: heads 294

Ramses III's Gifts of People
People whom he gave to the house of "Khonsu in Thebes, Beautiful Rest", Horus, lord of joy: persons 247
Syrians, and Negroes of the captivity of his majesty, L. P. H., whom he gave to the house of Amon-Re, king of gods, the house of Mut, and the house of Khonsu: persons 2,607
Bows of "Usermare-Meriamon,-L.-P.-H.,-Establisher-of-His-House-in-the-House-of-Amon"; people settled, whom he gave to this house: heads 770

Private Statues in Great Karnak Temple
The processional images, statues, and figures, to which the officials, standard-bearers, inspectors, and people of the

land pay impost, which the Pharaoh, L. P. H., gave; in the
ownership of the house of Amon-Re, king of gods, to
protect them and answer for them forever and ever;
2,756 gods, making: heads   5,164
Total   heads 86,486

Miscellaneous Property

Large and small cattle, various	421,362
Gardens and groves	433
Lands, stat	864,168¼
Transports and galleys	83
Workshops of cedar and acacia	46
Towns of Egypt	56
Towns of Syria and Kush	9
Total	65

Amon's Income

Things exacted, the impost of all the people and serf-
laborers of "The-House-of-King-Usermare-Meriamon,-
L.-P.-H.,-in-the-House-of-Amon" (Medinet Habu temple), in the South and North under charge of the officials;
the   "House-of-Usermare-Meriamon,-L.-P.-H.,-in-the-
House-of-Amon" (small Karnak temple), in the (residence) city; the "House-of-Ramses-Ruler-of-Heliopolis,-
L.-P.-H.,-in-the-House-of-Amon" (Luxor temple); the
"House-of-Ramses-Ruler-of-Heliopolis,-L.-P.-H.,-Pos-
sessed-of-Joy-in-the-House-of-Amon-of-Opet" (southern
Karnak temple); the "House-of-Ramses-Ruler-of-Heliopolis,-L.-P.-H.,-in-the-House-of-Khonsu" (Khonsu-temple);
the five herds made for this house, which King Usermare-Meriamon, L. P. H., the Great God, gave to their
treasuries, storehouses and granaries as their yearly dues:

Fine gold	217 deben,	5	kidet
Gold of the mountain, of Coptos	61 ″	3	″
Gold of Kush	290 ″	8½	″
Total, fine gold, and gold of the mountain	569 ″	6½	″
Silver	10,964 ″	9	″
Total, gold and silver	11,546 ″	8	″
Copper	26,320 ″		

Royal linen, mek-linen, fine southern linen, coloured southern linen, various garments	3,722
Yarn, deben	3,795
Incense, honey, oil, various jars	1,047
Shedeh and wine, various jars	25,405
Silver, being things of the impost of the people given for the divine offerings	3,606 deben, 1 kidet
Barley – of the impost of the peasants, 16-fold heket	309,950
Vegetables, bundles	24,650
Flax, bales	64,000
Water-fowl from the impost of the fowlers and fishermen	289,530
Bulls, bullocks of the bulls, heifers, calves, cows, cattle of—, cattle of—, of the herds of Egypt	847
Bulls, bullocks of the nege-bulls, heifers, calves, cows, being impost of the lands of Syria	19
Total	866

Live geese of the exactions   744
Cedar: tow-boats, and ferry-boats   11
Acacia: tow-boats, canal-boats, boats for the
   transportation of cattle, warships, and kara-boats: 71
Total, cedar and acacia: boats: 82
Products of the Oasis in many lists for the divine offer-
ings.

THE KING'S GIFTS TO AMON

Gold, silver, real lapis lazuli, real malachite, every real
costly stone, copper, garments of royal linen, mek-linen,
fine southern linen, southern linen, coloured garments,
jars, fowl, all the things which King Usermare-Meriamon,
L. P. H., the Great God, gave, as gifts of the king, L. P.
H., in order to provision the house of his august fathers,
Amon-Re, king of gods, Mut, and Khonsu, from the year
1 to the year 31, making 31 years.

Fine Ketem-gold; 42 —   making   21 deben
Fine gold in raised work,
   22 finger rings,   making   3   ″   3 kidet
Fine gold in inlay; 9
   finger rings,   making   1   ″   3½ ″
Fine gold in raised work,
   and in inlay of every
   real, costly stone; a ring
   of the column of Amon,   making   22   ″   5   ″
Fine gold in hammered
   work; a tablet,   making   9   ″   5½ ″
Total, fine gold in ornaments   57   ″   5[b] ″
Gold of two times; in raised
   work; and in inlay;

42 finger rings,	making	4	"	5 ½	"
Gold of two times; 2 vases		30	"	5	"
Total, gold of two times		35	"	½	"
White gold: 310 finger rings,	making	16	"	3 ½	"
White gold: 264 beads,	making	48	"	4	"
White gold in beaten work: 108 finger rings for the god,	making	19	"	8	"
White gold: 155 amulet cords,	making	6	"	2	"
Total, white gold		90	"	7 ½	"
Total, fine gold, gold of two times and white gold		183	"	5^c	"
Silver: a vase (with) the rim of gold, in raised work,	making	112	"	5	"
Silver: a sieve for the vase,	making	12	"	3	"
Silver: a sifting-vessel for the vase,	making	27	"	7	"
Silver: 4 vases,	making	57	"	4 ½	"
Silver: 31 large panniers with lids,	making	105	"	4	"
Silver: 31 caskets with lids,	making	74	"	4	"
Silver: 6 measuring-vases,	making	30	"	3	"
Silver: in hammered work, a tablet,	making	19	"	3 ½	"
Silver: in hammered work, 2 tablets,	making	287 deben		½ ki-det	
Silver in scraps		100	"		

Total, silver in vessels and scraps			827	"	1¼	"	
Total, gold and silver in vessels and scraps			1,010	"	6¼	"	
Real lapis lazuli: 2 blocks,	making		14	"	½	"	
Bronze, in hammered work: 4 tablets,	making		822	"			
Myrrh: deben							51,140
Myrrh: heket							3
Myrrh: hin							20
Myrrh wood: logs							15
Myrrh fruit in measures							100
Royal linen: garments							37
" " upper garments							94
" " hamen-garments							55
" " mantles							11
" " wrappings of Horus							2
" " — garments							1
" " garments							690
" " tunics							489
" " garments for the august [statue] of Amon							4
Total, royal linen, various garments							1,383
Mek-linen: a robe							1
Mek-linen: a mantle							1
" " in a cover: a garment for the august statue of Amon							1
Total, mek-linen: various garments							3
Fine southern linen: garments							2
" " " — garments							4
" " " upper garments							5
" " " garments							31

"	"	"	tunics	29
"	"	"	kilts	4

Total, fine southern linen, various garments   75

Coloured linen: mantles   876
     "   "   tunics   6,779

Total, coloured linen, various garments   7,125

Total, royal linen, mek-linen, fine southern linen,
   southern linen, coloured linen, various garments 8,586

White incense: jars   2,159
Whitc incense: jars   12
Honey: jars   1,065
Oil of Egypt: jars   2,743
Oil of Syria: jars   53
Oil of Syria: jars   1,757
White fat: jars   911
Goose fat: jars   385
Butter: jars   20
Total, filled jars   9,125
Shedeh: coloured jars   1,377
Shedeh: jars   1,111
Wine: jars   20,078
Total, shedeh and wine: jars   22,556

Hirset stone: sacred eye amulets   185
Lapis lazuli: sacred eye amulets   217
Red jasper: scarabs   62
Malachite: scarabs   224

Bronze and Minu stone: scarabs	224
Lapis lazuli: scarabs	62
Various costly stones: sacred eye amulets	165
Various costly stones: seals as pendants	62
Rock-crystal: seals	1,550
" " beads	155,000
" " cut: hin-jars	155
Wrought wood: seals	31
Alabaster: a block	1
Cedar:	6
Cedar: _t_	1
Neybu wood: 3 logs, making (deben)	610
Cassia wood: 1 log, making (deben)	800
Reeds: bundles	17
Cinnamon: measures	246
Cinnamon: bundles	82
Grapes: measures	52
Rosemary: measures	125
Yufiti plant: measures	101
Dom-palm fruit of Mehay: measures	26
Fruit: heket	46
Grapes: crates	1,809
Grapes: bunches	1,869
Pomegranates: crates	375
plant, in measures	1,668
—Various cattle	297
Live geese	2,940
Live turpu geese	5,200
Live water-fowl	126,300
Fat geese from the flocks	20
Natron: bricks	44,000
Salt: bricks	44,000
Palm-fibre: ropes	180

Palm-fibre: loads	50
Palm-fibre: [—]	77
Palm-fibre: cords	2
Sebkhet plants	60
Flax: bekhen	1,150
Ideninu	60
Hezet plant: measures	50
Pure [—], deben	750

Grain for the Old Feasts
Clean grain for the divine offerings of the feasts of the sky, and the feasts of the first of the seasons, which King Usermare-Meriamon L. P. H., the Great God, founded for his father, Amon-Re, king of gods, Mut, Khonsu, and all the gods of Thebes, as an increase of the divine offerings, as an increase of the daily offerings, in order to multiply that which was before, from the year 1 to the year 31, making 31 years: 2,981,674 16-fold heket.

Offerings for New Feasts Founded by Ramses III
Oblations of the festivals which King Usermare-Meriamon, L. P. H., the Great God, founded for his father, Amon-Re, king of gods, Mut, Khonsu, and all the gods of Thebes, during the 20 days of offering, of the festival (called): "Usermare-Meriamon,-L.-P.-H., Making-Festive-Thebes-for-Amon", from the first month of the third season, (ninth month), day 26, to the second month of the third season (tenth month), day 15; "making 20 days; from the year 22 to the year 32, making 11 years; together with the oblations of the feast of Southern Opet (Luxor), from the second month of the first season (second month), day 19, to the third month of the first season (third month), day 15, making 27 days, from the year 1 to the year 31, making 31 years.

Fine bread: large oblation-loaves	1,057
Fine bread: large loaves	1,277
" " large loaves	1,277
" " loaves	440
Bread: large oblation-loaves	43,620
Papyrus rind of the house of incense	685
Beer of the beer-cellar: 4,401 (jars), making	——
Fine bread, meat, rahusu cakes: measures for show	165
Fine bread, meat, rahusu-cakes: measures of gold	485
Fine bread, meat, rahusu-cakes: measures for eating	11,120
Fine bread, meat, rahusu-cakes: measures for the mouth of the eater	9,845
Fine bread, meat, rahusu-cakes: vases of the prince	3,720
Fine bread of the divine offerings: vases of gold, equipped	375
Fine bread of the divine offerings: loaves	62,540
" " " " " loaves	106,992
" " " " " white loaves	13,020
Fine bread: large loaves for eating	6,200
" " sweet loaves	24,800
" " loaves of the fire	16,665
" " large loaves	992,750
" " loaves of grain	17,340
" " white oblation-loaves	572,000
" " pyramidal loaves	46,500
" " kyllestis-loaves	441,800
" " loaves	127,400
Kunek bread: white loaves	116,400
Fine bread: loaves	262,000
Total of fine bread: various loaves	2,844,357

Rahusu-cakes: measures	344
Cakes: measures	48,420
Rahusu: measures	28,200
Flour: vessels	3,130
Shedeh: jars	2,210
Shedeh: jars	310
Wine: jars	39,510
Total, shedeh and wine: jars	42,030
Beer: various jars	219,215
Sweet oil: jars	93
Sweet oil: hin	1,100
White incense: jars	62
Incense: various measures	304,093
Inflammable incense: jars	778
Red oil: jars	31
Oil: jars	93
Oil: hin	110,000
Honey: jars	310
White fat: jars	93
Olives: jars	62
Southern linen: garments	155
Southern linen: garments	31
Coloured linen: garments	31
Coloured linen: tunics	44
Total	261
—Wax: deben	3,100
All (kinds of) fine fruit: measures	620
All (kinds of) fine fruit: measures	620
Fruit: measures	559,500

Fruit: measures	78,550
Figs of the impost: measures	310
" " " weights	1,410
" " " measures	55
Figs: in measures	15,500
Figs: measures	310
Mehiwet: cakes	3,100
Cinnamon: measures	220
Cinnamon: measures	155
Semu plant: measures	1,550
Cabbage: heket	620
Khithana fruit: heket	310
Khithana fruit: bundles	6,200
Grapes: measures	117
Grapes: measures	1,550
Southern fruit: heket	8,985
Enbu: measures	620
—Papyrus sandals: pairs	15,110
Salt: 16-fold heket	1,515
Salt: bricks	69,200
Natron: bricks	75,400
Thick stuff: garments	150
Flax: measures	265
Tamarisk: bundles	3,270
Reed-grass: bundles	4,200
Leather sandals: pairs	3,720
Dom-palm fruit: in measures	449,500
Pomegranates: in measures	15,500
Pomegranates: crates	1,240
Olives: jars	310
Jars and vessels of the mouth of the Heliopolitan canal	9,610
Papyrus rind: measures	3,782

Nebdu: measures	930
Bulls	419
Bullocks of the bulls	290
Oxen	18
Heifers	281
Two-year-olds (cattle)	3
Calves	740
Bullocks	19
Cows	1,122
Total, various cattle	2,892
Male of the white oryx	1
White oryxes	54
Male gazelle	1
Gazelles	81
Total	137
Total, various cattle	3,029
Live geese	6,820
" fowl	1,410
" turpu geese	1,534
Cranes	150
Live hatching-fowl	4,060
Live water-fowl	25,020
Pigeons	57,810
Live pedet birds	21,700
Live sesha birds	1,240
Doves	6,510
Total, various fowl	126,250
Jars of the canal filled with fish, having wooden lids	440
White fish	2,200

Dressed shene fish	15,500
Fish cut up	15,500
Fish, whole	441,000
Blossoms of the impost of flowers: sunshades	124
Blossoms: tall bouquets	3,100
Blossoms of the impost of flowers: "garden fragrance"	15,500
Isi-plant: measures	124,351
Flowers: garlands	60,450
Flowers: strings	620
Blue flowers: ropes	12,400
Flowers for the hand	46,500
Flowers: measures	110
Lotus flowers for the hand	144,720
" " bouquets	3,410
" " for the hand	110,000
Papyrus flowers: bouquets	68,200
Papyrus: stems	349,000
Large bouquets of the impost of flowers	19,150
Dates: measures	65,480
Dates: cut branches	3,100
Vegetables: measures	2,170
Vegetables: bundles	770,200
Isi-plant for the hand	128,650
Corn: bouquets	11,000
Ears of grain for the hand	31,000
Blossoms: bouquets	1,975,800
Blossoms: measures	1,975,800

Private Statues of Amon
The amount belonging to the 2,756 statues and figures which are above:

Fine gold and silver	18,252 deben,	1 ¼ kidet
Real costly stones:		
various blocks	18,214 "	3 "
Black copper, copper,		
lead, tin	112,132 "	
Cedar: various logs		328
Mastic tree: various logs		4,415

Ramses' Concluding Prayer to Amon

How happy is he who depends upon thee! O god, Amon, Bull of his mother, ruler of Thebes. Grant thou that I may arrive in safety, landing in peace, and resting in Tazoser like the gods. May I mingle with the excellent souls of Manu, who see thy radiance at early morning. Hear my petition! O my father, my lord, I am alone among the gods who are at thy side. Crown my son as king upon the throne of Atum, establish him as mighty Bull, lord, L. P. H., of the two shores, King of Upper and Lower Egypt, Lord of the Two Lands: Usermare-Setepnamon, L. P. H.: Son of Re, Lord of Diadems: Ramses (IV)-Hekma-Meriamon, L. P. H., emanation that came forth from thy limbs. Thou art the one who didst designate him to be king, while he was a youth. Appoint thou him to be ruler, L. P. H., of the Two Lands over the people. Give to him a reign of millions of years, his every limb being whole, in prosperity and health. Place thy crown upon his head, seated on thy throne; and may the serpent-goddess alight upon his brows. Make him divine more than any king, and great like thy reverence, as lord of the Nine Bows. Make his body to flourish and be youthful daily, while thou art a shield behind him for every day. Put his sword and his war-mace over the heads of the Bedwin; may they fall down in fear of him like Baal. Extend for him the boundaries as far as he desires; may the lands and countries fear in terror of him. Grant for him that Egypt may rejoice, ward off all evil, misfortune and destruction. Give to him joy abiding in his heart, jubilation, singing and dancing before his beautiful face. Put love of him in the hearts of the gods and goddesses; his kindness and his terror in the hearts of men. Complete the good things of which thou hast told me on earth for my son, who is upon my throne. Thou art the one who didst create him, confirm his kingdom to the son of his son, thou being to them a protector, answering for them and they being to thee servants with their eyes upon thee doing benefactions for thy *ka*, forever and ever. The things that thou ordainest, they come to pass, abiding and established; the things that thou sayest, they endure like gritstone. Thou didst adjudge to me a reign of 200 years; establish them for my son who is (still) upon earth; make his life longer than (that of) any king, in order to repay the benefactions which I have done for thy *ka*. Let him be king by reason of thy command; even thine, who crownest him; let him not reverse that which thou hast done, O lord of gods. Give great and rich Niles in his time, in order to supply his reign with plentiful food. Give to him the princes who have not known Egypt, with loads upon their backs for his august palace, King of Upper and Lower Egypt, Lord of the Two Lands: Usermare-Setepnamon, L. P. H.; Son of Re, Lord of Diadems: Ramses (IV)-Hekma-Meriamon, L. P. H.

THE FIGHT AGAINST THE SEA PEOPLES, c. 1174 BC

Anonymous

The reign of Ramses III (1182–1151 BC) coincided with demographic and political upheaval in the Mediterranean and Near East. The Libyans, as in the time of Merneptah, forced their way into Egypt, but were resoundingly beaten at

Usermare-Meriamon-is-Chastiser-of-Temeh, with a thousand Libyans taken into slavery. A more serious threat, however, came from the east: the Sea Peoples. They comprised a mass, if motley, confederation of tribes from southern Asia and the Aegean, including the Shekelesh (probably from Sicily), the Denyen, the Cretan Peleset (aka the Philistines), the Tjeker, the Weshesh. Initially, the Sea Peoples moved into north Syria, where they crushed the Hittites. Then they marched towards Egypt, their fleet following them at sea. Ramses III met them at the border and also in a naval engagement at the mouth of one of the eastern branches of the Nile.

Not one stood before their hands, from Kheta, Kode, Carchemish, Arvad, Alasa, they were wasted. They set up a camp in one place in Amor. They desolated his people and his land like that which is not. They came with fire prepared before them, forward to Egypt. Their main support was Peleset, Thekel, Shekelesh, Denyen, and Weshesh. These lands were united, and they laid their hands upon the land as far as the Circle of the Earth. Their hearts were confident, full of their plans.

Ramses' Preparations

"Now, it happened through this god, the lord of gods, that I was prepared and armed to trap them like wild fowl. He furnished my strength and caused my plans to prosper. I went forth, directing these marvellous things. I equipped my frontier in Zahi, prepared before them. The chiefs, the captains of infantry, the nobles, I caused to equip the harbour-mouths, like a strong wall, with warships, galleys, and barges. They were manned completely from bow to stern with valiant warriors bearing their arms, soldiers of all the choicest of Egypt, being like lions roaring upon the mountain-tops. The charioteers were warriors, and all good officers ready of hand. Their horses were quivering in their every limb, ready to crush the countries under their feet. I was the valiant Montu, stationed before them, that they might behold the hand-to-hand fighting of my arms. I, King Ramses III, was made a far-striding hero, conscious of his might, valiant to lead his army in the day of battle."

Defeat of the Enemy

"Those who reached my boundary, their seed is not; their heart and their soul are finished forever and ever. As for those who had assembled before them on the sea, the full flame[1] was in their front, before the harbour-mouths, and a wall of metal[2] upon the shore surrounded them. They were dragged, overturned, and laid low upon the beach; slain and made heaps from stern to bow of their galleys, while all their things were cast upon the water. Thus I turned back the waters to remember Egypt; when they mention my name in their land, may it consume them, while I sit upon the throne of Harakhte, and the serpent-diadem is fixed upon my head, like Re. I permit not the countries to see the boundaries of Egypt. As for the Nine Bows, I have taken away their land and their boundaries; they are added to mine. Their chiefs and their people (come) to me with praise. I carried out the plans of the All-Lord, the august, divine father, lord of the gods."

THE HAREM CONSPIRACY: THE PLOTTERS TRY MAGIC TO KILL RAMSES III, c. 1151 BC

The Court Recorder

The military victories of Ramses III were not enough to dispel the aura of crisis which hung over his reign. The economy was collapsing, harvests were bad, the priesthood at Thebes challenged his divine status. Even the royal palace was not

[1] "the full flame" = the Egyptian fleet in harbour
[2] "a wall of metal" = the Egyptian infantry ashore

barrier to decline in morale. Tiy, a secondary queen, plotted with allies to place her
son Pentaweret on the throne. At first the conspirators tried magic to dispatch the
incumbent pharaoh, as was recorded at their subsequent trial.

The First Case of Magic
Papyrus Rollin begins here. Thus the name of the accused is unknown.

He [the accused] began to make magic rolls for hindering
and terrifying, and to make some gods of wax, and some
people, for enfeebling the limbs of people; and gave them
into the hand of Pebekkamen, whom Re made not to be
chief of the chamber, and the other great criminals, saying:
"Take them in"; and they took them in. Now, when he set
himself to do the evil (deeds) which he did, in which Re did
not permit that he should succeed, he was examined. Truth
was found in every crime and in every evil (deed), which his
heart had devised to do. There was truth therein, he had
done them all, together with all the other great criminals.
They were great crimes of death, the great abominations of
the land, the things which he had done. Now, when he
learned of the great crimes of death which he had committed, he took his own life.

The Second Case of Magic
Papyrus Lee begins here; again the name of the accused is unknown.

Now, when Penhuibin, formerly overseer of herds, said to
him: "Give to me a roll for enduing me with strength and
might", she gave to him a magic roll of Usermare-Meriamon
(Ramses III), L. P. H., the Great God, his lord, L. P. H., and
he began to employ the magic powers of a god upon people.
He arrived at the side of the harem, this other large, deep
place. He began to make people of wax, inscribed, in order
that they might be taken in by the inspector, Errem, hinder-

ing one troop and bewitching the others, that a few words might be taken in, and others brought out. Now, when he was examined concerning them, truth was found in every crime and in every evil (deed), which his heart had devised to do. There was truth therein, he had done them all, together with the other great criminals, the abomination of every god and every goddess all together. The great punishments of death were executed upon him, of which the gods have said: "Execute them upon him."

THE HAREM CONSPIRATORS: THEIR CRIMES AND THEIR FATE, c. 1151 BC

The Court Recorder

Four people were implicated in the plot, the majority of them close to the king. The guilty were sentenced to death, some of them by suicide in the courtroom itself. Four court officials who knowingly consorted with some of the indicted women conspirators had their nose and ears amputated.

The Condemned of the First Prosecution
First Prosecution
Persons brought in because of the great crimes which they had committed, and placed in the court of examination before the great nobles of the court of examination, that they might be examined by:

   The overseer of the White House, Mentemtowe;
   The overseer of the White House, Pefroi;
   The standard-bearer, Kara;
   The butler, Pebes;
   The scribe of the archives, Mai;
   The standard-bearer, Hori.

They examined them; they found them guilty; they brought their punishment upon them; their crimes seized them.

The Condemned and Their Crimes
The great criminal, Pebekkamen, formerly chief of the chamber.

He was brought in because of his collusion with Tiy and the women of the harem. He made common cause with them, and began bringing out their words to their mothers and their brothers who were there, saying: "Stir up the people! Incite enemies to hostility against their lord." He was placed before the great nobles of the court of examination; they examined his crimes; they found that he had committed them. His crimes seized him; the nobles who examined him brought his punishment upon him.

The great criminal, Mesedsure, formerly butler. He was brought in because of his collusion [with] Pebekkamen, formerly chief of the chamber, and with the women, to stir up enemies to hostility against their lord. He was placed before the great nobles of the court of examination; they examined his crimes; they found him guilty; they brought his punishment upon him.

The great criminal, Peynok, formerly overseer of the king's harem.

He was brought in because of his making common cause with Pebekkamen and Mesedsure, to commit hostility against their lord. He was placed before the great nobles of the court of examination; they examined his crimes; they found him guilty; they brought his punishment upon him.

The great criminal, Pendua, formerly scribe of the king's harem.

He was brought in because of his making common cause

with Pebekkamen and Mesedsure, the other criminal, formerly overseer of the king's —, and the women of the harem, to make a conspiracy with them, to commit hostility against their lord. He was placed before the nobles of the court of examination; they examined his crimes; they found him guilty; they brought his punishment upon him.

The great criminal, Petewnteamon, formerly inspector of the harem.

He was brought in because of his hearing the words which the people discussed with the women of the harem, without reporting them. He was placed before the great nobles of the court of examination; they examined his crimes; they found him guilty; they brought his punishment upon him.

The great criminal, Kerpes, formerly inspector of the harem.

He was brought in because of the words which he had heard and had concealed. He was placed before the nobles of the court of examination. They found him guilty; they brought his punishment upon him.

The great criminal, Khamopet, formerly inspector of the harem.

He was brought in because of the words which he had heard and had concealed. He was placed before the nobles of the court of examination. They found him guilty; they brought his punishment upon him.

The great criminal, Khammale, formerly inspector of the harem.

He was brought in because of the words which he had heard and had concealed. He was placed before the nobles of the court of examination; they found him guilty; they brought his punishment upon him.

The great criminal, Setimperthoth, formerly inspector of the harem.

He was brought in because of the words which he had heard and had concealed. He was placed before the nobles of the court of examination; they found him guilty; they brought his punishment upon him.

The great criminal, Setimperamon, formerly inspector of the harem.

He was brought in because of the words which he had heard and had concealed. He was placed before the nobles of the court of examination; they found him guilty; they brought his punishment upon him.

The great criminal, Weren, who was butler.

He was brought in because of his hearing the words from the chief of the chamber, and when he had withdrawn from him, he concealed them and did not report them. He was placed before the nobles of the court of examination; they found him guilty; they brought his punishment upon him.

The great criminal, Eshehebsed, formerly assistant of Pebekkamen.

He was brought in because of his hearing the words from Pebekkamen; and when he had left him, he did not report them. He was placed before the nobles of the court of examination; they found him guilty; they brought his punishment upon him.

The great criminal, Peluka, formerly butler and scribe of the White House.

He was brought in because of his collusion with Pebekkamen, having heard the words from him, without reporting them. He was placed before the nobles of the court of examination; they found him guilty; they brought his punishment upon him.

The great criminal, the Libyan, Yenini, formerly butler.

He was brought in because of his collusion with Pebekkamen, having heard the words from him, without reporting them. He was placed before the nobles of the court of examination; they found him guilty; they brought his punishment upon him.

Wives of the people of the harem-gate, who united with the men, when the things were discussed; who were placed before the nobles of the court of examination; they found them guilty; they brought their punishment upon them: six women.

The great criminal, Pere, son of Ruma, formerly overseer of the White House.

He was brought in because of his collusion with the great criminal, Penhuibin, making common cause with him to stir up enemies to hostility against their lord. He was placed before the nobles of the court of examination; they found him guilty; they brought his punishment upon him.

The great criminal, Binemwese, formerly captain of archers in Nubia.

He was brought in because of the letter, which his sister, who was in the harem, had written to him, saying: "Incite the people to hostility! And come thou to begin hostility against thy lord." He was placed before Kedendenna, Maharbaal, Pirsun, and Thutrekhnefer; they examined him; they found him guilty; they brought his punishment upon him.

The Condemned of the Second Prosecution

Persons brought in because of their crimes and because of their collusion with Pebekkamen, Peyes, and Pentewere. They were placed before the nobles of the court of examination in order to examine them; they found them guilty; they left them in their own hands in the court of examination; they took their own lives; and no punishment was executed upon them.

The great criminal, Peyes, formerly commander of the army.

The great criminal, Messui, formerly scribe of the house of sacred writings.

The great criminal, Perekamenef, formerly chief.

The great criminal, Iroi, formerly overseer of the — of Sekhmet.

The great criminal, Nebzefai, formerly butler.

The great criminal, Shedmeszer, formerly scribe of the house of sacred writings.

Total, 6.

The Condemned of the Third Prosecution

Persons who were brought in, because of their crimes, to the court of examination, before Kedendenna, Maharbaal, Pirsun, Thutrekhnefer, and Mertusamon. They examined them concerning their crimes; they found them guilty; they left them in their place; they took their own lives.

Pentewere, who bore that other name.

He was brought in because of his collusion [with] Tiy, his mother, when she discussed the words with the women of the harem, being hostile against his lord. He was placed before the butlers, in order to examine him; they found him guilty; they left him in his place; he took his own life.

The great criminal, Henutenamon, formerly butler.

He was brought in because of the crimes of the women of the harem; having been among them and having heard (them), without reporting them. He was placed before the butlers, in order to examine him; they found him guilty; they left him in his place; he took his own life.

The great criminal, Amenkha, formerly deputy of the harem.

He was brought in because of the crimes of the women of

the harem; having been among them, and having heard (them), without reporting them. He was placed before the butlers, in order to examine him; they found him guilty; they left him in his place; he took his own life.

The great criminal, Pere, formerly scribe of the king's harem.

He was brought in because of the crimes of the women of the harem; having been among them, and having heard (them), without reporting them. He was placed before the butlers, in order to examine him; they found him guilty; they left him in his place; he took his own life.

The Condemned of the Fourth Prosecution

Persons upon whom punishment was executed by cutting off their noses and their ears, because of their forsaking the good testimony delivered to them. The women had gone; had arrived at their place of abode, and had there caroused with them and with Peyes. Their crime seized them.

This great criminal, Pebes, formerly butler. This punishment was executed upon him; he was left (alone); he took his own life.

The great criminal, Mai, formerly scribe of the archives.

The great criminal, Teynakhte, formerly officer of infantry.

The great criminal, Oneney, formerly captain of police.

The Acquitted

Person who had been connected with them; they had contended with him, with evil and violent words; he was dismissed; punishment was not executed upon him:

The great criminal, Hori, who was standard-bearer of the infantry.

PRAYER TO THOT FOR SKILL IN WRITING, c. 1150 BC

Anonymous

Come to me, Thot, O noble Ibis, O god who longs for Khmun, O dispatch-writer of the Ennead, the great one of Unu. Come to me that you may give advice and make me skilful in your office. Better is your profession than all professions. It makes (men) great. He who is skilled in it is found (fit) to exercise (the office of) magistrate. I have seen many for whom you have acted, and they are in the Council of the Thirty, they being strong and powerful through what you have done. You are the one who has given advice. You are the one who has given advice to the motherless man. Shay and Renenwetet are with you. Come to me that you may advise me. I am the servant of your house. Let me relate your prowess in whatever land I am. Then the multitude of men shall say: How great are the things that Thot has done. Then they shall come with their children to brand them with your profession, a calling good to the lord of victory. Joyful is the one who has exercised it.

PRAYER TO AMUN IN A YEAR OF NEED, c. 1150 BC

Anonymous

Come to me, Amun, save me in a year of need. The sun comes, but it does not rise. Winter is come in summer, the months come turned backward, and the hours are in disarray. The great ones call out to you, Amun, and the young seek you out. Those who are in the arms of their nurses [say]: Give breath, Amun. Perhaps Amun will come in peace, the sweet breeze before him. May he cause me to become the wing of a vulture, like an equipped *mesti*-boat, so say the herdsmen in the field, the washermen on the river-bank, the Madjoy who come from the district, and the gazelles on the desert.

THE ROBBING OF THE TOMB OF SOBEKEMSAF II, c. 1110 BC

Amenpanufer

The weakening of pharaonic authority and the Egyptian economy at the end of the 20th Dynasty prompted a wave of temple and tomb robberies at the royal necropolis at Thebes. Prominent among the robbers were those actually expected to build and guard the tombs, the workmen of the Deir el-Medina village. The stonemason Amenpanufer was one such worker turned tomb-thief. Called before a court, he admits to stealing from the tomb of the 17th Dynasty pharaoh Sobekemsaf II.

We went to rob the tombs as is our usual habit, and we found the pyramid tomb of King Sobekemsaf, this tomb being unlike the pyramids and tombs of the nobles which we usually rob. We took our copper tools and forced a way into the pyramid of this king through its innermost part. We located the underground chambers and, taking lighted candles in our hands, went down . . . [We] found the god lying at the back of his burial place. And we found the burial place of Queen Nubkhaas, his consort, beside him, it being protected and guarded by plaster and covered with rubble . . . We opened their sarcophagi and their coffins, and found the noble mummy of the king equipped with a sword. There were a large number of amulets and jewels of gold on his neck, and he wore a headpiece of gold. The noble mummy of the king was completely covered in gold and his coffins were decorated with gold and with silver inside and out, and inlaid with various precious stones. We collected the gold that we found on the mummy of the god including the amulets and jewels which were on his neck . . . We set fire to their coffins . . .

After some days the district officers of Thebes heard that we had been robbing in the west, and they arrested me and imprisoned me in the office of the mayor of Thebes. I took the twenty *deben* of gold that represented my share and I gave them to Khaemope, the district scribe of the landing quay of Thebes. He released me and I rejoined my colleagues and they compensated me with a share again. And so I got into the habit of robbing the tombs.

TOMB ROBBERS' CONFESSIONS, c. 1108 BC

The Court Recorder

As detailed in the Mayer Papyri.

Year 1, of Uhem-mesut, fourth month of the third season, day 15. On this day occurred the examination of the thieves of the tomb of King Usermare-Setepnere (Ramses II), L. P. H., the great god; and the tomb of King Menmare, L. P. H., Seti (I), L. P. H., which are recorded in the treasury of "The-House-of-King-Usermare-Meriamon (Ramses III),-L.-P.-H.", concerning whom the chief of police, Nesuamon, had reported, in this roll of names; for he was there, standing with the thieves, when they laid their hands upon the tombs; who were tortured at the examination on their feet and their hands, to make them tell the way they had done exactly.

Composition of the Court
By the governor of the city and vizier, Nibmarenakht;
 Overseer of the White House and overseer of the granary, Menmarenakht;

Steward and king's-butler, Ini, the herald of Pharaoh, L. P. H.;

Steward of the court, king's-butler, Pemeriamon, the scribe of Pharaoh.

Testimony of the Prisoner, Paykamen

Examination. The X,* Paykamen, under charge of the overseer of the cattle of Amon, was brought in; the oath of the king, L. P. H., was administered to him, not to tell a lie. He was asked: "What was the manner of thy going with the people who were with thee, when ye robbed the tombs of the kings which are recorded in the treasury of "The-House-of-King-Usermare-Meriamon,-L.-P.-H.?" He said: "I went with the priest Teshere, son of the divine father, Zedi, of 'The House'; Beki, son of Nesuamon, of this house; the X, Nesumontu of the house of Montu, lord of Erment; the X, Paynehsi of the vizier, formerly prophet of Sebek of Peronekh; Teti—who belonged to Paynehsi, of the vizier, formerly prophet of Sebek of Peronekh; in all six."

Testimony of the Chief of Police

The chief of police, Nesuamon, was brought in. He was asked: "How didst thou find these men?" He said: "I heard that these men had gone to rob this tomb. I went and found these six men. That which the thief, Paykamen, has said is correct. I took testimony from them on that day . . . The examination of the watchman of the house of Amon, the thief, Paykamen, under charge of the overseer of the cattle of Amon, was held by beating with a rod, the bastinade was applied to his feet. An oath was administered to him that he

---

* This is a title common among the people of the necropolis, and often occurring in these prosecutions. We have no hint as to its meaning, and I indicate it by X. [James Henry Breasted]

might be executed if he told a lie; he said: 'That which I did is exactly what I have said.' He confirmed it with his mouth, saying: 'As for me, that which I did is what [they] did; I was w[ith the]se six men, I stole a piece of copper therefrom, and I took possession of it.' "

Testimony of the Prisoner, Nesumontu

The X, the thief, Nesumontu, was brought in; the examination was held by beating with a rod; the bastinade was applied on (his) feet and his hand(s); the oath of the king, L. P. H., was administered to him, that he might be executed if he told a lie. He was asked: "What was the manner of thy going to rob in the tomb with thy companions?" He said: "I went and found these people; I was the sixth. I stole a piece of copper therefrom, I took possession of it."

Testimony of Karu

The watchman of the house of Amon, the X, Karu, was brought in; he was examined with the rod, the bastinade was applied to his feet and his hands; the oath of the king, L. P. H., was administered to him, that he might be executed if he told a lie. He was asked: "What was the manner of thy going with the companions when ye robbed in the tomb?" He said: "The thief, the X, Pehenui, he made me take some grain. I seized a sack of grain, and when I began to go down, I heard the voice of the men who were in this storehouse. I put my eye to the passage, and I saw Paybek and Teshere, who were within. I called to him, saying, 'Come!' and he came out to me, having two pieces of copper in his hand. He gave them to me, and I gave to him 1½ measures of spelt to pay for them. I took one of them, and I gave the other to the X, Enefsu.

Testimony of Nesuamon

The priest, Nesuamon, son of Paybek, was brought in, because of his father. He was examined by beating with the rod. They said to him: "Tell the manner of thy father's going with the men who were with him." He said: "My father was truly there. I was (only) a little child, and I know not how he did it." On being (further) examined, he said: "I saw the workman, Ehatinofer, while he was in the place where the tomb is, with the watchman, Nofer, son of Merwer, and the artisan, —, in all three (men). They are the ones I saw distinctly. Indeed, gold was taken, and they are the ones whom I know." On being (further) examined with a rod, he said: "These three men are the ones I saw distinctly."

Testimony of Wenpehti

The weaver of "The House", Wenpehti, son of—, was brought in. He was examined by beating with a rod, the bastinade was applied to his feet and his hands. The oath of the king, L. P. H., was administered, not to tell a lie. They said to him: "Tell what was the manner of thy father's going, when he committed theft in the tomb with his companions." He said: "My father was killed when I was a child. My mother told me: 'The chief of police, Nesuamon, gave some chisels of copper to thy father; then the captains of the archers and the X slew thy father.' They held the examination, and Nesuamon took the copper and gave it to me. It remains in the possession of my mother."

Testimony of Enroy

A Theban woman, Enroy, the mistress of the priest, Te-shere, son of Zedi, was brought in. She was examined by beating with a rod; the bastinade was applied to her feet and her hands. The oath of the king, L. P. H., not to tell a lie, was administered to her; she was asked: "What was the manner of thy husband's going when he broke into the tomb and carried away the copper from it?" She said: "He carried away some copper belonging to this tomb; we sold it and devoured it."

AN EGYPTIAN ABROAD: THE REPORT OF WENAMON c. 1093 BC

Wenamon

The author was sent by Ramses XI to Byblos to secure cedars for the barque of Amun (Amon) at Thebes. His subsequent report, preserved in a papyrus in Moscow, shows how low Egypt's standing had fallen in the Near East: despite being an official representative of the pharaoh, Wenamon is forced to pay Byblos for the wood. He is even robbed en route.

Year five, third month of the third season (eleventh month), day 16, day of the departure of the "eldest of the hall", of the house of Amon, the lord of the lands, Wenamon, to bring the timber for the great and august barge of Amon-Re, king of gods, which is on the river (called): "Userhet" of Amon.

On the day of my arrival at Tanis, at the place of abode of Nesubenebded and Tentamon, I gave to them the writings of Amon-Re, king of gods, which they caused to be read in their presence; and they said: "I will do (it), I will do it according to that which Amon-Re, king of gods, our lord, saith." I abode until the fourth month of the third season, being in Tanis.

Nesubenebded and Tentamon sent me with the ship-captain, Mengebet, and I descended into the great Syrian sea, in the fourth month of the third season, on the first day.

I arrived at Dor, a city of Thekel, and Bedel, its king, caused to be brought for me much bread, a jar of wine, and a joint of beef.

Then a man of my ship fled, having stolen:

vessels of gold, amounting to	5 deben
4 vessels of silver, amounting to	20 deben
A sack of silver	11 deben
Total of what he stole	5 deben of gold
	31 deben of silver

In the morning then I rose and went to the abode of the prince, and I said to him: "I have been robbed in thy harbour. Since thou art the king of this land, thou art therefore its investigator, who should search for my money. For the money belongs to Amon-Re, king of gods, the lord of the lands; it belongs to Nesubenebded, and it belongs to Hrihor, my lord, and the other magnates of Egypt; it belongs also to Weret, and to Mekmel, and to Zakar-Baal, the prince of Byblos." He said to me: "To thy honour and thy excellence! but, behold, I know nothing of this complaint which thou hast lodged with me. If the thief belonged to my land, he who went on board thy ship, that he might steal thy treasure, I would repay it to thee from my treasury till they find thy thief by name; but the thief who robbed thee belongs to thy ship. Tarry a few days here with me, and I will seek him." When I had spent nine days, moored in his harbour, I went to him, and said to him: "Behold, thou hast not found my money, therefore let me depart with the ship-captain, and with those who go to sea." He said to me, "Be silent."

[Wenamon then leaves impatiently for Tyre]

I went forth from Tyre at early dawn . . . I found 30 deben of silver [in the freighter in which Wenamon was travelling]. I seized it, saying to them: "I will take your money, and it shall remain with me until ye find my money. Was it not a man of Thekel who stole it? I will take [confiscate] this . . ." They went away.

I arrived in the harbour of Byblos. I made a place of concealment. I hid "Amon-of-the-way", and I placed his things in it.

The prince of Byblos sent to me, saying: "Betake thyself from my harbour." I sent to him, saying: ". . . if they sail, let them take me to Egypt." I spent nineteen days in his [harbour] and he continually sent to me daily, saying: "Betake thyself away from my harbour."

Now, when he sacrificed to his gods, the god seized one of his noble youths, making him frenzied, so that he said: "Bring the god hither! Bring the messenger of Amon who hath him.

"Send him, and let him go."

Now, while the frenzied (youth) continued in frenzy during this night, I found a ship bound for Egypt, and I loaded in all my belongings into it. I waited for the darkness, saying: "When it descends I will embark the god also, in order that no other eye may see him."

The harbour-master came to me, saying: "Remain until morning by the prince." I said to him: "Art not thou he who continually came to me daily, saying: 'Betake thyself away from my harbour'? Dost thou not say, 'Remain in the land' in order to let depart the ship that I have found? that thou mayest come and say again, 'Away!'?" He went and told it to the prince, and the prince sent to the captain of the ship, saying: "Remain until morning by the king."

When morning came he sent and had me brought up, when the divine offering occurred in the fortress wherein he was, on the shore of the sea. I found him sitting in his upper chamber, leaning his back against a window, while the waves of the great Syrian sea beat behind him. I said to him: "Kindness of Amon!" He said to me: "How long is it until this day since thou camest (away) from the abode of Amon?" I said: "Five months and one day until now."

He said to me: "Behold, if thou art true, where is the writing of Amon, which is in thy hand? Where is the letter of the High Priest of Amon, which is in thy hand?" I said to him: "I gave them to Nesubenebded and Tentamon." Then he was very wroth, and he said to me: "Now, behold, the writing and the letter are not in thy hand! Where is the ship of cedar, which Nesubenebded gave to thee? Where is its Syrian crew? He would not deliver thy business to this ship-captain to have thee killed, that they might cast thee into the sea. From whom would they have sought the god then? And thee, from whom would they have sought thee then?" So spake he to me. I said to him: "There are indeed Egyptian ships and Egyptian crews who sail under Nesu-benebded, (but) he hath no Syrian crews." He said to me: "There are surely twenty ships here in my harbour, which are in connection with Nesubenebded; and at this Sidon, whither thou also wouldst go, there are indeed 10,000 ships also which are in connection with Berket-el and sail to his house."

Then I was silent in this great hour. He answered and said to me: "On what business hast thou come hither?" I said to him: "I have come after the timber for the great and august barge of Amon-Re, king of gods. Thy father did it, thy grandfather did it, and thou wilt also do it." So spake I to him.

He said to me: "They did it, truly. If thou give me (something) for doing it, I will do it. Indeed, my agents transacted the business; the Pharaoh, L. P. H., sent six ships, laden with the products of Egypt, and they were unloaded into their storehouses. And thou also shalt bring something for me." He had the journal of his fathers brought in, and he had them read it before me. They found 1,000 deben of every (kind of) silver, which was in his book.

He said to me: "If the ruler of Egypt were the owner of my property, and I were also his servant, he would not send silver and gold, saying: 'Do the command of Amon.' It was not the payment of tribute which they exacted of my father. As for me, I am myself neither thy servant nor am I the servant of him that sent thee. If I cry out to the Lebanon, the heavens open, and the logs lie here on the shore of the sea.

"Give me the sails which thou hast brought to propel thy ships which bear thy logs to Egypt. Give me the cordage which thou hast brought to bind the trees which I fell, in order to make them fast for thee. I make them for thee into the sails of thy ships, and the tops are (too) heavy and they break, and thou die in the midst of the sea when Amon thunders in heaven, and puts Sutekh in his time.

"For Amon equips all lands; he equips them, having first equipped the land of Egypt, whence thou comest. For artisanship came forth from it, to reach my place of abode; and teaching came forth from it, to reach my place of abode. What (then) are these miserable journeys which they have had thee make?"

I said to him: "O guilty one! They are no miserable journeys on which I am. There is no ship upon the river, which Amon does not own. For his is the sea, and his is

Lebanon of which thou sayest, 'It is mine.' It grows for 'Userhet' (the barge) of Amon, the lord of every ship. Yea, so spake Amon-Re, king of gods, saying to Hrihor, my lord: 'Send me', and he made me go, bearing this great god. But, behold, thou hast let this great god wait twenty-nine days, when he had landed [in] thy harbour, although thou didst certainly know he was here. He is indeed (still) what he (once) was, while thou standest and bargainest for the Lebanon with Amon, its lord. As for what thou sayest, that the former kings sent silver and gold, if they had given life and health, they would not have sent the valuables; (but) they sent the valuables to thy fathers instead of life and health. Now, as for Amon-Re, king of gods, he is the lord of life and health, and he was the lord of thy fathers, who spent their lifetime offering to Amon. And thou also, thou art the servant of Amon. If thou sayest to Amon, 'I will do (it), I will do (it)', and thou executest his command, thou shalt live, and thou shalt be prosperous, and thou shalt be healthy, and thou shalt be pleasant to thy whole land and thy people. Wish not for thyself a thing belonging to Amon-Re, [king of] gods. Yea, the lion loves his own.

"Let my scribe be brought to me, that I may send him to Nesubenebded and Tentamon, the rulers whom Amon hath given to the North of his land, and they will send all that of which I shall write to them, saying: 'Let it be brought', until I return to the South and send thee all, all thy trifles again." So spake I to him.

He gave my letter into the hand of his messenger. He loaded in the keel, the head of the bow and the head of the stern, with four other hewn timbers, together seven; and he had them taken to Egypt. His messenger went to Egypt, and returned to me, to Syria in the first month of the second season. Nesubenebded and Tentamon sent:

Gold: 4 jars, 1 *kakmen*-vessel
Silver: 5 jars
Royal linen: 10 garments, ten veils of thin cloth
Papyrus: 500 rolls
Ox-hides: 500
Rope: 500 coils
Lentils: 20 measures
Fish: 30 measures
She sent me [personally]:
Linen: 5 garments, 5 veils of thin cloth
Lentils: 1 measure
Fish: 5 measures

The prince rejoiced, and detailed 300 men and 300 oxen, placing overseers over them, to have the trees felled. They spent the second season therewith. In the third month of the second season (seventh month) they dragged them [to] the shore of the sea. The prince came forth and stood by them.

He sent to me, saying: "Come." Now, when I had presented myself before him, the shadow of his sunshade fell upon me. Penamon, a butler, he stepped between me, saying: "The shadow of Pharaoh, L. P. H., thy lord, falls upon thee." He was angry with him, saying: "Let him alone!" I presented myself before him, and he answered and said to me: "Behold, the command which my fathers formerly executed, I have executed, although thou for thy part hast not done for me that which thy fathers did for me. Behold, there has arrived the last of thy timber, and there it lies. Do according to my desire and come to load it, for they will indeed give it to thee.

"Come not to contemplate the terror of the sea, (but) if thou dost contemplate the terror of the sea, thou shalt (also) contemplate my own. Indeed, I have not done to thee that which they did to the messengers of Khamwese, when they spent seventeen years in this land. They died in their place." He said to his butler: "Take him, and let him see their tomb, wherein they sleep."

I said to him: "Let me not see it! As for Khamwese, (mere) people were the messengers whom he sent to thee; but there was no [god among] his messengers. And yet thou sayest, 'Go and see thy companions.' Lo, art thou not glad? and dost thou not have made for thee a tablet, whereon thou sayest: 'Amon-Re, king of gods, sent to me "Amon-of-the-Way", his [divine] messenger, and Wenamon, his human messenger, after the timber for the great and august barge of Amon-Re, king of gods? I felled it, I loaded it, I supplied him (with) my ships and my crews, I brought them to Egypt, to beseech for me 10,000 years of life from Amon, more than my ordained (life), and it came to pass.' Then in future days when a messenger comes from the land of Egypt, who is able to write, and reads thy name upon the stela, thou shalt receive water in the West, like the gods who are "there". He said to me: "It is a great testimony which thou tellest me."

I said to him: "As for the many things which thou hast said to me, when I reach the place of abode of the High Priest of Amon, and he shall see thy command in thy command, [he] will have something delivered to thee."

I went to the shore of the sea, to the place where the timbers lay; I spied eleven ships coming from the sea, belonging to the Thekel, saying: "Arrest him! Let not a ship of his (pass) to Egypt!" I sat down and began to weep. The letter-scribe of the prince came out to me, and said to me: "What is the matter with thee?" I said to him: "Surely thou seest these birds which twice descend upon Egypt.

Behold them! They come to the pool, and how long shall I be here, forsaken? For thou seest surely those who come to arrest me again."

He went and told it to the prince. The prince began to weep at the evil words which they spoke to him. He sent out his letter-scribe to me, he brought me two jars of wine and a ram. He sent to me Tentno, an Egyptian singer (feminine), who was with him, saying: "Sing for him; let not his heart feel apprehension." He sent to me, saying: "Eat, drink, and let not thy heart feel apprehension. Thou shalt hear all that I have to say in the morning."

Morning came, he had (the Thekel) called into his —, he stood in their midst and said to the Thekel: "Why have ye come?" They said to him: "We have come after the stove-up ships which thou sendest to Egypt with our comrades." He said to them: "I cannot arrest the messenger of Amon in my land. Let me send him away, and ye shall pursue him, to arrest him."

He loaded me on board, he sent me away – to the harbour of the sea. The wind drove me to the land of Alasa; those of the city came forth to me to slay me. I was brought among them to the abode of Heteb, the queen of the city. I found her as she was going forth from one of her houses and entering into her other. I saluted her, I asked the people who stood about her: "There is surely one among you who understands Egyptian?" One among them said: "I understand (it)." I said to him: "Say to my mistress: 'I have heard as far as Thebes, the abode of Amon, that in every city injustice is done, but that justice is done in the land of Alasa; (but), lo, injustice is done every day here.'" She said: "Indeed! What is this that thou sayest?" I said to her: "If the sea raged and the wind drove me to the land where I am, thou wilt not let them

take advantage of me to slay me; I being a messenger of
Amon. I am one for whom they will seek unceasingly. As
for the crew of the prince of Byblos whom they sought to
kill, their lord will surely find 'ten crews of thine, and he
will slay them, on his part.' She had the people called and
stationed (before her); she said to me: "Pass the night —."

The remainder of the report is lost.

PART FOUR

Decline

*The Third Intermediate Period,
the Late Period and the
Ptolemaic Period, Egypt, 1069–30 BC*

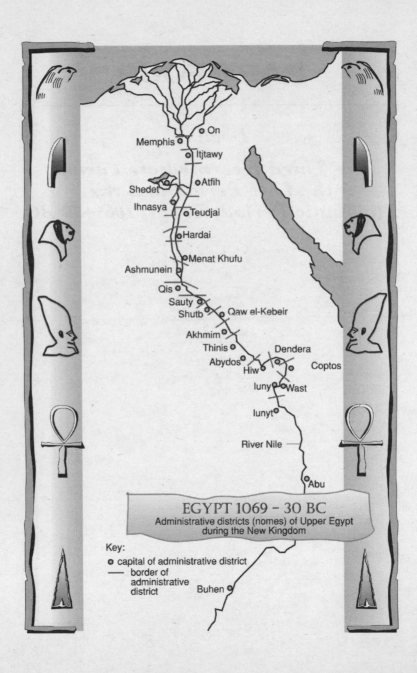

On
Memphis
Itjtawy
Atfih
Shedet
Ihnasya
Teudjai
Hardai
Menat Khufu
Ashmunein
Qis
Sauty
Shutb
Qaw el-Kebeir
Akhmim
Thinis
Dendera
Abydos
Hiw
Coptos
Iuny
Wast
Iunyt
River Nile
Abu

EGYPT 1069 – 30 BC
Administrative districts (nomes) of Upper Egypt
during the New Kingdom

Key:
○ capital of administrative district
— border of
administrative
district

Buhen

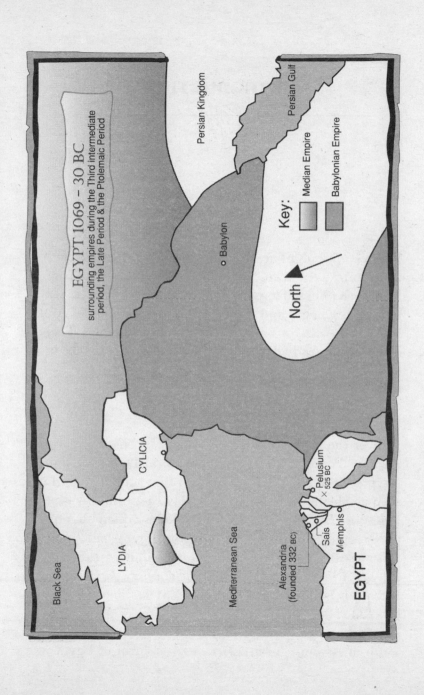

EGYPT 1069 – 30 BC
surrounding empires during the Third intermediate period, the Late Period & the Ptolemaic Period

Key:
Median Empire
Babylonian Empire

North

Black Sea

Mediterranean Sea

LYDIA

CYLICIA

Persian Kingdom

Babylon

Persian Gulf

Alexandria
(founded 332 BC)

Sais

Memphis

Pelusium
× 525 BC

EGYPT

INTRODUCTION

When Ramses XI "departed for the west", the Golden Age of Empire went with him. The country was bankrupt – Ramses XI himself had resorted to robbing ancestral tombs to keep it going – and the bumptious priesthood of Amun had set themselves up as *de facto* kingly rulers at Thebes. They certainly had the wherewithal to do so, for they owned two thirds of the land of Egypt. In the Delta, meanwhile, the 21st Dynasty announced itself as the official succession to Ramses XI. Once again, Egypt divided into Upper and Lower.

Over the next five hundred years of "The Third Intermediate Period", a series of ephemeral Dynasties stalked Egypt, one or two rulers of which grasped at old-style glory, such as Sheshonq I who led a highly successful invasion of Palestine (he is the Shisak of the Bible). Yet Sheshonq was also a signal illustration of how low Egypt had sunk; he wasn't really an Egyptian for all his hallowed titles, but a Libyan invader who had seized the country. No longer was Egypt an isolated Land of Lotus Eaters. The neighbours developed an unpleasant habit of breaking in. Ignominiously enough, these included the despised Nubians from south of Aswan who in 727 BC took control of Egypt and founded the 25th Dynasty. Alas for the Nubians, success went to their collective head and they proceeded to engage the fearsome Assyrian army in Palestine. Ashurbanipal retaliated by striking into Egypt, executing much of the nobility and even sacking Thebes, jewel of the Ancient World. Under Assyrian lordship, the 26th Dynasty however, whose capital was at Sais, brought a revival of sorts in art and commerce in Egypt, and when Assyria itself became preoccupied with internal strife the Saites stopped paying tribute to Nineveh. The Saites were efficient and even forward-thinking rulers (particularly in the realm of mercantilism, where they pursued trade links across the Mediterranean) but they were no match for the Persians when they appeared at Pelesium, the eastern portal to Egypt, in 525 BC.

Thus it was that Pharaoh Psmatik III fled and Cambysses walked in, won one quick battle, took charge. And then left. The Persian kings were not exactly smitten with Egypt; they were uniformly absentee overlords who left "satraps" in charge. Slighted by their provincial status, the Egyptians revolted in 405 BC and not until 343 BC did the Persians retake the country, forcing the latest self-proclaimed Egyptian pharaoh, Nakhthoreb (Nectanebo II), to flee to Nubia. As it would turn out, Nakhthoreb was the last Egyptian to rule Egypt for more than 2,000 years.

This second period of Persian rule was brief, lasting only until 332 BC when Alexander the Great invaded Egypt, seizing the land of the Nile for his Macedonian empire. After being crowned pharaoh, Alexander endeared himself to his new subjects by founding a city at the mouth of the Nile (Alexandria) and ordering the restoration of temples destroyed by the Persians. However, Alexander's life was cut short by illness in 323 BC and a cloudy succession condemned the Macedonian empire to be plucked apart by his generals. Egypt was obtained by Ptolemy I. Almost inevitably, like all previous incomer rulers, he sought legitimacy to his reign by according himself the title of pharaoh.

And the ensuing Ptolemaic dynasty began with panache; Ptolemy I commissioned the Pharos lighthouse, one of the Seven Wonders of the Ancient World, the Library at Alexandria and a spate of imposing temples. His immediate successors achieved a notable degree of prosperity, stability and territory. The rot began with Ptolemy IV (Philopator), who interrupted his indolence only to poison his mother and scald his brother to death. Internecine bickering and gargantuan dissolution (Ptolemy X was so fat he could not walk unaided) plagued the dynasty for the rest of its span. The belated attempt by the politicking Cleopatra to revive Ptolemaic power with Roman help was cursed by her bad luck in her choice of Latin lovers. Her affair with Julius Caesar – which bore a son, Ptolemy XV Caesarion – was terminated by his assassination. She then consorted with Mark Antony, one of the triumvirate who ruled Rome on Caesar's death. Unfortunately for Cleopatra, Antony's guile, power-base and ambition did not match that of his fellow triumvir Octavian, who declared war on Egypt and defeated Antony and Cleopatra at the naval battle of Actium in 31 BC. Misled by a false report of Cleopatra's death, Antony fell on his sword. When Octavian proved immune to her charms, Cleopatra took her own life by, legendarily, clasping an asp to her breast.

With Cleopatra died the last of Egyptian independence. The land of the pharaohs was unceremoniously annexed by the land of the emperors as its private granary.

DISASTER AT THEBES: THE CANAL WALL COLLAPSES, c. 1060 BC

Anonymous

Inscribed on a pillar in the quarry at Gebelen, where pharaoh Smendes of the 21st Dynasty sent his workmen for stone for rebuilding after the catastrophe narrated below.

Lo, his majesty sat, in the hall of his palace, when there came messengers, informing his majesty, that the canal-wall, forming the limits of Luxor, which King Menkhe-perre (Tuthmosis III) had built, had begun to fall to ruin— forming a great flood, and a powerful current therein, on the great pavement of the house of the temple. It encircled the front —. Said his majesty to them: "As for this matter reported to me, there has been nothing in the time of my majesty from of old, like it . . ."

His majesty dispatched master-builders and 3,000 men with them, of the choicest people of his majesty. The command of his majesty to them: "Hasten to . . . this quarry, from the time of the ancestors to the present day, Gebelen."

They engraved this decree, which perpetuates his majesty forever . . . His command arrived to beautify the work on the stele . . . never was done the like of it in the time of the ancestors.

FLOODS IN THEBES, c. 871 BC

Anonymous

An inscription from the hypostyle of the Luxor temple.

The flood came on, in this whole land; it invaded the two shores as in the beginning. This land was in his power like

the sea, there was no dyke of the people to withstand its
fury . . .

All the temples of Thebes were like marshes. On this day
Amon caused to appear in Opet, the [barque] of his
(portable) image —; when he had entered the "Great
House" of his barque of this temple.*

THE NUBIAN INVASION, 727 BC

Anonymous

*Nubia – the land of the Kush south of Aswan – secured independence from Egypt
during the 19th Dynasty to become the kingdom of Napata. Egyptian political
tutelage was easy to overthrow; religious ideas less so. Napata became a hotbed of
Amun-worship, with a massive temple to the god built at Gebel Barkal. When
Egypt fell into a squabble of competing kingdoms, the Nubians moved north not, as
they saw it, to conquer but restore the "old way" and the primacy of Amun. The
campaign of Piankhi against the coalition of northern kings under Tefnakhte is
enshrined on his "Victory Stele", a pink granite block nearly 6 feet long found in
1862 at Gebel Barkal.*

Announcement of Tefnakhte's Advance

One [messenger] came to say to his majesty: "A chief of the
west, the great prince in Neter, Tefnakhte . . . has seized
the whole west from the back-lands to Ithtowe, coming
southward with a numerous army, while the Two Lands
are united behind him, and the princes and rulers of walled
towns are as dogs at his heels. No stronghold has closed its
doors in the nomes of the South: Mer-Atum (Medûm), Per-
Sekhemkheperre, the temple of Sebek, Permezed, The-
knesh; and every city of the west; they have opened the

---

* Amon [Amun] was taken from the temple in his sacred barque, and the priests
prayed that he would end the flooding.

doors for fear of him. He turned to the east, they opened to him likewise: Hatbenu, Tozi, Hatseteni, Pernebtepih. Behold, he besieges Heracleopolis, he has completely invested it, not letting the comers-out come out, and not letting the goers-in go in, fighting every day. He measured it off in its whole circuit, every prince knows his wall; he stations every man of the princes and rulers of walled towns over his (respective) portion."

Piankhi's Indifference
Then his majesty heard the message with courageous heart, laughing, and joyous of heart.

Second Appeal of the North
These princes and commanders of the army who were in their cities sent to his majesty daily, saying: "Wilt thou be silent, even to forgetting the Southland, the nomes of the court? While Tefnakhte advances his conquest and finds none to repel his arm."

Submission of Hermopolis to Tefnakhte
"Namlot —, prince of Hatweret, he has overthrown the wall of Nefrus, he has demolished his own city, for fear of him who might take it from him, in order to besiege another city. Behold, he goes to follow at his (Tefnakhte's) heels, having cast off allegiance to his majesty (Piankhi). He tarries with him (Tefnakhte) like one of [his vassals in] the nome of Oxyrhyncus, and gives to him (Tefnakhte) gifts, as much as he desires, of everything that he has found."

Piankhi Commands the Capture of the Hare Nome
Then his majesty sent to the princes and commanders of the army who were in Egypt: the commander, Purem;

and the commander, Lemersekeny; and every commander of his majesty who was in Egypt (saying): "Hasten
into battle line, engage in battle, surround —, capture its
people, its cattle, its ships upon the river. Let not the
peasants go forth to the field, let not the ploughmen
plough, beset the frontier of the Hare nome, fight against
it daily." Then they did so.

Piankhi Sends His Army; His Instructions

Then his majesty sent an army to Egypt, charging them
earnestly: "Delay not day nor night, as at a game of
draughts; (but) fight ye on sight. Force battle upon him
from afar. If he says to the infantry and chariotry of another
city, 'Hasten'; (then) ye shall abide until his army comes,
that ye may fight as he says. But if his allies be in another
city, (then) let one hasten to them; these princes, whom he
has brought for his support: Libyans and favourite soldiers,
force battle upon them first. Say, 'We know not what he
cries in mustering troops. Yoke the war horses, the best of
thy stable; draw up the line of battle! Thou knowest that
Amon is the god who has sent us.'"

Instructions as to Thebes

"When ye arrive at Thebes, before Karnak, ye shall enter
into the water, ye shall bathe in the river, ye shall dress in
fine linen; unstring the bow, loosen the arrow. Let not the
chief boast as a mighty man; there is no strength to the
mighty without him (Amon). He maketh the weak-armed
into the strong-armed, so that multitudes flee from the
feeble, and one alone taketh a thousand men. Sprinkle
yourselves with the water of his altars, sniff the ground
before him. Say ye to him, 'Give to us the way, that we may
fight in the shadow of thy sword. (As for) the generation

whom thou hast sent out, when its attack occurs, multitudes flee before it.'"

Reply of the Army
Then they threw themselves upon their bellies before his majesty (saying): "It is thy name which endues us with might, and thy counsel is the mooring-post of thy army; thy bread is in our bellies on every march, thy beer quenches our thirst. It is thy valour that giveth us might, and there is strength at the remembrance of thy name; (for) no army prevails whose commander is a coward. Who is thy equal therein? Thou art a victorious king, achieving with his hands, chief of the work of war."

Advance to Thebes
They sailed down-stream, they arrived at Thebes, they did according to all that his majesty had said.

Battle on the River
They sailed down-stream upon the river; they found many ships coming up-stream bearing soldiers, sailors, and commanders; every valiant man of the Northland, equipped with weapons of war, to fight against the army of his majesty. Then there was made a great slaughter among them, (whose) number was unknown. Their troops and their ships were captured, and brought as living captives to the place where his majesty was.

Arrival at Heracleopolis
They went to the frontier of Heracleopolis, demanding battle.

List of the Northern Enemy

List of the princes and kings of the Northland, namely:
King Namlot and

   King Yewept

   Chief of Me, Sheshonk, of Per-Osiris (Busiris), lord of
Ded.

   Great chief of Me, Zeamonefonekh, of Per-Benebded
(Mendes), together with

   His eldest son, who was commander of the army of Per-
Thutuprehui.

   The army of the hereditary prince, Beknenef, together
with

   His eldest son, chief of Me, Nesnekedi in the nome of
Hesebka.

   Every chief wearing a feather who was in the Northland;
together with

   King Osorkon, who was in Per-Bast (Bubastis) and the
district of Ranofer.

   Every prince, the rulers of the walled towns in the West,
in the East, (and) the islands in the midst, were united of
one mind as followers of the great chief of the West, ruler of
the walled towns of the Northland, prophet of Neit, mistress of Sais, sem priest of Ptah, Tefnakhte.

Battle Opposite Heracleopolis

They went forth against them; then they made a great
slaughter among them, greater than anything. Their ships
were captured upon the river. The remnant crossed over
and landed on the west side before Per-Peg.

Battle at Per-Peg

When the land brightened early in the morning, the army
of his majesty crossed over against them. Army mingled

with army; they slew a multitude of people among them; horses of unknown number; a rout ensued among the remnant. They fled to the North-land, from the blow, great and evil beyond everything.

List of the slaughter made among them:

People: — men.

Hermopolis Besieged

King Namlot fled up-stream southward, when it was told him: "Hermopolis is in the midst of the foe from the army of his majesty, who capture its people and its cattle." Then he entered into Hermopolis, while the army of his majesty was upon the river, in the harbour of the Hare nome. Then they heard of it, and they surrounded the Hare nome on its four sides, not letting the comers-out come out, and not letting the goers-in go in.

Report to Piankhi

They sent to report to the majesty of the King of Upper and Lower Egypt, Meriamon-Piankhi, given life, on every conflict which they had fought, and on every victory of his majesty.

Piankhi Determines to go to Egypt Himself

Then his majesty was enraged thereat like a panther (saying): "Have they allowed a remnant of the army of the Northland to remain? Allowing him that went forth of them to go forth, to tell of his campaign? Not causing their death, in order to destroy the last of them? I swear: as Re loves me! As my father Amon favours me! I will myself go northward, that I may destroy that which he has done, that I may make him turn back from fighting, forever."

Piankhi Would Visit Thebes

"Now, afterward when the ceremonies of the New Year are celebrated, I will offer to my father, Amon, at his beautiful feast, when he makes his beautiful appearance of the New Year, that he may send me forth in peace, to behold Amon at the beautiful Feast of Opet; that I may bring his image forth in procession to Luxor at his beautiful feast (called): "Night of the Feast of Opet", and at the feast (called): "Abiding in Thebes", which Re made for him in the beginning; and that I may bring him in procession to his house, resting upon his throne, on the "Day of Bringing in the God", in the third month of the first season, second day; that I may make the Northland taste the taste of my fingers."

Capture of Oxyrhyncus

Then the army, which was there in Egypt, heard of the wrath which his majesty felt towards them. Then they fought against Per-Mezed of the Oxyrhynchite nome, they took it like a flood of water, and they sent to his majesty; (but) his heart was not satisfied therewith.

Capture of Tetehen

Then they fought against Tetehen, great in might. They found it filled with soldiers, with every valiant man of the Northland. Then the battering-ram was employed against it, its wall was overthrown, and a great slaughter was made among them, of unknown number; also the son of the chief of Me, Tefnakhte. Then they sent to his majesty concerning it, (but) his heart was not satisfied therewith.

Capture of Hatbenu

Then they fought against Hatbenu, its interior was breached, the army of his majesty entered into it. Then they sent to his majesty, (but) his heart was not satisfied there-with.

Piankhi Goes to Hermopolis

First month of the first season, ninth day; his majesty went northward to Thebes, and completed the Feast of Amon at the Feast of Opet. His majesty sailed northward to the city of the Hare nome (Hermopolis); his majesty came forth from the cabin of the ship, the horses were yoked up, the chariot was mounted, the terror of his majesty reached to the end of the Asiatics, every heart was heavy with the fear of him.

Piankhi Rebukes His Army

Then his majesty went forth — to hate his soldiers, enraged at them like a panther (saying): "Is the steadfastness of your fighting this slackness in my affairs? Has the year reached its end, when the fear of me has been inspired in the Northland? A great and evil blow shall be smitten them."

Siege of Hermopolis

He set up for himself the camp on the southwest of Hermopolis, and besieged it daily. An embankment was made, to inclose the wall; a tower was raised to elevate the archers while shooting, and the slingers while slinging stones, and slaying people among them daily.

The City Pleads for Mercy

Days passed, and Hermopolis was foul to the nose, without her (usual) fragrance. Then Hermopolis threw herself upon her belly, and plead before the king. Messengers came forth and descended bearing everything beautiful to behold:

gold, every splendid costly stone, clothing in a chest, and the diadem which was upon his head, the uraeus which inspired the fear of him; without ceasing during many days, pleading with his diadem.

Namlot's Queen Intercedes
Then they sent his wife, the kings'-wife, and king's-daughter, Nestent, to plead with the king's-wives, king's-concubines, king's-daughters, and king's-sisters, to throw herself upon her belly in the harem, before the king's-wives (saying): "We come to you, O king's-wives, king's-daughters, and king's-sisters, that ye may appease Horus,* lord of the palace, whose fame is great and his triumph mighty . . ."

Piankhi Addresses Namlot
"Lo, who has led thee? who has led thee? Who, then, has led thee? Who has led thee? — thou didst forsake the way of life. Did heaven rain with arrows? I am content when the Southerners do obeisance and the Northerners (say): 'Put us in thy shadow.' Lo, it is evil — bearing his food. The heart is a steering-oar; it capsizes its owner through that which is from the god. It seeth flame as coolness in the heart —. There is no old man, —. Thy nomes are full of youths."

Namlot's Reply to Piankhi
He threw himself upon his belly before his majesty (saying): "[Be appeased], Horus, lord of the palace, it is thy might which has done it. I am one of the king's slaves, paying impost into the treasury — their impost. I have brought for thee more than they."

Namlot's Gifts

Then he presented much silver, gold, lapis lazuli, malachite, bronze, and all costly stones. Then he filled the treasury with this tribute; he brought a horse in the right hand and a sistrum in the left hand, of gold and lapis lazuli.

Piankhi's Triumphant Entry into Hermopolis

Then his [majesty] appeared in splendour in his palace, proceeded to the house of Thoth, lord of Hermopolis, and he slew bulls, calves, and fowl for his father, lord of Hermopolis, and the eight gods in the house of the eight gods. The army of the Hare nome acclaimed and rejoiced, saying: "How beautiful is Horus, resting in his city, the Son of Re, Piankhi! Celebrate for us a jubilee, even as thou hast protected the Hare nome."

Piankhi Visits Namlot's Palace

His majesty proceeded to the house of King Namlot, he entered every chamber of the king's-house, his treasury and his magazines. He caused that there be brought to him; the king's-wives and king's-daughters; they saluted his majesty in the fashion of women, (but) his majesty turned not his face to them.

Piankhi Visits Namlot's Stables

His majesty proceeded to the stable of the horses and the quarters of the foals. When he saw that they had suffered hunger, he said: "I swear, as Re loves me, and as my nostrils are rejuvenated with life, it is more grievous in my heart that my horses have suffered hunger, than any evil deed that thou hast done, in the prosecution of thy desire. It has borne witness of thee to me, the fear of thy associates for thee. Didst thou not know that the god's shadow is over

me? and that my fortune never perishes because of him?
Would that another had done it to me! I could not but
condemn him on account of it. When I was being fashioned
in the womb, and created in the divine egg, the seed of the
god was in me. By his *ka*, I do nothing without him; he it is
who commands me to do it."

Disposal of Namlot's Property
Then his possessions were assigned to the treasury, and his
granary to the divine offerings of Amon in Karnak.

Loyalty of Heracleopolis
The ruler of Heracleopolis Pefnefdibast came, bearing
tribute to the palace: gold, silver, every costly stone, and
horses of the choicest of the stable. He threw himself upon
his belly before his majesty; he said: "Hail to thee, Horus,
mighty king, Bull subduer of Bulls! The Nether World had
seized me, and I was submerged in darkness, upon which
the light has (now) shone. I found not a friend in the evil
day, who was steadfast in the day of battle; but thou, O
mighty king, thou hast expelled the darkness from me. I
will labour together with (thy) subjects, and Heracleopolis
shall pay taxes into thy treasury, thou likeness of Harakhte,
chief of the imperishable stars. As he was, so art thou king;
as he perishes not so thou shalt not perish, O King of Upper
and Lower Egypt, Piankhi, living forever.

Per-Sekhemkheperre is Summoned to Surrender
His majesty sailed north to the opening of the canal beside
Illahun; he found Per-Sekhemkhperre with its wall raised,
and its stronghold closed, filled with every valiant man of
the Northland. Then his majesty sent to them, saying: "Ye
living in death! Ye living in death! Ye insignificant — and

miserable ones! Ye living in death! If an hour passes without opening to me, behold, ye are of the number of the fallen; and that is painful to the king. Close not the gates of your life, to be brought to the block this day. Love not death, nor hate life — before the whole land."

Surrender of Per-Sekhemkheperre

Then they sent to his majesty, saying: "Lo, the shadow of the god is over thee; the son of Nut, he gives to thee his two arms; the thought of thy heart comes to pass immediately, like that which comes forth from the mouth of a god. Lo, thou art fashioned as the face of a god; we see by the decree of thy hands. Lo, thy city, his stronghold; do thy pleasure therewith. Let the goers-in go in there, and the comers-out come out. Let his majesty do what he will." Then they came out, with the son of the chief of Me, Tefnakhte. The army of his majesty entered into it, without slaying one of all the people. He found — and treasures to seal his possessions. His treasures were assigned to the Treasury, and his granaries to the divine offerings of his father, Amon-Re, lord of Thebes.

Surrender of Medûm

His majesty sailed northward; he found that Mer-Atum (Medûm), the house of Sokar, lord of Sehez, had been closed, and was inaccessible. It had set fighting in its heart, taking — Fear seized them; terror sealed their mouth. Then his majesty sent to them, saying: "Behold, two ways are before you; choose ye as ye will: open, and ye shall live; close, and ye shall die. My majesty will not pass by a closed city." Then they opened immediately; his majesty entered into this city, and offered — [to] Menhy of Sehez. His treasury was assigned [to the Treasury], his granaries to the divine offerings of Amon of Karnak.

Surrender of Ithtowe

His majesty sailed north to Ithtowe; he found the rampart closed, and the walls filled with the valiant troops of the Northland. Then they opened the stronghold, and threw themselves upon [their] bellies before his majesty (saying): "Thy father has assigned to thee his inheritance. Thine are the Two Lands, thine is what is therein, thine is all that is on earth." His majesty entered to cause a great oblation to be offered to the gods residing in this city, consisting of bulls, calves, fowl, and everything good and pure. Then his treasury was assigned to the Treasury, and his granaries to the divine offerings of Amon.

Piankhi Demands the Surrender of Memphis

His majesty sailed north to Memphis; then he sent to them, saying: "Shut not up, fight not, thou abode of Shu in the beginning. As for him that would go in, let him go in; as for him that would come out, let him come out; and let not them that would leave be hindered. I would offer an oblation to Ptah and to the gods dwelling in Memphis, I would sacrifice to Sokar in the mysterious place, I would behold 'Him-Who-is-South-of-His-Wall', that I may sail north in peace. The people of Memphis shall be safe and sound; not (even) a child shall weep. Look ye to the nomes of the South; not a single one has been slain therein, except the enemies who blasphemed against the god, who were dispatched as rebels."

Memphis Resists and Makes a Sortie

Then they closed their stronghold; they sent forth an army against some of the soldiers of his majesty, being artisans, chief builders and sailors — the harbour of Memphis.

Tefnakhte Enters Memphis

Lo, that chief of Sais (Tefnakhte) arrived at Memphis in the night, charging his infantry and his sailors, all the best of his army, a total of 8,000 men, charging them very earnestly: "Behold, Memphis is filled with troops of all the best of the Northland; (with) barley and spelt and all kinds of grain, the granaries are running over; (with) all weapons of war. It is fortified with a wall; a great battlement has been built, executed with skilful workmanship. The river flows around the east side, and no (opportunity of) attack is found there. Cattle yards are there, filled with oxen; the treasury is supplied with everything: silver, gold, copper, clothing, incense, honey, oil."

Tefnakhte Goes for Reinforcements

"I will go, and I will give something to the chiefs of the North, and I will open to them their nomes. I will be —. There will be but a few days until I return." He mounted upon a horse, he asked not for his chariot, he went north in fear of his majesty.

Plans for Taking Memphis

When day broke, at early morning, his majesty reached Memphis. When he had landed on the north of it, he found that the water had approached to the walls, the ships mooring at the walls of Memphis. Then his majesty saw that it was strong, and that the wall was raised by a new rampart, and battlements manned with mighty men. There was found no way of attacking it. Every man told his opinion among the army of his majesty, according to every rule of war. Every man said: "Let us besiege [it] —; lo, its troops are numerous." Others said: "Let a causeway be made against it; let us elevate the ground to its walls. Let

us bind together a tower; let us erect masts and make the
spars into a bridge to it. We will divide it on this (plan) on
every side of it, on the high ground and — on the north of
it, in order to elevate the ground at its walls, that we may
find a way for our feet."

Piankhi Decides to Assault

Then his majesty was enraged against it like a panther; he
said: "I swear, as Re loves me, as my father, Amon who
fashioned me, favours me, this shall befall it, according to
the command of Amon. This is what men say: 'The Northland and the nomes of the South, they opened to him from
afar, they did not set Amon in their heart, they knew not
what he commanded. He (Amon) made him (Piankhi) to
show forth his fame, to cause his might to be seen.' I will
take it like a flood of water. I have commanded —."

Harbour of Memphis Captured

Then he sent forth his fleet and his army to assault the
harbor of Memphis; they brought to him every ferry-boat,
every cargo-boat, every transport, and the ships, as many
as there were, which had moored in the harbour of Memphis, with the bow-rope fastened among its houses. There
was not a citizen who wept, among all the soldiers of his
majesty.

Piankhi Orders Assault of Memphis

His majesty himself came to line up the ships, as many as
there were. His majesty commanded his army (saying):
"Forward against it! Mount the walls! Penetrate the houses
over the river. If one of you gets through upon the wall, let
him not halt before it, so that the (hostile) troops may not
repulse you. It were vile that we should close up the South,

should land [in] the North and lay siege in 'Balances of the Two Lands'."

Capture of Memphis
Then Memphis was taken as (by) a flood of water, a multitude of people were slain therein, and brought as living captives to the place where his majesty was.

Protection of Memphis
Now, afterward, when it dawned, and the second day came, his majesty sent people into it, protecting the temples of the god. He — the holy of holies of the gods, offered to the community of gods of Hatkeptah (Memphis), cleansed Memphis with natron and incense, installed the priests in their places.

Piankhi's Recognition by Ptah
His majesty proceeded to the house of Ptah, his purification was performed in the Dewat-chamber, and every custom that is practised upon a king was fulfilled upon him. He entered into the temple, and a great oblation was made for his father, "Ptah-South-of-His-Wall", consisting of bulls, calves, fowl, and everything good. His majesty proceeded to his house.

Region of Memphis Surrenders
Then all the nomes which were in the district of Memphis, heard (of it): Herypedemy, Penineywe, the Tower of Beyew, the Oasis of Bit; they opened the strongholds, and fled away; none knew the place whither they had gone.

Submission of Delta Dynasts
King Yewepet came, and the chief of Me, Akenesh, and the hereditary prince, Pediese, together with all the princes of

the Northland, bearing their tribute to behold the beauty
of his majesty.

Wealth of Memphis Assigned

Then the treasuries and granaries of Memphis were assigned to the divine offerings of Amon, of Ptah, and of the
gods dwelling in Hatkeptah (Memphis).

Piankhi Worships in Khereha

When the land brightened, very early in the morning, his
majesty proceeded eastward, and an offering was made for
Atum in Khereha, the divine ennead in the house of the ennead,
the cavern and the gods dwelling in it; consisting of bulls, calves,
and fowl; that they might give life, prosperity, and health to the
King of Upper and Lower Egypt, Piankhi, living forever.

Piankhi Goes to Heliopolis

His majesty proceeded to Heliopolis, upon that mount of
Khereha, on the highway of (the god) Sep to Khereha. His
majesty proceeded to the camp, which was on the west of
Eti. His purification was performed, and he was cleansed in
the pool of Kebeh, and he bathed his face in the river of
Nun, in which Re bathes his face.

Ceremonies in Heliopolis: the "Sand-hill"

Proceeding to the Sand-hill in Heliopolis, a great oblation
was made upon the Sand-hill in Heliopolis, in the presence
of Re, at his rising, consisting of white oxen, milk, myrrh,
incense, and every sweet-smelling wood.

Temple of Re

He came proceeding to the house of Re, and entered into the
temple with great praise. The chief ritual priest praised the

god, that rebels might be repelled from the king. The Dewat-chamber was visited, that the sedeb-garment might be fastened on; he was purified with incense and libations; garlands for the pyramidion-house were presented to him, and flowers were brought to him. He ascended the steps to the great window, to behold Re in the pyramidion-house. The king himself stood alone, he broke through the bolts, opened the double doors, and beheld his father, Re, in the glorious pyramidion-house, the Morning-Barque of Re, and the Evening-Barque of Atum. He closed the double doors, applied the clay, and sealed (them) with the king's own seal. He charged the priests: "I have proved the seal; no other shall enter therein, of all the kings who shall arise." They threw themselves upon their bellies before his majesty, saying: "To abide, to endure, without perishing, O Horus, beloved of Heliopolis."

Temple of Atum
He came and entered into the house of Atum, following the image of his father, Atum-Khepri the Great, of Heliopolis.

Submission of Osorkon
King Osorkon came to see the beauty of his majesty.

Piankhi Camps near Athribis
When the land brightened, very early in the morning, his majesty proceeded to the harbour, and the best of his ships crossed over to the harbour of the nome of Athribis. The camp of his majesty was set up on the south of Keheni, on the east of the nome of Athribis.

Submission of Delta Dynasts
Then came those kings and princes of the Northland, all the chiefs who wore the feather, every vizier, all chiefs, and

every king's-confidant, from the west, from the east, and from the islands in the midst, to see the beauty of his majesty.

Piankhi is Invited to Athribis

The hereditary prince, Pediese, threw himself upon his belly before his majesty, and said: "Come to Athribis, that thou mayest see Khentikhet, that thou mayest worship Khuyet, that thou mayest offer an oblation to Horus in his house, consisting of: bulls, calves, and fowl; and that thou mayest enter my house. My treasury is open to thee, to — thyself with my paternal possessions. I will give to thee gold, as much as thou desirest; malachite shall be heaped up before thee; many horses of the best of the stable, and the first of the stall."

Piankhi in Athribis

His majesty proceeded to the house of Harkhentikhet, and there were offered bulls, calves, and fowl to his father, Harkhentikhet, lord of Kemwer. His majesty went to the house of the hereditary prince, Pediese; he (Pediese) presented to him silver, gold, lapis lazuli, and malachite, a great heap of everything; clothing of royal linen of every number; couches laid with fine linen; myrrh and ointment in jars; horses, both stallions and mares, of all the best of his stable.

Speech of Pediese of Athribis

He (Pediese) purified himself by a divine oath, before these kings and great chiefs of the Northland (saying): "Every one of them, if he conceals his horses and hides his obligation shall die the death of his father. So be it to me, till ye bear witness of the servant there, in all that ye know of me;

say ye, (whether) I have concealed (aught) from his majesty, of all the possessions of my father's house: [of] gold, silver; of costly stone; of all kinds of vessels, —; of golden bracelets, of necklaces, and collars wrought with costly stones; amulets for every limb, chaplets for the head, rings for the ears: all the adornments of a king; all the vessels of the king's purification, in gold and — all costly stones. All these I have presented in the (royal) presence: garments of royal linen by thousands of all the best of my house, wherewith I knew thou wouldst be pleased. Go to the stable that thou mayest choose as thou desirest, of all the horses that thou willst." Then his majesty did so.

Delta Dynasts Dismissed
Said these kings and princes to his majesty: "Dismiss us to our cities, that we may open our treasuries, that we may choose as much as thy heart desires, that we may bring to thee the best of our stables, the first of our horses." Then his majesty did so.

List of Delta Dynasts
List of names belonging thereto:

1. King Osorkon in Bubastis, the district of Ranofer.
2. King Yewepet in Tentremu and Tayan.
3. The prince, Zeamonefonekh in "The Granary of Re", of Per-Benehded (Mendes).
4. His eldest son, commander of the army, in Per-Thutuprehui, Enekhhor.
5. The prince, Akenesh in Sebennytos, in Per-heby, and in Samhudet.
6. The prince, chief of Me, Pethenef, in Per-Soped and in "Granary of Memphis".

7. The prince, chief of Me, Pemou, in Per-Osiris (Busiris), lord of Ded.
8. The prince, chief of Me, Nesnekedy in the nome of Hesebka.
9. The prince, chief of Me, Nekhtharneshenu in Per-Gerer.
10. The chief of Me, Pentewere.
11. The chief of Me, Pentibekhenet.
12. The prophet of Horus, lord of Letopolis, Pediharsomtous.
13. The prince, Hurabes in the house of Sekhmet, mistress of Sais, and the house of Sekhmet, mistress of Rehesu.
14. The prince, Zedkhiyu in Khentnofer.
15. The prince Pebes in Khereha in Per-Hapi.

Bearing all their good tribute: gold, silver, —, couches laid with fine linen, myrrh in jars, —, as goodly dues; horses of —.

Revolt of Mesed

Many days after this, came one to say to his majesty: "The — army — his wall for fear of thee; he has set fire to his treasury and to the ships upon the river. He has garrisoned Mesed with soldiers and —. Then his majesty caused his warriors to go and see what had happened there, among the force of the hereditary prince, Pediese. One came to report to his majesty, saying: "We have slain every man whom we found there." His majesty gave it as a reward to the hereditary prince, Pediese.

Tefnakhte's Message of Submission

Then the chief of Me, Tefnakhte, heard of it and caused a messenger to come to the place where his majesty was, with flattery, saying: "Be thou appeased! I have not beheld thy face for shame; I cannot stand before thy flame, I tremble at thy might. Lo, thou art Nubti, presiding over the Southland, Montu, the Bull of mighty arm. To whatsoever city thou hast turned thy face, thou hast not found the servant there, until I reached the islands of the sea, trembling before thy might, and saying, 'His flame is hostile to me.' Is not the heart of thy majesty appeased, with these things that thou hast done to me? For I am verily a wretched man. Thou shouldst not smite me according to the measure of the crime; weighing with the balances, knowing with the kidet-weights. Thou increasest it to me threefold; leave the seed that thou mayest spare it in time; do not hew down the grove to its root. By thy *ka*, the terror of thee is in my body, and the fear of thee in my bones. I have not sat in the beer-hall, nor has the harp been played for me; but I have eaten bread in hunger, and I have drunk water in thirst, since that day when thou heardest my name. Disease is in my bones, my head is bare, my clothing is rags, till Neit is appeased toward me. Long is the course which thou hast brought to me; thy face is against me — the year has undone me. Cleanse (thy) servant of his fault, let my possessions be received into the Treasury, of gold and every costly stone, and the best of the horses, (even) payment for everything. Send to me a messenger quickly, that he may expel fear from my heart. Let me go forth before him to the temple, that I may cleanse myself with a divine oath."

Tefnakhte Takes Oath of Allegiance

His majesty dispatched the chief ritual priest, Pediamenesttowe, and the commander of the army, Purme. He presented him with silver and gold, clothing and every splendid, costly stone. He went forth to the temple, he worshipped the god, he cleansed himself with a divine oath, saying: "I will not transgress the command of the king, I will not overstep that which the king saith. I will not do a hostile act against a prince without thy knowledge; I will do according to that which the king says, and I will not transgress that which he has commanded." Then his majesty was satisfied therewith.

Submission of the Fayûm, Atfih, and the Last Kings of the Delta
One came to say to his majesty: "The temple of Sebek, they have opened its stronghold, Metenu throws itself upon its belly, there is not a nome closed against his majesty of the nomes of the South and North; the west, the east, and the islands in the midst are upon their bellies in fear of him, causing that their possessions be presented at the place where his majesty is, like subjects of the palace." When the land brightened, very early in the morning these two rulers of the South and two rulers of the North, with serpent-crests (uraei), came to sniff the ground before the fame of his majesty, while, as for these kings and princes of the Northland who came to behold the beauty of his majesty, their legs were as the legs of women. They entered not into the king's-house, because they were unclean and eaters of fish; which is an abomination for the palace. Lo, King Namlot, he entered into the king's-house, because he was pure, and he ate not fish. There stood three upon their feet, (but only) one entered the king's-house.

Piankhi's Return to the South
Then the ships were laden with silver, gold, copper, clothing, and everything of the Northland, every product of Syria, and all sweet woods of God's-Land. His majesty

sailed up-stream, with glad heart, the shores on his either side were jubilating. West and east, they seized the —, jubilating in the presence of his majesty; singing and jubilating as they said: "O mighty, mighty Ruler, Piankhi, O mighty Ruler; thou comest, having gained the dominion of the Northland. Thou makest bulls into women. Happy the heart of the mother who bore thee, and the man who begat thee. Those who are in the valley give to her praise, the cow that hath borne a bull. Thou art unto eternity, thy might endureth, O Ruler, beloved of Thebes."

THE BATTLE OF CARCHEMISH, 605 BC

Anonymous

The resounding victory of Nebuchadrezzar over Pharaoh Necho at Carchemish established Babylonian hegemony in Syria and Palestine. From Carchemish onwards, Egypt was a second-rate power. Within four years, Nebuchadrezzar attacked Egypt itself, although desperate Egyptian defence persuaded him to withdraw. Much of the history of Egypt's 7th-century involvement in the Near East is chronicled in the Bible's Second Book of Kings. *The account of Carchemish below is from a Babylonian clay tablet.*

In the twenty-first year the king of Babylon stayed in his own country while the crown-prince Nebuchadrezzar, his eldest son, took personal command of his troops and marched to Carchemish which lay on the bank of the river Euphrates. He crossed the river (to go) against the Egyptian army which was situated in Carchemish and . . . they fought with each other and the Egyptian army withdrew before him. He defeated them (smashing) them out of existence. As for the remnant of the Egyptian army which had escaped from the defeat so (hastily) that no weapon had touched them, the Babylonian army overtook and defeated them in the district of Hamath, so that not a single man [escaped] to his own country. At that time Nebuchadrezzar conquered the whole of the land of Hatti.*

CIVIL WAR: GENERAL AMASIS USURPS THE THRONE, 570 BC

Herodotus

The Greek historian Herodotus visited Egypt in c. 450 BC. Despite his pro-Hellenistic bias and occasional credulity, he remains the best source for the detail and the colour of the implosion of the 26th Dynasty (and the Persian invasion) of a century before. As Herodotus relates below, the pharaoh Apries (Wahibre) was beset by a military uprising after the army was mauled fighting Dorian Greek invaders in Libya. The Egyptian soldiery turned for leadership to the veteran general, Amasis. Only the mercenaries remained loyal to Apries.

An army despatched by Apries to attack Cyrene, having met with a terrible reverse, the Egyptians laid the blame on him, imagining that he had, of *malice prepense*, sent the troops into the jaws of destruction. They believed he had wished a vast number of them to be slain, in order that he himself might reign with more security over the rest of the Egyptians. Indignant therefore at this usage, the soldiers who returned and the friends of the slain broke instantly into revolt.

Apries, on learning these circumstances, sent Amasis to the rebels, to appease the tumult by persuasion. Upon his arrival, as he was seeking to restrain the malcontents by his exhortations, one of them, coming behind him, put a helmet on his head, saying, as he put it on, that he thereby crowned him king. Amasis was not altogether displeased at

* i.e. Syria and Palestine

the action, as his conduct soon made manifest: for no sooner had the insurgents agreed to make him actually their king, than he prepared to march with them against Apries. That monarch, on tidings of these events reaching him, sent Patarbemis, one of his courtiers, a man of high rank, to Amasis, with orders to bring him alive into his presence. Patarbemis, on arriving at the place where Amasis was, called on him to come back with him to the king, whereupon Amasis broke a coarse jest, and said, "Prithee take that back to thy master." When the envoy, notwithstanding this reply, persisted in his request, exhorting Amasis to obey the summons of the king, he made answer, "that this was exactly what he had long been intending to do; Apries would have no reason to complain of him on the score of delay; he would shortly come himself to the king, and bring others with him." Patarbemis, upon this, comprehending the intention of Amasis, partly from his replies, and partly from the preparations which he saw in progress, departed hastily, wishing to inform the king with all speed of what was going on. Apries, however, when he saw him approaching without Amasis, fell into a paroxysm of rage; and, not giving himself time for reflection, commanded the nose and ears of Patarbemis to be cut off. Then the rest of the Egyptians, who had hitherto espoused the cause of Apries, when they saw a man of such note among them so shamefully outraged, without a moment's hesitation went over to the rebels, and put themselves at the disposal of Amasis.

Apries, informed of this new calamity, armed his mercenaries, and led them against the Egyptians: this was a body of Carians and Ionians, numbering thirty thousand men, which was now with him at Saïs, where his palace stood – a vast building, well worthy of notice. The army of

Apries marched out to attack the host of the Egyptians, while that of Amasis went forth to fight the strangers; and now both armies drew near the city of Momemphis, and prepared for the coming fight.

When Apries, at the head of his mercenaries, and Amasis, in command of the whole native force of the Egyptians, encountered one another near the city of Momemphis, an engagement presently took place. The foreign troops fought bravely, but were overpowered by numbers, in which they fell very far short of their adversaries. It is said that Apries believed that there was not a god who could cast him down from his eminence, so firmly did he think that he had established himself in his kingdom. But at this time the battle went against him; and, his army being worsted, he fell into the enemy's hands, and was brought back a prisoner to Saïs, where he was lodged in what had been his own house, but was now the palace of Amasis. Amasis treated him with kindness, and kept him in the palace for a while; but finding his conduct blamed by the Egyptians, who charged him with acting unjustly in preserving a man who had shown himself so bitter an enemy both to them and him, he gave Apries over into the hands of his former subjects, to deal with as they chose. Then the Egyptians took him and strangled him, but having so done they buried him in the sepulchre of his fathers. This tomb is in the temple of Athene, very near the sanctuary, on the left hand as one enters. The Saïtes buried all the kings who belonged to their canton inside this temple; and thus it even contains the tomb of Amasis, as well as that of Apries and his family. The latter is not so close to the sanctuary as the former, but still it is within the temple. It stands in the court, and is a spacious cloister, built of stone, and adorned with pillars carved so as to resemble palm trees, and with other sumptuous ornaments. Within the cloister is a chamber with folding doors, behind which lies the sepulchre of the king.

A GRAFFITO: WE WERE HERE, 529 BC

Greek Mercenaries

Scratched by a Greek mercenary on the colossal statue of Ramses II at Abu Simbel. The purpose of Pharaoh Psamtik [Psammetichus] II's excursion to Nubia is unclear.

When King Psammetichus came to Elephantine, this was written by those who sailed with Psammetichus the son of Theocles, and they came beyond Kerkis as far as the river permits. Those who spoke foreign tongues [i.e. Greeks and Carians who also scratched their names on the statue] were led by Potasimto, the Egyptians by Amasis.

THE PERSIAN CONQUEST OF EGYPT, 525 BC

Herodotus

The Achaemenid Persian army swept the Near East and Western Asia like a tidal wave in the 6th century BC, to create the greatest empire the world had yet seen. Divided and ruined, the Egyptians were no match for Cambyses when he marched upon them from Palestine. The reasons given for the Persian invasion by Herodotus are mythical, but the manner of the actual attack across the desert, with the defecting general Phanes and the bedouin guides, is almost certainly accurate. So too, the fate of defeated pharaoh Psamtik III (Psammetichus III).

1.   The above-mentioned Amasis was the Egyptian king against whom Cambyses, son of Cyrus, made his expedition; and with him went an army composed of the many nations under his rule, among them being included both Ionic and Aeolic Greeks. The reason of the invasion was the

following. Cambyses, by the advice of a certain Egyptian, who was angry with Amasis for having torn him from his wife and children, and given him over to the Persians, had sent a herald to Amasis to ask his daughter in marriage. His adviser was a physician, whom Amasis, when Cyrus had requested that he would send him the most skilful of all the Egyptian eye-doctors, singled out as the best from the whole number. Therefore the Egyptian bore Amasis a grudge, and his reason for urging Cambyses to ask the hand of the king's daughter was, that if he complied, it might cause him annoyance; if he refused, it might make Cambyses his enemy. When the message came, Amasis, who much dreaded the power of the Persians, was greatly perplexed whether to give his daughter or no; for that Cambyses did not intend to make her his wife, but would only receive her as his concubine, he knew for certain. He therefore cast the matter in his mind, and finally resolved what he would do. There was a daughter of the late king Apries, named Nitetis, a tall and beautiful woman, the last survivor of that royal house. Amasis took this woman, and, decking her out with gold and costly garments, sent her to Persia as if she had been his own child. Some time afterwards, Cambyses, as he gave her an embrace, happened to call her by her father's name, whereupon she said to him, "I see, o king, thou knowest not how thou hast been cheated by Amasis; who took me, and, tricking me out with gauds, sent me to thee as his own daughter. But I am in truth the child of Apries, who was his lord and master, until he rebelled against him, together with the rest of the Egyptians, and put him to death." It was this speech, and the cause of quarrel it disclosed, which roused the anger of Cambyses, son of Cyrus, and brought his arms upon Egypt. Such is the Persian story.

2.   The Egyptians, however, claim Cambyses as belonging to them, declaring that he was the son of this Nitetis. It was Cyrus, they say, and not Cambyses, who sent to Amasis for his daughter. But here they mis-state the truth. Acquainted as they are beyond all other men with the laws and customs of the Persians, they cannot but be well aware, first, that it is not the Persian wont to allow a bastard to reign when there is a legitimate heir, and next, that Cambyses was the son of Cassandane, the daughter of Pharnaspes, an Achaemenian, and not of this Egyptian. But the fact is, that they pervert history, in order to claim relationship with the house of Cyrus. Such is the truth of this matter.

3.   I have also heard another account, which I do not at all believe – that a Persian lady came to visit the wives of Cyrus, and seeing how tall and beautiful were the children of Cassandane, then standing by, broke out into loud praise of them, and admired them exceedingly. But Cassandane, wife of Cyrus, answered, "Though such the children I have borne him, yet Cyrus slights me and gives all his regard to the newcomer from Egypt." Thus did she express her vexation on account of Nitetis: whereupon Cambyses, the eldest of her boys, exclaimed, "Mother, when I am a man, I will turn Egypt upside down for you." He was but ten years old, as the tale runs, when he said this, and astonished all the women, yet he never forgot it afterwards; and on this account, they say, when he came to be a man, and mounted the throne, he made his expedition against Egypt.

4.   There was another matter, quite distinct, which helped to bring about the expedition. One of the mercenaries of Amasis, a Halicarnassian, Phanes by name, a man of good judgment, and a brave warrior, dissatisfied for some reason or other with his master, deserted the service, and, taking

ship, fled to Cambyses, wishing to get speech with him. As he was a person of no small account among the mercenaries, and one who could give very exact intelligence about Egypt, Amasis, anxious to recover him, ordered that he should be pursued. He gave the matter in charge to one of the most trusty of the eunuchs, who went in quest of the Halicarnassian in a vessel of war. The eunuch caught him in Lycia, but did not contrive to bring him back to Egypt, for Phanes outwitted him by making his guards drunk, and then escaping into Persia. Now it happened that Cambyses was meditating his attack on Egypt, and doubting how he might best pass the desert, when Phanes arrived, and not only told him all the secrets of Amasis, but advised him also how the desert might be crossed. He counselled him to send an ambassador to the king of the Arabs, and ask him for safe-conduct through the region.

5.   Now the only entrance into Egypt is by this desert: the country from Phoenicia to the borders of the city Cadytis belongs to the people called the Palaestine Syrians; from Cadytis, which it appears to me is a city almost as large as Sardis, the marts upon the coast till you reach Jenysus are the Arabian king's; after Jenysus the Syrians again come in, and extend to lake Serbonis, near the place where Mount Casius juts out into the sea. At Lake Serbonis, where the tale goes that Typhon hid himself, Egypt begins. Now the whole tract between Jenysus on the one side, and Lake Serbonis and Mount Casius on the other, and this is no small space, being as much as three days' journey, is a dry desert without a drop of water.

6.   I shall now mention a thing of which few of those who sail to Egypt are aware. Twice a year wine is brought into Egypt from every part of Greece, as well as from Phoenicia, in earthen jars; and yet in the whole country you will

nowhere see, as I may say, a single jar. What then, every one will ask, becomes of the jars? This, too, I will clear up. The burgomaster of each town has to collect the wine-jars within his district, and to carry them to Memphis, where they are all filled with water by the Memphians, who then convey them to this desert tract of Syria. And so it comes to pass that all the jars which enter Egypt year by year, and are there put up to sale, find their way into Syria, whither all the old jars have gone before them.

7.   This way of keeping the passage into Egypt fit for use by storing water there, was begun by the Persians so soon as they became masters of that country. As, however, at the time of which we speak the tract had not yet been so supplied, Cambyses took the advice of his Halicarnassian guest, and sent messengers to the Arabian to beg a safe-conduct through the region. The Arabian granted his prayer, and each pledged faith to the other.

8.   The Arabs keep such pledges more religiously than almost any other people. They plight faith with the forms following. When two men would swear a friendship, they stand on each side of a third: he with a sharp stone makes a cut on the inside of the hand of each near the middle finger, and, taking a piece from their dress, dips it in the blood of each, and moistens therewith seven stones lying in the midst, calling the while on Dionysus and Urania. After this, the man who makes the pledge commends the stranger (or the citizen, if citizen he be) to all his friends, and they deem themselves bound to stand to the engagement. They have but these two gods, to wit, Dionysus and Urania; and they say that in their mode of cutting the hair, they follow Dionysus. Now their practice is to cut it in a ring, away from the temples. Dionysus they call in their language Orotal, and Urania, Alilat.

9.   When, therefore, the Arabian had pledged his faith to the messengers of Cambyses, he straightway contrived as follows: he filled a number of camels' skins with water, and loading therewith all the live camels that he possessed, drove them into the desert, and awaited the coming of the army. This is the more likely of the two tales that are told. The other is an improbable story, but, as it is related, I think that I ought not to pass it by. There is a great river in Arabia, called the Corys, which empties itself into the Erythraean sea. The Arabian king, they say, made a pipe of the skins of oxen and other beasts, reaching from this river all the way to the desert, and so brought the water to certain cisterns which he had had dug in the desert to receive it. It is a twelve days' journey from the river to this desert tract. And the water, they say, was brought through three different pipes to three separate places.

10.   Psammenitus, son of Amasis, lay encamped at the mouth of the Nile, called the Pelusiac, awaiting Cambyses. For Cambyses, when he went up against Egypt, found Amasis no longer in life: he had died after ruling Egypt forty and four years, during all which time no great misfortune had befallen him. When he died, his body was embalmed, and buried in the tomb which he had himself caused to be made in the temple. After his son Psammenitus had mounted the throne, a strange prodigy occurred in Egypt: Rain fell at Egyptian Thebes, a thing which never happened before, and which, to the present time, has never happened again, as the Thebans themselves testify. In Upper Egypt it does not usually rain at all; but on this occasion, rain fell at Thebes in small drops.

11.   The Persians crossed the desert, and, pitching their camp close to the Egyptians, made ready for battle. Hereupon the mercenaries in the pay of Psammenitus, who were

Greeks and Carians, full of anger against Phanes for having brought a foreign army upon Egypt, bethought themselves of a mode whereby they might be revenged on him. Phanes had left sons in Egypt. The mercenaries took these, and leading them to the camp, displayed them before the eyes of their father, after which they brought out a bowl, and, placing it in the space between the two hosts, they led the sons of Phanes, one by one, to the vessel, and slew them over it. When the last was dead, water and wine were poured into the bowl, and all the soldiers tasted of the blood, and so they went to the battle. Stubborn was the fight which followed, and it was not till vast numbers had been slain upon both sides, that the Egyptians turned and fled.

12.   On the field where this battle was fought I saw a very wonderful thing which the natives pointed out to me. The bones of the slain lie scattered upon the field in two lots, those of the Persians in one place by themselves, as the bodies lay at the first – those of the Egyptians in another place apart from them: If, then, you strike the Persian skulls, even with a pebble, they are so weak, that you break a hole in them; but the Egyptian skulls are so strong, that you may smite them with a stone and you will scarcely break them in. They gave me the following reason for this difference, which seemed to me likely enough: The Egyptians (they said) from early childhood have the head shaved, and so by the action of the sun the skull becomes thick and hard. The same cause prevents baldness in Egypt, where you see fewer bald men than in any other land. Such, then, is the reason why the skulls of the Egyptians are so strong. The Persians, on the other hand, have feeble skulls, because they keep themselves shaded from the first, wearing turbans upon their heads. What I

have here mentioned I saw with my own eyes, and I
observed also the like at Papremis, in the case of the
Persians who were killed with Achaemenes, the son of
Darius by Inarus the Libyan.

13.   The Egyptians who fought in the battle, no sooner
turned their backs upon the enemy, than they fled away in
complete disorder to Memphis, where they shut themselves
up within the walls. Hereupon Cambyses sent a Mytilenaean vessel, with a Persian herald on board, who was to
sail up the Nile to Memphis, and invite the Egyptians to a
surrender. They, however, when they saw the vessel entering the town, poured forth in crowds from the castle,
destroyed the ship, and, tearing the crew limb from limb, so
bore them into the fortress. After this Memphis was besieged, and in due time surrendered. Hereon the Libyans
who bordered upon Egypt, fearing the fate of that country,
gave themselves up to Cambyses without a battle, made an
agreement to pay tribute to him, and forthwith sent him
gifts. The Cyrenaeans too, and the Barcaeans, having the
same fear as the Libyans, immediately did the like. Cambyses received the Libyan presents very graciously, but not
so the gifts of the Cyrenaeans. They had sent no more than
five hundred minae of silver, which Cambyses, I imagine,
thought too little. He therefore snatched the money from
them, and with his own hands scattered it among his
soldiers.

14.   Ten days after the fort had fallen, Cambyses resolved
to try the spirit of Psammenitus, the Egyptian king, whose
whole reign had been but six months. He therefore had him
set in one of the suburbs, and many other Egyptians with
him, and here subjected him to insult. First of all he sent his
daughter out from the city, clothed in the garb of a slave,
with a pitcher to draw water. Many virgins, the daughters

of the chief nobles, accompanied her, wearing the same dress. When the damsels came opposite the place where their fathers sat, shedding tears and uttering cries of woe, the fathers, all but Psammenitus, wept and wailed in return, grieving to see their children in so sad a plight; but he, when he had looked and seen, bent his head towards the ground. In this way passed by the water-carriers. Next to them came Psammenitus' son, and two thousand Egyptians of the same age with him – all of them having ropes round their necks and bridles in their mouths – and they too passed by on their way to suffer death for the murder of the Mytilenaeans who were destroyed, with their vessel, in Memphis. For so had the royal judges given their sentence – "for each Mytilenaean ten of the noblest Egyptians must forfeit life." King Psammenitus saw the train pass on, and knew his son was being led to death, but, while the other Egyptians who sat around him wept and were sorely troubled, he showed no further sign than when he saw his daughter. And now, when they too were gone, it chanced that one of his former boon-companions, a man advanced in years, who had been stripped of all that he had and was a beggar, came where Psammenitus, son of Amasis, and the rest of the Egyptians were, asking alms from the soldiers. At this sight the king burst into tears, and, weeping out aloud, called his friend by his name, and smote himself on the head. Now there were some who had been set to watch Psammenitus and see what he would do as each train went by; so these persons went and told Cambyses of his behaviour. Then he, astonished at what was done, sent a messenger to Psammenitus, and questioned him, saying, "Psammenitus, thy lord Cambyses asketh thee why, when thou sawest thy daughter brought to shame, and thy son on his way to death, thou didst neither utter cry nor shed tear, while to a beggar, who is, he hears, a stranger to thy race, thou gavest those marks of honour." To this question Psammenitus made answer, "O son of Cyrus, my own misfortunes were too great for tears; but the woe of my friend deserved them. When a man falls from splendour and plenty into beggary at the threshold of old age, one may well weep for him." When the messenger brought back this answer, Cambyses owned it was just; Croesus, likewise, the Egyptians say, burst into tears – for he too had come into Egypt with Cambyses – and the Persians who were present wept. Even Cambyses himself was touched with pity, and he forthwith gave an order, that the son of Psammenitus should be spared from the number of those appointed to die, and Psammenitus himself brought from the suburb into his presence.

15. The messengers were too late to save the life of Psammenitus' son, who had been cut in pieces the first of all; but they took Psammenitus himself and brought him before the king. Cambyses allowed him to live with him, and gave him no more harsh treatment; nay, could he have kept from intermeddling with affairs, he might have recovered Egypt, and ruled it as governor. For the Persian wont is to treat the sons of kings with honour, and even to give their fathers' kingdoms to the children of such as revolt from them. There are many cases from which one may collect that this is the Persian rule, and especially those of Pausiris and Thannyras. Thannyras was son of Inarus the Libyan, and was allowed to succeed his father, as was also Pausiris, son of Amyrtaeus; yet certainly no two persons ever did the Persians more damage than Amyrtaeus and Inarus. In this case Psammenitus plotted evil, and received his reward accordingly. He was discovered to be stirring up revolt in Egypt, wherefore Cambyses, when his guilt clearly

appeared, compelled him to drink bull's blood, which presently caused his death. Such was the end of Psammenitus.

A TRAVELLER'S EGYPT, c. 440 BC

Herodotus

As recounted in Book 2 of Herodotus' History.

For any one who sees Egypt, without having heard a word about it before, must perceive, if he has only common powers of observation, that the Egypt to which the Greeks go in their ships is an acquired country, the gift of the river. The same is true of the land above the lake to the distance of three days' voyage, concerning which the Egyptians say nothing, but which is exactly the same kind of country.

The following is the general character of the region. In the first place, on approaching it by sea, when you are still a day's sail from the land, if you let down a sounding-line you will bring up mud, and find yourself in eleven fathoms' water, which shows that the soil washed down by the stream extends to that distance.

The length of the country along shore, according to the bounds that we assign to Egypt, namely from the Plinthinetic gulf to lake Serbonis, which extends along the base of Mount Casius, is sixty schoenes. The nations whose territories are scanty measure them by the fathom; those whose bounds are less confined, by the furlong; those who have an ample territory, by the parasang; but if men have a country which is very vast, they measure it by the schoene. Now the length of the parasang is thirty furlongs, but the schoene, which is an Egyptian measure, is sixty furlongs. Thus the coast-line of Egypt would extend a length of three thousand six hundred furlongs.

From the coast inland as far as Heliopolis the breadth of Egypt is considerable, the country is flat, without springs, and full of swamps. The length of the route from the sea up to Heliopolis is almost exactly the same as that of the road which runs from the altar of the twelve gods at Athens to the temple of Olympian Zeus at Pisa. If a person made a calculation he would find but a very little difference between the two routes, not more than about fifteen furlongs; for the road from Athens to Pisa falls short of fifteen hundred furlongs by exactly fifteen, whereas the distance of Heliopolis from the sea is just the round number.

As one proceeds beyond Heliopolis up the country, Egypt becomes narrow, the Arabian range of hills, which has a direction from north to south, shutting it in upon the one side, and the Libyan range upon the other. The former ridge runs on without a break, and stretches away to the sea called the Erythraean; it contains the quarries whence the stone was cut for the pyramids of Memphis: and this is the point where it ceases its first direction, and bends away in the manner above indicated. In its greatest length from east to west it is, as I have been informed, a distance of two months' journey; towards the extreme east its skirts produce frankincense. Such are the chief features of this range. On the Libyan side, the other ridge whereon the pyramids stand is rocky and covered with sand; its direction is the same as that of the Arabian ridge in the first part of its course. Above Heliopolis, then, there is no great breadth of territory for such a country as Egypt, but during four days' sail Egypt is narrow; the valley between the two ranges is a level plain, and seemed to me to be, at the narrowest point, not more than two hundred furlongs across from the

Arabian to the Libyan hills. Above this point Egypt again widens.

From Heliopolis to Thebes is nine days' sail up the river; the distance is eighty-one schoenes, or 4,860 furlongs. If we now put together the several measurements of the country we shall find that the distance along shore is, as I stated above, 3,600 furlongs, and the distance from the sea inland to Thebes 6,120 furlongs. Further, it is a distance of eighteen hundred furlongs from Thebes to the place called Elephantine.

When the Nile overflows, the country is converted into a sea, and nothing appears but the cities, which look like the islands in the Aegean. At this season boats no longer keep the course of the river, but sail right across the plain. On the voyage from Naucratis to Memphis at this season, you pass close to the pyramids, whereas the usual course is by the apex of the Delta, and the city of Cercasorus. You can sail also from the maritime town of Canobus across the flat to Naucratis, passing by the cities of Anthylla and Archandropolis.

"EXACTLY THE REVERSE OF THE COMMON PRACTICE OF MANKIND": THE CUSTOMS OF THE EGYPTIANS, c. 440 BC

Herodotus

Not only is the climate different from that of the rest of the world, and the rivers unlike any other rivers, but the people also, in most of their manners and customs, exactly reverse the common practice of mankind. The women attend the markets and trade, while the men sit at home at the loom, and here, while the rest of the world works the woof up the warp, the Egyptians work it down; the women likewise carry burthens upon their shoulders, while the men carry them upon their heads. They eat their food out of doors in the streets, but retire for private purposes to their houses, giving as a reason that what is unseemly, but necessary, ought to be done in secret, but what has nothing unseemly about it, should be done openly. A woman cannot serve the priestly office, either for god or goddess, but men are priests to both; sons need not support their parents unless they choose, but daughters must, whether they choose or no.

In other countries the priests have long hair, in Egypt their heads are shaven; elsewhere it is customary, in mourning, for near relations to cut their hair close: the Egyptians, who wear no hair at any other time, when they lose a relative, let their beards and the hair of their heads grow long. All other men pass their lives separate from animals, the Egyptians have animals always living with them, others make barley and wheat their food; it is a disgrace to do so in Egypt, where the grain they live on is spelt, which some call *zea*. Dough they knead with their feet; but they mix mud, and even take up dirt, with their hands. They are the only people in the world – they at least, and such as have learnt the practice from them – who use circumcision. Their men wear two garments apiece, their women but one. They put on the rings and fasten the ropes to sails inside; others put them outside. When they write or calculate, instead of going, like the Greeks, from left to right, they move their hand from right to left; and they insist, notwithstanding, that it is they who go to the right, and the Greeks who go to the left. They have two quite different kinds of writing, one of which is called sacred, the other common . . .

It is to be remarked that those who live in the corn

country, devoting themselves, as they do, far more than any other people in the world, to the preservation of the memory of past actions, are the best skilled in history of any men that I have ever met. The following is the mode of life habitual to them. For three successive days in each month they purge the body by means of emetics and clysters, which is done out of a regard for their health, since they have a persuasion that every disease to which men are liable is occasioned by the substances whereon they feed. Apart from any such precautions, they are, I believe, next to the Libyans, the healthiest people in the world – an effect of their climate, in my opinion, which has no sudden changes. Diseases almost always attack men when they are exposed to a change, and never more than during changes of the weather. They live on bread made of spelt, which they form into loaves called in their own tongue *cyllestis*. Their drink is a wine which they obtain from barley, as they have no vines in their country. Many kinds of fish they eat raw, either salted or dried in the sun. Quails also, and ducks and small birds, they eat uncooked, merely first salting them. All other birds and fishes, excepting those which are set apart as sacred, are eaten either roasted or boiled.

In social meetings among the rich, when the banquet is ended, a servant carries round to the several guests a coffin, in which there is a wooden image of a corpse, carved and painted to resemble nature as nearly as possible, about a cubit or two cubits in length. As he shows it to each guest in turn, the servant says, "Gaze here, and drink and be merry; for when you die, such will you be."

The Egyptians adhere to their own national customs, and adopt no foreign usages. Many of these customs are worthy of note: among others their song, the Linus, which is

sung under various names not only in Egypt but in Phoenicia, in Cyprus, and in other places; and which seems to be
exactly the same as that in use among the Greeks, and by
them called Linus. There were very many things in Egypt
which filled me with astonishment, and this was one of
them. Whence could the Egyptians have got the Linus? It
appears to have been sung by them from the very earliest
times. For the Linus in Egyptian is called Maneros; and
they told me that Maneros was the only son of their first
king, and that on his untimely death he was honoured by
the Egyptians with these dirgelike strains, and in this way
they got their first and only melody.

There is another custom in which the Egyptians resemble a particular Greek people, namely the Lacedaemo-
nians. Their young men, when they meet their elders in the
streets, give way to them and step aside; and if an elder
come in where young men are present, these latter rise from
their seats. In a third point they differ entirely from all the
nations of Greece. Instead of speaking to each other when
they meet in the streets, they make an obeisance, sinking
the hand to the knee.

They wear a linen tunic fringed about the legs, and
called *calasiris*; over this they have a white woollen garment
thrown on afterwards. Nothing of woollen, however, is
taken into their temples or buried with them, as their
religion forbids it. Here their practice resembles the rites
called Orphic and Bacchic, but which are in reality Egyptian and Pythagorean; for no one initiated in these mysteries can be buried in a woollen shroud, a religious reason
being assigned for the observance.

The Egyptians likewise discovered to which of the gods
each month and day is sacred, and found out from the day
of a man's birth, what he will meet with in the course of his

life, and how he will end his days, and what sort of man he will be – discoveries whereof the Greeks engaged in poetry have made a use. The Egyptians have also discovered more prognostics than all the rest of mankind besides. Whenever a prodigy takes place, they watch and record the result; then, if anything similar ever happens again, they expect the same consequences.

The following is the way in which they conduct their mournings and their funerals: on the death in any house of a man of consequence, forthwith the women of the family beplaster their heads, and sometimes even their faces, with mud; and then, leaving the body indoors, sally forth and wander through the city, with their dress fastened by a band, and their bosoms bare, beating themselves as they walk. All the female relations join them and do the same. The men too, similarly begirt, beat their breasts separately. When these ceremonies are over, the body is carried away to be embalmed.

ANIMAL SACRIFICE, c. 440 BC

Herodotus

They are religious to excess, far beyond any other race of men, and use the following ceremonies: They drink out of brazen cups, which they scour every day: there is no exception to this practice. They wear linen garments, which they are specially careful to have always fresh washed. They practise circumcision for the sake of cleanliness, considering it better to be cleanly than comely. The priests shave their whole body every other day, that no lice or other impure thing may adhere to them when they are engaged in the service of the gods. Their dress is entirely of linen, and their shoes of the papyrus plant: it is not lawful for them to wear either dress or shoes of any other material. They bathe twice every day in cold water, and twice each night; besides which they observe, so to speak, thousands of ceremonies. They enjoy, however, not a few advantages. They consume none of their own property, and are at no expense for anything, but every day bread is baked for them of the sacred corn, and a plentiful supply of beef and of goose's flesh is assigned to each, and also a portion of wine made from the grape. Fish they are not allowed to eat; and beans – which none of the Egyptians ever sow, or eat, if they come up of their own accord, either raw or boiled – the priests will not even endure to look on, since they consider it an unclean kind of pulse. Instead of a single priest, each god has the attendance of a college, at the head of which is a chief priest; when one of these dies, his son is appointed in his room.

Male kine are reckoned to belong to Epaphus, and are therefore tested in the following manner. One of the priests appointed for the purpose searches to see if there is a single black hair on the whole body, since in that case the beast is unclean. He examines him all over, standing on his legs, and again laid upon his back; after which he takes the tongue out of his mouth, to see if it be clean in respect of the prescribed marks (what they are I will mention elsewhere); he also inspects the hairs of the tail, to observe if they grow naturally. If the animal is pronounced clean in all these various points, the priest marks him by twisting a piece of papyrus round his horns, and attaching thereto some sealing-clay, which he then stamps with his own signet-ring. After this the beast is led away; and it is forbidden, under the penalty of death, to sacrifice an animal which has not been marked in this way.

The following is their manner of sacrifice: They lead the victim, marked with their signet, to the altar where they are about to offer it, and setting the wood alight, pour a libation of wine upon the altar in front of the victim, and at the same time invoke the god. Then they slay the animal, and cutting off his head, proceed to flay the body. Next they take the head, and heaping imprecations on it, if there is a market-place and a body of Greek traders in the city, they carry it there and sell it instantly; if, however, there are no Greeks among them, they throw the head into the river. The imprecation is to this effect: They pray that if any evil is impending either over those who sacrifice, or over universal Egypt, it may be made to fall upon that head. These practices, the imprecations upon the heads, and the libations of wine, prevail all over Egypt, and extend to victims of all sorts; and hence the Egyptians will never eat the head of any animal.

The disembowelling and burning are, however, different in different sacrifices. I will mention the mode in use with respect to the goddess whom they regard as the greatest, and honour with the chiefest festival. When they have flayed their steer they pray, and when their prayer is ended they take the paunch of the animal out entire, leaving the intestines and the fat inside the body; they then cut off the legs, the ends of the loins, the shoulders, and the neck; and having so done, they fill the body of the steer with clean bread, honey, raisins, figs, frankincense, myrrh, and other aromatics. Thus filled, they burn the body, pouring over it great quantities of oil. Before offering the sacrifice they fast, and while the bodies of the victims are being consumed they beat themselves. Afterwards, when they have concluded this part of the ceremony, they have the other parts of the victim served up to them for a repast.

The male kine, therefore, if clean, and the male calves, are used for sacrifice by the Egyptians universally; but the females they are not allowed to sacrifice, since they are sacred to Isis. The statue of this goddess has the form of a woman but with horns like a cow, resembling thus the Greek representations of Io; and the Egyptians, one and all, venerate cows much more highly than any other animal. This is the reason why no native of Egypt, whether man or woman, will give a Greek a kiss, or use the knife of a Greek, or his spit, or his cauldron, or taste the flesh of an ox, known to be pure, if it has been cut with a Greek knife. When kine die, the following is the manner of their sepulture: The females are thrown into the river, the males are buried in the suburbs of the towns, with one or both of their horns appearing above the surface of the ground to mark the place. When the bodies are decayed, a boat comes, at an appointed time, from the island called Prosopitis – which is a portion of the Delta, nine schoenes in circumference – and calls at the several cities in turn to collect the bones of the oxen. Prosopitis is a district containing several cities; the name of that from which the boats come is Atarbechis. Aphrodite has a temple there of much sanctity. Great numbers of men go forth from this city and proceed to the other towns, where they dig up the bones, which they take away with them and bury together in one place. The same practice prevails with respect to the interment of all other cattle – the law so determining; they do not slaughter any of them.

The pig is regarded among them as an unclean animal, so much so that if a man in passing accidentally touch a pig, he instantly hurries to the river, and plunges in with all his clothes on. Hence, too, the swineherds, notwithstanding that they are of pure Egyptian blood, are forbidden to enter into any of the temples, which are open to all other Egyptians; and further, no one will give his daughter in marriage to a swineherd, or take a wife from among them, so that the swineherds are forced to intermarry among themselves. They do not offer swine in sacrifice to any of their gods, excepting Dionysus and the Moon, whom they honour in this way at the same time, sacrificing pigs to both of them at the same full moon, and afterwards eating of the flesh. There is a reason alleged by them for their detestation of swine at all other seasons, and their use of them at this festival, with which I am well acquainted, but which I do not think it proper to mention. The following is the mode in which they sacrifice the swine to the Moon: As soon as the victim is slain, the tip of the tail, the spleen, and the caul are put together, and having been covered with all the fat that has been found in the animal's belly, are straightaway burnt. The remainder of the flesh is eaten on the same day that the sacrifice is offered, which is the day of the full moon: at any other time they would not so much as taste it. The poorer sort, who cannot afford live pigs, form pigs of dough, which they bake and offer in sacrifice.

To Dionysus, on the eve of his feast, every Egyptian sacrifices a hog before the door of his house, which is then given back to the swineherd by whom it was furnished, and by him carried away. In other respects the festival is celebrated almost exactly as Dionysian festivals are in Greece, excepting that the Egyptians have no choral dances. They also use instead of phalli another invention, consisting of images a cubit high, pulled by strings, which the women carry round to the villages. A piper goes in front, and the women follow, singing hymns in honour of Dionysus. They give a religious reason for the peculiarities of the image.

RELIGIOUS FESTIVALS, c. 440 BC

Herodotus

The Egyptians were also the first to introduce solemn assemblies, processions, and litanies to the gods; of all which the Greeks were taught the use by them. It seems to me a sufficient proof of this, that in Egypt these practices have been established from remote antiquity, while in Greece they are only recently known.

The Egyptians do not hold a single solemn assembly, but several in the course of the year. Of these the chief, which is better attended than any other, is held at the city of Bubastis in honour of Artemis. The next in importance is that which takes place at Busiris, a city situated in the very middle of the Delta; it is in honour of Isis, who is called in the Greek tongue Demeter. There is a third great festival in Saïs to Athene, a fourth in Heliopolis to the Sun, a fifth in Buto to Leto, and a sixth in Papremis to Ares.

The following are the proceedings on occasion of the assembly at Bubastis: Men and women come sailing all together, vast numbers in each boat, many of the women with castanets, which they strike, while some of the men pipe during the whole time of the voyage; the remainder of the voyagers, male and female, sing the while, and make a clapping with their hands. When they arrive opposite any of the towns upon the banks of the stream, they approach the shore, and, while some of the women continue to play and sing, others call aloud to the females of the place and load them with abuse, while a certain number dance, and some standing up uncover themselves. After proceeding in this way all along the river-course, they reach Bubastis, where they celebrate the feast with abundant sacrifices. More grape-wine is consumed at this festival than in all the rest of the year besides. The number of those who attend, counting only the men and women and omitting the children, amounts, according to the native reports, to seven hundred thousand.

The ceremonies at the feast of Isis in the city of Busiris have been already spoken of. It is there that the whole multitude, both of men and women, many thousands in number, beat themselves at the close of the sacrifice, in honour of a god, whose name a religious scruple forbids me to mention. The Carian dwellers in Egypt proceed on this occasion to still greater lengths, even cutting their faces with their knives, whereby they let it be seen that they are not Egyptians but foreigners.

At Saïs, when the assembly takes place for the sacrifices, there is one night on which the inhabitants all burn a multitude of lights in the open air round their houses. They use lamps in the shape of flat saucers filled with a mixture of oil and salt, on the top of which the wick floats. These burn the whole night, and give to the festival the name of the Feast of Lamps. The Egyptians who are absent from the festival observe the night of the sacrifice, no less than the rest, by a general lighting of lamps, so that the illumination is not confined to the city of Saïs, but extends over the whole of Egypt. And there is a religious reason assigned for the special honour paid to this night, as well as for the illumination which accompanies it.

At Heliopolis and Buto the assemblies are merely for the purpose of sacrifice; but at Papremis, besides the sacrifices and other rites which are performed there as elsewhere, the following custom is observed: When the sun is getting low, a few only of the priests continue occupied about the image of the god, while the greater number, armed with wooden clubs, take their station at the portal of the temple. Opposite to them is drawn up a body of men, in number above a thousand, armed, like the others, with clubs, consisting of persons engaged in the performance of their vows. The image of the god, which is kept in a small wooden shrine covered with plates of gold, is conveyed from the temple into a second sacred building the day before the festival begins. The few priests still in attendance upon the image place it, together with the shrine containing it, on a four-wheeled car, and begin to drag it along; the others, stationed at the gateway of the temple, oppose its admission. Then the votaries come forward to espouse the quarrel of the god, and set upon the opponents, who are sure to offer resistance. A sharp fight with clubs ensues, in which heads are commonly broken on both sides. Many, I am convinced, die of the wounds that they receive, though the Egyptians insist that no one is ever killed.

CATS AND DOGS, c. 440 BC

Herodotus

The number of domestic animals in Egypt is very great, and would be still greater were it not for what befalls the cats. As the females, when they have kittened, no longer seek the company of the males, these last, to obtain once more their companionship, practise a curious artifice. They seize the kittens, carry them off, and kill them, but do not eat them afterwards. Upon this the females, being deprived of their young, and longing to supply their place, seek the males once more, since they are particularly fond of their offspring. On every occasion of a fire in Egypt the strangest prodigy occurs with the cats. The inhabitants allow the fire to rage as it pleases, while they stand about at intervals and watch these animals, which, slipping by the men or else leaping over them, rush headlong into the flames. When this happens, the Egyptians are in deep affliction. If a cat dies in a private house by a natural death, all the inmates of the house shave their eyebrows; on the death of a dog they shave the head and the whole of the body.

The cats on their decease are taken to the city of Bubastis, where they are embalmed, after which they are buried in certain sacred repositories. The dogs are interred in the cities to which they belong, also in sacred burial-places. The same practice obtains with respect to the ichneumons; the hawks and shrew-mice, on the contrary, are conveyed to the city of Buto for burial, and the ibises to Hermopolis. The bears, which are scarce in Egypt, and the wolves, which are not much bigger than foxes, they bury wherever they happen to find them lying.

HUNTING CROCODILES ON THE NILE, c. 440 BC

Herodotus

The following are the peculiarities of the crocodile: During the four winter months they eat nothing; they are four-footed, and live indifferently on land or in the water. The female lays and hatches her eggs ashore, passing the greater portion of the day on dry land, but at night retiring to the river, the water of which is warmer than the night-air and the dew. Of all known animals this is the one which from the smallest size grows to be the greatest: for the egg of the crocodile is but little bigger than that of the goose, and the young crocodile is in proportion to the egg; yet when it is full grown, the animal measures frequently seventeen cubits and even more. It has the eyes of a pig, teeth large and tusk-like, of a size proportioned to its frame; unlike any other animal, it is without a tongue; it cannot move its under-jaw, and in this respect too it is singular, being the only animal in the world which moves the upper-jaw but not the under. It has strong claws and a scaly skin, impenetrable upon the back. In the water it is blind, but on land it is very keen of sight. As it lives chiefly in the river, it has the inside of its mouth constantly covered with leeches; hence it happens that, while all the other birds and beasts avoid it, with the trochilus it lives at peace, since it owes much to that bird: for the crocodile, when he leaves the water and comes out upon the land, is in the habit of lying with his mouth wide open, facing the western breeze: at such times the trochilus goes into his mouth and devours the leeches. This benefits the crocodile, who is pleased, and takes care not to hurt the trochilus.

The crocodile is esteemed sacred by some of the Egyptians, by others he is treated as an enemy. Those who live near Thebes, and those who dwell around Lake Moeris, regard them with especial veneration. In each of these places they keep one crocodile in particular, who is taught to be tame and tractable. They adorn his ears with ear-rings of molten stone or gold, and put bracelets on his fore-paws, giving him daily a set portion of bread, with a certain number of victims; and, after having thus treated him with the greatest possible attention while alive, they embalm him when he dies and bury him in a sacred repository. The people of Elephantine, on the other hand, are so far from considering these animals as sacred that they even eat their flesh. In the Egyptian language they are not called crocodiles, but *champsae*. The name of crocodiles was given them by the Ionians, who remarked their resemblance to the lizards, which in Iònia live in the walls, and are called crocodiles.

The modes of catching the crocodile are many and various. I shall only describe the one which seems to me most worthy of mention. They bait a hook with a chine of pork and let the meat be carried out into the middle of the stream, while the hunter upon the bank holds a living pig, which he belabours. The crocodile hears its cries, and, making for the sound, encounters the pork, which he instantly swallows down. The men on the shore haul, and when they have got him to land, the first thing the hunter does is to plaster his eyes with mud. This once accomplished, the animal is despatched with ease, otherwise he gives great trouble.

MUMMIFICATION, c. 440 BC

Herodotus

The word "mummy" appears to derive from the Arabic-Persian word for bitumen, "moumiya". From modern laboratory analysis, Herodotus' description of the process of mummification appears generally accurate.

There are a set of men in Egypt who practise the art of embalming, and make it their proper business. These persons, when a body is brought to them, show the bearers various models of corpses, made in wood, and painted so as to resemble nature. The most perfect is said to be after the manner of him whom I do not think it religious to name in connection with such a matter; the second sort is inferior to the first, and less costly; the third is the cheapest of all. All this the embalmers explain, and then ask in which way it is wished that the corpse should be prepared. The bearers tell them, and having concluded their bargain, take their departure, while the embalmers, left to themselves, proceed to their task. The mode of embalming, according to the

most perfect process, is the following: They take first a
crooked piece of iron, and with it draw out the brain
through the nostrils, thus getting rid of a portion, while
the skull is cleared of the rest by rinsing with drugs; next
they make a cut along the flank with a sharp Ethiopian
stone, and take out the whole contents of the abdomen,
which they then cleanse, washing it thoroughly with palm
wine, and again frequently with an infusion of pounded
aromatics. After this they fill the cavity with the purest
bruised myrrh, with cassia, and every other sort of spicery
except frankincense, and seal up the opening. Then the
body is placed in natrum for seventy days, and covered
entirely over. After the expiration of that space of time,
which must not be exceeded, the body is washed, and
wrapped round, from head to foot, with bandages of fine
linen cloth, smeared over with gum, which is used generally
by the Egyptians in the place of glue, and in this state it is
given back to the relations, who enclose it in a wooden case
which they have had made for the purpose, shaped into the
figure of a man. Then, fastening the case, they place it in a
sepulchral chamber, upright against the wall. Such is the
most costly way of embalming the dead.

If persons wish to avoid expense, and choose the second
process, the following is the method pursued: syringes are
filled with oil made from the cedar-tree, which is then,
without any incision or disembowelling, injected into the
abdomen. The passage by which it might be likely to return
is stopped, and the body laid in natrum the prescribed
number of days. At the end of the time the cedar-oil is
allowed to make its escape; and such is its power that it
brings with it the whole stomach and intestines in a liquid
state. The natrum meanwhile has dissolved the flesh, and so
nothing is left of the dead body but the skin and the bones.

It is returned in this condition to the relatives, without any further trouble being bestowed upon it.

The third method of embalming, which is practised in the case of the poorer classes, is to clear out the intestines with a clyster, and let the body lie in natrum the seventy days, after which it is at once given to those who come to fetch it away.

The wives of men of rank are not given to be embalmed immediately after death, nor indeed are any of the more beautiful and valued women. It is not till they have been dead three or four days that they are carried to the embalmers. This is done to prevent indignities from being offered them. It is said that once a case of this kind occurred: the man was detected by the information of his fellow-workman.

Whensoever any one, Egyptian or foreigner, has lost his life by falling a prey to a crocodile, or by drowning in the river, the law compels the inhabitants of the city near which the body is cast up to have it embalmed, and to bury it in one of the sacred repositories with all possible magnificence. No one may touch the corpse, not even any of the friends or relatives, but only the priests of the Nile, who prepare it for burial with their own hands – regarding it as something more than the mere body of a man – and themselves lay it in the tomb.

THE DESTRUCTION OF THE JEWISH TEMPLE AT ELEPHANTINE, 410 BC

Yedoniah

The temple belonged to a longstanding Jewish military colony at Elephantine. On Cambyses II's seizure of Egypt, the colony became integrated into the Persian

*defence. The letter below recounting the Egyptian destruction of the temple of Yahu
is addressed to Bagoas, the Persian governor of Judea.*

To our lord Bagoas, governor of Judaea, your servants
Yedoniah and his colleagues, the priests who are in the
fortress of Elephantine. The welfare of your lordship may
the God of Heaven seek abundantly at all times, and give
you favour before King Darius and the court circles a
thousand times more than at present, and may He grant
you long life and may you be happy and prosperous at all
times.

Now your servant Yedoniah and his colleagues depose as
follows: In the month of Tammuz in the fourteenth year of
King Darius when Arsames departed and went to the
King, the priests of the god Khnub in the fortress of
Elephantine combined with Widrang, who was governor
here, saying: ("Let the temple of the God Yahu in the
fortress of Elephantine be done away with.") Then Widrang, that scoundrel, sent a letter to his son Nephayan,
who was in command of the garrison in the fortress of
Elephantine, saying: "Let the temple which is in Elephantine, the fortress, be destroyed." Thereupon Nephayan led
the Egyptians with the other troops. They came to the
fortress of Elephantine with their weapons, entered that
temple, razed it to the ground, and broke the stone pillars
which were there. Moreover five gateways of stone, built
with hewn blocks of stone, which were in that temple, they
destroyed, and their doors were set up, and the hinges of
those doors were of bronze, and the roof of cedar wood, all
of it, with the rest of the timber-work and other things
which were there, was entirely burned with fire, and the
basins of gold and silver and everything whatsoever that
was in that temple they took and made their own. Our

fathers built this temple in the fortress of Elephantine in the days of the Kings of Egypt, and when Cambyses entered Egypt he found that temple already built, and though all the temples of the Egyptian gods were destroyed, no one did any harm to that temple.

When this was done we, with our wives and children, put on sackcloth and fasted and prayed to Yahu, the Lord of Heaven, who let us see our desire upon that hound Widrang. The anklet was torn from his legs, and all the wealth he had acquired was lost, and all the men who had sought to do harm to that temple were all killed, and we saw our desire upon them. Further, before this, at the time when this evil was done to us, we sent a letter to your lordship and to the High Priest Johanan and his colleagues the priests in Jerusalem and to Ostanes, the brother of Anani, and the leaders of the Jews. They have not sent any letter to us. Moreover from the month of Tammuz in the fourteenth year of King Darius until this day we have worn sackcloth and fasted. Our wives are made as widows, we do not anoint ourselves with oil, and we drink no wine. Also from then till the present day, in the seventeenth year of King Darius, meal-offering and inc[en]se and burnt-offering have not been offered in this temple. Now your servants Yedoniah and his colleagues and the Jews, all citizens of Elephantine, say: "If it seems good to your lordship, take thought for that temple to rebuild it, since they do not permit us to rebuild it. Look upon your well wishers and friends here in Egypt. Let a letter be sent from you to them concerning this temple of the God Yahu that it be rebuilt in the fortress of Elephantine as it was built before, and let meal-offering, incense and burnt-offering be offered upon the altar of the God Yahu in your name, and we will pray for you continually, we, our wives, and our children and all the Jews who are here, if it is so arranged that this temple be rebuilt, and it shall be a merit to you before Yahu, the God of Heaven, greater than that of a man who offers Him a burnt-offering and sacrifices worth as much as a thousand talents of silver." Now concerning gold, concerning this we have sent and given instructions. Further we have set out the whole matter in a letter sent in our name to Delaiah and Shelemaiah, the sons of Sanballat the governor of Samaria.

Also Arsames knew nothing of all this that was done to us. Dated the twentieth of Marchesvan in the seventeenth year of King Darius.

"SHALL SUPPLY ALL THAT IS PROPER FOR A FREEBORN WIFE": THE MARRIAGE CONTRACT OF HERACLIDES AND DEMETRIA, 311 BC

Anonymous

311 B.C.

In the 7th year of the reign of Alexander son of Alexander, the 14th year of the satrapship of Ptolemy,* in the month Dius. Marriage contract of Heraclides and Demetria. Heraclides takes as his lawful wife Demetria, Coan, both being freeborn, from her father Leptines, Coan, and her mother Philotis, bringing clothing and ornaments to the value of 1,000 drachmae, and Heraclides shall supply to Demetria all that is proper for a freeborn wife, and we shall live together wherever it seems best to Leptines and Heraclides consulting in common. If Demetria is discovered doing any evil to the shame of her husband Heraclides, she shall be

---

* Ptolemy Soter, who, though practically an independent sovereign, retained the title of satrap till 305 BC

deprived of all that she brought, but Heraclides shall prove whatever he alleges against Demetria before three men whom they both accept. It shall not be lawful for Heraclides to bring home another wife in insult of Demetria nor to have children by another woman nor to do any evil against Demetria on any pretext. If Heraclides is discovered doing any of these things and Demetria proves it before three men whom they both accept, Heraclides shall give back to Demetria the dowry of 1,000 drachmae which she brought and shall moreover forfeit 1,000 drachmae of the silver coinage of Alexander. Demetria and those aiding Demetria to exact payment shall have the right of execution, as if derived from a legally decided action, upon the person of Heraclides and upon all the property of Heraclides both on land and on water. This contract shall be valid in every respect, wherever Heraclides may produce it against Demetria, or Demetria and those aiding Demetria to exact payment may produce it against Heraclides, as if the agreement had been made in that place. Heraclides and Demetria shall have the right to keep the contracts severally in their own custody and to produce them against each other. Witnesses: Cleon, Gelan; Anticrates, Temnian; Lysis, Temnian; Dionysius, Temnian; Aristomachus, Cyrenaean; Aristodicus, Coan.

THE MAGNIFICENT PROCESSION OF PTOLEMY II PHILADELPHUS, 285 BC

Athanaeus

At Alexandria.

First I will describe the tent prepared inside the citadel, apart from the place provided to receive the soldiers, artisans, and foreigners. For it was wonderfully beautiful, and worth talking of. Its size was such that it could accommodate one hundred and thirty couches [for ban-queters] arranged in a circle. The roof was upborne on wooden pillars fifty cubits high of which four were arranged to look like palm trees. On the outside of the pillars ran a portico, adorned with a peristyle on three sides with a vaulted roof. Here it was the feasters could sit down. The interior of this was surrounded with scarlet curtains; in the middle of the space, however, were suspended strange hides of beasts, strange both for their variegated colour, and their remarkable size. The part which surrounded this portico in the open air was shaded by myrtle trees and laurels, and other suitable shrubs.

As for the whole floor, it was strewed with every kind of flower; for Egypt, thanks to its mild climate, and the fondness of its people for gardening, produces abundantly, and all the year round, those flowers which are scarce in other lands, and then come only at special seasons. Roses, white lilies, and many another flower never lack in that country. Wherefore, although this entertainment took place in midwinter, there was a show of flowers that was quite incredible to the foreigners. For flowers of which one could not easily have found enough to make one chaplet in any other city, were here in vast abundance, to make chaplets for the guests . . . and were thickly strewn over the whole floor of the tent; so as really to give the appear-ance of a most divine meadow.

By the posts around the tent were placed animals carved in marble by the first artists, a full hundred in number; while in the spaces between the posts were hung pictures by the Sicyonian painters. And alternately with these were carefully selected images of every kind, and garments embroidered with gold and splendid cloaks, some having portraits of the kings of Egypt wrought upon them, and some stories from mythology. Above these were placed gold and silver shields alternately.

There follows a detailed account of the gold, silver and be-jewelled dishes and cutlery provided for the guests.

And now to go on to the shows and processions exhibited; for they passed through the Stadium of the city. First of all there went the procession of Lucifer [the name given to the planet Venus] for the fête began at the time when that star first appears. Then came processions in honour of the several gods. In the Dionysus procession, first of all went the Sileni to keep off the multitude, some clad in purple cloaks, and some in scarlet ones. These were followed by Satyrs, bearing gilded lamps made of ivy wood. After them came images of Victory, having golden wings, and they bore in their hands incense burners, six cubits in height, adorned with branches made of ivy wood and gold, and clad in tunics embroidered with figures of animals, and they themselves also had a deal of gold ornament about them. After them followed an altar six cubits high, a double altar, all covered with gilded ivy leaves, having a crown of vine leaves upon it all in gold. Next came boys in purple tunics, bearing frankincense and myrrh, and saffron on golden dishes. And then advanced forty Satyrs, crowned with golden ivy garlands; their bodies were painted some with purple, some with vermilion, and some with other colours. They wore each a golden crown, made to imitate vine leaves and ivy leaves. Presently also came Philiscus the Poet, who was a priest of Dionysus, and with him all the artisans employed in the service of that god; and following were the

Delphian tripods as prizes to the trainers of the athletes, one for the trainer of the youths, nine cubits high, the other for the trainer of the men, twelve cubits.

The next was a four-wheeled wagon fourteen cubits high and eight cubits wide; it was drawn by one hundred and eighty men. On it was an image of Dionysus – ten cubits high. He was pouring libations from a golden goblet, and had a purple tunic reaching to his feet . . . In front of him lay a Lacedaemonian goblet of gold, holding fifteen measures of wine, and a golden tripod, in which was a golden incense burner, and two golden bowls full of cassia and saffron; and a shade covered it round adorned with ivy and vine leaves, and all other kinds of greenery. To it were fastened chaplets and fillets, and ivy wands, drums, turbans, and actors' masks. After many other wagons came one twenty-five cubits long, and fifteen broad; and this was drawn by six hundred men. On this wagon was a sack, holding three thousand measures of wine, and consisting of leopards' skins sewn together. This sack allowed its liquor to escape, and it gradually flowed over the whole road.

More wonders followed, including chariots drawn by elephants, by ostriches, by zebras.

After these came a procession of troops – both horsemen and footmen, all superbly armed and appointed. There were 57,600 infantry, and 23,200 cavalry. All these marched in the procession. . . . all in their appointed armour . . .

The cost of this great occasion was 2,239 talents and 50 minae.

MEN, CLOTHES, CHATTERING: TWO WOMEN
FESTIVAL-GOERS, ALEXANDRIA, c. 275 BC

Theocritus

From *Theocritus' Idyll 15. Gorgo and Praxinoa are attending the Festival of Adonis.*

(Gorgo, with her maid Eutychis, calls on Praxinoa whose maid Eunoa answers the door.)

GORGO: Is Praxinoa at home?

PRAXINOA: Ah, Gorgo dear, here you are at last; I thought you were never coming. Yes, I'm here. Eunoa, see to a chair for her, and put a cushion on it.

GORGO: Thank you, it's very nice as it is.

PRAXINOA: Well, do sit down.

GORGO: My word, what an ass I've been. You should have seen the men and chariots; boots and long tunics all over the place. I only just got here alive. The road seemed endless, and your house would be the farthest of all.

PRAXINOA: That's my fool of a husband; came and took a place at the world's end, fit only for animals not human beings, just to stop us being neighbours and to stir up trouble, the old spoil-sport. He's always the same!

GORGO: Careful! Don't call your Dinon such things while Baby's around. Just look, dear, how he's watching you. Cheer up, little Zopyrus, my darling. She's not speaking of da-da.

PRAXINOA: Good Lord, the baby understands.

GORGO: Nice da-da.

PRAXINOA: That nice da-da of his! – the other day I said to him, "Daddy, please buy some soap and rouge from the shop." Do you know what he did? He came back with some salt, and him a grown man.

GORGO: Mine's just the same; he's terribly close with money, is Diocleidas. Yesterday he went and bought five old purses, shoddy old bits of dog's hair, all got to be repaired. And he paid 7/6d. apiece for them. But come on, get your dress and coat on. We're off to see the Adonis of the mighty king Ptolemy. I hear the Queen's outfit's pretty staggering.

PRAXINOA: Oh, I don't know. I expect it's just the same as usual.

GORGO: But if you've been and someone else hasn't, you can have a fine old gossip about it all. We must get a move on.

PRAXINOA: I suppose that those with nothing to do are always on holiday. Oh, all right then. Eunoa, you go and put that spinning back with the rest and stop picking your spots. Cats love to have a nice soft sleep. Here, get busy, and hurry up with some water. Heavens, we first want the water, and she brings the soap. Give it me, then. Not too much, wastrel. Now pour out the water. You slut, you've wet my dress, stop. Now I'm clean and sweet, thank God. Where's the key of the large chest? Bring it here.

GORGO: I like that folding dress, Praxinoa. It suits you. Tell me, how much did you pay for the material?

PRAXINOA: Don't remind me, Gorgo. Well over a fiver, and I put my heart and soul into making it up.

GORGO: Well, it's come out excellently.

PRAXINOA: Very kind of you to say so. Fetch me my cloak and arrange my hat properly. I'm leaving you here, baba. Horses bite little boys. You can squawl as much as you like, but I won't have you lamed. We're off! Phrygia,

take the baby and play with him; call in the dog and lock the outside door.

Heavens, what a crowd! How on earth are we to get through this mass? They're like ants. You've done us some wonderful good, Ptolemy, since your father was exalted to heaven. There aren't any crooks nowadays creeping around Egyptian-style, fleecing the pedestrians, and playing the sort of horrible games the dreadful, deceitful rascals played before.

Dear Gorgo, what's to become of us? Here are the king's war horses. Good sir, don't trample me down. Look how fierce the chestnut is and how he's rearing up. Eunoa, don't be so reckless; get out of the way. He'll finish off his leader. I thank my lucky stars that I left baby at home.

GORGO: Cheer up, Praxinoa; we've got left behind now and they've reached their places.

PRAXINOA: And I'm nearly myself again too. Ever since a child I've had a special dread of horses and clammy snakes. Hurry up! A big crowd's pushing down on us.

GORGO: Have you come from the Court, dear?

OLD WOMAN: Yes, ducks.

GORGO: Easy to get there?

OLD WOMAN: The Greeks got into Troy by trying, didn't they? Where there's a will there's a way.

GORGO: The old woman's gone off with her proverbs.

PRAXINOA: Women know everything, even about Adam and Eve.

GORGO: Oh, look, Praxinoa; what a crowd around the doors!

PRAXINOA: Staggering! Give me your hand, Gorgo. And you, Eunoa, take hold of Eutychis's. Hold on, lest you get separated. Let's all go in together. Hold on to me

tight, Eunoa. Damn, my summer coat's already split, Gorgo. Heavens, man, take care of my coat, if you want to live.

IST STRANGER: It's really out of my power, but I'll try.

PRAXINOA: What a mass! They're shoving like pigs.

STRANGER: Chin up, ladies; we're OK.

PRAXINOA: God bless you, Sir, for ever for looking after us. What a good, kind man! Eunoa's getting squashed. Come on, you coward, give a push.

Hurrah! "Everyone in", as the bridegroom said as he shut the door on the bride.

GORGO: Praxinoa, do come here. Just have a look at the decorations, so light and graceful. You'd say that they were some god's work.

PRAXINOA: The goddess of handicraft! The weavers and embroiderers that worked on those detailed pictures must have been marvels. How real everything seems, standing still or moving about. And how alive they look, quite unlike things spun. What a wonderful piece of work is man! And just look at the Adonis on his silver bed, with the first down just coming on his cheeks. Oh, thrice-loved Adonis, loved even in Hell!

2ND STRANGER: Do stop chattering like a lot of birds. They'll bore the pants off me with their platitudes.

PRAXINOA: Ha, where's he from? What's it to him if we do chatter. Go and lord it over your own slaves. You're talking to ladies from Syracuse. Actually we are Corinthian by birth like Bellerophon. We are talking Peloponnesian. I suppose Dorians are allowed to talk Doric? Let's pray only to have one boss. Don't you waste your time on me, sir.

GORGO: Hush, Praxinoa. The Argive lady's daughter is about to sing the *Adonis*. She's a pretty skilled singer and

won the competition for the dirge last year. She will do it beautifully, I'm sure. She's clearing her throat.

(The dirge is sung)

GORGO: Praxinoa, how wonderful we women are. She's lucky to know all that, and luckier still to be able to sing it so well. But it's time to go home. Diocleidas will be wanting his lunch. The man's as sharp as vinegar; you can't come near him when he's hungry. Good-bye, lovely Adonis, and I hope you find us well when you come again.

THE SALE OF A SLAVE GIRL, 259 BC

Anonymous

An official deed of sale.

In the 27th year of the reign of Ptolemy* son of Ptolemy and of his son Ptolemy, the priest of Alexander and of the gods Adelphi and the canephorus of Arsinoe Philadelphus being those in office in Alexandria, in the month Xandicus, at Birta in the land of Ammon. Nicanor son of Xenocles, Cnidian, in the service of Tobias, has sold to Zenon son of Agreophon, Caunian, in the service of Apollonius the dioecetes, a Babylonian girl named Sphragis, about seven years of age, for fifty drachmae. Guarantor . . . son of Ananias, Persian, of the troop of Tobias, cleruch. Witnesses: . . . judge; Polemon son of Straton, Macedonian, of the cavalrymen of Tobias, cleruch; Timopolis son of Botes, Milesian, Heraclitus son of Philippus, Athenian, Zenon son

* Ptolemy Philadelphus.

of Timarchus, Colophonian, Demostratus son of Dionysius, Aspendian, all four in the service of Apollonius the dioecetes. (Endorsed) Deed of sale of a girl.

ONE MAN'S CLOTHES: ZENON'S WARDROBE, 250 BC

Pisicles

Zenon's trunk in which are contained: 1 linen wrap, washed; 1 clay-coloured cloak, for winter, washed, and 1 worn, 1 for summer, half-worn, 1 natural-coloured, for winter, washed, and 1 worn, 1 vetch-coloured, for summer, new; 1 white tunic for winter, with sleeves, washed, 1 natural-coloured, for winter, with sleeves, worn, 1 natural-coloured, for winter, worn, 2 white, for winter, washed, and 1 half-worn, 3 for summer, white, new, 1 unbleached, 1 half-worn; 1 outer garment, white, for winter, washed; 1 coarse mantle; 1 summer garment, white, washed, and 1 half-worn; 1 pair of Sardian pillow-cases; 2 pairs of socks, clay-coloured, new, 2 pairs of white, new; 2 girdles, white, new. (Endorsed) From Pisicles, a list of Zenon's clothes.

COMPENSATIONS FOR CRIMES, ALEXANDRIA, 250 BC

Anonymous

Egypt under the Hellenes adopted Greek political institutions and laws (such as those below), but retained much of its old cultural and religious life. Alexandria, the capital of Hellenistic Egypt, was founded by Alexander the Great at the mouth of the Nile in 332 BC.

Threatening with Iron

If a freeman threatens a freeman with iron or copper or stone or . . . or wood, he shall forfeit a hundred drachmae, if he is worsted in the suit. But if a male slave or a female slave does any of these things to a freeman or a freewoman, they shall receive not less than a hundred stripes, or else the master of the offender, if he is defeated in the suit, shall forfeit to the injured party twice the amount of the penalty which is prescribed for a freeman.

Injuries done in Drunkenness

Whoever commits a personal injury in drunkenness or by night or in a temple or in the market-place shall forfeit twice the amount of the prescribed penalty.

Slave Striking Freemen

If a male slave or a female slave strikes a freeman or a freewoman, they shall receive not less than a hundred stripes, or else the master, if he acknowledges the fact, shall pay on behalf of his slave twice the amount of the penalty which is prescribed for a freeman. But if he disputes it, the plaintiff shall indict him, claiming for one blow a hundred drachmae, and if the master is condemned, he shall forfeit three times that amount without assessment; and for a greater number of blows the plaintiff shall himself assess the injury when he brings the suit, and whatever assessment is fixed by the court, the master shall forfeit three times that amount.

Blows between Freemen

If a freeman or a freewoman, making an unjust attack, strikes a freeman or a freewoman, they shall forfeit a hundred drachmae without assessment, if they are defeated in the suit. But if they strike more than one blow, the plaintiff in bringing the suit shall himself assess the damage caused by the blows, and whatever assessment is fixed by the court, the accused shall forfeit twice that amount. And if anyone strikes one of the magistrates while executing the administrative duties prescribed to the magistracy, he shall pay the penalties trebled, if he is defeated in the suit.

Outrages

If any person commits against another an outrage not provided for in the code, the injured party shall himself assess the damage in bringing his suit, but he shall further state specifically in what manner he claims to have been outraged and the date on which he was outraged. And the offender if condemned shall pay twice the amount of the assessment fixed by the court.

"SEND ME ZENOBIUS THE EFFEMINATE DANCER": A BILL OF ENTERTAINMENT, c. 245 BC

Demophon

The author and recipient of the below letter were government employees.

Demophon to Ptolemaeus greeting. Send me by hook or crook the flute-player Petous with both the Phrygian and the other flutes; and if any expenditure is necessary, pay and you shall recover from me.

Send me also Zenobius the effeminate dancer with a drum and cymbals and castanets, for the women want him for the sacrifice; and let him be dressed as finely as possible. Get the kid also from Aristion and send it to me. And if you have arrested the slave, hand him over to Semphtheus to bring to me. Send me also as many cheeses as you can, empty jars, vegetables of all sorts, and any delicacies that you may have. Goodbye. Put them on board with policemen who will help to bring the boat along. (Addressed) To Ptolemaeus.

A PETITION FROM A SCALDED WOMAN, 220 BC

Philista

Sent to Ptolemy Philopator.

To King Ptolemy greeting from Philista daughter of Lysias resident in Tricomia. I am wronged by Petechon. For as I was bathing in the baths of the aforesaid village on Tubi 7 of year 1, and had stepped out to soap myself, he being bathman in the women's rotunda and having brought in the jugs of hot water emptied one (?) over me and scalded my belly and my left thigh down to the knee, so that my life was in danger. On finding him I gave him into the custody of Nechthosiris the chief policeman of the village in the presence of Simon the epistates. I beg you therefore, O king, if it please you, as a suppliant who has sought your protection, not to suffer me, who am a working woman, to be thus lawlessly treated, but to order Diophanes the strategus to write to Simon the epistates and Nechthosiris the policeman that they are to bring Petechon before him in order that Diophanes may inquire into the case, hoping that having sought the protection of you, O king, the common benefactor of all, I may obtain justice. Farewell. (Docketed) To Simon. Send the accused. Year 1, Gorpiaeus 28 Tubi 12.

(Endorsed) Year 1, Gorpiaeus 28 Tubi 12. Philista against Petechon, bathman, about having been scalded.

"I BEG YOU, O KING, NOT TO SUFFER ME TO BE WRONGED BY MY DAUGHTER": A PETITION FROM AN AGED AND INFIRM FATHER, 220 BC

Ctesicles

Again sent to Ptolemy Philopator.

To King Ptolemy greeting from Ctesicles. I am being wronged by Dionysius and my daughter. Nice. For though I had nurtured her, being my own daughter and educated her and brought her up to womanhood, when I was stricken with bodily infirmity and my eyesight enfeebled she would not furnish me with any of the necessaries of life. And when I wished to obtain justice from her in Alexandria, she begged my pardon and in year 18 she gave me in the temple of Arsinoe Actia a written oath by the king that she would pay me twenty drachmae every month by means of her own bodily labour; if she failed to do so or transgressed any of the terms of her bond, she was to forfeit to me 500 drachmae on pain of incurring the consequences of the oath. Now, however, corrupted by Dionysius, who is a comedian, she is not keeping any of her engagements to me, in contempt of my old age and my present infirmity. I beg you therefore, O king, not to suffer me to be wronged by my daughter and Dionysius the comedian who has corrupted her, but to order Diophanes the strategus to summon them and hear our case; and if my words are true, let Diophanes deal with her corrupter as seems good to him and compel my daughter Nice to yield me my rights . . . For by this means I shall no longer be wronged, but having sought your protection, O king, I shall obtain justice.

ROBBERY IN A VINEYARD, 210 BC

Amosis

Memorandum to Teos the royal scribe. Amosis, village scribe of Apollonias,* to Teos greeting. I subjoin for your information a copy of the notification presented to me by Heracon the superintendent of the estate of Pitholaus. Goodbye. (Year) 12, Epeiph 9.

Notification to Amosis, scribe of the village of Apollonias, from Heracon, superintendent of the estate of Pitholaus. On the . . . of Epeiph Theophilus son of Dositheus, Philistion son of . . ., and Timaeus son of Telouphis, all three Jews of the Epigone, raided the fruit-garden of the aforesaid Pitholaus, which is in the bounds of the aforesaid village, and stripped the grapes from ten vines; and when Horus the guard ran out against them, they maltreated him and struck him on any part of the body that offered; and they carried off a vine-dresser's pruning-hook. The aforesaid robbers are living in Kerkeosiris. I estimate the grapes gathered as enough to make 6 metretae of wine. (Endorsed) To the royal scribe. Year 12, Epeiph 10. Concerning a vineyard of Pitholaus stripped of its grapes.

THE DRINKS BILL FOR A WAKE, 2ND CENTURY BC

Anonymous

Held by a social club for its late member, Kalatutis.

Hathur 17. For the funeral feast of Kalatutis: 1 six-chous jar of wine 2000 drachmae, 6 dinner loaves 190 dr., total 2190

* A village in the Fayum.

dr. 22 persons present, of whom 18 were members and 4
were guests, the latter being T . . . son of Numenius, Kames
son of Harphaesis, Teos son of Petechon, Papnebtunis son
of Sokeus, total 4. Total 22 at 100 dr. each, 2200 dr.;
remaining with treasurer 10 dr. 20th. 1 six-chous jar of wine
2000 dr., a garland 120 dr., total 2120 dr. Persons present,
18 members and . . . Nephoreges son of Kera . . . and Sen
. . . son of . . ., and guests Marres son of Pet . . ., Pete-
souchus son of Melas, Chaeremon son of Di . . ., total 23 at
100 dr. each, 2300 dr.; remaining with treasurer 180 dr.
Tubi 25. 1 jar of wine 2000 dr., a garland 120 dr., total
2120 dr. Persons present 21 at 100 dr. each, 2100 dr.; spent
in excess 20 dr.

"TRY GOING FROM PLACE TO PLACE TO CHEER EVERYBODY UP": THE DUTIES OF A PTOLEMAIC OECONOMUS, c. 200 BC

Anonymous

*An oeconomus was an interior financial official. The instruction below seems to
have been standard issue for each newly appointed oeconomus from his boss, the
Ptolemaic minister of finance.*

In your tours of inspection try in going from place to place
to cheer everybody up and to put them in better heart; and
not only should you do this by words but also, if any of
them complain of the village scribes or the comarchs about
any matter touching agricultural work, you should make
inquiry and put a stop to such doings as far as possible.

When the sowing has been completed it would be no bad
thing if you were to make a careful round of inspection; for
thus you will get an accurate view of the sprouting of the
crops and will easily notice the lands which are badly sown

or are not sown at all, and you will thus know those who have neglected their duty and will become aware if any have used the seed for other purposes.

You must regard it as one of your most indispensable duties to see that the nome be sown with the kinds of crops prescribed by the sowing-schedule. And if there be any who are hard pressed by their rents or are completely exhausted, you must not leave it unexamined.

Make a list of the cattle employed in cultivation, both the royal and the private, and take the utmost care that the progeny of the royal cattle, when old enough to eat hay, be consigned to the calf-byres . . .

Take care also that the prescribed supplies of corn, of which I send you a list, are brought down to Alexandria punctually, not only correct in amount but also tested and fit for use.

Visit also the weaving-establishments in which the linen is woven, and do your utmost to have the largest possible number of looms in operation, the weavers supplying the full amount of embroidered stuffs prescribed for the nome. If any of them are in arrears with the pieces ordered, let the prices fixed by the ordinance for each kind of stuff be exacted from them. Take especial care, too, that the linen is good and has the prescribed number of weft-threads . . .

Since the revenue from the pasturage dues, too, is one of the most important, it will most readily be increased if you carry out the registration (of cattle) in the best possible way. The most favourable season for one so engaged is about the month of Mesore; for the whole country in this month being covered with water, it happens that cattle-breeders send their flocks to the highest places, being unable to scatter them on other places.

See to it, too, that the goods for sale be not sold at prices

higher than those prescribed. Make also a careful investigation of those goods which have no fixed prices and on
which the dealers may put what prices they like; and after
having put a fair surplus on the wares being sold, make the
. . . dispose of them.

"BUT YOU HAVE NOT EVEN THOUGHT OF RETURNING HOME": A WIFE WRITES TO HER HUSBAND SOJOURNING AT THE TEMPLE OF SERAPIS, 168 BC

Isias

Isias' husband was "in retreat" at the Serapeum, Memphis, home of a religious community.

Isias to Hephaestion her brother,* greeting. If you are well,
and things in general are going right, it is as I am continually praying the gods. I myself am in good health, and
the child, and all at home; we talk of you continually.
When I got your letter from Horus, in which you explained
that you were in retreat at the Serapeum at Memphis, I
immediately gave thanks to the gods that you were well,
but that you did not return when all those who were in
retreat with you returned, distresses me. For having piloted
myself and your child out of such a crisis, and come to the
last extremity because of the high price of corn, I thought
that now at last on your return I should obtain some relief.
But you have never even thought of returning, nor spared a
look for our helpless state. While you were still at home, I
went short altogether, not to mention how long a time has
passed since then, and such disasters befallen, and you

* i.e. her husband

having sent us nothing. And now that Horus who brought
the letter has told me that you have been released from
your retreat, I am utterly distressed. Nor is this all, but
since your mother is in great trouble about it, I entreat you
for her sake and for ours to return to the city, unless indeed
something most pressing occupies you. Pray take care of
yourself that you may be in health. Good-bye.
To Hephaestion.
Year 2 Epeiph 30.

SUSPECTED MURDER, 178/167 BC

Anonymous police officer

4th year, Hathur 6. To Osoroeris, royal scribe. On the 5th
of the present month when patrolling the fields near the
village I found an effusion of blood (deleted: but no body),
and I learn from the villagers that Theodotus son of
Dositheus, having set out in that direction, has not yet
returned. I make this report.

REWARD: FOR RECOVERY OF ESCAPED
SLAVE, 156 BC

Anonymous

The 25th year, Epeiph 16. A slave of Aristogenes son of
Chrysippus, of Alabanda, ambassador, has escaped in
Alexandria, by name Hermon also called Nilus, by birth
a Syrian from Bambyce, about 18 years old, of medium
stature, beardless, with good legs, a dimple on the chin, a
mole by the left side of the nose, a scar above the left corner
of the mouth, tattooed on the right wrist with two barbaric
letters. He has taken with him 3 octadrachms of coined

gold, 10 pearls, an iron ring on which an oil-flask and strigils are represented, and is wearing a cloak and a loincloth. Whoever brings back this slave shall receive 3 talents of copper; if he points him out in a temple, 2 talents; if in the house of a substantial and actionable man, 5 talents. Whoever wishes to give information shall do so to the agents of the strategus.

There is also another who has escaped with him, Bion, a slave of Callicrates, one of the chief stewards at court, short of stature, broad at the shoulders, stout-legged, bright-eyed, who has gone off with an outer garment and a slave's wrap and a woman's dress (?) worth 6 talents 5,000 drachmae of copper.

Whoever brings back this slave shall receive the same rewards as for the above-mentioned. Information about this one also is to be given to the agents of the strategus.

THE WILL OF A SOLDIER, 126 BC

Dryton

The 44th year, Pauni 9, at Pathyris, before Asclepiades the agoranomus. Dryton son of Pamphilus, Cretan, one of the *diadochi*[1] and belonging to the reserve, hipparch over men, being sound of body, sane and sensible, has made the following will. May it be mine to own my property in good health, but if I should suffer the lot of man, I bequeath and give my property in land and movable objects and cattle and whatever else I may have acquired, first my war-horse and all my armour to Esthladas my son by my former wife Sarapias daughter of Esthladas son of Theon, of civic rank,[2] in accordance with the laws and with the will which

1 An honorific title.
2 That is, belonging to a family which possessed the citizenship in one of the Greek cities in Egypt.

has been made through the record-office at Diospolis Parva before Dionysius the agoranomus in the 6th year of the reign of Philometor, which will besides the other matters which it sets forth appointed as his guardian (?) . . . being a kinsman, and of the household slaves I give him 4, whose names are Myrsine and her 3 children (?) – but the remaining two females, whose names are Irene and Ampelion, I give to Apollonia and her sisters, being 5 in all – also the vineyard site belonging to me at . . . in the Pathyrite nome and the wells therein of baked brick and the other appurtenances and the cart with the harness and the dove-cote and the other half-finished one and a yard of which the boundaries are, on the south waste grounds of the said Esthladas, on the north a vaulted room of Apollonia the younger, on the east waste ground of Petras . . . son of Esthladas, on the west waste ground of Esthladas up to the door opening to the west. The remaining rooms and fixtures and . . . and the waste ground assigned for a dovecote down beyond the door of Esthladas and to the west of the vaulted chamber I give to Apollonia and Aristo and Aphrodisia and Nicarion and Apollonia the younger, being 5 in all, my daughters by my present wife Apollonia also called Semmonthis, in accordance with the laws, and they shall own the 2 female slaves and the cow in equal shares for their households, according to the division which I have made. Esthladas shall give up from the waste ground given to him opposite his door which opens to the west 4 square cubits for the site of an oven. Of the remaining buildings and waste grounds at Diospolis Magna in the Ammonium[3] and in the potters' quarter Esthladas shall receive half and Apollonia and her sisters half, and of all my

3 At Thebes

other property in corn and money contracts and all movable objects each party shall take half. Esthladas and
Apollonia with her sisters shall provide funds in common
for the building of a dove-cote on the site assigned until
they finish it; and to my wife Apollonia also called Semmonthis, if she stays at home living irreproachably, they
shall give every month for 4 years, for the maintenance of
herself and for her 2 daughters, 2½ artabae of wheat, $^1/_{12}$ of
croton, and 200 copper drachmae; and after 4 years they
shall give the same amounts in common to the two younger
daughters for 11 years. They shall give to Tachratis for a
dowry 12 copper talents out of the common funds. Whatever property Semmonthis may have manifestly acquired
for herself while living with Dryton, she shall continue to
own, and anyone who takes proceedings against her about
this . . . Year 44, Pauni 9.

ARRANGEMENTS FOR A ROMAN TOURIST, 112 BC

Hermias

A letter concerning the visit to the Fayum of the Roman senator Lucius Memmius.

Hermias to Horus, greeting. Appended is a copy of the
letter to Asclepiades. Take care therefore that action is
taken in accordance with it. Goodbye. The 5th year,
Xandicus 17, Mecheir 17.

To Asclepiades. Lucius Memmius a Roman Senator,
who occupies a position of highest rank and honour, is
making the voyage from the city as far as the Arsinoite
nome to see the sights. Let him be received with the utmost
magnificence, and take care that at the proper places the
guest-chambers be got ready, and the landing-stages to

them be completed, and that there be brought to him at the landing-stage the appended gifts of hospitality, and that the things for the furnishing of the guest-chamber, and the customary tit-bits for Petesuchus and the crocodiles, and the necessaries for the view of the labyrinth, and the offerings and sacrifices, be provided. In short, take the greatest care on all points that the visitor may thereby be well satisfied, and display the utmost zeal . . .

"NOR TO KEEP A CONCUBINE OR BOY": THE MARRIAGE CONTRACT OF PHILISCUS AND APOLLONIA, 92 BC

Dionysius

Year 22, Mecheir 11. Philiscus son of Apollonius, Persian of the Epigone, acknowledges to Apollonia also called Kellauthis, daughter of Heraclides, Persian, having with her as guardian her brother Apollonius, that he has received from her in copper money 2 talents 4000 drachmae, the dowry for herself, Apollonia, agreed upon with him . . . Keeper of the contract: Dionysius.

(Text of contract) In the 22nd year of the reign of Ptolemy also called Alexander, the god Philometor, the priest of Alexander and the other priests being as written in Alexandria, the 11th of the month Xandicus, which is the 11th of Mecheir, at Kerkeosiris in the division of Polemon of the Arsinoite nome. Philiscus son of Apollonius, Persian of the Epigone, acknowledges to Apollonia, also called Kellauthis, daughter of Heraclides, Persian, having with her as guardian her brother Apollonius, that he has received from her in copper money 2 talents 4,000 drachmae, the dowry for herself, Apollonia, agreed upon with him. Apollonia shall live with Philiscus, obeying him as a wife should her husband, owning their property in common with him. All necessaries and clothing and whatever else is proper for a wedded wife Philiscus shall supply to Apollonia, whether he is at home or abroad, in proportion to their means. It shall not be lawful for Philiscus to bring in another wife besides Apollonia, nor to keep a concubine or boy, nor to have children by another woman while Apollonia lives, nor to inhabit another house over which Apollonia is not mistress, nor to eject or insult or ill-treat her, nor to alienate any of their property to the detriment of Apollonia. If he is proved to be doing any of these things or fails to supply her with necessaries or clothing or other things as stated, Philiscus shall forthwith forfeit to Apollonia the dowry of 2 talents 4,000 drachmae of copper. In like manner it shall not be lawful for Apollonia to spend the night or day away from the house of Philiscus without Philiscus's consent or to consort with another man or to dishonour the common home or to cause Philiscus to be shamed by any act that brings shame upon a husband. If Apollonia chooses of her own will to separate from Philiscus, Philiscus shall repay her the bare dowry within ten days from the date of the demand. If he does not repay as stated, he shall forthwith forfeit to her one and a half times the amount of the dowry which he has received. Witnesses: Dionysius son of Patron, Dionysius son of Hermaiscus, Theon son of Ptolemaeus, Didymus son of Ptolemaeus, Dionysius son of Dionysius, Heraclius son of Diocles, all six Macedonians of the Epigone. Keeper of the contract: Dionysius. (Acknowledgement) I, Philiscus son of Apollonius, Persian of the Epigone, acknowledge that I have received the dowry of 2 talents 4,000 drachmae of copper as is stated above, and I have deposited the contract, being valid, with Dionysius. Dionysius son of Hermaiscus, the aforesaid, wrote for him, as he is illiterate. (Receipt) I, Dionysius, have received the contract, being valid. (Docketed) Deposited for registration on Mecheir 11 of year 22. (Endorsed) Marriage compact of Apollonia with Philiscus . . .

CLEOPATRA IN ROME, c. 45 BC

Cicero

The Egyptian queen had been brought to Rome by Caesar as his mistress. To the distaste of the statesman, orator and lawyer Marcus Tullius Cicero.

. . . I detest the Queen: let Hammonius, the voucher for her promises, vouch that I have good cause for saying so.* For all the presents she promised were things of a learned kind, and consistent with my character, such as I could proclaim on the housetops. As for Sara I know him to be not only an unprincipled rascal but aggressively insolent to me. Only once have I seen him at my house, and when I asked him politely what I could do for him, he said he was looking for Atticus. And the insolence of the Queen herself when she was living in Caesar's trans-Tiberine villa, the recollection of it is painful to me. So I will have nothing to do with any of them. They think me devoid not only of spirit, but of the ordinary feelings of a human being.

HOW CLEOPATRA BEWITCHED ANTONY, 41 BC

Plutarch

Plutarch wrote a century after the event, but his account of Antony and Cleopatra in Parallel Lives *seems to have embodied contemporaneous records. It without doubt*

* Presents from Cleopatra to Cicero had miscarried.

fuelled the Antony and Cleopatra legend. At the time, Mark Antony was one of the triumvirate who ruled Rome after Caesar's assassination.

When making preparation for the Parthian war, Antony sent to command her to make her personal appearance in Cilicia, to answer an accusation, that she had given great assistance, in the late wars, to Cassius. Dellius, who was sent on this message, had no sooner seen her face, and remarked her adroitness and subtlety in speech, but he felt convinced that Antony would not so much as think of giving any molestation to a woman like this; on the contrary, she would be the first in favour with him. So he set himself at once to pay his court to the Egyptian, and gave her his advice, "to go", in the Homeric style, to Cilicia, "in her best attire", and bade her fear nothing from Antony, the gentlest and kindest of soldiers.

She had some faith in the words of Dellius, but more in her own attractions, which, having formerly recommended her to Cæsar and the young Cnæus Pompey, she did not doubt might prove yet more successful with Antony. Their acquaintance was with her when a girl, young, and ignorant of the world, but she was to meet Antony in the time of life when women's beauty is most splendid, and their intellects are in full maturity.* She made great preparations for her journey, of money, gifts, and ornaments of value, such as so wealthy a kingdom might afford, but she brought with her her surest hopes in her own magic arts and charms.

She received several letters, both from Antony and from his friends, to summon her, but she took no account of these orders; and at last, as if in mockery of them, she came

---

* She was then about twenty-eight years old.

sailing up the river Cydnus, in a barge with gilded stern and outspread sails of purple, while oars of silver beat time to the music of flutes and fifes and harps. She herself lay all along, under a canopy of cloth of gold, dressed as Venus in a picture, and beautiful young boys, like painted Cupids, stood on each side to fan her. Her maids were dressed like Sea Nymphs and Graces, some steering at the rudder, some working at the ropes. The perfumes diffused themselves from the vessel to the shore, which was covered with multitudes, part following the galley up the river on either bank, part running out of the city to see the sight. The market place was quite emptied, and Antony at last was left alone sitting upon the tribunal; while the word went through all the multitude, that Venus was come to feast with Bacchus for the common good of Asia.

On her arrival, Antony sent to invite her to supper. She thought it fitter he should come to her; so, willing to show his good humour and courtesy, he complied, and went. He found the preparations to receive him magnificent beyond expression, but nothing so admirable as the great number of lights; for on a sudden there was let down altogether so great a number of branches with lights in them so ingeniously disposed, some in squares, and some in circles, that the whole thing was a spectacle that has seldom been equalled for beauty.

The next day, Antony invited her to supper, and was very desirous to outdo her as well in magnificence as contrivance; but he found he was altogether beaten in both, and was so well convinced of it, that he was himself the first to jest and mock at his poverty of wit, and his rustic awkwardness. She, perceiving that his raillery was broad and gross, and savoured more of the soldier than the courtier, rejoined in the same taste, and fell into it at once, without any sort of reluctance or reserve.

For her actual beauty, it is said, was not in itself so
remarkable that none could be compared with her, or that
no one could see her without being struck by it, but the
contact of her presence, if you lived with her, was irresistible; the attraction of her person, joining with the charm of
her conversation, and the character that attended all she
said or did, was something bewitching. It was a pleasure
merely to hear the sound of her voice, with which, like an
instrument of many strings, she could pass from one language to another; so that there were few of the barbarian
nations that she answered by an interpreter; to most of
them she spoke herself, as to the Æthiopians, Troglodytes,
Hebrews, Arabians, Syrians, Medes, Parthians, and many
others, whose language she had learnt; which was all the
more surprising, because most of the kings, her predecessors, scarcely gave themselves the trouble to acquire the
Egyptian tongue, and several of them quite abandoned the
Macedonian.

Antony was so captivated by her, that while Fulvia his
wife maintained his quarrels in Rome against Cæsar by
actual force of arms, and the Parthian troops, commanded
by Labienus (the king's generals having made him com-
mander-in-chief), were assembled in Mesopotamia, and
ready to enter Syria, he could yet suffer himself to be
carried away by her to Alexandria, there to keep holiday,
like a boy, in play and diversion, squandering and fooling
away in enjoyment that most costly, as Antiphon says, of all
valuables, time. They had a sort of company, to which they
gave a particular name, calling it that of the "Inimitable
Livers". The members entertained one another daily in
turn, with an extravagance of expenditure beyond measure
or belief.

Philotas, a physician of Amphissa, who was at that time a

student of medicine in Alexandria, used to tell my [Plutarch's] grandfather Lamprias, that, having some acquaintance with one of the royal cooks, he was invited by him, being a young man, to come and see the sumptuous preparations for supper. So he was taken into the kitchen, where he admired the prodigious variety of all things; but particularly, seeing eight wild boars roasting whole, says he, "Surely you have a great number of guests." The cook laughed at his simplicity, and told him there were not above twelve to sup, but that every dish was to be served up just roasted to a turn, and if any thing was but one minute ill timed, it was spoiled; "And," said he, "maybe Antony will sup just now, maybe not this hour, maybe he will call for wine, or begin to talk, and will put it off. So that," he continued, "it is not one, but many suppers must be had in readiness, as it is impossible to guess at his hour."

To return to Cleopatra; Plato admits four sorts of flattery, but she had a thousand. Were Antony serious or disposed to mirth, she had at any moment some new delight or charm to meet his wishes; at every turn she was upon him, and let him escape her neither by day nor by night. She played at dice with him, drank with him, hunted with him; and when he exercised in arms, she was there to see. At night she would go rambling with him to disturb and torment people at their doors and windows, dressed like a servant woman, for Antony also went in servant's disguise, and from these expeditions he often came home very scurvily answered, and sometimes even beaten severely, though most people guessed who it was. However, the Alexandrians in general liked it all well enough, and joined good-humouredly and kindly in his frolic and play, saying they were much obliged to Antony for acting his tragic parts at Rome, and keeping his comedy for them.

It would be trifling without end to be particular in his follies, but his fishing must not be forgotten. He went out one day to angle with Cleopatra, and, being so unfortunate as to catch nothing in the presence of his mistress, he gave secret orders to the fishermen to dive under water, and put fishes that had been already taken upon his hooks; and these he drew so fast that the Egyptian perceived it. But, feigning great admiration, she told everybody how dexterous Antony was, and invited them next day to come and see him again. So, when a number of them had come on board the fishing boats, as soon as he had let down his hook, one of her servants was beforehand with his divers, and fixed upon his hook a salted fish from Pontus. Antony, feeling his line give, drew up the prey, and when, as may be imagined, great laughter ensued, "Leave," said Cleopatra, "the fishing-rod, general, to us poor sovereigns of Pharos and Canopus; your game is cities, provinces, and kingdoms."

ON GOING TO BED WITH CLEOPATRA, 33 BC

Mark Antony

The letter below is addressed to Antony's fellow triumvir, Octavian. The two men went to war in 32 BC, not least because of Antony's relationship with Cleopatra; to enjoy her charms fully, Antony divorced his wife — who happened to be the sister of Octavian.

What's upset you? Because I go to bed with Cleopatra? But she's my wife, and I've been doing so for nine years, not just recently. And, anyway, is Livia your only pleasure? I expect that you will have managed, by the time you read this, to have hopped into bed with Tertulla, Terentilla, Rufilla, Salvia Titisenia, or the whole lot of them. Does it really matter where, or with what women, you get your excitement?

ENVOI: EGYPT AND ITS CONDITION UNDER ROME, c. AD 1

Strabo

At present [in Augustus's time] Egypt is a Roman province, and pays considerable tribute, and is well governed by prudent persons sent there in succession. The governor thus sent out has the rank of king. Subordinate to him is the administrator of justice, who is the supreme judge in many cases. There is another officer called the Idologus whose business is to inquire into property for which there is no claimant, and which of right falls to Cæsar. These are accompanied by Cæsar's freedmen and stewards, who are intrusted with affairs of more or less importance.

Three legions are stationed in Egypt, one in the city of Alexandria, the rest in the country. Besides these, there are also nine Roman cohorts quartered in the city, three on the borders of Ethiopia in Syene, as a guard to that tract, and three in other parts of the country. There are also three bodies of cavalry distributed at convenient posts.

Of the native magistrates in the cities, the first is the "Expounder of the Law" – who is dressed in scarlet. He receives the customary honours of the land, and has the care of providing what is necessary for the city. The second is the "Writer of the Records"; the third is the "Chief Judge"; the fourth is the "Commander of the Night Guard". These officials existed in the time of the Ptolemaic kings, but in consequence of the bad administration of the public affairs by the latter, the prosperity of the city of Alexandria was ruined by licentiousness. Polybius expresses his indignation at the state of things when he was there. He describes the inhabitants of Alexandria as being composed of three classes, – first the Egyptians and natives, acute in mind, but very poor citizens, and wrongfully meddlesome in civic affairs. Second were the mercenaries, – a numerous and undisciplined body, – for it was an old custom to keep foreign soldiers – who from the worthlessness of their sovrans knew better how to lord it than to obey. The third were the [so-called] "Alexandrines", who, for the same reason, were not orderly citizens; however they were better than the mercenaries, for although they were a mixed race, yet being of Greek origin they still retained the usual Hellenic customs.

Such, then, if not worse, were the conditions of Alexandria under the last kings. The Romans, as far as they were able, corrected – as I have said – many abuses, and established an orderly government – by setting up vice-governors, "nomarchs", and "ethnarchs", whose business it was to attend to the details of administration.

APPENDIX

APPENDIX I: THE LEGEND OF OSIRIS

Donald A. Mackenzie

In the beginning of Egyptian mythology, Osiris was merely one of the gods of the king's afterlife. During the Middle Kingdom, when the afterlife became "democratized", Osiris became the "King of the Dead" for all (correctly buried) Egyptians. He also took on many of the functions of Neper, the "grain-god who lives after death". Thus Osiris became not only the god of death but of agriculture. The myth of Osiris – in which he is killed, dismembered and resurrected – is a complete analogy of the crop cycle, with its reaping, threashing, planting and new growth. Accordingly, Osiris was frequently portrayed as having a skin of black (the colour of fertile Nile mud) or green (the colour of plant growth). By legend, the head of Osiris was buried at Abydos, which became one of the most sacred places in Egypt, the site of the great Festival of Osiris and necropolis of kings and nobles.

When Osiris was born, a voice from out of the heavens proclaimed: "Now hath come the lord of all things." The wise man Pamyles had knowledge of the tidings in a holy place at Thebes, and he uttered a cry of gladness, and told the people that a good and wise king had appeared among men.

When Ra grew old and ascended unto heaven, Osiris sat in his throne and ruled over the land of Egypt. Men were but savages when he first came amongst them. They hunted wild animals, they wandered in broken tribes hither and thither, up and down the valley and among the mountains, and the tribes contended fiercely in battle. Evil were their ways and their desires were sinful.

Osiris ushered in a new age. He made good and binding laws, he uttered just decrees, and he judged with wisdom between men. He caused peace to prevail at length over all the land of Egypt.

Isis was the queen consort of Osiris, and she was a

woman of exceeding great wisdom. Perceiving the need of
mankind, she gathered the ears of barley and wheat which
she found growing wild, and these she gave unto the king.
Then Osiris taught men to break up the land which had
been under flood, to sow the seed, and, in due season, to
reap the harvest. He instructed them also how to grind corn
and knead flour and meal so that they might have food in
plenty. By the wise ruler was the vine trained upon poles,
and he cultivated fruit trees and caused the fruit to be
gathered. A father was he unto his people, and he taught
them to worship the gods, to erect temples, and to live holy
lives. The hand of man was no longer lifted against his
brother. There was prosperity in the land of Egypt in the
days of Osiris the Good.

When the king perceived the excellent works which he
had accomplished in Egypt, he went forth to traverse the
whole world with purpose to teach wisdom unto all men,
and prevail upon them to abandon their evil ways. Not by
battle conquest did he achieve his triumphs, but by reason
of gentle and persuasive speech and by music and song.
Peace followed in his footsteps, and men learned wisdom
from his lips.

Isis reigned over the land of Egypt until his return. She
was stronger than Set, who regarded with jealous eyes the
good works of his brother, for his heart was full of evil and
he loved warfare better than peace. He desired to stir up
rebellion in the kingdom. The queen frustrated his wicked
designs. He sought in vain to prevail in battle against her,
so he plotted to overcome Osiris by guile. His followers
were seventy and two men who were subjects of the dusky
queen of Ethiopia.[1]

1 After the period of Ethiopian supremacy (Twenty-fifth Dynasty) Set was identified
with the Ethiopians.

When Osiris returned from his mission, there was great rejoicing in the land. A royal feast was held, and Set came to make merry, and with him were his fellow conspirators. He brought a shapely and decorated chest, which he had caused to be made according to the measurements of the king's body. All men praised it at the feast, admiring its beauty, and many desired greatly to possess it. When hearts were made glad with beer-drinking, Set proclaimed that he would gift the chest unto him whose body fitted its proportions with exactness. There was no suspicion of evil design among the faithful subjects of Osiris. The guests spoke lightly, uttering jests one against another, and all were eager to make trial as Set had desired. So it happened that one after another entered the chest on that fateful night, until it seemed that no man could be found to win it for himself. Then Osiris came forward. He lay down within the chest, and he filled it in every part. But dearly was his triumph won in that dark hour which was his hour of doom. Ere he could raise his body, the evil followers of Set sprang suddenly forward and shut down the lid, which they nailed fast and soldered with lead. So the richly decorated chest became the coffin of the good king Osiris, from whom departed the breath of life.

The feast was broken up in confusion. Merry-making ended in sorrow, and blood flowed after that instead of beer. Set commanded his followers to carry away the chest and dispose of it secretly. As he bade them, so did they do. They hastened through the night and flung it into the Nile. The current bore it away in the darkness, and when morning came it reached the great ocean and was driven hither and thither, tossing among the waves. So ended the days of Osiris and the years of his wise and prosperous reign in the land of Egypt.

When the grievous tidings were borne unto Isis, she was

stricken with great sorrow and refused to be comforted. She wept bitter tears and cried aloud. Then she uttered a binding vow, cut off a lock of her shining hair, and put on the garments of mourning. Thereafter the widowed queen wandered up and down the land, seeking for the body of Osiris.

Nor would she rest nor stay until she found what she sought. She questioned each one she encountered, and one after another they answered her without knowledge. Long she made search in vain, but at length she was told by shoreland children that they had beheld the chest floating down the Nile and entering the sea by the Delta mouth which takes its name from the city of Tanis.[2]

Meanwhile Set, the usurper, ascended the throne of Osiris and reigned over the land of Egypt. Men were wronged and despoiled of their possessions. Tyranny prevailed and great disorder, and the followers of Osiris suffered persecution. The good queen Isis became a fugitive in the kingdom, and she sought concealment from her enemies in the swamps and deep jungle of the Delta. Seven scorpions followed her, and these were her protectors. Ra, looking down from heaven, was moved to pity because of her sore distress, and he sent to her aid Anubis, "the opener of the ways", who was the son of Osiris and Nepthys, and he became her guide.

One day Isis sought shelter at the house of a poor woman, who was stricken with such great fear when she beheld the fearsome scorpions that she closed the door against the wandering queen. But a scorpion gained entrance, and bit her child so that he died. Then loud and long were the lamentations of the stricken mother. The heart of Isis was touched with pity, and she uttered magical

2 Tanis was during the later Dynasties associated with the worship of Set as Sutekh.

words which caused the child to come to life again, and the woman ministered unto the queen with gratitude while she remained in the house.

Then Isis gave birth unto her son Horus; but Set came to know where the mother and babe were concealed, and he made them prisoners in the house.[3]

It was his desire to put Horus to death, lest he should become his enemy and the claimant of the throne of Osiris. But wise Thoth came out of heaven and gave warning unto Isis, and she fled with her child into the night. She took refuge in Buto, where she gave Horus into the keeping of Uazit, the virgin goddess of the city, who was a serpent,[4] so that he might have protection against the jealous wrath of Set, his wicked uncle, while she went forth to search for the body of Osiris. But one day, when she came to gaze upon the child, she found him lying dead. A scorpion had bitten him, nor was it in her power to restore him to life again. In her bitter grief she called upon the great god Ra. Her voice ascended to high heaven, and the sun boat was stayed in its course. Then wise Thoth came down to give aid. He worked a mighty spell; he spoke magical words over the child Horus, who was immediately restored to life again.[5] It was the will of the gods that he should grow into strong manhood and then smite his father's slayer.

The coffin of Osiris was driven by the waves to Byblos, in Syria, and it was cast upon the shore. A sacred tree sprang up and grew round it, and the body of the dead ruler was enclosed in its great trunk. The king of that alien land marvelled greatly at the wonderful tree, because that it had

3 Another version of the myth places the birth of Horus after the body of Osiris was found.
4 She took the form of a shrew mouse to escape Set when he searched for Horus.
5 Thoth in his lunar character as divine physician.

such rapid growth, and he gave command that it should be cut down. As he desired, so it was done. Then was the trunk erected in his house as a sacred pillar, but to no man was given knowledge of the secret which it contained.

A revelation came unto Isis, and she set out towards Byblos in a ship. When she reached the Syrian coast she went ashore clad in common raiment, and she sat beside a well, weeping bitterly. Women came to draw water, and they spoke to her with pity, but Isis answered not, nor ceased to grieve, until the handmaidens of the queen drew nigh. Unto them she gave kindly greetings. When they had spoken gently unto her she braided their hair, and into each lock she breathed sweet and alluring perfume. So it chanced that when the maidens returned unto the king's house the queen smelt the perfume, and commanded that the strange woman should be brought before her. Then it was that Isis found favour in the eyes of the queen, who chose her to be the foster-mother of the royal babe.

But Isis refused to suckle the child, and to silence his cries for milk she put her finger into his mouth. When night came she caused fire to burn away his flesh, and she took the form of a swallow and flew, uttering broken cries of sorrow, round about the sacred pillar which contained the body of Osiris. It chanced that the queen came nigh and beheld her babe in the flames. She immediately plucked him forth; but although she rescued his body she caused him to be denied immortality.[6]

Isis again assumed her wonted form, and she confessed unto the queen who she was. Then she asked the king that the sacred pillar be given unto her. The boon was granted,

---

6 We have here a suggestion of belief in cremation, which was practised by the cave-dwellers of southern Palestine. The ghost of Patroklos says: "Never again will I return from Hades when I receive from you my meed of fire." – *Iliad*, xxiii, 75.

and she cut deep into the trunk and took forth the chest which was concealed therein. Embracing it tenderly, she uttered cries of lamentation that were so bitter and keen that the royal babe died with terror. Then she consecrated the sacred pillar, which she wrapped in linen and anointed with myrrh, and it was afterwards placed in a temple which the king caused to be erected to Isis, and for long centuries it was worshipped by the people of Byblos.

The coffin of Osiris was borne to the ship in which the queen goddess had sailed unto Syria. Then she went aboard, and took with her Maneros, the king's first-born, and put forth to sea. The ship sped on, and the land faded from sight. Isis yearned to behold once again the face of her dead husband, and she opened the chest and kissed passionately his cold lips, while tears streamed from her eyes. Maneros, son of the King of Byblos, came stealthily behind her, wondering what secret the chest contained. Isis looked round with anger, her bright eyes blinded him, and he fell back dead into the sea.

When Isis reached the land of Egypt she concealed the body of the dead king in a secret place, and hastened towards the city of Buto to embrace her son Horus; but shortlived was her triumph. It chanced that Set came hunting the boar[7] at full moon in the Delta jungle, and he found the chest which Isis had taken back from Syria. He caused it to be opened, and the body of Osiris was taken forth and rent into fourteen pieces, which he cast into the Nile, so that the crocodiles might devour them. But these reptiles had fear of Isis and touched them not, and they were scattered along the river banks.[8] A fish (Oxyrhynchus) swallowed the phallus.

7 The Osiris boar.
8 The crocodile worshippers held that their sacred reptile recovered the body of Osiris for Isis.

The heart of Isis was filled with grief when she came to know what Set had done. She had made for herself a papyrus boat and sailed up and down the Delta waters, searching for the fragments of her husband's body, and at length she recovered them all, save the part which had been swallowed by the fish. She buried the fragments where they were found, and for each she made a tomb. In after days temples were erected over the tombs, and in these Osiris was worshipped by the people for long centuries.

Set continued to rule over Egypt, and he persecuted the followers of Osiris and Isis in the Delta swamps and along the seacoast to the north. But Horus, who was rightful king, grew into strong manhood. He prepared for the coming conflict, and became a strong and brave warrior. Among his followers were cunning workers in metal who were called Mesniu (smiths), and bright and keen were their weapons of war. The sun hawk was blazoned on their battle banners.

One night there appeared to Horus in a dream a vision of his father Osiris.[9] The ghost urged him to overthrow Set, by whom he had been so treacherously put to death, and Horus vowed to drive his wicked uncle and all his followers out of the land of Egypt. So he gathered his army together and went forth to battle. Set came against him at Edfu and slew many of his followers. But Horus secured the aid of the tribes that remained faithful to Osiris and Isis, and Set was again attacked and driven towards the eastern frontier. The usurper uttered a great cry of grief when he was forced to take flight. He rested at Zaru, and there was the last battle fought. It was waged for many days, and Horus lost an eye. But Set was still more grievously wounded,[10] and he was at length driven with his army out of the kingdom.

9 This is the earliest known form of the Hamlet myth.
10 He was mutilated by Horus as he himself had mutilated Osiris.

It is told that the god Thoth descended out of heaven and healed the wounds of Horus and Set. Then the slayer of Osiris appeared before the divine council and claimed the throne. But the gods gave judgment that Horus was the rightful king, and he established his power in the land of Egypt, and became a wise and strong ruler like to his father Osiris.

Another version of the legend relates that when the fragments of the body of Osiris were recovered from the Nile, Isis and Nepthys lamented over them, weeping bitterly. In one of the temple chants Isis exclaims:

> Gods, and men before the face of the gods, are weeping for thee at the same time when they behold me!
> Lo! I invoke thee with wailing that reacheth high as heaven —
> Yet thou hearest not my voice. Lo! I, thy sister, I love thee more than all the earth —
> And thou lovest not another as thou dost thy sister!

Nepthys cries,

> Subdue every sorrow which is in the hearts of us thy sisters . . .
> Live before us, desiring to behold thee.[11]

The lamentations of the goddesses were heard by Ra, and he sent down from heaven the god Anubis, who, with the assistance of Thoth and Horus, united the severed portions of the body of Osiris, which they wrapped in linen bandages. Thus had origin the mummy form of the god.

---

11 *The Burden of Isis*, translated by J. T. Dennis (Wisdom of the East Series).

Then the winged Isis hovered over the body, and the air from her wings entered the nostrils of Osiris so that he was imbued with life once again. He afterwards became the Judge and King of the Dead.

Egyptian burial rites were based upon this legend. At the ceremony enacted in the tomb chapel two female relatives of the deceased took the parts of Isis and Nepthys, and recited magical formulæ so that the dead might be imbued with vitality and enabled to pass to the Judgment Hall and Paradise.

Osiris and Isis, the traditional king and queen of ancient Egyptian tribes, were identified with the deities who symbolized the forces of Nature, and were accordingly associated with agricultural rites.

The fertility of the narrow strip of country in the Nile valley depends upon the River Nile, which overflows its banks every year and brings down fresh soil from the hills. The river is at its lowest between April and June, the period of winter. Fed by the melting snows on the Abyssinian hills, and by the equatorial lakes, which are flooded during the rainy season, the gradual rise of the river becomes perceptible about the middle of June. The waters first assume a reddish tint on account of the clay which they carry. For a short period they then become greenish and unwholesome. Ere that change took place the Ancient Egyptians were wont to store up water for domestic use in large jars. By the beginning of August the Nile runs high. It was then that the canals were opened in ancient days, so that the waters might fertilize the fields.

"As the Nile rose," writes Wilkinson,[12] "the peasants were careful to remove the flocks and herds from the

12 *The Ancient Egyptians*, Sir J. Gardner Wilkinson.

lowlands; and when a sudden irruption of the water, owing to the bursting of a dike, or an unexpected and unusual increase of the river, overflowed the fields and pastures, they were seen hurrying to the spot, on foot or in boats, to rescue the animals and to remove them to the high grounds above the reach of the inundation . . . And though some suppose the inundation does not now attain the same height as of old, those who have lived in the country have frequently seen the villages of the Delta standing, as Herodotus describes them, like islands in the Ægean Sea, with the same scenes of rescuing the cattle from the water." According to Pliny, "a proper inundation is of 16 cubits . . . in 12 cubits the country suffers from famine, and feels a deficiency even in 13; 14 causes joy, 15 scarcity, 16 delight; the greatest rise of the river to this period was of 18 cubits."

When the river rose very high in the days of the Pharaohs, "the lives and property of the inhabitants", says Wilkinson, "were endangered"; in some villages the houses collapsed. Hence the legend that Ra sought to destroy his enemies among mankind.

The inundation is at its height by the end of September, and continues stationary for about a month. Not until the end of September does the river resume normal proportions. November is the month for sowing; the harvest is reaped in Upper Egypt by March and in Lower Egypt by April.

It was believed by the ancient agriculturists that the tears of Isis caused the river to increase in volume. When Sirius rose before dawn about the middle of July it was identified with the goddess. In the sun-cult legend this star is Hathor, "the eye of Ra", who comes to slaughter mankind. There are evidences that human sacrifices were offered to the sun god at this period.

E. W. Lane, in his *Manners and Customs of the Modern*

Egyptians, tells that the night of 17 June is called "Leyleten-Nuktah", or "the Night of the Drop", because "it is believed that a miraculous drop then falls into the Nile and causes it to rise." An interesting ceremony used to be performed at "the cutting of the dam" in old Cairo. A round pillar of earth was formed, and it was called the "bride", and seeds were sown on the top of it. Lane says that an ancient Arabian historian "was told that the Egyptians were accustomed, at the period when the Nile began to rise, to deck a young virgin in gay apparel, and throw her into the river, as a sacrifice to obtain a plentiful inundation."

When the ancient Egyptians had ploughed their fields they held a great festival at which the moon god, who, in his animal form, symbolized the generative principle, was invoked and worshipped. Then the sowing took place, amidst lamentations and mourning for the death of Osiris. The divine being was buried in the earth; the seeds were the fragments of his body. Reference is made to this old custom in Psalm cxxvi: "They that sow in tears shall reap in joy. He that goeth forth and weepeth, bearing precious seed, shall doubtless come again with rejoicing, bringing his sheaves with him."

When harvest operations began, the Egyptians mourned because they were slaying the corn spirit. Diodorus Siculus tells that when the first handful of grain was cut, the Egyptian reapers beat their breasts and lamented, calling upon Isis. When, however, all the sheaves were brought in from the fields, they rejoiced greatly and held their "harvest home".

Both Osiris and Isis were originally identified with the spirits of the corn. The former represented the earth god and the latter the earth goddess. But after the union of the tribes which worshipped the human incarnations of ancient deities, the rival conceptions were fused. As a result we find that the inundation is symbolized now as the male principle and now as the female principle; the Nile god, Hapi, is depicted as a man with female breasts. In an Abydos temple chant Isis makes reference to herself as "the woman who was made a male by her father, Osiris."

Source: Egyptian Myth and Legend,. *Donald A. Mackenzie, Gresham Publishing, London, 1907.*

APPENDIX II: THE DISCOVERY AND OPENING OF TUTANKHAMUN'S TOMB, LUXOR, NOVEMBER 1922–FEBRUARY 1924

Howard Carter

The tomb of the 19th Dynasty boy pharaoh Tutankhamun [Tutankamen, Tutankaten] was discovered in the Valley of the Kings by Egyptologist Howard Carter in November 1922.

[The history of The Valley of the Tombs of the Kings]. has never lacked the dramatic element, and in this, the latest episode, it has held to its traditions. For consider the circumstances. This was to be our final season in The Valley. Six full seasons we had excavated there, and season after season had drawn a blank; we had worked for months at a stretch and found nothing, and only an excavator knows how desperately depressing that can be; we had almost made up our minds that we were beaten, and were preparing to leave The Valley and try our luck elsewhere; and then – hardly had we set hoe to ground in our last despairing effort than we made a discovery that far exceeded our wildest dreams. Surely, never before in the whole history of excavation has a full digging season been compressed within the space of five days.

Let me try and tell the story of it all. It will not be easy, for the dramatic suddenness of the initial discovery left me in a dazed condition, and the months that have followed have been so crowded with incident that I have hardly had time to think. Setting it down on paper will perhaps give me a chance to realize what has happened and all that it means.

I arrived in Luxor on October 28th [1922], and by November 1st I had enrolled my workmen and was ready to begin. Our former excavations had stopped short at the north-east corner of the tomb of Ramses VI, and from this point I started trenching southwards . . . In this area there were a number of roughly constructed workmen's huts, used probably by the labourers in the tomb of Ramses. These huts, built about three feet above bed-rock, covered the whole area in front of the Ramseside tomb, and continued in a southerly direction to join up with a similar group of huts on the opposite side of The Valley, discovered by Davis . . . By the evening of November 3rd we had laid bare a sufficient number of these huts for experimental purposes, so, after we had planned and noted them, they were removed, and we were ready to clear away the three feet of soil that lay beneath them.

Hardly had I arrived on the work next morning (November 4th) than the unusual silence, due to the stoppage of the work, made me realize that something out of the ordinary had happened, and I was greeted by the announcement that a step cut in the rock had been discovered underneath the very first hut to be attacked. This seemed too good to be true, but a short amount of extra clearing revealed the fact that we were actually in the entrance of a steep cut in the rock, some thirteen feet below the entrance to the tomb of Ramses VI, and a similar depth from the present bed level of The Valley. The manner of cutting was that of the sunken stairway entrance so common in The Valley, and I almost dared to hope that we had found our tomb at last. Work continued feverishly throughout the whole of that day and the morning of the next, but it was not until the afternoon of November 5th that we succeeded in clearing away the masses of rubbish that overlay the cut, and were able to demarcate the upper edges of the stairway on all its four sides.

It was clear by now beyond any question that we actually had before us the entrance to a tomb, but doubts, born of previous disappointments, persisted in creeping in. There was always the horrible possibility that the tomb was an unfinished one, never completed and never used: if it had been finished there was the depressing probability that it had been completely plundered in ancient times. On the other hand, there was just the chance of an untouched or only partially plundered tomb, and it was with ill-suppressed excitement that I watched the descending steps of the staircase, as one by one they came to light. The cutting was excavated in the side of a small hillock, and, as the work progressed, its western edge receded under the slope of the rock until it was, first partially, and then completely, roofed in, and became a passage, ten feet high by six feet wide. Work progressed more rapidly now; step succeeded step, and at the level of the twelfth, towards sunset, there was disclosed the upper part of a doorway, blocked, plastered, and sealed.

A sealed doorway – it was actually true, then! Our years of patient labour were to be rewarded after all, and I think my first feeling was one of congratulation that my faith in The Valley had not been unjustified. With excitement growing to fever heat I searched the seal impressions of the door for evidence of the identity of the owner, but could find no name: the only decipherable ones were those of the well-known royal necropolis seal, the jackal and nine captives. Two facts, however, were clear: first, the employment of this royal seal was certain evidence that the tomb had been constructed for a person of very high standing; and second, that the sealed door was entirely screened from above by workmen's huts of the Twentieth Dynasty was sufficiently clear proof that at least from that date it had never been entered. With that for the moment I had to be content.

While examining the seals I noticed, at the top of the doorway, where some of the plaster had fallen away, a heavy wooden lintel. Under this, to assure myself of the method by which the doorway had been blocked, I made a small peephole, just large enough to insert an electric torch, and discovered that the passage beyond the door was filled completely from floor to ceiling with stones and rubble – additional proof this of the care with which the tomb had been protected.

It was a thrilling moment for an excavator. Alone, save for my native workmen, I found myself, after years of comparatively unproductive labour, on the threshold of what might prove to be a magnificent discovery. Anything, literally anything, might lie beyond that passage, and it needed all my self-control to keep from breaking down the doorway, and investigating then and there.

One thing puzzled me, and that was the *smallness of the opening in comparison with* the ordinary Valley tombs. The design was certainly of the Eighteenth Dynasty. Could it be the tomb of a noble buried here by royal consent? Was it a royal cache, a hiding-place to which a mummy and its equipment had been removed for safety? Or was it actually the tomb of the king for whom I had spent so many years in search?

Once more I examined the seal impressions for a clue, but on the part of the door so far laid bare only those of the royal necropolis seal already mentioned were clear enough to read. Had I but known that a few inches lower down there was a perfectly clear and distinct impression of the seal of Tut-ankh-Amen [Tutankhamun], the king I most desired to find, I would have cleared on, had a much better night's rest in consequence, and saved myself nearly three weeks of uncertainty. It was late, however, and darkness was already upon us. With some reluctance I reclosed the small hole that I had made, filled in our excavation for protection during the night, selected the most trustworthy of my workmen – themselves almost as excited as I was – to watch all night above the tomb, and so home by moonlight, riding down The Valley.

Naturally my wish was to go straight ahead with our clearing to find out the full extent of the discovery, but Lord Carnarvon* was in England, and in fairness to him I had to delay matters until he could come. Accordingly, on the morning of November 6th I sent him the following cable: "At last have made wonderful discovery in Valley; a magnificent tomb with seals intact; re-covered same for your arrival; congratulations."

My next task was to secure the doorway against interference until such time as it could finally be re-opened. This we did by filling our excavation up again to surface level, and rolling on top of it the large flint boulders of which the workmen's huts had been composed. By the evening of the same day, exactly forty-eight hours after we had discovered the first step of the staircase, this was accomplished. The tomb had vanished. So far as the appearance of the ground was concerned there never had been any tomb, and I found it hard to persuade myself at times that the whole episode had not been a dream.

I was soon to be reassured on this point. News travels fast in Egypt, and within two days of the discovery congratulations, inquiries, and offers of help descended upon me in a steady stream from all directions. It became clear, even at

* Carter's patron

this early stage, that I was in for a job that could not be tackled single-handed, so I wired to Callender, who had helped me on various previous occasions, asking him if possible to join me without delay, and to my relief he arrived on the very next day. On the 8th I had received two messages from Lord Carnarvon in answer to my cable, the first of which read, "Possibly come soon", and the second, received a little later, "Propose arrive Alexandria 20th."

We had thus nearly a fortnight's grace, and we devoted it to making preparations of various kinds, so that when the time of reopening came, we should be able, with the least possible delay, to handle any situation that might arise. On the night of the 18th I went to Cairo for three days, to meet Lord Carnarvon and make a number of necessary purchases, returning to Luxor on the 21st. On the 23rd Lord Carnarvon arrived in Luxor with his daughter, Lady Evelyn Herbert, his devoted companion in all his Egyptian work, and everything was in hand for the beginning of the second chapter of the discovery of the tomb. Callender had been busy all day clearing away the upper layer of rubbish, so that by morning we should be able to get into the staircase without any delay.

By the afternoon of the 24th the whole staircase was clear, sixteen steps in all, and we were able to make a proper examination of the sealed doorway. On the lower part the seal impressions were much clearer, and we were able without any difficulty to make out on several of them the name of Tut-ankh-Amen. This added enormously to the interest of the discovery. If we had found, as seemed almost certain, the tomb of that shadowy monarch, whose tenure of the throne coincided with one of the most interesting periods in the whole of Egyptian history, we should indeed have reason to congratulate ourselves.

With heightened interest, if that was possible, we renewed our investigation of the doorway. Here for the first
time a disquieting element made its appearance. Now that
the whole door was exposed to light it was possible to
discern a fact that had hitherto escaped notice – that there
had been two successive openings and re-closing of a part of
its surface: furthermore, that the sealing originally discovered, the jackal and nine captives, had been applied to the
re-closed portions, whereas the sealings of Tut-ankh-Amen
covered the untouched part of the doorway, and were
therefore those with which the tomb had been originally
secured. The tomb then was not absolutely intact, as we
had hoped. Plunderers had entered it, and entered it more
than once – from the evidence of the huts above, plunderers
of a date not later than the reign of Ramses VI – but that
they had not rifled it completely was evident from the fact
that it had been re-sealed.

Then came another puzzle. In the lower strata of rubbish
that filled the staircase we found masses of broken potsherds
and boxes, the latter bearing the names of Akh-en-Aten,
Smenkh-ka-Re and Tut-ankh-Amen, and, what was much
more upsetting, a scarab of Thothmes III and a fragment
with the name of Amenhetep II. Why this mixture of
names? The balance of evidence so far would seem to
indicate a cache rather than a tomb, and at this stage in
the proceedings we inclined more and more to the opinion
that we were about to find a miscellaneous collection of
objects of the Eighteenth Dynasty kings, brought from Tell
el Amarna by Tut-ankh-Amen and deposited here for
safety.

So matters stood on the evening of the 24th. On the
following day the sealed doorway was to be removed, so
Callender set carpenters to work making a heavy wooden

grille to be set up in its place. Mr Engelbach, Chief Inspector of the Antiquities Department, paid us a visit during the afternoon, and witnessed part of the final clearing of rubbish from the doorway.

On the morning of the 25th the seal impressions on the doorway were carefully noted and photographed, and then we removed the actual blocking of the door, consisting of rough stones carefully built from floor to lintel, and heavily plastered on their outer faces to take the seal impressions.

This disclosed the beginning of a descending passage (not a staircase), the same width as the entrance stairway, and nearly seven feet high. As I had already discovered from my hole in the doorway, it was filled completely with stone and rubble, probably the chip from its own excavation. This filling, like the doorway, showed distinct signs of more than one opening and re-closing of the tomb, the untouched part consisting of clean white chip, mingled with dust, whereas the disturbed part was composed mainly of dark flint. It was clear that an irregular tunnel had been cut through the original filling at the upper corner on the left side, a tunnel corresponding in position with that of the hole in the doorway.

As we cleared the passage we found, mixed with the rubble of the lower levels, broken potsherds, jar sealings, alabaster jars, whole and broken, vases of painted pottery, numerous fragments of smaller articles, and water skins, these last having obviously been used to bring up the water needed for the plastering of the doorways. These were clear evidence of plundering, and we eyed them askance. By night we had cleared a considerable distance down the passage, but as yet saw no sign of second doorway or of chamber.

The day following (November 26th) was the day of days,

the most wonderful that I have ever lived through, and certainly one whose like I can never hope to see again. Throughout the morning the work of clearing continued, slowly perforce, on account of the delicate objects that were mixed with the filling. Then, in the middle of the afternoon, thirty feet down from the outer door, we came upon a second sealed doorway, almost an exact replica of the first. The seal impressions in this case were less distinct, but still recognizable as those of Tut-ankh-Amen and of the royal necropolis. Here again the signs of opening and re-closing were clearly marked upon the plaster. We were firmly convinced by this time that it was a cache that we were about to open, and not a tomb . . . We were soon to know. There lay the sealed doorway, and behind it was the answer to the question.

Slowly, desperately slowly it seemed to us as we watched, the remains of passage debris that encumbered the lower part of the doorway were removed, until at last we had the whole door clear before us. The decisive moment had arrived. With trembling hands I made a tiny breach in the upper left-hand corner. Darkness and blank space, as far as an iron testing-rod could reach showed that whatever lay beyond was empty, and not filled like the passage we had just cleared. Candle tests were applied as a precaution against possible foul gases, and then, widening the hole a little, I inserted the candle and peered in, Lord Carnarvon, Lady Evelyn and Callender standing anxiously beside me to hear the verdict. At first I could see nothing, the hot air escaping from the chamber causing the candle flame to flicker, but presently, as my eyes grew accustomed to the light, details of the room within emerged slowly from the mist, strange animals, statues, and gold – everywhere the glint of gold. For the moment – an eternity it must have seemed to the others standing by – I was struck dumb with amazement, and when Lord Carnarvon, unable to stand the suspense any longer, inquired anxiously, "Can you see anything?" it was all I could do to get out the words, "Yes, wonderful things." Then widening the hole a little further, so that we both could see, we inserted an electric torch.

I suppose most excavators would confess to a feeling of awe – embarrassment almost – when they break into a chamber closed and sealed by pious hands so many centuries ago. For the moment, time as a factor in human life has lost its meaning. Three thousand, four thousand years maybe, have passed and gone since human feet last trod the floor on which you stand, and yet, as you note the signs of recent life around you – the half-filled bowl of mortar for the door, the blackened lamp, the finger-mark upon the freshly painted surface, the farewell garland dropped upon the threshold – you feel it might have been but yesterday. The very air you breathe, unchanged throughout the centuries, you share with those who laid the mummy to its rest. Time is annihilated by little intimate details such as these, and you feel an intruder.

That is perhaps the first dominant sensation, but others follow thick and fast – the exhilaration of discovery, the fever of suspense, the almost overmastering impulse, born of curiosity, to break down seals and lift the lids of boxes, the thought – pure joy to the investigator – that you are about to add a page to history, or solve some problem of research, the strained expectancy – why not confess it? – of the treasure-seeker. Did these thoughts actually pass through our minds at the time, or have I imagined them since? I cannot tell. It was the discovery that my memory was blank, and not the mere desire for dramatic chapter-ending, that occasioned this digression.

Surely never before in the whole history of excavation had such an amazing sight been seen as the light of our torch revealed to us. The reader can get some idea of it by reference to the photographs, but these were taken afterwards when the tomb had been opened and electric light installed. Let him imagine how they appeared to us as we looked down upon them from our spy-hole in the blocked doorway, casting the beam of light from our torch – the first light that had pierced the darkness of the chamber for three thousand years – from one group of objects to another, in a vain attempt to interpret the treasure that lay before us. The effect was bewildering, overwhelming. I suppose we had never formulated exactly in our minds just what we had expected or hoped to see, but certainly we had never dreamed of anything like this, a roomful – a whole museumful it seemed – of objects, some familiar, but some the like of which we had never seen, piled one upon another in seemingly endless profusion.

Gradually the scene grew clearer, and we could pick out individual objects. First, right opposite to us – we had been conscious of them all the while, but refused to believe in them – were three great gilt couches, their sides carved in the form of monstrous animals, curiously attenuated in body, as they had to be to serve their purpose, but with heads of startling realism. Uncanny beasts enough to look upon at any time: seen as we saw them, their brilliant gilded surfaces picked out of the darkness by our electric torch, as though by limelight, their heads throwing grotesque distorted shadows on the wall behind them, they were almost terrifying. Next, on the right, two statues caught and held our attention; two life-sized figures of a king in black, facing each other like sentinels, gold kilted, gold sandalled, armed with mace and staff, the protective sacred cobra upon their foreheads.

These were the dominant objects that caught the eye at first. Between them, around them, piled on top of them, there were countless others – exquisitely painted and inlaid caskets; alabaster vases, some beautifully carved in open-work designs; strange black shrines, from the open door of one a great gilt snake peeping out; bouquets of flowers or leaves; beds; chairs beautifully carved; a golden inlaid throne; a heap of curious white oviform boxes; staves of all shapes and designs; beneath our eyes, on the very threshold of the chamber, a beautiful lotiform cup of translucent alabaster; on the left a confused pile of over-turned chariots, glistening with gold and inlay; and peeping from behind them another portrait of a king.

Such were some of the objects that lay before us. Whether we noted them all at the time I cannot say for certain, as our minds were in much too excited and con-fused a state to register accurately. Presently it dawned upon our bewildered brains that in all this medley of objects before us there was no coffin or trace of mummy, and the much-debated question of tomb or cache began to intrigue us afresh. With this question in view we re-ex-amined the scene before us, and noticed for the first time that between the two black sentinel statues on the right there was another sealed doorway. The explanation gradually dawned upon us. We were but on the threshold of our discovery. What we saw was merely an antecham-ber. Behind the guarded door there were to be other chambers, possibly a succession of them, and in one of them, beyond any shadow of doubt, in all his magnificent panoply of death, we should find the Pharaoh lying.

We had seen enough, and our brains began to reel at the thought of the task in front of us. We re-closed the hole, locked the wooden grille that had been placed upon the

first doorway, left our native staff on guard, mounted our
donkeys and rode home down The Valley, strangely silent
and subdued . . .

Our natural impulse was to break down the door, and
get to the bottom of the matter at once, but to do so would
have entailed serious risk of damage to many of the objects
in the Antechamber, a risk which we were by no means
prepared to face. Nor could we move the objects in question
out of the way, for it was imperative that a plan and
complete photographic record should be made before anything was touched, and this was a task involving a considerable amount of time, even if we had had sufficient
plant available – which we had not – to carry it through
immediately. Reluctantly we decided to abandon the opening of this inner sealed door until we had cleared the
Antechamber of all its contents.

*In fact, Carter did not "abandon the opening" of the inner-sealed door; that night or
the next day, Carter, Carnavon and Lady Evelyn opened up a small hole made by
tomb-robbers and secretly accessed the burial chamber.*

Clearing the objects from the Antechamber was like playing a gigantic game of spillikins. So crowded were they that
it was a matter of extreme difficulty to move one without
running serious risk of damaging others, and in some cases
they were so inextricably tangled that an elaborate system
of props and supports had to be devised to hold one object
or group of objects in place while another was being
removed. At such times life was a nightmare. One was
afraid to move lest one should kick against a prop and bring
the whole thing crashing down. Nor, in many cases, could
one tell without experiment whether a particular object
was strong enough to bear its own weight. Certain of the
things were in beautiful condition, as strong as when they

first were made, but others were in a most precarious state, and the problem constantly arose whether it would be better to apply preservative treatment to an object *in situ*, or to wait until it could be dealt with in more convenient surroundings in the laboratory. The latter course was adopted whenever possible, but there were cases in which the removal of an object without treatment would have meant almost certain destruction.

There were sandals, for instance, of patterned bead-work, of which the threading had entirely rotted away. As they lay on the floor of the chamber they looked in perfectly sound condition, but, try to pick one up, and it crumbled at the touch, and all you had for your pains was a handful of loose, meaningless beads. This was a clear case for treatment on the spot – a spirit stove, some paraffin wax, an hour or two to harden, and the sandal could be removed intact, and handled with the utmost freedom. The funerary bouquets again: without treatment as they stood they would have ceased to exist; subjected to three or four sprayings of celluloid solution they bore removal well, and were subsequently packed with scarcely any injury. Occasionally, particularly with the larger objects, it was found better to apply local treatment in the tomb, just sufficient to ensure a safe removal to the laboratory, where more drastic measures were possible. Each object presented a separate problem, and there were cases in which only experiment could show the proper treatment.

It was slow work, painfully slow, and nerve-racking at that, for one felt all the time a heavy weight of responsibility. Every excavator must, if he have any archaeological conscience at all. The things he finds are not his own property, to treat as he pleases, or neglect as he chooses. They are a direct legacy from the past to the present age, he but the privileged intermediary through whose hands they come; and if, by carelessness, slackness, or ignorance, he lessens the sum of knowledge that might have been obtained from them, he knows himself to be guilty of an archaeological crime of the first magnitude. Destruction of evidence is so painfully easy, and yet so hopelessly irreparable. Tired or pressed for time, you shirk a tedious piece of cleaning, or do it in a half-hearted, perfunctory sort of way, and you will perhaps have thrown away the one chance that will ever occur of gaining some important piece of knowledge.

Too many people – unfortunately there are so-called archaeologists among them – are apparently under the impression that the object bought from a dealer's shop is just as valuable as one which has been found in actual excavation, and that until the object in question has been cleaned, entered in the books, marked with an accession number, and placed in a tidy museum case, it is not a proper subject for study at all. There was never a greater mistake. Field-work is all-important, and it is a sure and certain fact that if every excavation had been properly, systematically, and conscientiously carried out, our knowledge of Egyptian archaeology would be at least 50 per cent greater than it is. There are numberless derelict objects in the storerooms of our museums which would give us valuable information could they but tell us whence they came, and box after box full of fragments which a few notes at the time of finding would have rendered capable of reconstruction.

Granting, then, that a heavy weight of responsibility must at all times rest upon the excavator, our own feelings on this occasion will easily be realized. It had been our privilege to find the most important collection of Egyptian antiquities that had ever seen the light, and it was for us to show that we were worthy of the trust. So many things there were that might go wrong. Danger of theft, for instance, was an ever-present anxiety. The whole country-side was agog with excitement about the tomb; all sorts of extravagant tales were current about the gold and jewels it contained; and, as past experience had shown, it was only too possible that there might be a serious attempt to raid the tomb by night. This possibility of robbery on a large scale was negatived, so far as was humanly possible, by a complicated system of guarding, there being present in The Valley, day and night, three independent groups of watch-men, each answerable to a different authority – the Gov-ernment Antiquities Guards, a squad of soldiers supplied by the Mudir of Kena, and a selected group of the most trustworthy of our own staff. In addition, we had a heavy wooden grille at the entrance to the passage, and a massive steel gate at the inner doorway, each secured by four padlocked chains; and, that there might never be any mistake about these latter, the keys were in the permanent charge of one particular member of the European staff, who never parted with them for a moment, even to lend them to a colleague. Petty or casual theft we guarded against by doing all the handling of the objects ourselves.

Another and perhaps an even greater cause for anxiety was the condition of many of the objects. It was manifest with some of them that their very existence depended on careful manipulation and correct preservative treatment, and there were moments when our hearts were in our mouths . . .

By the middle of February [1923] our work in the Antechamber was finished. With the exception of the two sentinel statues . . . all its contents had been removed to the laboratory, every inch of its floor had been swept and sifted for the last bead or fallen piece of inlay, and it now stood bare and empty. We were ready at last to penetrate the mystery of the sealed door.

Friday, the 17th, was the day appointed, and at two o'clock those who were to be privileged to witness the ceremony met by appointment above the tomb . . .

In the Antechamber everything was prepared and ready, and to those who had not visited it since the original opening of the tomb it must have presented a strange sight. We had screened the statues with boarding to protect them from possible damage, and between them we had erected a small platform, just high enough to enable us to reach the upper part of the doorway, having determined, as the safest plan, to work from the top downwards. A short distance back from the platform there was a barrier, and beyond, knowing that there might be hours of work ahead of us, we had provided chairs for the visitors. On either side standards had been set up for our lamps, their light shining full upon the doorway. Looking back, we realize what a strange, incongruous picture the chamber must have presented, but at the time I question whether such an idea even crossed our minds. One thought and one only was possible. There before us lay the sealed door, and with its opening we were to blot out the centuries and stand in the presence of a king who reigned three thousand years ago. My own feelings as I mounted the platform were a strange mixture, and it was with a trembling hand that I struck the first blow.

My first care was to locate the wooden lintel above the door: then very carefully I chipped away the plaster and picked out the small stones which formed the uppermost layer of the filling. The temptation to stop and peer inside at every moment was irresistible, and when, after about ten minutes' work, I had made a hole large enough to enable me to do so, I inserted an electric torch. An astonishing sight its light revealed, for there, within a yard of the doorway, stretching as far as one could see and blocking the entrance to the chamber, stood what to all appearance was a solid wall of gold. For the moment there was no clue as to its meaning, so as quickly as I dared I set to work to widen the hole. This had now become an operation of considerable difficulty, for the stones of the masonry were not accurately squared blocks built regularly upon one another, but rough slabs of varying size, some so heavy that it took all one's strength to lift them: many of them, too, as the weight above was removed, were left so precariously balanced that the least false movement would have sent them sliding inwards to crash upon the contents of the chamber below. We were also endeavouring to preserve the seal-impressions upon the thick mortar of the outer face, and this added considerably to the difficulty of handling the stones. Mace and Callender were helping me by this time, and each stone was cleared on a regular system. With a crowbar I gently eased it up, Mace holding it to prevent it falling forwards; then he and I lifted it out and passed it back to Callender, who transferred it on to one of the foremen, and so, by a chain of workmen, up the passage and out of the tomb altogether.

With the removal of a very few stones the mystery of the golden wall was solved. We were at the entrance of the actual burial-chamber of the king, and that which barred our way was the side of an immense gilt shrine built to cover and protect the sarcophagus. It was visible now from the Antechamber by the light of the standard lamps, and as stone after stone was removed, and its gilded surface came gradually into view, we could, as though by electric current, feel the tingle of excitement which thrilled the spectators behind the barrier . . . We who were doing the work were probably less excited, for our whole energies were taken up with the task in hand – that of removing the blocking without an accident. The fall of a single stone might have done irreparable damage to the delicate surface of the shrine, so, directly the hole was large enough, we made an additional protection for it by inserting a mattress on the inner side of the door-blocking, suspending it from the wooden lintel of the doorway. Two hours of hard work it took us to clear away the blocking, or at least as much of it as was necessary for the moment; and at one point, when near the bottom, we had to delay operations for a space while we collected the scattered beads from a necklace brought by the plunderers from the chamber within and dropped upon the threshold. This last was a terrible trial to our patience, for it was a slow business, and we were all of us excited to see what might be within; but finally it was done, the last stones were removed, and the way to the innermost chamber lay open before us . . .

Lord Carnarvon and M. Lacau [Director-General of the Service of Antiquities] now joined me, and, picking our way along the narrow passage between shrine and wall, paying out the wire of our light behind us, we investigated further.

It was, beyond any question, the sepulchral chamber in which we stood, for there, towering above us, was one of the great gilt shrines beneath which kings were laid. So enormous was this structure (seventeen feet by eleven feet, and nine feet high, we found afterwards) that it filled within a little the entire area of the chamber, a space of some two feet only separating it from the walls on all four sides, while its roof, with cornice top and torus moulding, reached almost to the ceiling. From top to bottom it was overlaid with gold, and upon its sides there were inlaid panels of brilliant blue faience, in which were represented, repeated over and over, the magic symbols which would ensure its strength and safety. Around the shrine, resting upon the ground, there were a number of funerary emblems, and, at the north end, the seven magic oars the king would need to ferry himself across the waters of the underworld. The walls of the chamber, unlike those of the Antechamber, were decorated with brightly painted scenes and inscriptions, brilliant in their colours, but evidently somewhat hastily executed.

These last details we must have noticed subsequently, for at the time our one thought was of the shrine and of its safety. Had the thieves penetrated within it and disturbed the royal burial? Here, on the eastern end, were the great folding doors, closed and bolted, but not sealed, that would answer the question for us. Eagerly we drew the bolts, swung back the doors, and there within was a second shrine with similar bolted doors, and upon the bolts a seal, intact. This seal we determined not to break, for our doubts were resolved, and we could not penetrate further without risk of serious damage to the monument. I think at the moment we did not even want to break the seal, for a feeling of intrusion had descended heavily upon us with the opening of the doors, heightened, probably, by the almost painful impressiveness of a linen pall, decorated with golden rosettes, which drooped above the inner shrine. We felt that we were in the presence of the dead King and must do him reverence, and in imagination could see the doors of the successive shrines open one after the other till the innermost disclosed the King himself. Carefully, and as silently as possible, we re-closed the great swing doors, and passed on to the farther end of the chamber.

Here a surprise awaited us, for a low door, eastwards from the sepulchral chamber, gave entrance to yet another chamber, smaller than the outer ones and not so lofty. This doorway, unlike the others, had not been closed and sealed. We were able, from where we stood, to get a clear view of the whole of the contents, and a single glance sufficed to tell us that here, within this little chamber, lay the greatest treasures of the tomb. Facing the doorway, on the farther side, stood the most beautiful monument that I have ever seen – so lovely that it made one gasp with wonder and admiration. The central portion of it consisted of a large shrine-shaped chest, completely overlaid with gold, and surmounted by a cornice of sacred cobras. Surrounding this, free-standing, were statues of the four tutelary goddesses of the dead – gracious figures with outstretched protective arms, so natural and lifelike in their pose, so pitiful and compassionate the expression upon their faces, that one felt it almost sacrilege to look at them. One guarded the shrine on each of its four sides, but whereas the figures at front and back kept their gaze firmly fixed upon their charge, an additional note of touching realism was imparted by the other two, for their heads were turned sideways, looking over their shoulders towards the entrance, as though to watch against surprise. There is a simple grandeur about this monument that made an irresistible appeal to the imagination, and I am not ashamed to confess that it brought a lump to my throat.

The second season's work actually began in the laboratory, under Mr Mace, who dealt with the magnificent chariots and the ceremonial couches that were left over from the first season. While he was carrying out this work of preservation and packing, with the aid of Mr Callender, I began by removing the two guardian statues that stood before the doorway of the Burial Chamber, and then, as it was necessary, demolished the partition wall dividing it from the Antechamber.

Without first demolishing that partition wall, it would have been impossible to have dealt with the great shrines within the Burial Chamber, or to remove many of the funereal paraphernalia therein. Even then our great difficulty was due to the confined space in which we had to carry out the most difficult task of dismantling those shrines, which proved to be four in number, nested one within the other.

Beyond the very limited space and high temperature which prevailed, our difficulties were further increased by the great weight of the various sections and panels of which those complex shrines were constructed. These were made of 2¼-inch oak planking, and overlaid with superbly delicate gold-work upon gesso. The wood-planking, though perfectly sound, had shrunk in the course of three thousand three hundred years in that very dry atmosphere, the gold-work upon the gesso had, if at all, slightly expanded; the result in any case was a space between the basic wood-planking and the ornamented gold surface which, when touched, tended to crush and fall away. Thus our problem was how to deal in that very limited space with those sections of the shrines, weighing from a quarter to three-quarters of a ton, when taking them apart and removing them, without causing them undue damage.

Other complications arose during this undertaking, and one of them was due to the fact that those sections were held together by means of secret wooden tongues let into the thickness of the wood-planking of the panels, roof sections, cornice pieces and "styles". It was only by slightly forcing open the cracks between those different sections, and by that means discovering the positions of the tongues that held them together, inserting a fine saw and severing them, that we were able to free them and take them apart. No sooner had we discovered the method of overcoming this complication, had dealt with the various sections of the great outermost shrine, and become proud of ourselves, anticipating that we had learnt how to treat the next shrine or shrines, than we found that, in the very next shrine, although held together in a similar manner, many of the hidden tongues were of solid bronze, inscribed with the names of Tut-ankh-Amen. These could not of course be sawn through as in the first case. We had therefore to find other methods. In fact, contrary to our expectations, the farther we proceeded, although the space in which we could work had been increased, new and unforeseen obstacles continually occurred.

For instance, after our scaffolding and hoisting tackle had been introduced it occupied practically all the available space, leaving little for ourselves in which to work. When some of the parts were freed, there was insufficient room to remove them from the chamber. We bumped our heads, nipped our fingers, we had to squeeze in and out like weasels, and work in all kinds of embarrassing positions. I think I remember that one of the eminent chemists assisting us in the preservation work, when taking records of various phenomena in the tomb, found that he had also recorded a certain percentage of profanity! Nevertheless, I am glad to say that in the conflict we did more harm to ourselves than to the shrines.

Such was our task during the second season's work in the Burial Chamber . . .

At this point of our undertaking we realized that it would now be possible, by opening those further doors, to solve the secret the shrines had so jealously guarded throughout the centuries. I therefore decided before any other procedure to make the experiment. It was an exciting moment in our arduous task that cannot easily be forgotten. We were to witness a spectacle such as no other man in our times has been privileged to see. With suppressed excitement I carefully cut the cord, removed that precious seal, drew back the bolts, and opened the doors, when a fourth shrine was revealed, similar in design and even more brilliant in workmanship than the last. The decisive moment was at hand! An indescribable moment for an archaeologist! What was beneath and what did that fourth shrine contain? With intense excitement I drew back the bolts of the last and unsealed doors; they slowly swung open, and there, filling the entire area within, effectually barring any further progress, stood an immense yellow quartzite sarcophagus, intact, with the lid still firmly fixed in its place, just as the pious hands had left it. It was certainly a thrilling moment, as we gazed upon the spectacle enhanced by the striking contrast – the glitter of metal – of the golden shrines shielding it. Especially striking were the outstretched hand and wing of a goddess sculptured on the end of the sarcophagus, as if to ward off an intruder. It symbolized an idea beautiful in conception, and, indeed, seemed an eloquent illustration of the perfect faith and tender solicitude for the well-being of their loved one, that animated the people who dwelt in that land over thirty centuries ago.

We were now able to profit by the experience we had

acquired and had a much clearer conception of the operation immediately before us: the three remaining shrines
would have to be taken to pieces and removed before the
problem of the sarcophagus could be contemplated . . .

Many strange scenes must have happened in the Valley
of the Tombs of the Kings since it became the royal burial
ground of the Theban New Empire, but one may be
pardoned for thinking that the present scene [the official
opening of the sarcophagus] was not the least interesting or
dramatic. For ourselves it was the one supreme and cul-
minating moment – a moment looked forward to ever since
it became evident that the chambers discovered, in November, 1922, must be the tomb of Tutankh-Amen, and
not a cache of his furniture as had been claimed. None of us
but felt the solemnity of the occasion, none of us but was
affected by the prospect of what we were about to see – the
burial custom of a king of ancient Egypt of thirty-three
centuries ago. How would the king be found? Such were the
anticipatory speculations running in our minds during the
silence maintained.

The tackle for raising the lid was in position. I gave the
word. Amid intense silence the huge slab, broken in two,
weighing over a ton and a quarter, rose from its bed. The
light shone into the sarcophagus. A sight met our eyes that
at first puzzled us. It was a little disappointing. The
contents were completely covered by fine linen shrouds.
The lid being suspended in mid-air, we rolled back those
covering shrouds, one by one, and as the last was removed a
gasp of wonderment escaped our lips, so gorgeous was the
sight that met our eyes: a golden effigy of the young boy
king, of most magnificent workmanship, filled the whole of
the interior of the sarcophagus. This was the lid of a
wonderful anthropoid coffin some seven feet in length,

resting upon a low bier in the form of a lion, and no doubt the outermost coffin of a series of coffins, nested one within the other, enclosing the mortal remains of the king. Enclasping the body of this magnificent monument are two winged goddesses, Isis and Neith, wrought in rich goldwork upon gesso, as brilliant as the day the coffin was made. To it an additional charm was added, by the fact that, while this decoration was rendered in fine low bas-relief, the head and hands of the king were in the round, in massive gold of the finest sculpture, surpassing anything we could have imagined. The hands, crossed over the breast, held the royal emblems – the Crook and the Flail – encrusted with deep blue faience. The face and features were wonderfully wrought in sheet-gold. The eyes were of aragonite and obsidian, the eyebrows and eyelids inlaid with lapis lazuli glass. There was a touch of realism, for while the rest of this anthropoid coffin, covered with feathered ornament, was a brilliant gold, that of the bare face and hands seemed different, the gold of the flesh being of different alloy, thus conveying an impression of the greyness of death. Upon the forehead of this recumbent figure of the young boy king were two emblems delicately worked in brilliant inlay – the Cobra and the Vulture – symbols of Upper and Lower Egypt, but perhaps the most touching by its human simplicity was the tiny wreath of flowers around these symbols, as it pleased us to think, the last farewell offering of the widowed girl queen to her husband, the youthful representative of the "Two Kingdoms".

Among all that regal splendour, that royal magnificence – everywhere the glint of gold – there was nothing so beautiful as those few withered flowers, still retaining their tinge of colour. They told us what a short period three thousand three hundred years really was – but Yesterday and the Morrow. In fact, that little touch of nature made that ancient and our modern civilization kin . . .

The lid was fastened to the shell by means of eight gold tenons (four on each side), which were held in their corresponding sockets by nails. Thus, if the nails could be extracted the lid could be raised. In the narrow space between the two coffins ordinary implements for extracting metal pins were useless, and others had to be devised. With long screwdrivers converted to meet the conditions, the nails or pins of solid gold, that unfortunately had to be sacrificed, were removed piecemeal. The lid was raised by its golden handles and the mummy of the king disclosed.

At such moments the emotions evade verbal expression, complex and stirring as they are. Three thousand years and more had elapsed since men's eyes had gazed into that golden coffin. Time, measured by the brevity of human life, seemed to lose its common perspectives before a spectacle so vividly recalling the solemn religious rites of a vanished civilization. But it is useless to dwell on such sentiments, based as they are on feelings of awe and human pity. The emotional side is no part of archaeological research. Here at last lay all that was left of the youthful Pharaoh, hitherto little more to us than the shadow of a name.

Before us, occupying the whole of the interior of the golden coffin, was an impressive, neat and carefully made mummy, over which had been poured anointing unguents as in the case of the outside of its coffin – again in great quantity – consolidated and blackened by age. In contra-distinction to the general dark and sombre effect, due to these unguents, was a brilliant, one might say magnificent, burnished gold mask or similitude of the king, covering his head and shoulders, which, like the feet, had been intentionally avoided when using the unguents. The mummy was fashioned to symbolize Osiris. The beaten gold mask, a beautiful and unique specimen of ancient portraiture, bears a sad but calm expression suggestive of youth overtaken prematurely by death. Upon its forehead wrought in massive gold were the royal insignia – the Nekhebet vulture and Buto serpent – emblems of the Two Kingdoms over which he had reigned. To the chin was attached the conventional Osiride beard, wrought in gold and lapis-lazuli-coloured glass; around the throat was a triple necklace of yellow and red gold and blue faience disk-shaped beads; pendent from the neck by flexible gold inlaid straps was a large black resin scarab that rested between the hands and bore the *Bennu* ritual. The burnished gold hands, crossed over the breast, separate from the mask, were sewn to the material of the linen wrappings, and grasped the Flagellum and Crozier – the emblems of Osiris . . .

But, alas! both the mask and the mummy were stuck fast to the bottom of the coffin by the consolidated residue of the unguents, and no amount of legitimate force could move them. What was to be done?

Since it was known that this adhesive material could be softened by heat, it was hoped that an exposure to the midday sun would melt it sufficiently to allow the mummy to be raised. A trial therefore was made for several hours in sun temperature reaching as high as 149° Fahrenheit (65°C) without any success and, as other means were not practicable, it became evident that we should have to make all further examination of the king's remains as they lay within the two coffins.

As a matter of fact, after the scientific examination of the king's mummy *in situ*, and its final removal from the gold coffin, that very difficult question of removing the gold mask and extricating the gold coffin from the shell of the second coffin had to be solved.

Originally something like two bucketsful of the liquid unguents had been poured over the golden coffin, and a similar amount over the body inside. As heat was the only practical means of melting this material and rendering it amenable, in order to apply a temperature sufficiently high for the purpose, without causing damage to those wonderful specimens of ancient Egyptian arts and crafts, the interior of the golden coffin had to be completely lined with thick plates of zinc, which would not melt under a temperature of 968° Fahrenheit (520°C). The coffins were then reversed upon trestles, the outside one being protected against undue heat and fire by several blankets saturated and kept wet with water. Our next procedure was to place under the hollow of the gold coffin several Primus paraffin lamps burning at full blast. The heat from the lamps had to be regulated so as to keep the temperature well within the melting-point of zinc. It should be noted here that the coating of wax upon the surface of the second coffin acted as a pyrometer – while it remained unmelted under the wet blanketing there was manifestly no fear of injury.

Although the temperature arrived at was some 932° Fahrenheit (500°C), it took several hours before any real effect was noticeable. The moment signs of movement became apparent, the lamps were turned out, and the coffins left suspended upon the trestles, when, after an hour, they began to fall apart. The movement at first was almost imperceptible owing to the tenacity of the material, but we were able to separate them by lifting up the wooden shell of the second coffin, thus leaving the shell of the gold coffin resting upon the trestles. Its very nature was hardly recognizable, and all we could see was a dripping mass of viscous pitch-like material which proved very difficult to remove, even with quantities of various solvents – the principal of which was acetone.

In the same manner that the outside of the golden coffin was covered with a viscid mass, so was the interior, to which still adhered the gold mask. This mask had also been protected by being bound with a folded wet blanket continually fed with water, its face padded with wet wadding. As it had necessarily been subjected to the full power of the heat collected in the interior of the coffin, it was freed and lifted away with comparative ease, though to its back, as in the case of the coffin, there adhered a great mass of viscous unguents, which had eventually to be removed with the aid of a blast lamp and cleaning solvents . . .

The more one considers it the more deeply one is impressed by the extreme care and enormous costliness lavished by this ancient people on the enshrinement of their dead. Barrier after barrier was raised to guard their remains from the predatory hands against which, in death, these great kings too ineffectually sought protection. The process was as elaborate as it was costly.

First we have the golden shrines profusely decorated and of magnificent workmanship. They were sealed and nested one in the other over an immense and superbly sculptured monolithic quartzite sarcophagus. The sarcophagus, in its turn, contained three great anthropoid coffins of wood and gold which bear the likeness of the king with repeated *Rishi* and Osiride symbolism.

Everywhere there was evidence of the accomplished artist and skilful craftsman, intent on the mysteries of a vanished religion, and the problems of death. Finally we reach the monarch himself, profusely anointed with sacred unguents and covered with numberless amulets and emblems for his betterment, as well as personal ornaments for his glory.

The modern observer indeed is astounded at the enormous labour and expense bestowed on these royal burials, even when the titanic excavations of their rock-cut tombs is disregarded. Consider the carving and gilding of the elaborate shrines; the hewing and transport of that quartzite sarcophagus; the moulding, carving, inlaying of the magnificent coffins, the costly and intricate goldsmith's work expended upon them, the crowd of craftsmen employed, the precious metal and material so generously devoted to the princely dead . . .

Around the forehead [of the mummy itself] underneath a few more layers of linen, was a broad temple-band of burnished gold terminating behind and above the ears. At its extremities are slots through which linen tapes were passed and tied in a bow at the back of the head. This band held in place, over the brow and temples, a fine cambric-like linen *Khat* head-dress, unfortunately reduced by decay to such an irreparable condition that it was only recognizable from a portion of the kind of pigtail at the back common to this head-dress. Sewn to this *Khat* head-dress were the royal insignia, being a second set found upon the king. The uraeus, with body and tail in flexible sections of gold-work threaded together, and bordered with minute beads, was passed over the axis of the crown of the head as far back as the *lambda*, whilst the Nekhebet vulture (in this case with open wings, and with characteristics identical with those already described) covered the top of the head-dress, its body being parallel with the uraeus. In order that the soft linen of this head-dress should take its conventional shape, pads of linen had been placed under it and above the temples.

Beneath the *Khat* head-dress were further layers of bandaging that covered a skull-cap of the fine linen fabric, fitting tightly over the shaven head of the king, and embroidered with an elaborate device of uraei in minute gold and faience beads. The cap was kept in place by a gold temple-band similar to that just described. Each uraeus of the device bears in its centre the *Aten* cartouche of the Sun. The fabric of the cap was unfortunately much carbonized and decayed, but the bead-work had suffered far less, the device being practically perfect, since it adhered to the head of the king. To have attempted to remove this exquisite piece of work would have been disastrous, so it was treated with a thin coating of wax and left as it was found.

The removal of the final wrappings that protected the face of the king needed the utmost care, as owing to the carbonized state of the head there was always the risk of injury to the very fragile features. We realized the peculiar importance and responsibility attached to our task. At the touch of a sable brush the last few fragments of decayed fabric fell away, revealing a serene and placid countenance, that of a young man . . .

Source: The Discovery of the Tomb of Tutankamen, Howard Carter, 1933.

APPENDIX III: PRIVATE LETTERS FROM ROMAN EGYPT, AD 1st–3rd CENTURIES

Various

1. A Request: Ilarion to his Sister (and Wife)
Ilarion to his sister Alis, greetings, and to my dear Berous and Apollonarion. Know that I am still, even now, at Alexandria; and do not worry if they come back altogether, but I remain at Alexandria. I urge and entreat you to be careful of the child, and if I receive a present soon, I will send it up to you. If Apollonarion has a child, if it is a male let it be, if a female, expose it. You told Aphrodisias, "Don't forget me." How can I forget you? I urge you therefore not to worry. The 29th year of Caesar, Pauni 23.

Deliver to Alis from Ilarion.

2. Domestic Matters: Isidora to Asclepiades
Isidora to Asclepiades her brother, greeting, and good health, as I pray always.

I got your letter on November 4th, the letter you wrote on October 24th. Kindly write me exactly about the trouble in regard to the lentils and the pease, for in your letter to Paniscus you contradict yourself, saying first "I sold", and then "I did not sell." In any case do as you think best. Only be industrious over payments and takings, so that when Paniscus comes to Memphis you may not be in difficulties.

I sent you the money, 120 drachmae, for the quilt, but you must find out, if you come, who obtained it: it is worth no more than 50 drachmae. Give another quilt to Alexion, the dyer, on my account for my boy Artemas; it must be good, and not worthless, at 100 drachmae. Do not detain

Achilleus, but give him two boats, so he can travel to Hermupolis, and take care of your health. Good-bye.

3. Beware of the Jewish Money-Lenders: Sarapion to Heraclides
Sarapion to our Heraclides, greeting. I sent you two other letters, one by the hand of Nedymus, one by the hand of Cronius, the sword-bearer. Finally I received your letter from the Arab, and read it and was grieved. Stick to Ptolarion at all times; perhaps he can set you free. Say to him, "I am not like anyone else, I am but a lad; with the exception of one talent's worth, I have sold you everything: we have many creditors, do not drive us out." Beseech him from day to day; perhaps he will have pity on you. If not, like everyone else, beware of the Jews. Better stick to Ptolarion, so you may become his friend. Notice that the document can be signed by Diodorus or the headman's wife. If you manage your affairs by yourself, you are not to be blamed. Greet Diodorus with the others. Farewell. Greet Harpocrates.

4. House Decorating: Capito to Teres
Capito to his dear friend Teres, many greetings. First of all, I was greatly delighted to get your letter, and to hear that you are well and that you found your wife and your child the same. With regard to the dining-room (for I will do nothing but what you require) I have of course had everything put in hand – in fact, rather more. For I greatly value and cherish your friendship, and everything that you enjoined on me in your first letter you will find accomplished. And I hope that when you come you will find things still further forward. I am immensely grateful to Primus and Tycharion for their assiduity in following your instructions, and for their attention to me. And the plas-

terers have done everything in bright colours and are still at it. With regard to the terrace portico, as you are intending to redecorate it, write me what you want done, what you mean to have there, whether the siege of Troy or some other subject. The space demands something of the kind. Farewell. Sertorius and his household greet you, greetings to all your family.

5. Poor Husbandry: Lucius Bellenus Gemellus to his Nephew, Epagathus

Lucius Bellenus Gemellus to his own Epagathus, greeting. I blame you greatly for the loss of two pigs owing to the fatigue of the journey, when you had in the village ten animals fit for work. Heracleides, the donkey-driver, shifted the blame from himself, saying that you had told him to drive the pigs on foot. I have already more than sufficiently enjoined you to stay at Dionysias a couple of days, till you have bought 20 artabae of lotus, believing it to be essential. Hasten with the flooding of all the olive yards . . . and water the row of trees at "the Prophet". Do not neglect these instructions. Good-bye.

The 15th year of the Emperor Caesar Domitianus Augustus Germanicus, the 15th of the Germanic month.

6. More Agricultural Matters: Lucius Bellenus Gemellus to his son, Sabinus

Lucius Bellenus Gemellus to his son Sabinus, greeting.

Aunes, the donkey-driver, has brought a rotten bundle of hay at 12 drachmae; the bundle is small and the hay rotten, the whole of it decayed – no better than dung. Sabinus, son of Psellus of Psinachis, who is with you, brought to the city a letter of the prefect to Dionysus, the strategus, telling him to hear . . . Where did you put the notice of payment of the hay, and the contract for his loan of a mina? Send the key, and let me know where they lie, so that I may get them out in order to have them if I am about to settle accounts with him. Do not neglect these instructions. Greet Epagathus and those who love us truly. Good-bye. Send ten cocks from the market for the Saturnalia, and send some delicacies for Gemella's birthday feast . . . and an artaba of wheaten bread. Send the animals to carry manure at the vegetable ground at Psinachis and the manure carts, for Pasis is crying out that we must not allow it to be dissolved by the water, and let them fetch his hay. Send the animals at once.

Deliver to Sabinus my son from Lucius Bellenus Gemellus.

7. *Payment for a Mouse-Catcher: Horus to Apion*
Horus to his esteemed Apion, greeting.

Regarding Lampon, the mouse-catcher, I paid him for you as earnest money 8 drachmae in order that he may catch the mice while they are with young. Please send me the money. I have also lent Dionysus, the chief man of Nemerae, 8 drachmae, and he has not repaid them, to which I call your attention. Goodbye. Payni 24th.[1]

8. *Concerning a Debt: Pisais to Heracleus*
Pisais to Heracleus, greeting. Whenever in necessity you want to borrow anything from me, I at once give in to you; and now please give to Cleon the three staters which Seleucus told you to give me, and consider that you are lending them to me, even if you have to pawn your cloak; for I have settled accounts with his father, and he has allowed me to remain in arrears, and now I want to get a receipt. Seleucus has evaded paying the money by saying that you have made an ar-

rangement with him to pay instead. Now, therefore, please consider that you are lending the money to me, and don't keep Cleon waiting, but go and meet him, and ask Saras for the twelve silver drachmae. On no account fail to do this. The 20th year, Payni 25th.[2]

9. Hoping for Promotion: From Apion, a Soldier in Italy to his Father

Apion to Epimachus, his father and lord, heartiest greetings. First of all I pray that you are in health and continually prosper and fare well, with my sister and her daughter and my brother. I thank the lord Serapis that when I was in danger at sea he saved me. Straightway upon entering Misenum I received my travelling money from Caesar, three gold pieces. And I am well. I beg you, therefore, honoured father, write me a few lines, first regarding your health, secondly regarding that of my brother and sister, thirdly that I may kiss your hand, because you have brought me up so well, and on this account I hope for early promotion, if the gods will. Greetings to Capito, to my brother and sister, to Serenilla and to my friends. I send you by Euctemon a little portrait of myself. My military name is Antonius Maximus. I pray for your good health.

Athenonike company.

P.S. – Greetings from Serenus, son of Agathus Daemon, and from Turbo, son of Gallonius.

To Philadelphia for Epimachus from his son Apion.

To be handed to the office of the first cohort of the Apamaeans to Julianus, paymaster, from Apion, to be forwarded to Epimachus his father.

1 June 19th.
2 c. June 20th.

10. A Prodigal Son: Antonis to his Mother, Nilous

Antonis Longus to Nilous, his mother, many greetings. Continually I pray for your health. Every day I make supplication to the Lord Serapis on your behalf. I wish you to know that I had no hope that you would come up to the metropolis, and on this account neither did I myself go to the city. And I was ashamed to come to Karanis, because I am going about in rags. I wrote to you to tell you that I am naked. I beseech you, mother, be reconciled to me. I know now what I have brought on myself. Punished I have been every way. I know that I have sinned. I heard from Postumus, who met you in the district of Arsinoe, how he inopportunely told you everything. Do you not know that I would rather be a cripple than have it on my mind that I still owe anyone a penny? . . . Come to me yourself . . .

To his mother, from Antonius Longus, her son.

11. To an Errant Wife: Serenus to Isidora

Serenus to his beloved sister[3] Isidora, many greetings.

Before all else I pray for your health, and every day and evening I perform the act of veneration on your behalf to Thoeris who loves you. I assure you that ever since you left me I have been in mourning, weeping by night and lamenting by day. Since we bathed together on Phaophi 12th, I never bathed nor anointed myself till Athur 12th. You sent me letters which would have shaken a stone, so much did your words move me. Instantly I answered you and gave the letter sealed to the messenger on the 12th, together with letters for you. Apart from your saying and writing: "Colobus has made me a prostitute", he (Colobus)

3 Probably also his wife.

said to me: "Your wife sent me a message saying 'He himself (Serenus) has sold the chain, and himself put me in the boat.'" You say this to prevent my being believed any longer with regard to my embarkation. See how many things I have sent to you! Whether you are coming or not, let me know.

Deliver to Isidora from Serenus.

12. *Housekeeping: Corbolon to Heraclides*

Corbolon to Heraclides, greeting. I send you the key by Horion, and a piece of the lock by Onnophris, the camel-driver of Apollonius. I enclosed in the former packet a pattern of white violet colour. I beg you to be good enough to match it for me and buy me two drachmas' weight, and send it to me at once by any messenger you can find, for the tunic is to be woven immediately. I received safely everything you told me to expect by Onnophris. I send you by the same Onnophris six quarts of good apples. Do not think that I took no trouble about the key. The reason is that the smith is a long way from us. I wonder that you did not see your way to let me have what I asked you to send by Corbolon, especially when I wanted it for a festival. I beg you to buy me a silver seal and to send it me with all speed. Take care that Onnophris buys me what Irene's mother told him. I told him that Syntrophus said that nothing more was to be given to Amaranthus on my account. Let me know what you have given him, that I may settle accounts with him. Otherwise I and my son will come for this purpose. I received the large cheeses from Corbolon. I did not, however, want large ones, but small.

Let me know of anything that you want, and I will gladly do it. Farewell.

Payni 1st.

P.S. – Send me an obol's worth of cake for my nephew. To the Lord Heraclides, son of Ammonius.

12. *A Boy's Petition to his Father for a Lyre: Theon to his Father, Theon*

Theon to his father Theon, greeting. It was a fine thing of you not to take me with you to the city! If you won't take me with you to Alexandria I won't write to you, or speak to you, or say good-bye to you, and if you go to Alexandria I won't take your hand nor ever greet you again. That is what will happen if you won't take me. Mother said to Achelaus: "It quite upsets him to be left behind." It was good of you to send me presents . . . on the 12th, the day you sailed. Send me a lyre, I implore you. If you won't, I won't eat, I won't drink; there, now!

13. *Forging Temple Accounts: Serenus to Theon*

Serenus to his dearest Theon, greeting. I have sent you other letters about the six robes of Pyrrhus, and the two cloaks, telling you to send them to me at any cost, and I am now writing in haste to prevent your being anxious, for I will see that you are not worried. You must know that an inspector of finance in the temples has arrived and intends to go to your division also. Do not be disturbed on this account, as I will get you off. So if you have time, write up your books and come to me; for he is a very stern fellow. If anything detains you, send them on to me, and I will see you through, as he has become my friend. If you are in any difficulty about expense, and at present have no funds, write to me, and I will get you off now as I did the first time. I am making haste to write to you in order that you may not put in an appearance yourself; for I will make him let you through before he comes to you. He has instructions to send recalcitrants under guard to the high priest. But do not neglect yourself, nor what I wrote to you to buy for me; and if you have any figs, bring what you have, as I am in need of them. Good-bye, most honoured friend.

14. Friendship: Flavius Herculanus to Aplonarion

Flavius Herculanus to the sweetest and most honoured Aplonarion, very many greetings.

I rejoiced greatly at receiving your letter, which was given me by the cutler; I have not, however, received that which you say you sent by Plato, the dancer's son. But I was very much grieved that you did not come for my boy's birthday, both you and your husband, for you would have been able to have many days' enjoyment with him. But you doubtless had better things to do, that was why you neglected us. I wish you to be happy always, as I wish it for myself, but yet I am grieved that you are away from me. If you are not unhappy away from me, I rejoice for your happiness, but still I am vexed at not seeing you. Do what suits you; for when you wish to see us, always we shall receive you with the greatest pleasure. You will therefore do well to come to us in Messore, in order that we may really see you. Salute your mother and father and Callias. My son salutes you, and his mother and Dionysus, my fellow-worker, who serves me in the stable. Salute all your friends. I pray for your health.

Deliver to Aplonarion from her patron Herculanus. From Flavius Herculanus.

15. Farm Matters: Isidorus to Aurelius

Isidorus to his brother Aurelius, many greetings. I told you about the two acanthus trees, that they were to give them to us; let them be dug round to-day. Let Phanias himself have them dug round. If he refuses, write and let me know. I shall perhaps come to-morrow for the sealing; so make haste with this in order that I may know. As to the bulls, make them work, don't allow them to be entirely idle. Carry all the branches into the road and have them tied together by threes and dragged along. You will find this of service. Don't make over anything to their masters. I shall perhaps give him nothing. I am causing them much trouble. Don't allow the carpenters to be altogether idle. Worry them. I pray for your health.

16 Pawned Property: Eunoea to a Friend

Eunoea to a friend. Now please redeem my property from Sarapion. It is pledged for two minae. I have paid the interest up to Epeiph, at the rate of a stater per mina. There is a casket of incense-wood, another of onyx, a tunic, a white veil with a real purple border, a handkerchief, a tunic with a Laconian stripe, a garment of purple linen, two armlets, a necklace, a coverlet, a figure of Aphrodite, a cup, a big tin flask and a wine jar. From Onetor get the two bracelets. They have been pledged since Tybi of last year . . . at the rate of a stater per mina. If the cash is insufficient owing to the carelessness of Theagenis, if, I say, it is insufficient, sell the bracelets to make up the money. Many salutations to Aia and Eutychia and Alexandra. Xanthilla salutes Aia and all her friends. I pray for your health.

Source: Private Letters Pagan and Christian, ed. Dorothy Brooke, Ernest Benn Ltd., 1929. Letters 1, 2, 5, 6, 7, 8, 11, 12, 14, 15, 16 translated by B.P. Grenfell and A.S. Hunt; letters 3, 4, 9, 10 translated by G. Milligan; letter 13 translated by B.P. Grenfell, A.S. Hunt and J.G. Smyly.

APPENDIX IV: EXODUS

Donald A. Mackenzie

The Hebrew Exodus from Egypt was a minor matter in Egyptian annals, if a major one in the Bible and Israeli history. Here the Egyptologist Donald Mackenzie explores the evidence.

In the familiar Bible story of Joseph, the young Hebrew slave who became grand vizier in the land of the Nile, there is a significant reference to the nationality of his master Potiphar. Although that dignitary was "an officer of Pharaoh, captain of the guard", he was not of alien origin; we are pointedly informed that he was "an Egyptian". We also gather that Hyksos jurisdiction extended beyond the Delta region. During the dry cycle, when the great famine prevailed, Joseph "gathered up all the money that was found in the land of Egypt and in the land of Canaan" for the corn which the people purchased. Then he proceeded to acquire for the Crown all the privately owned estates in the Nile Valley and Delta region, with purpose, it would appear, to abolish the feudal system. An exception was made, however, of the lands attached to the temples. Apparently Pharaoh desired to conciliate the priests, whose political influence was very great, because we find that he allowed them free supplies of corn; indeed he had previously selected for Joseph's wife, "Asenath, the daughter of Potiphera, priest of On"; an indication that he specially favoured the influential sun cult of Heliopolis. Queen Hatshepsut's assertion that the foreign kings ruled in ignorance of Ra was manifestly neither strictly accurate nor unbiased.

The inference drawn from the Biblical narrative that the Hyksos Pharaohs adopted a policy of conciliation is confirmed by the evidence gleaned amidst the scanty records of the period. We find that some of these rulers assumed Ra titles, although they were also "beloved of Set" (Sutekh), and that one of them actually restored the tomb of Queen Apuit of the Sixth Dynasty. The Egyptians apparently indulged in pious exaggerations. That the Hyksos influence was not averse to culture is evidenced by the fact that the name of King Apepa Ra-aa-user is associated with a mathematical treatise which is preserved in the British Museum.

If learning was fostered, the arts and industries could not have been neglected. The Egyptian iconoclasts systematically destroyed practically all the monuments of the period, so that we have no direct evidence to support the assumption that it was characterized by a spirit of decadence due to the influence of uncultured desert dwellers. The skill displayed at the beginning of the Eighteenth Dynasty was too great to be of sudden growth, and certainly does not suggest that for about two centuries there had existed no appreciation of, or demand for, works of art. Although sculpture had grown mechanical, there had been, apparently, progressive development in other directions. We find, for instance, a marked and increased appreciation of colour, suggesting influence from a district where Nature presents more variety and distinguishing beauty than the somewhat monotonous valley of the Nile; ware was being highly glazed and tinted with taste and skill unknown in the Twelfth Dynasty, and painting had become more popular.

But, perhaps, it was in the work of administration that the Egyptians learned most from their Hyksos rulers. Joseph, who was undoubtedly a great statesman, must have impressed them greatly with his sound doctrines of political economy. That sagacious young vizier displayed an acute and far-sighted appreciation of the real needs of

Egypt, a country which cannot be made prosperous under divided rule. No doubt he was guided by the experienced councillors at Court, but had he not been gifted with singular intelligence and strong force of character, he could never have performed his onerous duties with so much distinction and success. He fostered the agricultural industry during the years of plenty, and "gathered corn as the sand of the sea, very much, until he left numbering; for it was without number".

Then came the seven years of famine. "And when all the land of Egypt was famished, the people cried to Pharaoh for bread . . . And Joseph opened all the storehouses and sold unto the Egyptians." Much wealth poured into the Imperial Exchequer. "All countries came into Egypt to Joseph for to buy corn." The dry cycle prevailed apparently over a considerable area, and it must have propelled the migrations of pastoral peoples which subsequently effected so great a change in the political conditions of Asia.

It is interesting to note that at this period the horse was known in Egypt. On the occasion of Joseph's elevation to the post of grand vizier, Pharaoh "made him to ride in the second chariot which he had". Then when the Egyptians, who found it necessary to continue purchasing corn, cried out "the money faileth", the young Hebrew "gave them bread in exchange for horses", &c.

The wholesale purchase of estates followed. "Buy us and our land for bread," said the Egyptians, "and we and our land will be servants unto Pharaoh . . . So the land became Pharaoh's . . . And as for the people, he (Joseph) removed them to cities from one end of the borders of Egypt even to the other end thereof."

The work of reorganization proceeded apace. Joseph in due season distributed seed, and made it conditional that a fifth part of the produce of all farms should be paid in taxation. A strong central government was thus established upon a sound economic basis, and it may have flourished until some change occurred of which we have no knowledge. Perhaps the decline of the Hyksos power was not wholly due to a revolt in the south; it may have been contributed to as well by interference from without.

Meanwhile the children of Israel "dwelt in the land of Egypt, in the country of Goshen; and they had possessions therein and multiplied exceedingly." Josephus's statement that they were identical with the Hyksos hardly accords with the evidence of the Bible. It is possible, however, that other Semites besides Joseph attained high positions during the period of foreign control. In fact, one of the Pharaohs was named Jacobher, or possibly, as Breasted suggests, "Jacob-El". Such a choice of ruler would not be inconsistent with the policy of the Hittites, who allowed subject peoples to control their own affairs so long as they adhered to the treaty of alliance and recognized the suzerainty of the supreme Power.

It is impossible to fix with any certainty the time at which the Israelites settled in Egypt. They came, not as conquerors, but after the Hyksos had seized the crown. Apparently, too, they had no intention of effecting permanent settlement, because the bodies of Jacob and Joseph, having been embalmed, were carried to the family cave tomb "in the land of Canaan", which Abraham had purchased from "Ephron the Hittite".

No inscription regarding Joseph or the great famine has survived. But the Egyptians were not likely to preserve any record of a grand vizier who starved them into submission. A tablet which makes reference to a seven years' famine during the Third Dynasty has been proved to be a pious fraud of the Roman period. It was based, in all probability, on the Joseph story. The alleged record sets forth that King Zoser, who was greatly distressed regarding the condition of the country, sent a message to the Governor of Nubia, asking for information regarding the rise of the Nile. Statistics were duly supplied according to his desire. Then Pharaoh "dreamed a dream", and saw the god Khnûmû, who informed him that Egypt was being afflicted because no temples had been erected to the gods. As soon as he woke up, His Majesty made gifts of land to the priests of Khnû-mû, and arranged that they should receive a certain proportion of all the fish and game caught in the vicinity of the first cataract.

There is no agreement as to when the Exodus of the Israelites took place. Some authorities are of opinion that it coincided with the expulsion of the Hyksos. Such a view, however, conflicts with the Biblical reference to a period of bondage. The Pharaoh of the Oppression was a "new king" and he "knew not Joseph". He enslaved and oppressed the Israelites, who had been so singularly favoured by the foreign rulers. According to tradition, he was Ramses II, during whose reign Moses acquired "all the wisdom of the Egyptians" and became "mighty in words and deeds". The next king was Mene-ptah, but he cannot be regarded as the Pharaoh of the Exodus. He reigned little over ten years, and one of his inscriptions makes reference to the Israelites as a people resident in Canaan, where they were attacked by the Egyptian army during a Syrian campaign. It is probable that the Hebrews were the Khabri mentioned in the Tell el Amarna letters, two centuries before Mene-ptah's time. They were then waging war against Canaa-nitish allies of Egypt, and the Prince of Gezer sent an urgent but ineffectual appeal to the Pharaoh Akenaton for assistance. The Exodus must have taken place in the early part of the Eighteenth Dynasty, and possibly during the reign of Thothmes I – about a generation after Ahmes expelled the Asiatics from Avaris.

During the latter part of the Hyksos period the Theban princes, whom Manetho gives as the kings of the Seventeenth Dynasty, were tributary rulers over a goodly part of Upper Egypt. Reinforced from Nubia, and aided by the princes of certain of the nomes, they suddenly rose against their oppressors, and began to wage the War of Independence, which lasted for about a quarter of a century.

An interesting papyrus, preserved in the British Museum, contains a fragmentary folktale, which indicates that the immediate cause of the rising was an attempt on the part of the Hyksos overlord to compel the Egyptians to worship the god Sutekh.

"It came to pass," we read, "that Egypt was possessed by the Impure, and there was no lord and king."

This may mean that either the Hyksos rule had limited power in Upper Egypt or was subject to a higher authority in Asia. The folktale proceeds:

"Now King Sekenenra was lord of the south . . . Impure Asiatics were in the cities (? as garrisons), and Apepa was lord in Avaris. They worked their will in the land, and enjoyed all the good things of Egypt. The god Sutekh was Apepa's master, for he worshipped Sutekh alone, and erected for him an enduring temple . . . He sacrificed and gave offerings every day unto Sutekh . . ."

The tale then goes on to relate that Apepa sent a messenger to Sekenenra, the lord of Thebes, "the city of the south", with an important document which had been prepared after lengthy consultation with a number of learned scribes.

Sekenenra appears to have received the messenger with undisguised alarm. He asked: "What order do you bring? Why have you made this journey?"

The document was read, and, so far as can be gathered from the blurred and mutilated papyrus, it was something to the following effect: –

The King Ra Apepa sends to you to say: Let the hippopotami, be put out of the pool in the city of Thebes. I cannot get sleep, either by day or by night, because their roaring is in my ear.

No wonder that "the lord of the south" was astounded. The sacred animals at Thebes could not possibly be disturbing the slumbers of a monarch residing on the Delta frontier. Apepa was evidently anxious to pick a quarrel with the Thebans, for his hypocritical complaint was, in effect, an express order to accomplish the suppression of a popular form of worship. Well he knew that he could not adopt more direct means to stir up a spirit of rebellion among his Egyptian subjects. Possibly the growing power of the Theban ruler may have caused him to feel somewhat alarmed, and he desired to shatter it before it became too strong for him.

Sekenenra was unable for a time to decide what reply he should make. At length, having entertained the messenger, he bade him to convey the following brief but pointed answer to Apepa: "I intend to do as is your wish."

Apparently he desired to gain time, for there could remain no doubt that a serious crisis was approaching. No sooner did the messenger take his departure than the Theban ruler summoned before him all the great lords in the district, and to them he related "what had come to pass". These men were likewise "astounded"; they heard what Sekenenra had to tell them "with feelings of sorrow, but were silent, for none knew what to say".

The fragmentary tale then ends abruptly with the words: "The King Ra Apepa sent to –"

We can infer, however, that his second message roused a storm of opposition, and that whatever demand it contained was met with a blank refusal. King Ra Apepa must have then sent southward a strong army to enforce his decree and subdue the subject princes who dared to have minds of their own.

If we identify Sekenenra with the Theban king of that name, whose mummy was found at Der el Bahari, and is now in the Cairo museum, we can conclude that the ancient folktale contained a popular account of the brief but glorious career and tragic death of a national hero, who, like the Scottish Sir William Wallace, inspired his countrymen with the desire for freedom and independence.

Sekenenra died on the battlefield. We can see him pressing forward at the head of the Egyptian army, fighting with indomitable courage and accomplishing mighty deeds. Accompanied by his most valiant followers, he hews his way through the Hyksos force. But "one by one they fall around him" . . . Now he is alone. He is surrounded . . . The warriors in front of him are mowed down, for none can withstand his blows. But an Asiatic creeps up on his left side, swings his battleaxe, and smites a glancing blow. Sekenenra totters; his check bone and teeth have been laid bare. Another Asiatic on his right leaps up and stabs him on the forehead. Ere he falls, his first successful assailant strikes again, and the battleaxe crashes through the left side of the hero's skull. The Hyksos shout triumphantly, but the Egyptians are not dismayed; clamouring in battle fury, they rush on to avenge the death of Sekenenra . . . That hero has not died in vain.

The mummy of the great prince bears the evidence of the terrible wounds he received. In his agony he had bitten his tongue between his teeth. But it is apparent that before he fell he turned the tide of battle, and that the Hyksos were compelled to retreat, for his body was recovered and carried back to Thebes, where it was embalmed after putrefaction had set in.

Sekenenra appears to have been a handsome and dashing soldier. He was tall, slim, and active, with a strong, refined face of dark Mediterranean type. Probably he was a descendant of one of the ancient families which had taken refuge in the south after the Hyksos invaders had accomplished the fall of the native monarchy.

His queen, Ah-hotep, who was a hereditary princess in her own right, lived until she was a hundred years old. Her three sons reigned in succession, and continued the war against the Hyksos. The youngest of these was Ahmes I, and he was the first Pharaoh of the Eighteenth Dynasty. Ah-hotep must have followed his career with pride, for he drove the Asiatics across the frontier. She survived him, and then lived through the reign of Amenhotep I also, for she did not pass away until Thotmes I ruled in splendour over united Egypt, and caused its name to be dreaded in western Asia.

Ahmes I, like the heroic Sekenenra, received the support of the El Kab family, which was descended from one of the old feudal lords. His successes are recorded in the tomb of his namesake, the son of Ebana, a princess, and of Baba, the lord of El Kab, who had served under Sekenenra. This El Kab Ahmes was quite a youth – he tells us that he was "too young to have a wife" – when he fought on foot behind the chariot of the Pharaoh. He was afterwards promoted to the rank of admiral, and won a naval victory on a canal. So greatly did the young nobleman distinguish himself that he received a decoration – a golden collar, the equivalent of our "Victoria Cross". Indeed he was similarly honoured for performing feats of valour on four subsequent occasions, and he also received gifts of land and of male and female slaves who had been taken captive.

The progress northward of Ahmes I, with army and river fleet, was accompanied by much hard fighting. But at length he compelled the Hyksos force, which had suffered heavily, to take refuge in the fortified town of Avaris. After a prolonged siege the enemy took flight, and he pursued them across the frontier.

We have followed, so far, the narrative of Ahmes, son of Ebana. According to Manetho's account of the expulsion, as quoted by Josephus, who, perhaps, tampered with it, King Ahmes was unable to do more than shut up the Asiatics in Avaris. Then Thummosis (Thothmes), successor of Ahmes, endeavoured to carry the town by assault, but failed in the attempt. Just when he was beginning to despair of accomplishing his purpose, the enemy offered to capitulate if they would be allowed to depart in peace. This condition was accepted, whereupon 240,000 men, women, and children evacuated Avaris and crossed the frontier into Syria. Manetho adds that they migrated to the district afterwards known as Judea, and built Jerusalem, because "they were in dread of the Assyrians". But, as we have seen, the Assyrians were not at this period the predominating power in the East. Manetho (or Josephus) was plainly wrong. A new and hostile enemy, however, had appeared at Mitanni – the dreaded Aryans, who worshipped the strange gods Indra, Mithra, and Varuna.

After clearing the Delta of Asiatic soldiers, Ahmes I turned his attention to Nubia. He did not meet with much opposition, and succeeded in extending the southern frontier to the second cataract, thus recovering the area which had been controlled by the great Pharaohs of the Twelfth Dynasty. He had afterwards to suppress two abortive risings in the heart of the kingdom, which may have been engineered by Hyksos sympathizers. Then he devoted himself to the work of restoring the monuments of his ancestors and the temples of the gods. After a strenuous reign of over twenty years he died in the prime of life, lamented, no doubt, by the people whom he had set free, and especially by the queen mother, Ah-hotep, that wife of a mighty leader and nurse of valiant heroes – one of the first great women in history.

The military successes of the Egyptians were largely contributed to by their use of the horse, which the Aryans had introduced into the West.

New methods of fighting had also been adopted by the Egyptians. When the Eighteenth-Dynasty soldiers were depicted on the monuments and in the tombs the artists had for their models highly disciplined and well-organized bodies of men who had undergone a rigorous training. The infantry were marshalled in regular lines, and on battlefields made vigorous and orderly charges. Charioteers gathered into action with the dash and combination of modern-day cavalry. Had this new military system evolved in Upper Egypt as a result of the example shown by the Hyksos? Or had the trade in horses brought into the Nile valley Aryan warriors who became the drill sergeants and adjutants of the army which drove the Hyksos from the land of the Pharaohs?

Source: Egyptian Myth and Legend, *Donald A. Mackenzie, Gresham Publishing, London, 1907*

APPENDIX V: EGYPTIAN MAGIC
By E.A. Wallis Budge, 1901

The "magic" of the Egyptians was of two kinds: (1) that
which was employed for legitimate purposes and with the
idea of benefiting either the living or the dead, and (2) that
which was made use of in the furtherance of nefarious plots
and schemes and was intended to bring calamities upon
those against whom it was directed. In the religious texts
and works we see how magic is made to be the handmaiden
of religion, and how it appears in certain passages side by
side with the most exalted spiritual conceptions; and there
can be no doubt that the chief object of magical books and
ceremonies was to benefit those who had by some means
attained sufficient knowledge to make use of them. But the
Egyptians were unfortunate enough not to be understood
by many of the strangers who found their way into their
country, and as a result wrong and exaggerated ideas of
their religion were circulated among the surrounding
nations, and the magical ceremonies which were performed
at their funerals were represented by the ignorant either as
silly acts of superstition or as tricks of the "black" art. But
whereas the magic of every other nation of the ancient East
was directed entirely against the powers of darkness, and
was invented in order to frustrate their fell designs by
invoking a class of benevolent beings to their aid, the
Egyptians aimed at being able to command their gods
to work for them, and to compel them to appear at their
desire. These great results were to be obtained by the use of
certain words which, to be efficacious, must be uttered in a
proper tone of voice by a duly qualified man; such words
might be written upon some substance, papyrus, precious

stones, and the like, and worn on the person, when their effect could be transmitted to any distance. As almost every man, woman, and child in Egypt who could afford it wore some such charm or talisman, it is not to be wondered at that the Egyptians were at a very early period regarded as a nation of magicians and sorcerers. Hebrew, and Greek, and Roman writers referred to them as experts in the occult sciences, and as the possessors of powers which could, according to circumstances, be employed to do either good or harm to man.

From the Hebrews we receive, incidentally, it is true, considerable information about the powers of the Egyptian magician. Saint Stephen boasts that the great legislator Moses "was learned in all the wisdom of the Egyptians", and declares that he "was mighty in words and in deeds", and there are numerous features in the life of this remarkable man which show that he was acquainted with many of the practices of Egyptian magic. The phrase "mighty in words" probably means that, like the goddess Isis, he was "strong of tongue" and uttered the words of power which he knew with correct pronunciation, and halted not in his speech, and was perfect both in giving the command and in saying the word. The turning of a serpent into what is apparently an inanimate, wooden stick, and the turning of the stick back into a writhing snake, are feats which have been performed in the East from the most ancient period; and the power to control and direct the movements of such venomous reptiles was one of the things of which the Egyptian was most proud, and in which he was most skilful, already in the time when the pyramids were being built. But this was by no means the only proof which Moses gives that he was versed in the magic of the Egyptians, for, like the sage Âba-aner and king Nectanebus, and all the

other magicians of Egypt from time immemorial, he and
Aaron possessed a wonderful rod by means of which they
worked their wonders. At the word of Moses, Aaron lifted
up his rod and smote the waters and they became blood; he
stretched it out over the waters, and frogs innumerable
appeared; when the dust was smitten by the rod it became
lice; and so on. Moses sprinkled ashes "toward heaven",
and it became boils and blains upon man and beast; he
stretched out his rod, and there was "hail, and fire mingled
with the hail, very grievous", and the "flax and the barley
was smitten"; he stretched out his rod and the locusts came,
and after them the darkness. Now Moses did all these
things, and brought about the death of the firstborn among
the Egyptians by the command of his God, and by means of
the words which He told him to speak. But although we are
told by the Hebrew writer that the Egyptian magicians
could not imitate all the miracles of Moses, it is quite
certain that every Egyptian magician believed that he
could perform things equally marvellous by merely uttering the name of one of his gods, or through the words of
power which he had learned to recite; and there are many
instances on record of Egyptian magicians utterly destroy-
ing their enemies by the recital of a few words possessed of
magical power, and, by the performance of some, apparently, simple ceremony. But one great distinction must be
made between the magic of Moses and that of the Egyptians among whom he lived; the former was wrought by the
command of the God of the Hebrews, but the latter by the
gods of Egypt at the command of man.

Later on in the history of Moses' dealings with the
Egyptians we find the account of how "he stretched out
his hand over the sea, and the Lord caused the sea to go
back by a strong east wind all that night, and made the sea

dry *land*, and the waters were divided. And the children of
Israel went into the midst of the sea upon the dry *ground*;
and the waters *were* a wall unto them on their right hand,
and on their left." When the Egyptians had come between
the two walls of water, by God's command Moses stretched
forth his hand over the sea, "and the sea returned to his
strength," and the "waters returned, and covered the
chariots, and the horsemen, *and* all the host of Pharaoh
that came into the sea after them". But the command of the
waters of the sea or river was claimed by the Egyptian
magician long before the time of Moses, as we may see from
an interesting story preserved in the Westcar Papyrus. This
document was written in the early part of the 20th Dynasty, about 1550 BC but it is clear that the stories in it date
from the Early Empire, and are in fact as old as the Great
Pyramid. The story is related to king Khufu (Cheops) by
Baiu-f-Râ as an event which happened in the time of the
king's father, and as a proof of the wonderful powers of
magic which were possessed by the priest called Tchatcha-
em-ânkh. It seems that on a certain day king Seneferu was
in low spirits, and he applied to the nobles of his royal
household expecting that they would find some means
whereby his heart might be made glad; but as they could
do nothing to cheer up the king, he gave orders that the
priest and writer of books, Tchatcha-em-ânkh, should be
brought into his presence immediately, and in accordance
with the royal command he was at once brought. When he
had arrived, Seneferu said to him, "My brother, I turned to
the nobles of my royal household seeking for some means
whereby I might cheer my heart, but they have found
nothing for me." Then the priest made answer and advised
the king to betake himself to the lake near the palace, and
to go for a sail on it in a boat which had been comfortably

furnished with things from the royal house. "For," said he, "the heart of thy Majesty will rejoice and be glad when thou sailest about hither and thither, and dost see the beautiful thickets which are on the lake, and when thou seest the pretty banks thereof and the beautiful fields then shall thy heart feel happiness." He next begged that the king would allow him to organize the journey, and asked his permission to let him bring twenty ebony paddles inlaid with gold, and also twenty young virgins having beautiful heads of hair and lovely forms and shapely limbs, and twenty nets wherein these virgins may array themselves instead of in their own ordinary garments. The virgins were to row and sing to his Majesty. To these proposals the king assented, and when all was ready he took his place in the boat; while the young women were rowing him about hither and thither the king watched them, and his heart became released from care. Now as one of the young women was rowing, she entangled herself in some way in her hair, and one of her ornaments which was made of "new turquoise" fell into the water and sank; she ceased to row, and not herself only, but all the other maidens ceased to row also. When the king saw that the maidens had ceased from their work, he said to them, "Will ye not row?" and they replied, "Our leader has ceased to row." Then turning to the maiden who had dropped her ornament overboard, he asked her why she was not rowing, where- upon she told him what had happened. On this the king promised that he would get back the ornament for her.

Then the king commanded that Tchatcha-em-ânkh should appear before him at once, and as soon as the sage had been brought into his presence he said to him, "O Tchatcha-em-ânkh, my brother, I have done according to thy words, and the heart of my Majesty became glad when

I saw how the maidens rowed. But now, an ornament which is made of new turquoise and belongeth to one of the maidens who row hath fallen into the water, and she hath in consequence become silent, and hath ceased to row, and hath disturbed the rowing of those in her company. I said to her, 'Why dost thou not row?' and she replied, 'An ornament [of mine] made of new turquoise hath fallen into the water.' Then I said to her, 'I will get it back for thee.'" Thereupon the priest and writer of books Tchatcha-em-ânkh spake certain words of power (*hekau*), and having thus caused one section of the water of the lake to go up upon the other, he found the ornament lying upon a pot-sherd, and he took it and gave it to the maiden. Now the water was twelve cubits deep, but when Tchatcha-em-ânkh had lifted up one section of the water on to the other, that portion became four and twenty cubits deep. The magician again uttered certain words of power, and the water of the lake became as it had been before he had caused one portion of it to go up on to the other; and the king prepared a feast for all his royal household, and rewarded Tchatcha-em-ânkh with gifts of every kind. Such is a story of the power possessed by a magician in the time of king Khufu (Cheops), who reigned at the beginning of the 14th Dynasty, about 3800 BC. The copy of the story which we possess is older than the period when Moses lived, and thus there can be no possibility of our seeing in it a distorted version of the miracle of the waters of the sea standing like walls, one on the right hand and one on the left; on the other hand Moses' miracle may well have some connexion with that of Tchatcha-em-ânkh.

Among the Greeks and Romans considerable respect was entertained, not only for the "wisdom" of the Egyptians, but also for the powers of working magic which they were supposed to possess. The Greek travellers who visited Egypt brought back to their own country much information concerning its religion and civilization, and, though they misunderstood many things which they saw and heard there, some of the greatest of thinkers among the Greeks regarded that country not only as the home of knowledge and the source of civilization and of the arts, but also as the fountain head of what has been called "white magic", and the "black art". In some respects they exaggerated the powers of the, Egyptians, but frequently when the classical writers were well informed they only ascribed to them the magical knowledge which the Egyptian magicians themselves claimed to possess. A striking instance of this is given in the second book of the *Metamorphoses of Apuleius* where, it will be remembered, the following is narrated. The student Telephron arrived one day at Larissa, and as he was wandering about in an almost penniless condition he saw an old man standing on a large block of stone issuing a proclamation to the effect that any one who would undertake to guard a dead body should receive a good reward. When Telephron asked if dead men were in the habit of running away the old man replied testily to the effect that the witches all over Thessaly used to tear off pieces of flesh from the faces of the dead with their teeth, in order to make magical spells by means of them, and to prevent this dead bodies must needs be watched at night. The young man then asked what his duties would be if he undertook the post, and he was told that he would have to keep thoroughly awake all night, to gaze fixedly upon the dead body, to look neither to the right hand nor to the left, and not to close the eyes even to wink. This was absolutely necessary because the witches were able to get out of their skins and to take the form of a bird, or dog, or mouse, and their craftiness was such that they could take the forms of flies and cast sleep upon the watcher. If the watcher relaxed his attention and the body became mutilated by the witches, the pieces of flesh torn away would have to be made good from the body of the watcher. Telephron agreed to undertake the duty for one thousand nummi, and was led by the old man to a house, and, having been taken into the room where the dead body was, found a man making notes on tablets to the effect that nose, eyes, ears, lips, chin, etc., were untouched and whole. Having been provided with a lamp and some oil that night he began his watch, and all went well, notwithstanding that he was greatly afraid, until the dead of night when a weasel came into the chamber and looked confidingly at the watcher; but he drove the animal – which was no doubt a witch – from the room, and then fell fast asleep. In the early morning he was suddenly wakened by the trumpets of the soldiers, and almost immediately the widow of the dead man came to him with seven witnesses, and began to examine the body to see if it was intact; finding that no injury had been done to it she ordered her steward to pay Telephron his fee, and was so grateful to him that she promised to make him one of her household. In attempting to express his thanks, however, he made use of some inauspicious words, and immediately the servants of the house fell upon him, and buffeted him, and plucked out his hair by the roots, and tore his clothes, and finally cast him out of the house. Soon afterwards, whilst wandering about, he saw the funeral procession pass through the forum, and at that moment an old man went to the bier, and with sobs and tears accused the widow of poisoning his nephew so that she might inherit his property and marry her lover. Presently the mob which had gathered together wanted to set her house on fire, and some people began to stone her; the small boys also threw stones at her. When she had denied the accusation, and had called upon the gods to be witnesses of her innocence, the old man cried out, "Let, then, Divine Providence decide the truth, in answer to her denial. Behold, the famous prophet Zaclas the Egyptian, dwelleth among us, and he hath promised me that for much money he will make the soul of the dead man to return from the place of death in the underworld, and to make it to dwell in his body again for a short time." With these words, he led forward a man dressed in linen, and wearing palm-leaf sandals, who, like all the Egyptian priests, had his head shaved, and having kissed his hands and embraced his legs he implored him by the stars, and by the gods of the underworld, and by the island of the Nile, and by the Inundation, etc., to restore life to the dead body, if only for the smallest possible time, so that the truth of his accusation against the widow might be proved. Thus adjured Zaclas touched the mouth and the breast of the dead man three times with some plant, and having turned his face to the East and prayed, the lungs of the corpse began to fill with breath, and his heart to beat, and raising his head and shoulders he asked why he had been called back to life, and then he begged to be allowed to rest in peace. At this moment Zaclas addressed him, and telling him that he had the power, through his prayers, to cause the fiends to come and torture him, ordered, him to make known the means by which he had died. With a groan he replied that the wife whom he had recently married gave him poison to drink, and that he died as a consequence. The wife at once contradicted the words of her husband, and of the people who were standing round some took one side and some another. At length the husband declared that he would

prove the truth of his own words, and pointing to Telephron, who had attempted to guard his body, told those
present that the witches after making many attempts to
elude his vigilance had cast deep sleep upon him. They next
called upon himself by his name, which happened to be
Telephron, like that of his watcher, and whilst he was
endeavouring feebly to obey their spells, his watcher rose
up unconsciously and walked about. Seeing this the witches
forced their way into the room through some unknown
place, and having taken off the nose and ears of the watcher
they placed models of these members in their places. Those
who heard these words looked fixedly at the young man,
who at once put up his hands and touched the members,
whereupon his nose came off in his hand, and his ears
slipped through his fingers on to the ground.

The end of the story does not concern us, and so we pass
on to note that the act of touching the mouth which Zaclas
performed is, of course, a part of the ceremony of "opening
the mouth" which is so often referred to in religious texts,
and was considered of extreme importance for the welfare
of the dead, and that the power of bringing back the dead
to life which Apuleius ascribes to the priest or magician was
actually claimed some thousands of years before Christ by
the sages of Egypt, as we may see from the following story in
the Westcar Papyrus.

A son of king Khufu (or Cheops, who reigned about 3800
BC) called Herutâtâf, who was famous as a learned man and
whose name is preserved in the "Book of the Dead" in
connection with the "discovery" of certain Chapters of that
wonderful compilation, was one day talking to his father,
presumably on the subject of the powers of working magic
possessed by the ancients. In answer to some remark by
Khufu he replied, "Up to the present thou hast only heard

reports concerning the things which the men of olden time knew, and man knoweth not whether they are true or not; but now I will cause thy Majesty to see a sage in thine own time, and one who knoweth thee not." In reply to Khufu's question, "Who is this man, O Herutâtâf?" the young man replied, "It is a certain man called Teta, who dwelleth in Tet-Seneferu, and is one hundred and ten years old, and to this very day he eateth five hundred loaves of bread, and the shoulder of an ox, and he drinketh one hundred measures of ale. He knoweth how to fasten on again to its body a head that hath been cut off; he knoweth how to make a lion follow him whilst his snare is trailing on the ground; and he knoweth the number of the *aptet* of the sanctuary of Thoth." Now Khufu had for a long time past sought out the aptet of the sanctuary of Thoth, because he was anxious to make one similar for his own "horizon". Though at the present it is impossible to say what the *aptet* was, it is quite clear that it was an object or instrument used in connection with the working of magic of some sort, and it is clear that the king was as much interested in the pursuit as his subjects. In reply to his son's words Khufu told him to go and bring the sage into his presence, and the royal barge or boat having been brought, Herutâtâf set out for the place where the sage dwelt. Having sailed up the river some distance he and his party arrived at Tet-Seneferu, and when the boats had been tied to the quay the prince set out to perform the rest of the Journey, which was overland, in a sort of litter made of ebony, which was borne by men by means of poles of *sesnetchem* wood, inlaid with gold. When he had arrived at the abode of Teta, the litter was set down upon the ground, and the prince came out to greet the sage, whom he found lying upon a basket-work bed or mattress, which had been placed for him in the courtyard of his house, whilst one servant shampooed his head, and another rubbed his feet. After a suitable greeting and reference to the sage's honourable condition had been made, Herutâtâf told him that he had come from a great distance in order to bring to him a message from Khufu his father, and the sage bade him "Welcome" heartily, and prophesied that Khufu would greatly exalt his rank. The greetings ended, Herutâtâf assisted Teta to rise, and the old man set out for the quay leaning upon the arm of the king's son, and when he had arrived there he asked that a boat might be provided for the transport of his children and his books. Two boats were at once prepared and filled with their complement of sailors, and Teta sailed down the Nile with Herutâtâf, while his family followed.

After a time the party arrived at Khufu's palace, and Herutâtâf went into the presence of his father, and reported to him that he had brought Teta the sage for him to see; Khufu gave orders that he was to be brought before him quickly, and having gone forth into the colonnade of the palace, Teta was led in to him. Khufu said to him, "How is it, Teta, that I have never seen thee?" and the sage replied, "O Prince, he who is called cometh; and since thou hast called me, behold, here I am." Khufu said to him, "Is it true, according to what is reported, that thou knowest how to fasten on again to its body the head which hath been cut off?" and the sage replied, "Yea, verily, O my lord the Prince, I do know how to do this thing." And Khufu said, "Let a captive who is shut up in prison be brought to me so that I may inflict his doom upon him," but Teta made answer, "Nay, my lord the king let not this thing be performed upon man, but upon some creature that belongeth to the sacred animals." Then some one brought to him a goose, and having cut off its head, he laid the body of the goose on the west side of the colonnade, and the head on the east side. Teta then stood up and spake certain words of magical power, whereupon the body began to move and the head likewise, and each time that they moved the one came nearer to the other, until at length the head moved to its right place on the bird, which straightway cackled. After this Teta had a *khet-âa* bird brought to him, and upon it he performed the same miracle which he had wrought upon the goose; and to prove that he had similar power over the animal creation, an ox was brought to him, and having cut off its head, which fell upon the ground, he uttered words of magical power, and the ox stood up and lived as before.

The two stories from the Westcar Papyrus given above are sufficient to prove that already in the Fourth Dynasty the working of magic was a recognized art among the Egyptians, and everything we learn from later texts indicates that it is well-nigh impossible to imagine a time in Egypt when such was not the case. But the "wisdom" of the Egyptians was of two kinds, that is to say, they were possessed of the two kinds of "wisdom" which enabled them to deal with both the material world and the spiritual world; the nations around, however, confused the two kinds, and misunderstood matters in consequence.

One of the oldest names of Egypt is "Kamt" or "Qemt", a word which means "black" or "dusky", and it was applied to the country on account of the dark colour of the mud which forms the land on each side of the Nile; the Christian Egyptians or Copts transmitted the word under the form Khême to the Greeks, Romans, Syrians, and

Arabs. At a very early period the Egyptians were famous for their skill in the working of metals and in their attempts to transmute them, and, according to Greek writers, they employed quicksilver in the processes whereby they separated the metals gold and silver from the native ore. From these processes there resulted a "black" powder or substance which was supposed to possess the most marvellous powers, and to contain in it the individualities of the various metals; and in it their actual substances were incorporated. In a mystical manner this "black" powder was identified with the body which the god Osiris was known to possess in the underworld, and to both were attributed magical qualities, and both were thought to be sources of life and power. Thus, side by side with the growth of skill in performing the ordinary processes of metal-working, in Egypt, there grew up in that country the belief that magical powers existed in fluxes and alloys; and the art of manipulating the metals, and the knowledge of the chemistry of the metals and of their magical powers were described by the name "Khemeia", that is to say "the preparation of the black ore" (or "powder") which was regarded as the transmutation of metals. To this name the Arabs affixed the article *al*, and thus we obtain the word Al-Khemeia, or Alchemy, which will perpetuate the reputation of the Egyptians as successful students both of "white magic" and of the "black" art.

But in addition to their skill as handicraftsmen and artisans the Egyptians were skilled in literary composition, and in the production of books, especially of that class which related to the ceremonies which were performed for the benefit of the dead. We have, unfortunately, no means of knowing what early contemporary peoples thought of the Egyptian funeral ceremonies, but it seems to be certain that it was chiefly by means of these that they obtained their reputation as workers of miracles. If by chance any members of a desert tribe had been permitted to behold the ceremonies which were performed when the kings for whom the Pyramids had been built were laid to rest in them, the stories that they took back to their kinsmen would be received as sure proofs that the Egyptians had the power to give life to the dead, to animate statues, and to command the services of their gods by the mere utterance of their names as words of power. The columns of hieroglyphics with which the walls of the tombs were often covered, and the figures of the gods, painted or sculptured upon stelæ or sarcophagi, would still further impress the barbarian folk who always regard the written letter and those who understand it with great awe. The following story from Mas'ûdî will illustrate the views which the Arabs held concerning the inscriptions and figures of gods in the temples of Egypt. It seems that when the army of Pharaoh had been drowned in the Red Sea, the women and slaves feared lest they should be attacked by the kings of Syria and the West; in this difficulty they elected a woman called Dalûkah as their queen, because she was wise and prudent and skilled in magic. Dalûkah's first act was to surround all Egypt with a wall, which she guarded by men who were stationed along it at short intervals, her object being as much to protect her son, who was addicted to the chase, from the attacks of wild beasts as Egypt from invasion by nomad tribes; besides this she placed round the enclosure figures of crocodiles and other formidable animals. During the course of her reign of thirty years she filled Egypt with her temples and with figures of animals; she also made figures of men in the form of the dwellers in the countries round about Egypt, and in Syria, and in the West, and of the beasts which they rode. In the temples she collected all the secrets of nature and all the attracting or repelling powers which were contained in minerals, plants, and animals. She performed her sorceries at the moment in the revolution of the celestial bodies when they would be amenable to a higher power. And it came to pass that if an army set out from any part of Arabia or Syria to attack Egypt, the queen made the figures of its soldiers and of the animals which they were riding to disappear beneath the ground, and the same fate immediately overtook the living creatures which they represented, wherever they might be on their journey, and the destruction of the figures on sculptures entailed the destruction of the hostile host. In brief, the large figures of the gods which were sculptured or painted on the walls, and the hieroglyphic inscriptions which accompanied them, were considered by those who could neither understand nor read them to be nothing more nor less than magical figures and formulæ which were intended to serve as talismans.

The historian Mas'ûdî mentions an instance of the powers of working magic possessed by a certain Jew, which proves that the magical practices of the Egyptians had passed eastwards and had found a congenial home among the Jews who lived in and about Babylon. This man was a native of the village of Zurârah in the district of Kûfa, and he employed his time in working magic. In the Mosque at Kûfa, and in the presence of Walîd ibn Ukbah, he raised up several apparitions, and made a king of huge stature, who was mounted upon a horse, gallop about in the courtyard of the Mosque. He then transformed himself into a camel and walked upon a rope; and made the phantom of an ass to pass through his body; and finally having slain a man, he cut off the head and removed it from the trunk, and then by passing his sword over the two parts, they united and the man came alive again. This last act recalls the joining of the head of the dead goose to its body and the coming back of the bird to life which has been described above.

We have now to describe briefly the principal means upon which the Egyptians relied for working magic, that is to say, magical stones or amulets, magical figures, magical pictures and formulæ, magical names, magical ceremonies, etc., and such portions of the Book of the Dead as bear upon these subjects generally.

The Egyptians, like most Oriental nations, attached very great importance to the knowledge of names, and the knowledge of how to use and to make mention of names which possessed magical powers was a necessity both for the living and the dead. It was believed that if a man knew the name of a god or a devil, and addressed him by it, he was bound to answer him and to do whatever he wished; and the possession of the knowledge of the name of a man enabled his neighbour to do him good or evil. The name that was the object of a curse brought down evil upon its owner, and similarly the name that was the object of a blessing or prayer for benefits secured for its master many good things. To the Egyptian the name was as much a part of a man's being as his soul, or his double (ka), or his body, and it is quite certain that this view was held by him in the earliest times. Thus in the text which is inscribed on the walls inside the pyramid of Pepi L, king of Egypt about 3200 BC, we read, "Pepi hath been purified. He hath taken in his hand the mâh staff, he hath provided himself with his throne, and he hath taken

his seat in the boat of the great and little companies of
the gods. Ed maketh Pepi to sail to the West, he
stablisheth his seat above those of the lords of doubles,
and he writeth down Pepi at the head of those who live.
The doors of Pekh-ka which are in the abyss open
themselves to Pepi, the doors of the iron which is the
ceiling of the sky open themselves to Pepi, and he passeth
through them; he hath his panther skin upon him, and
the staff and whip are in his hand. Pepi goeth forward
with his flesh, Pepi is happy with his name, and he liveth
with his *ka* (double)." Curiously enough only the body
and name and double of the king are mentioned, just as
if these three constituted his whole economy; and it is
noteworthy what importance is attached to the name in
this passage. In the text from the pyramid of another
king we have a prayer concerning the preservation of the
name, which is of such interest that a rendering of it in
full is here given: it reads, "O Great Company of the
gods who dwell in Annu (Heliopolis), grant that Pepi
Nefer-ka-Râ may flourish (*literally* 'germinate'), and that
his pyramid, his ever lasting building, may flourish, even
as the name of Temu, the chief of the nine gods, doth
flourish. If the name of Shu, the lord of the upper shrine
in Annu, flourisheth, then Pepi shall flourish, and his
pyramid, his everlasting building, shall flourish! If the
name of Tefnut, the lady of the lower shrine in Annu,
flourisheth, the name of Pepi shall be established, and
this his pyramid shall be established to all eternity! If the
name of Seb flourisheth at the 'homage of the earth',
then the name of Pepi shall flourish, and this his pyramid
shall flourish, and this his building shall flourish unto all
eternity! If the name of Nut in the House of Shenth in
Annu flourisheth, the name of Pepi shall flourish, and

this his pyramid shall flourish, and this his building shall flourish unto all eternity! If the name of Osiris flourisheth in the nome of Abydos, then the name of Pepi shall flourish, and this his pyramid shall flourish, and this his building shall flourish unto all eternity! If the name of Osiris Khent-Amentet flourisheth, then the name of Pepi shall flourish, and this his pyramid shall flourish, and this his building shall flourish unto all eternity! If the name of Set, the dweller in Nubt (Ombos) flourisheth, then the name of Pepi shall flourish, and this his pyramid shall flourish, and this his building shall flourish unto all eternity! If the name of Horus flourisheth, then the name of Pepi shall flourish, and this his pyramid shall flourish, and this his building shall flourish unto all eternity! If the name of Râ flourisheth in the horizon, then the name of Pepi shall flourish, and this his pyramid shall flourish, and this his building shall flourish unto all eternity! If the name of Khent-merti flourisheth in Sekhem (Letopolis), then the name of Pepi shall flourish, and this his pyramid shall flourish, and this his building shall flourish unto all eternity! If the name of Uatchet in Tep flourisheth, then the name of Pepi shall flourish, and this his pyramid shall flourish, and this his building shall flourish unto all eternity!" The above prayer or formula was the origin of most of the prayers and texts which had for their object the "making the name to germinate or flourish", and which were copied so frequently in the Saïte, Ptolemaic, and Roman periods. All these compositions show that from the earliest to the latest times the belief as to the importance of the preservation of the name never changed in Egypt, and the son who assisted in keeping green his father's name, and in consequence his memory, performed a most meritorious duty. But in the present chapter we are not so much concerned with the ordinary as with the extraordinary uses to which a name might be put, and the above facts have only been mentioned to prove that a man's name was regarded as an essential part of himself, and that the blotting out of the name of an individual was synonymous with his destruction. Without a name no man could be identified in the judgment, and as a man only came into being upon this earth when his name had been pronounced, so the future life could only be attained after the gods of the world beyond the grave had become acquainted with it and had uttered it.

According to the story of the Creation which is related in the Papyrus of Nesi-Amsu, before the world and all that therein is came into being, only the great god Neb-er-tcher existed, for even the gods were not born. Now when the time had come for the god to create all things he says, "I brought (*i.e.*, fashioned) my mouth, and I uttered my own name as a word of power, and thus I evolved myself under the evolutions of the god Khepera, and I developed myself out of the primeval matter which had evolved multitudes of evolutions from the beginning of time. Nothing existed on this earth [before me], I made all things. There was none other who worked with me at that time. Elsewhere, that is to say, in the other version of the story, the god Khepera says, I developed myself from the primeval matter which I made, I developed myself out of the primeval matter. My name is 'Osiris', the germ of primeval matter." Here, then, we have a proof that the Egyptians regarded the creation as the result of the utterance of the name of the god Neb-er-tcher or Khepera by himself. In the story of Râ and Isis we see that although Isis was able to make a serpent and to cause it to bite Râ, and to make him very ill, she was powerless to do as she wished in heaven and upon earth until she had persuaded the god to reveal to her his name by which he ruled the universe. In yielding up his name to the goddess he placed himself in her power, and in this example we have a striking instance of the belief that the knowledge of the name of god, or devil, or human being, implied dominion over that being. Râ, the type and symbol of God, is described as the god of "many names," and in that wonderful composition the XVIIth Chapter of the Book of the Dead, we have the following statement: "I am the great god Nu, who gave birth unto himself, and who made his name to become the company of the gods." Then the question, "What does this mean?" or "Who is this?" is asked. And this is the answer: "It is Râ, the creator of the name[s] of his limbs, which came into being in the form of the gods who are in the following of Râ." From this we see that all the "gods" of Egypt were merely personifications of the names of Râ, and that each god was one of his members, and that a name of a god was the god himself. Without the knowledge of the names of the gods and devils of the underworld the dead Egyptian would have fared badly, for his personal liberty would have been fettered, the roads and paths would have been blocked to him, the gates of the mansions of the underworld would have been irrevocably shut in his face, and the hostile powers which dogged his footsteps would have made an end of him; these facts are best illustrated by the following examples:

When the deceased comes to the Hall of Judgment, at the very beginning of his speech he says, "Homage to thee, O Great God, thou Lord of Maâti, I have come to thee, O my Lord, and I have brought myself hither that I may behold thy beauties. I know thee, and I know thy name, and I know the names of the two and forty gods who exist with thee in this Hall of Maâti." But although the gods may be favourable to him, and he be found righteous in the judgment, he cannot make his way among the other gods of the underworld without a knowledge of the names of certain parts of the Hall of Maâti. After the judgment he acquires the mystical name of "He who is equipped with the flowers and the dweller in his olive tree", and it is only after he has uttered this name that the gods say "Pass onwards." Next the gods invite him to enter the Hall of Maâti, but he is not allowed to pass in until he has, in answer to questions asked by the bolts, lintels, threshold, fastenings, socket, door-leaves, and door-posts, told their names. The floor of the Hall will not permit him to walk upon it unless he tells not only its name, but also the mystical names of his two legs and feet wherewith he is about to tread upon it. When all this has been done the guardian of the Hall says to him, "I will not announce thy name [to the god] unless thou tellest me my name"; and the deceased replies, "'Discerner of hearts and searcher of the reins' is thy name." In reply to this the guardian says, "If I announce thy name thou must utter the name of the god who dwelleth in his hour," and the deceased utters the name "Mâau-Taui". But still the guardian is not satisfied, and he says, "If I announce thy name thou must tell me who is he whose heaven is of fire, whose walls [are sur-mounted by] living uraei, and the floor of whose house is a stream of water. Who is he, I say? (*i.e.*, what is his name?)" But the deceased has, of course, learnt the name of the Great God, and he replies, "Osiris." The guardian of the Hall is now content, and he says, "Advance, verily thy name shall be mentioned to him"; and he further promises that the cakes, and ale, and sepulchral meals which the deceased shall enjoy shall come from the "Eye of Râ",

In another Chapter, the deceased addresses seven gods, and says, "Hail, ye seven beings who make decrees, who support the Balance on the night of the judgment of the Utchat, who cut off heads, who hack necks in pieces, who take possession of hearts by violence and rend the places where hearts are fixed, who make slaughterings in the Lake of Fire, I know you, and I know your names; therefore know ye me, even as I know your names." The deceased, having declared that the seven gods know his name and he their names, has no further apprehension that evil will befall him.

In one portion of the kingdom of Osiris there existed seven halls or mansions through which the deceased was anxious to pass, but each of the gates was guarded by a doorkeeper, a watcher, and a herald, and it required special provision on the part of the deceased to satisfy these beings that he had a right to pass them. In the first place, figures of the seven gates had to be made in some substance (or painted upon papyrus), as well as a figure of the deceased: the latter was made to approach each of the gates and to stand before it and to recite an address which had been specially prepared for the purpose. Meanwhile the thigh, the head, the heart, and the hoof of a red bull were offered at each gate, as well as a very large number of miscellaneous offerings which need not be described in detail. But all these ceremonies would not help the deceased to pass through the gates, unless he knew the names of the seven doorkeepers, and the seven watchers, and the seven heralds who guarded them. The gods of the first gate were: – Sekhet-hra-âsht-aru, Semetu, and Hukheru; those of the second, Tun-hât, Seqet-hra, and Sabes; of the third, Am-huat-ent-pehfi, Res-hra, and Uâau; of the fourth, Khesef-hra-âsht-kheru, Res-ab, and Neteka-hra-khesef-atu; of the fifth, Ânkh-em-fentu, Ashebu, and Tebherkehaat; of the sixth, Akentauk-ha-kheru, An-hra, and Metes-hra-ari-she; of the seventh, Metes-sen, Ââa-kheru, and Khesef-hra-khemiu. And the text, which the deceased recites to the Halls collectively, begins, "Hail, ye Halls! Hail, ye who made the Halls for Osiris! Hail, ye who watch your Halls! Hail, ye who herald the affairs of the two lands for the god Osiris each day, the deceased knoweth you, and he knoweth your names." The names having been uttered, and the addresses duly recited, the deceased went wherever he pleased in the seven Halls of Osiris.

But besides the seven halls, the deceased had to pass through the twenty-one hidden pylons of the house of Osiris in the Elysian Fields, and in order to do so he had to declare the names of the pylon and the doorkeeper of each, and to make a short address besides. Thus to the first pylon he says, "I have made my way, I know thee and I know thy name, and I know the name of the god who guardeth thee. Thy name is 'Lady of tremblings, with lofty walls, the sovereign lady, the mistress of destruction, who setteth in order the words which drive back the whirlwind and the storm, who delivereth from destruction him that travelleth along the way'; and the name of thy doorkeeper is Neri." At the second pylon he says, "I have made [my] way, I know thee, and I know thy name, and I know the name of the god who guardeth thee. Thy name is 'Lady of heaven, the mistress of the world, who devoureth with fire, the lady of mortals, who knoweth mankind'. The name of thy doorkeeper is Mes-Ptah," and so on at each of the pylons. In the later and longer version of the chapter which was written to supply the deceased with this knowledge he informs the god of each pylon what purification he has undergone; thus to the god of the first pylon he says, "I have anointed myself with *hâti* "unguent [made from] the cedar, I have arrayed myself in apparel of *menkh* (linen), and I have with me my sceptre made of *heti* wood." After the speech the god of the pylon says, "Pass on, then, thou art pure."

When we remember that one of the oldest beliefs as to the future life made it appear that it would be lived by man in the Sekhet-Aaru, or Field of Reeds, a region which, as we know from the drawings of it which have come down to us, was intersected by canals and streams, it is at once clear that in order to pass from one part of it to another the deceased would need a boat. Even assuming that he was fortunate enough to have made his own way into this region, it was not possible for him to take a boat with him. To meet this difficulty, a boat and all its various parts were drawn upon the papyrus, upon which the selection of Chapters from the Book of the Dead had been inscribed for him, and a knowledge of the text of the chapter which belonged to it made the drawing to become an actual boat. But before he could enter it, the post to which it was tied up, and every part of the boat itself, demanded that he should tell them their names, thus:

Post at which to tie up. "Tell me my name." D. "Lord of the two lands, dweller in the shrine" is thy name.

Rudder. "Tell me my name." D. "Leg of Hâpiu" is thy name.

Rope. "Tell me my name." D. "Hairs with which Anpu finisheth the work of my embalmment" is thy name.

Oar-ruts. "Tell us our name." D. "Pillars of the under-world" is your name.

Hold. "Tell me my name." D. "Akau" is thy name.

Mast. "Tell me my name." D. "Bringer back of the lady after her departure" is thy name.

Lower deck. "Tell me my name." D. "Standard of Ap-uat" is thy name.

Upper Post. "Tell me my name." D. "Throat of Mestha" is thy name.

Sail. "Tell me my name." D. "Nut" is thy name.

Leather Straps. "Tell us our name." D. "Those who are made from the hide of the Mnevis Bull, which was burned by Suti" is your name.

Paddles. "Tell us our name." D. "Fingers of Horus the firstborn" is your name.

Pump (?). "Tell me my name." D. "The hand of Isis which wipeth away the blood of the Eye of Horus" is thy name.

Planks. "Tell us our names." D. "Mestha, Hâpi, Tua-mutef, Qebhsennuf, Haqau, Thet-em-âua, Maa-an-tef, Ari-nef-tchesef" are your names.

Rows. "Tell us our name." D. "He who is at the head of his nomes" is your name.

Hull. "Tell me my name." D. "Mert" is thy name.

Rudder. "Tell me my name." D. "Âqa" is thy name; Shiner in the water, hidden beam" is thy name.

Keel. "Tell me my name." D. "Thigh of Isis, which Râ cut off with the knife to bring blood into the Sektet boat" is thy name.

Sailor. "Tell me my name." D. "Traveller" is thy name.

Wind. "Tell me my name." D. "The North Wind, which cometh from Tem to the nostrils of Osiris" is thy name.

And when the deceased had declared to these their names, before he could set out on his journey he was obliged to tell the river, and the river-banks, and the ground their mystical names. This done, the boat admitted him as a passenger, and he was able to sail about to any part of the Elysian Fields at will.

But among the beings whom the deceased wished to avoid in the underworld were the beings who "lay snares, and who work the nets, and who are fishers", and who would draw him into their nets. It seems as if it were absolutely necessary that he should fall in with these beings and their nets, for a whole chapter of the Book of the Dead was written with the view of enabling him to escape from them unharmed; the god their leader is called "the god whose face is behind him", and "the god who hath gained the mastery over his heart." To escape from the net which was worked by "the fishers who lay snares with their nets and who go round about in the chambers of the waters", the deceased had to know the names of the net, and of the ropes, and of the pole, and of the hooks, and of each and every part of it; without this knowledge nothing could save him from calamity. We unfortunately understand very few of the allusions to mythological events which are contained in the names of the various parts of the machinery which work the net, but it is quite certain that they have reference to certain events in the lives of the gods who are mentioned, and that these were well known to the writers and readers of religious texts.

From the above descriptions of the means whereby the deceased made his way through the gates and the halls of the underworld and escaped from the fowler and his net, it will be readily understood that the knowledge of the name alone was, in some cases, sufficient to help him out of his difficulties; but in others it was necessary to have the name which was possessed of magical power inscribed upon some object, amulet or otherwise. Moreover, some gods and devils were thought to have the power to assume different forms, and as each form carried with it its own name, to have absolute power over a god of many forms it was necessary to know all his names. Thus in the "Book of Overthrowing Âpep" we are told not only to make a wax figure of the monster, but also to write his name upon it, so that when the figure is destroyed by being burnt in the fire his name also may be destroyed; this is a striking example of the belief that the name was an integral part of the economy of a living creature. But Âpep possessed many forms and therefore many names, and unless he could be invoked by these names he still had the power to do evil; the above-mentioned book therefore supplies us with a list of his names, among which occur the following: "Tutu (*i.e.*, Doubly evil one), Hau-hra (*i.e.*, Backward Face), Hem-hemti (*i.e.*, Roarer), Qetu (*i.e.*, Evil-doer), Âmam (*i.e.*, Devourer), Saatet-ta (*i.e.*, Darkener of earth), Iubani, Khermuti, Unti, Karauememti, Khesef-hra, Sekhem-hra, Khak-ab, Nâi, Uai, Beteshu, Kharebutu the fourfold fiend", etc. All these names represent, as may be seen from the few of which translations are given, various aspects of Âpep, the devil of thunder, lightning, cloud, rain, mist, storm, and the like, and the anxiety to personify these so that the personifications might be attacked by means of magical ceremonies and words of power seems positively childish.

Passing now to certain chapters of the Book of the Dead which are rich in names of magical power, we notice that the god Amen, whose name meant the "hidden one", possessed numerous names, upon the knowledge of which the deceased relied for protection. Thus he says, "O Amen, Amen; O Re-Iukasa; O God, Prince of the gods of the east, thy name is Na-ari-k, or (as others say) Ka-ari-ka, Kasaika is thy name. Arethi-kasathika is thy name. Amen-na-an-ka-entek-share, or (as others say) Thek-share-Amen-kerethi, is thy name. O

Amen, let me make supplication unto thee, for I, even I, know thy name. Amen is thy name. Ireqai is thy name. Marqathai is thy name. Rerei is thy name. Nasaqbubu is thy name. Thanasa-Thanasa is thy name. Shareshatha-katha is thy name. O Amen, O Amen, O God, O God, O Amen, I adore thy name." In another place the deceased addresses Sekhet-Bast-Râ, saying, "Thou art the fire-goddess Ami-seshet, whose opportunity escapeth her not; thy name is Kaharesapusaremkakaremet, Thou art like unto the mighty flame of Saqenaqat which is in the bow of the boat of thy father Harepukakashareshabaiu, for behold, thus is [the name uttered] in the speech of the Negroes, and of the Anti, and of the people of Nubia. Sefiperemhesihrahaputchetef is thy name; Atareamtcherqemturennuparsheta is the name of one of thy divine sons, and Panemma that of the other." And in yet another chapter the deceased addressing the god Par says, "Thou art the mighty one of names among the gods, the mighty runner whose strides are might thou art the god the mighty one who comest and rescuest the needy one and the afflicted from him that oppresseth him; give heed to my cry. I am the Cow, and thy divine name is in my mouth, and I will utter it; Haqabakaher is thy name; Âurauaaqersaanqrebathi is thy name; Kherserau is thy name; Kharsatha is thy name. I praise thy name . . . O be gracious unto the deceased, and cause thou heat to exist under his head, for, indeed, he is the soul of the great divine Body which resteth in Annu (Heliopolis), whose names are Khukheperuru and Barekathatchara."

The examples of the use of names possessing magical powers described above illustrate the semi-religious views on the subject of names which the Egyptians held, and we have now to consider briefly the manner in which the knowledge of a name was employed in uses less important than those which had for their object the attainment of life and happiness in the world to come. In the famous magical papyrus which Chabas published we find a series of interesting charms and magical formulæ which were written to preserve its possessor from the attacks of sea and river monsters of every kind, of which the following is an example. "Hail, lord of the gods! Drive away from me the lions of the country of Meru (Meroë?), and the crocodiles which come forth from the river, and the bite of all poisonous reptiles which crawl forth from their holes. Get thee back, O crocodile Mâk, thou son of Set! Move not by means of thy tail! Work not thy legs and feet! Open not thy mouth! Let the water which is before thee turn into a consuming fire, O thou whom the thirty-seven gods did make, and whom the serpent of Râ did put in chains, O thou who wast fettered with links of iron before the boat of Râ! Get thee back, O crocodile Mâk, thou son of Set!" These words were to be said over a figure of the god Amen painted on clay; the rod was to have four rams' heads upon one neck, under his feet was to be a figure of the crocodile Mâk, and to the right and left of him were to be the dog-headed apes, i.e., the transformed spirits of the dawn, who sang hymns of praise to Râ when he rose daily. Again, let us suppose that some water monster wished to attack a man in a boat. To avoid this the man stood before the cabin of the boat and, taking a hard egg in his hand, he said, "O egg of the water which hath been spread over the earth, essence of the divine apes, the great one in the heaven above and in the earth beneath, who dost dwell in the nests which are in the waters, I have come forth with thee from the water, I have been with thee in thy nest, I am

Amsu of Coptos, I am Amsu, lord of Kebu." When he had said these words he would appear to the animal in the water in the form of the god Amsu, with whom he had identified himself, and it would be afraid and flee. At the end of the papyrus in which the above extracts occur we find a series of magical names which may be read thus: – Atir-Atisa, Atirkaha-Atisa, Samumatnatmu-Atisa, Samuanemui-Atisa, Samutekaari-Atisa, Samutekabaiu-Atisa, Samutchakaretcha-Atisa, Tâuuarehasa, Qina, Hama, Senentuta-Batetsataiu, Anrehakatha-sataiu, Haubailra-Haari. From these and similar magical names it is quite certain that the Gnostics and other sects which held views akin to theirs obtained the names which they were so fond of inscribing upon their amulets and upon the so-called magical papyri. The last class of documents undoubtedly contains a very large proportion of the magical ideas, beliefs, formulæ, etc., which were current in Egypt from the time of the Ptolemies to the end of the Roman Period, but from about 150 BC to A.D. 200 the papyri exhibit traces of the influence of Greek, Hebrew, and Syrian philosophers and magicians, and from a passage like the following we may get a proof of this: "I call thee, the headless one, that didst create earth and heaven, that didst create night and day, thee the creator of light and darkness. Thou art Osoronnophris, whom no man hath seen at any time; thou art Iabas, thou art Iapôs, thou hast distinguished the just and the unjust, thou didst make female and male, thou didst produce seeds and fruits, thou didst make men to love one another and to hate one another. I am Moses thy prophet, to whom thou didst commit thy mysteries, the ceremonies of Israel; thou didst produce the moist and the dry and all manner of food. Listen to me: I am an angel of Phapro Osoronnophris; this is thy true name, handed

down to the prophets of Israel. Listen to me . . ." In this
passage the name Osoronnophris is clearly a corruption of
the old Egyptian names of the great god of the dead
"Ausar Unnefer", and Phapro seems to represent the
Egyptian *Per-âa* (literally, "great house") or "Pharaoh,"
with the article *pa* "the" prefixed. It is interesting to note
that Moses is mentioned, a fact which seems to indicate
Jewish influence.

In another magical formula we read, "I call upon thee
that didst create the earth and bones, and all flesh and all
spirit, that didst establish the sea and that shakest the
heavens, that didst divide the light from the darkness,
the great regulative mind, that disposest everything, eye
of the world, spirit of spirits, god of gods, the lord of spirits,
the immoveable Aeon, Iaoouêi, hear my voice. I call upon
thee, the ruler of the gods, high-thundering Zeus, Zeus,
king, Adonai, lord, Iaoouêe. I am he that invokes thee in
the Syrian tongue, the great god, Zaalaêr, Iphphou, do
thou not disregard the Hebrew appellation Ablanathanalb,
Abrasilôa. For I am Silthakhôoukh, Lailam, Blasalôth, Iaô,
Ieô, Nebouth, Sabiothar, Bôth, Arbathiaô, Iaoth, Sabaôth,
Patoure, Zagourê, Baroukh Adonai, Elôai, Iabraam, Bar-
barauô, Nau, Siph", etc. The spell ends with the statement
that it "loosens chains, blinds, brings dreams, creates
favour; it may be used in common for whatever purpose
you will." In the above we notice at once the use of the
seven vowels which form "a name wherein be contained all
Names, and all Lights, and all Powers". The seven vowels
have, of course, reference to the three vowels "Iaô" which
were intended to represent one of the Hebrew names for
Almighty God, "Jâh." The names "Adonai, Elôai," are
also derived through the Hebrew from the Bible, and
Sabaôth is another well-known Hebrew word meaning

"hosts"; some of the remaining names could be explained, if space permitted, by Hebrew and Syriac words. On papyri and amulets the vowels are written in magical combinations in such a manner as to form triangles and other shapes; with them are often found the names of the seven archangels of God . . .

In combination with a number of signs which owe their origin to the Gnostics the seven vowels were sometimes engraved upon plaques, or written upon papyri, with the view of giving the possessor power over gods or demons or his fellow creatures.

But of all the names found upon Gnostic gems two, *i.e.*, Khnoubis (or Khnoumis), and Abrasax (or Abraxas), are of the most frequent occurrence. The first is usually represented as a huge serpent having the head of a lion surrounded by seven or twelve rays. Over the seven rays, one on the point of each, are the seven vowels of the Greek alphabet, which some suppose to refer to the seven heavens; and on the back of the amulet, on which the figure of Khnoumis occurs, is usually found the sign of the triple S and bar. Khnoumis is, of course, a form of the ancient Egyptian god Khnemu, or "Fashioner" of man and beast, the god to whom many of the attributes of the Creator of the universe were ascribed. Khnemu is, however, often depicted with the head of a ram, and in the later times, as the "beautiful ram of Râ", he has four heads; in the Egyptian monuments he has at times the head of a hawk, but never that of a lion. The god Abrasax is represented in a form which has a human body, the beak of a hawk or cock, and legs terminating in serpents; in one hand he holds a knife or dagger, and in the other a shield upon which is inscribed the great name *IAW*, or JÂH. Considerable difference of opinion exists as to the meaning and derivation of the name

Abrasax, but there is no doubt that the god who bore it was a form of the Sun-god, and that he was intended to represent some aspect of the Creator of the world. The name was believed to possess magical powers of the highest class, and Basileides, who gave it currency in the second century, seems to have regarded it as an invincible name. It is probable, however, that its exact meaning was lost at an early date, and that it soon degenerated into a mere magical symbol, for it is often found inscribed on amulets side by side with scenes and figures with which, seemingly, it cannot have any connexion whatever. Judging from certain Gnostic gems in the British Museum, Abrasax is to be identified with the polytheistic figure that stands in the upper part of the Metternich stele. This figure has two bodies, one being that of a man, and the other that of a bird; from these extend four wings, and from each of his knees projects a serpent. He has two pairs of hands and arms; one pair is extended along the wings, each hand holding the symbols of "life", "stability", and "power", and two knives and two serpents; the other pair is pendent, the right hand grasping the sign of life, and the other a sceptre. His face is grotesque, and probably represents that of Bes, or the sun as an old man; on his head is a pylon-shaped object with figures of various animals, and above it a pair of horns which support eight knives and the figure of a god with raised hands and arms, which typifies "millions of years". The god stands upon an oval wherein are depicted figures of various "typhonic" animals, and from each side of his crown proceed several symbols of fire. Whether in the Gnostic system Abraxas absorbed all the names and attributes of this god of many forms cannot be said with certainty.

When we think of the sublime character of the life which the souls of the blessed dead were believed to lead in heaven with the gods, it is hard to understand why the Egyptians took such pains to preserve the physical body from decay. No Egyptian who believed his Scriptures ever expected that his corruptible body would ascend into heaven and live with the gods, for they declare in no uncertain manner that it remains upon the earth whilst the soul dwells in heaven. But that the preservation of the body was in some way or for some reason absolutely necessary is certain, for the art of mummification flourished for several thousands of years, and unless there was some good reason, besides the observance of conservative custom and traditional use, why it should do so, king and priest, gentle and simple, and rich and poor, would never have burdened their relatives and heirs with the expense of costly funeral ceremonies, and with the performance of rites which were of no avail. At first sight, too, it seems strange to find the Egyptians studying carefully how best to provide the dead with a regular supply of sepulchral offerings, for when we come to think about it we notice that in arranging for the well-being of the dead nothing whatever was left to chance. For example, a papyrus will contain several prayers and pictures with appropriate formulæ, the object of each of which is to give the deceased meat and drink; any one of these would have been enough for the purpose, but it was thought best in such an important matter to make assurance doubly sure, and if there was the least doubt about the efficacy of one chapter, one or more of the same class were added. Similarly, the tendency of the natural body after death being to decay, the greatest care was taken in mummifying its various members, lest perchance any one of them should be neglected accidentally, and should, either by the omission of the words of power that ought to have been said over it, or through the lax performance of some ceremony, decay and perish. The Egyptian declared that he was immortal, and believed that he would enjoy eternal life in a spiritual body; yet he attempted by the performance of magical ceremonies and the recital of words of power to make his corruptible body to endure for ever. He believed that he would feed upon the celestial and imperishable food whereon the gods lived, but at the same time he spared no effort or expense to provide for his tomb being supplied at stated intervals throughout the year with perishable food in the shape of offerings of oxen, feathered fowl, cakes, bread, and the like. He mummified his dead and swathed them in linen bandages, and then by the performance of magical ceremonies and by the recital of words of power sought to give back to their members the strength to eat, and drink, and talk, and think, and move at will. Indeed, all the evidence now forthcoming seems to prove that he never succeeded in bringing himself to think that the gods could do without his help, or that the pictures or representations of the scenes which took place in the life, and death, and burial, and resurrection of Osiris, upon which he relied so implicitly, could possibly fail to be as efficacious as the actual power of the god himself.

The examination of mummies has shown us with tolerable clearness what methods were adopted in preparing bodies for bandaging and final ornamentation, and the means adopted for disposing of the more corruptible portions of the body are well known from classical and other writers. But for an account of the manner in which the body was bandaged, and a list of the unguents and other materials employed in the process, and the words of power which were spoken as each bandage was laid in its place, we must have recourse to a very interesting papyrus which has been edited and translated by M. Maspero under the title of *Le Rituel de l'Embaumement*. The first part of the papyrus, which probably gave instructions for the evisceration of the body, is wanting, and only the section which refers to the bandaging is at all perfect. The text opens with an address to the deceased in which it is said, "The perfume of Arabia hath been brought to thee to make perfect thy smell through the scent of the god. Here are brought to thee liquids which have come forth from Râ, to make perfect . . . thy smell in the Hall [of Judgment]. O sweet-smelling soul of the great god, thou dost contain such a sweet odour that thy face shall neither change nor perish . . . Thy members shall become young in Arabia, and thy soul shall appear over thy body in Ta-neter (*i.e.*, the 'divine land')." After this the priest or mummifier was to take a vase of liquid which contained ten perfumes, and to smear therewith the body from head to foot twice, taking especial care to anoint the head thoroughly. He was then to say, Osiris (*i.e.*, the deceased), thou hast received the perfume which shall make thy members perfect. Thou receivest the source [of life] and thou takest the form of the great Disk (*i.e.*, Aten), which uniteth itself unto thee to give enduring form to thy members; thou shalt unite with Osiris in the great Hall. The unguent cometh unto thee to fashion thy members and to gladden thy heart, and thou shalt appear in the form of Râ; it shall make thee to be sound when thou settest in the sky at eventide, and it shall spread abroad the smell of thee in the nomes of Aqert . . . Thou receivest the oil of the cedar in Amentet, and the cedar which came forth from Osiris cometh unto thee; it delivereth thee from thy enemies, and it protecteth thee in the nomes. Thy soul alighteth upon the venerable sycamores. Thou criest to Isis, and Osiris heareth thy voice, and Anubis cometh unto thee to invoke thee. Thou receivest the oil of the country of Manu which hath come from the East, and Râ riseth upon thee at the gates of the horizon, at the holy doors of Neith. Thou goest therein, thy soul is in the upper heaven, and thy body is in the lower heaven . . . O Osiris, may the Eye of Horus cause that which floweth forth from it to come to thee, and to thy heart for ever!" These words having been said, the whole ceremony was repeated, and then the internal organs which had been removed from the body were placed in the "liquid of the children of Horus", so that the liquid of this god might enter into them, and whilst they were being thus treated a chapter was read over them and they were put in the funeral chest. When this was done the internal organs were placed on the body, and the body having been made to lie straight the backbone was immersed in holy oil, and the face of the deceased was turned towards the sky; the bandage of Sebek and Sedi was then laid upon the backbone. In a long speech the deceased is addressed and told that the liquid is "secret", and that it is an emanation of the gods Shu and Seb, and that the resin of Phoenicia and the bitumen of Byblos will make his burial perfect in the underworld, and give him his legs, and facilitate his movements, and sanctify his steps in the Hall of Seb. Next gold, silver, lapis-lazuli, and turquoise are brought to the deceased, and crystal to lighten his face, and carnelian to strengthen his steps; these form amulets which will secure for him a free passage in the underworld. Meanwhile the backbone is kept in oil, and the face of the deceased is turned towards the heavens; and next the gilding of the nails of the fingers and toes begins. When this has been done, and portions of the fingers have been wrapped in linen made at Saïs, the following address is made to the deceased: "O Osiris, thou receivest thy nails of gold, thy fingers of gold, and thy thumb of *smu* (or *uasm*) metal; the liquid of Râ entereth into thee as well as into the divine members of Osiris, and thou journeyest on thy legs to the immortal abode. Thou hast carried thy hands to the house of eternity, thou art made perfect in gold, thou dost shine brightly in *smu* metal, and thy fingers shine in the dwelling of Osiris, in the sanctuary of Horus himself. O Osiris, the gold of the mountains cometh to thee; it is a holy talisman of the gods in their abodes, and it lighteneth thy face in the lower heaven. Thou breathest in gold, thou appearest in *smu* metal, and the dwellers in Re-stau receive thee; those who are in the funeral chest rejoice because thou hast transformed thyself into a hawk of gold by means of thy amulets (or talismans) of the City of Gold," etc. When these words have been said, a priest who is made to personify Anubis comes to the deceased and performs certain symbolical ceremonies by his head, and lays certain bandages upon it. When the head and mouth and face have been well oiled the bandage of Nekheb is laid on the forehead, the bandage of Hathor on the face, the bandage of Thoth upon the two ears, and the bandage of Nebt-hetep on the nape of the neck. Over the head was laid the bandage of Sekhet, in two pieces, and over each ear, and each nostril, and each cheek was fastened a bandage or strip of linen; over the forehead went four pieces of linen, on the top of the head two, outside the mouth two, and inside two, over the chin two, and over the nape of the neck four large pieces; there were to be twenty-two pieces to the right and to the left of the face passing over the two ears. The Lady of the West is then addressed in these words: "Grant thou that breathing may take place in the head of the deceased in the underworld, and that he may see with his eyes, and that he may hear with his two ears; and that he may breathe through his nose; and that he may be able to utter sounds with his mouth; and that he may be able to speak with his tongue in the underworld. Receive thou his voice in the Hall of Maâti and his speech in the Hall of Seb in the presence of the Great God, the lord of Amentet." The addresses which follow these words have, reference to the delights and pleasures of the future life which shall be secured for him through the oil and unguents, which are duly specified and described, and through the magical figures which are drawn upon the bandages. The protecting properties of the turquoise and other precious stones are alluded to, and after a further anointing with oil and the placing of grains of myrrh and resin, the deceased is declared to have "received his head", and he is promised that it shall nevermore depart from him. On the conclusion of the ceremonies which concern the head the deceased has the power to go in among the holy and perfect spirits, his name is exalted among men, the denizens of heaven receive his soul, the beings of the underworld bow down before his body, the dwellers upon earth adore him, and the inhabitants of the funeral mountain renew for him his youth. Besides these things, Anubis and Horus make perfect his bandages, and the god Thoth protects his members by his words of magical power; and he himself has learned the magical formulæ which are necessary to make his path straight in the underworld, and also the proper way in which to utter them. All these benefits were secured for him by the use of bandages and unguents which possess both magical names and properties, and by the words of power uttered by the priests who recited the Ritual of Embalmment, and by the ceremonies which the priest who personated Anubis performed beside the body of the deceased in imitation of those which the god Anubis performed for the dead god Osiris in remote days.

Next the left hand of the deceased was mummified and bandaged according to the instructions given in the Ritual of Embalmment. The hand was stretched out on a piece of linen, and a ring was passed over the fingers; it was then filled with thirty-six of the substances which were used in embalming, according to the number of the forms of the god Osiris. This done, the hand was bandaged with a strip of linen in six folds, upon which were drawn figures of Isis and Hâpi. The right hand was treated in a similar way, only the figures drawn upon the bandages were those of Râ and Amsu; and when the appropriate words had been recited over both hands divine protection was assured them. After these things the ceremonies concerning the right and left arms were performed, and these were followed by rubbing the soles of the feet and the legs and the thighs, first with black-stone oil, and secondly with holy oil. The toes were wrapped in linen, and a piece of linen was laid on each leg; on each piece was drawn the figure of a jackal, that on the right leg representing Anubis, and that on the left Horus. When flowers of the ânkham plant and other substances had been laid beside and on the legs, and they had been treated with ebony-gum water and holy oil, and appropriate addresses had been said, the ceremony of bandaging the body was ended. Everything that could be done to preserve the body was now done, and every member of it was, by means of the words of power which changed perishable substances into imperishable, protected to all eternity; when the final covering of purple or white linen had been fastened upon it, the body was ready for the tomb.

But the Ritual of Embalmment which has been briefly described above seems to belong to a late period of Egyptian history, and although the ideas and beliefs contained in it are as old as Egyptian civilization itself, it seems as if it was intended to take the place of a much older and more elaborate work which was in use as far back as the period in which the Great Pyramid was built, and which was intended to be recited during the performance of a complex series of ceremonies, some of which are still not completely understood. It seems as if the performance of all the ceremonies would require several days, and it is clear that only the wealthy could afford the expense which must have attended such elaborate obsequies; for the poorer classes of men the various ceremonies must have been greatly curtailed, and at a very early period we find that a shortened form of ritual had taken their place. Of all the ceremonies, the most important was that of the "Opening of the Mouth and Eyes", which was performed either on the mummy itself or upon a statue which represented it. It has already been stated that the Egyptians believed that they could transmit to a statue the attributes of the person in whose image it was made, and similarly that that which was done to the statue of the mummified person was also done to it. The use of a statue instead of the actual mummy has obvious advantages, for the ceremony could be performed at any time and in any place, and the presence of the mummy was unnecessary. As a matter of fact the ceremony was performed in a chamber at the entrance to the tomb, or outside the tomb at a place which had been made ceremonially pure or consecrated, and those who took part in it were: (1) The *Kher-heb*, or chief officiating priest, who held a roll of papyrus in his hand (2) The *Sem* priest (3) The *Smer*, who was, perhaps, some intimate friend of the deceased (4) *The Sa-mer-ef*, or man who was either the son of the deceased or his representative (5) The *Tcherau-ur*, or woman who represented Isis (6) The *Tcherau-sheraut*, or woman who represented Nephthys (7) The *Menhu*, or slaughterer (8) The *Am-asi* priest (9) The *Am-khent* priest and (10) A number of people who represented the armed guard of Horus. All these became actors in scenes which were intended to represent the events which took place in connexion with the burial of Osiris, with whom the deceased is now identified; the two women took the parts of the goddesses Isis and Nephthys, and the men those of the gods who helped them in the performance of their pious duties. From the scenes which accompany the texts relating to the ceremony of opening the mouth and eyes we see that it began with the sprinkling of water round about the statue or mummy from four vessels, one for each quarter of the earth, and with the recital of addresses to the gods Horus, Set, Thoth, and Sept; this act restored to the deceased the use of his head. The sprinkling of water was followed by a purification by means of incense, also contained in four vases, one for each of the four quarters of the earth. The burning of this sweet-smelling substance assisted in opening the mouth of the deceased and in strengthening his heart. At this stage the *Sem* priest dressed himself in the skin of a cow, and lying down upon a kind of couch pretended to be asleep; but he was roused up by the *Am-asi* priest in the presence of the *Kher-heb* and the *Am-khent* priest, and when the *Sem* priest had seated himself upon a seat, the four men together represented the four children of Horus, or the gods with the heads of a hawk, an ape, a jackal, and a man respectively. The *Sem* priest then said, "I have seen my father in all his forms," which the other men in turn repeat. The meaning of this portion of the ceremony is hard to explain, but M. Maspero thinks that it was intended to bring back to the body of the deceased its shadow (*khaibit*), which had departed from it when it died. The preliminary purifications being ended, and the shadow having been joined to the body once more, the statue or mummy is approached by the men who represent the armed guard of Horus; and one of their number, having taken upon himself the character of Horus, the son of Osiris and Isis, touches its mouth with his finger. The *Kher-heb* next made ready to perform the sacrifice which was intended to commemorate the slaughter, at some very early period, of the fiends who were the friends of Set. It seems that the soul of Horus dwelt in an eye, and that Set nearly succeeded in devouring it; but Horus vanquished Set and saved his eye. Set's associates then changed themselves into the forms of animals, and birds, and fish, but they were caught, and their heads were cut off; Set, however, who was concealed in the form of a pig, contrived to escape. The sacrifice consisted of a bull (or cow) or two, two gazelles or antelopes, and ducks. When the bull had been slain, one of the forelegs was cut off, and the heart taken out, and offered to the statue or mummy; the *Sem* priest then took the bleeding leg and touched, or pretended to touch, the mouth and eyes with it four times. The slaughtered gazelles or antelopes and ducks were simply offered before the statue. The *Sem* priest next said to the statue, "I have come to embrace thee, I am thy son Horus, I have pressed thy mouth; I am thy son, I love thee. . . . Thy mouth was closed, but I have set in order for thee thy mouth and thy teeth." He then brought two instruments, "Seb-ur" and "Tuntet" respectively, and touched the mouth of the statue or mummy with them, whilst the Kher-heb said, "Thy mouth was closed, but I have set in order for thee thy mouth and thy teeth. I open for thee thy mouth, I open for thee thy two eyes. I have opened for thee thy mouth with the instrument of Anubis. I have opened thy mouth with the instrument of Anubis, with the iron implement with which the mouths of the gods were opened. Horus, open the mouth! Horus, open the mouth! Horus hath opened the mouth of the dead, as he in times of old opened the mouth of Osiris, with the iron which came forth from Set, with the iron instrument with which he opened the mouths of the gods. He hath opened thy mouth with it. The deceased shall walk and shall speak, and his body shall be with the great company of the gods in the Great House of the Aged One in Annu, and he shall receive there the *ureret* crown from Horus, the lord of mankind." Thus the mouth and the eyes of the deceased are opened. The *Sem* priest then took in his hand the instrument called *ur hekau*, *i.e.*, the "mighty one of enchantments", a curious, sinuous piece of wood, one end of which is in the form of a ram's head surmounted by a uraeus, and touched the mouth and the, eyes of the statue or mummy four times, whilst the *Kher-heb* recited a long address in which he declared that this portion of the ceremony had secured for the deceased all the benefits which accrued to the god Osiris from the actions of Nut, Horus, and Set, when he was in a similar state. It has been said above that every dead man hoped to be provided with the hekau, or words of power, which were necessary for him in the next world, but without a mouth it was impossible for him to utter them. Now that the mouth, or rather the use of it, was restored to the deceased, it was all important to give him not only the words of power, but also the ability to utter them correctly and in such wise that the gods and other beings would hearken to them and obey them; four touches of the *ur hekau* instrument on the lips endowed the deceased with the faculty of uttering the proper words in the proper manner in each of the four quarters of the world. When this had been done, several

other ceremonies were performed with the object of allowing the "son who loveth him" or his representative to take
part in the opening of the mouth of his father. In order to
do this he took in his hand a metal chisel and touched the
openings of the mouth and of the eyes, and then the *Sem*
priest touched them first with his little finger, and afterwards with a little bag filled with pieces of red stone or
carnelian, with the idea, M. Maspero thinks, of restoring to
the lips and eyelids the colour which they had lost during
the process of mummification. The "son who loves him"
then took four objects called "iron of the South, and iron of
the North", and laid each of them four times upon the
mouth and the eyes while the Kher-heb recited the proper
address in which the mummy or statue is said to have had
his mouth and lips established firmly. This done, the *Sem*
priest brings an instrument called the "Pesh-en-kef", and
touches the mouth of the mummy or statue therewith, and
says, "O Osiris, I have stablished for thee the two jaw-
bones in thy face, and they are now separated"; that is to
say, the bandages with which they have been tied up can no
longer prevent their movement when the deceased wishes
to eat. After the Pesh-en-kef had been used the *Sem* priest
brought forward a basket or vessel of some kind of food in
the shape of balls, and by the order of the *Kher-heb* offered
them to the mouth of the mummy, and when this portion of
the ceremony was ended, the *Sem* priest took an ostrich
feather, and waved it before its face four times, but with
what object is not clear. Such are the ceremonies which it
was thought necessary to perform in order to restore to the
deceased the functions which his body possessed upon
earth. But it must be remembered that hitherto only the
"bull of the south" has been sacrificed, and that the "bull of
the north" has yet to be offered up; and all the ceremonies

which have been already performed must be repeated if the deceased would have the power to go forth at will over the whole earth. From the earliest times the South and the North were the two great sections into which the world was divided, and each section possessed its own special gods, all of whom had to be propitiated by the deceased; hence most religious ceremonies were ordered to be performed in duplicate. In later days each section was divided into two parts, and the four divisions thus made were apportioned to the four children of Horus; hence prayers and formulæ were usually said four times, once in honour of each god, and the rubrical directions on this point are definite.

The Egyptians, in common with many other Eastern nations, believed that certain sicknesses and diseases might be cured by certain medicaments pure and simple, but that others needed not only drugs but the recital of words of power to effect their cure. There is good reason for thinking that some diseases were attributed to the action of evil spirits or demons, which had the power of entering into human bodies and of vexing them in proportion to their malignant nature and influence, but the texts do not afford much information on the matter. Incidentally, however, we have one interesting proof that foreign peoples believed that the Egyptians were able to cure the diseases caused by demoniacal possession, and the exercise of their power on the occasion described was considered to be so noteworthy that the narrative of it was inscribed upon a stele and set up in the temple of the god Khonsu at Thebes, so that all men might read and know what a marvellous cure his priests had effected. It appears that King Ramses II was in Mesopotamia "according to his wont, year by year", and all the chiefs of the countries round about came to pay their respects to him, and they sought to obtain his goodwill and protection, probably even an alliance, by bringing to him gifts of gold, and lapis-lazuli, and turquoise, and of every kind of valuable thing which the land produced, and every man sought to outdo his neighbour by the lavishness of his gifts. Among others there came the Prince of Bekhten, and at the head of all the offerings which he presented to His Majesty he placed his eldest daughter, who was very beautiful. When the king saw her he thought her the most beautiful girl he had ever seen, and he bestowed upon her the title of "Royal spouse, chief lady, Râ-neferu" (i.e., "the beauties of Râ", the Sun-god), and took her to Egypt; and when they arrived in that country the king married her. One day during the fifteenth year of the king's reign, when His Majesty was in Thebes celebrating the festival of Amen-Râ, a messenger came to the king and reported the arrival of an ambassador from the Prince of Bekhten who had brought rich gifts for the royal lady Râ-neferu. When he had been led into the king's presence, he did homage before him, saying, "Glory and praise be unto thee, O thou Sun of the nations; grant that we may live before thee!" Having said these words be bowed down and touched the ground with his head three times, and said, "I have come unto thee, O my sovereign Lord, on behalf of the lady Bent-ent-resht, the younger sister of the royal spouse Râ-neferu, for, behold, an evil disease hath laid hold upon her body; I beseech thy Majesty to send a physician to see her." Then the king straightway ordered the books of the "double house of life" to be brought and the learned men to appear, and when they had come into his presence he ordered them to choose from among their number a man "wise of heart and cunning of finger", that he might send him to Bekhten; they did so, and their choice fell upon one Tehuti-em-heb. This sage having come before the king was ordered to set out for Bekhten in company with the ambassador, and he departed; and when they had arrived there the Egyptian priest found the lady Bent-ent-resht to be possessed of a demon or spirit over which he was powerless. The Prince of Bekhten, seeing that the priest was unable to afford relief to his daughter, sent once again to the king, and entreated him to send a god to his help.

When the ambassador from Bekhten arrived in Egypt the king was in Thebes, and on hearing what was asked he went into the temple of Khonsu Nefer-hetep, and besought that god to allow his counterpart Khonsu to depart to Bekhten and to deliver the daughter of the prince of that country from the power of the demon that possessed her. It seems as if the sage Tehuti-em-heb had been sent to Bekhten by the advice of the god, for the king says, in addressing the god, "I have come once again into thy presence"; but in any case Khonsu Nefer-hetep agreed to his request, and a fourfold measure of magical power was imparted to the statue of the god which was to go to Bekhten. The god, seated in his boat, and five other boats with figures of gods in them, accompanied by chariots and horses on the right hand and on the left, set out from Egypt, and after travelling for seventeen months arrived in Bekhten, where they were received with great honour. The god Khonsu went to the place where Bent-ent-resht was, and, having performed a magical ceremony over her, the demon departed from her and she was cured straightway. Then the demon addressed the Egyptian god, saying, "Grateful and welcome is thy coming unto us, O great god, thou vanquisher of the hosts of darkness! Bekhten is thy city, the inhabitants thereof are thy slaves, and I am thy servant; and I will depart unto the place whence I came that I may gratify thee, for unto this end hast thou come thither. And I beseech thy Majesty to command that the Prince of Bekhten and I may hold a festival together." To the demon's request Khonsu agreed, and he commanded his priest to tell the Prince of Bekhten to make a great festival in honour of the demon; this having been done by the command of Khonsu the demon departed to his own place.

When the Prince of Bekhten saw that Khonsu was thus powerful, he and all his people rejoiced exceedingly, and he determined that the god should not be allowed to return to Egypt, and as a result Khonsu remained in Bekhten for three years, four months, and five days. On a certain day, however, the Prince was sleeping., and he dreamed a dream in which he saw the god Khonsu come forth from his shrine in the form of a hawk of gold, and having mounted into the air he flew away to Egypt. The Prince woke up in a state of great perturbation, and having inquired of the Egyptian priest was told by him that the god had departed to Egypt, and that his chariot must now be sent back. Then the Prince gave to Khonsu great gifts, and they were taken to Egypt and laid before the god Khonsu Nefer-hetep in his temple at Thebes. In early Christian literatures we find a number of examples of demoniacal possession in which the demon who has entered the body yields it up before a demon of greater power than himself, but the demon who is expelled is invariably hostile to him that expels him, and he departs from before him with every sign of wrath and shame. The fact that it was believed possible for the demon of Bekhten and the god

Khonsu to fraternize, and to be present together at a festival made by the Prince of the country, shews that the people of Bekhten ascribed the same attributes to spirits or demons as they did to men. The demon who possessed the princess recognized in Khonsu a being who was mightier than himself, and, like a vanquished king, he wished to make the best terms he could with his conqueror, and to be on good terms with him.

The Egyptians believed that the divine powers frequently made known their will to them by means of dreams, and they attached considerable importance to them; the figures of the gods and the scenes which they saw when dreaming seemed to them to prove the existence of another world which was not greatly unlike that already known to them. The knowledge of the art of procuring dreams and the skill to interpret them were greatly prized in Egypt as elsewhere in the East, and the priest or official who possessed such gifts sometimes rose to places of high honour in the state, as we may see from the example of Joseph, for it was universally believed that glimpses of the future were revealed to man in dreams. As instances of dreams recorded in the Egyptian texts may be quoted those of Thothmes IV, king of Egypt about 1450 BC, and Nut-Amen, king of the Eastern Sûdân and Egypt, about 670 BC. A prince, according to the stele which he set up before the breast of the Sphinx at Gizeh, was one day hunting near this emblem of Râ-Harmachis, and he sat down to rest under its shadow and fell asleep and dreamed a dream. In it the god appeared to him, and, having declared that he was the god Harmachis-Khepera-Râ-Temu, promised him that if he would clear away from the Sphinx, his own image, the drift sand in which it was becoming buried, he would give to him the sovereignty of the lands of the South and of the North, *i.e.*, of all Egypt. In due course the prince became king of Egypt under the title of Thothmes IV, and the stele which is dated on the 19th day of the month Hathor of the first year of Thothmes IV. proves that the royal dreamer carried out the wishes of the god. Of Nut-Amen, the successor of the great Piânkhi who came down from Gebel Barkal and conquered all Egypt from Syene to the sea, we read that in the first year of his reign he one night dreamed a dream wherein he saw two serpents, one on his right hand and the other on his left; when he awoke they had disappeared. Having asked for an interpretation of the dream he was told: "The land of the South is thine, and thou shalt have dominion over the land of the North: the White Crown and the Red Crown shall adorn thy head. The length and the breadth of the land shall be given unto thee, and the god Amen, the only god, shall be with thee." The two serpents were the symbols of the goddesses Nekhebet and Uatchet, the mistresses of the South and North respectively. As the result of his dream Nut-Amen invaded Egypt successfully and brought back much spoil, a portion of which he dedicated to the service of his god Amen.

Since dreams and visions in which the future might be revealed to the sleeper were greatly desired, the Egyptian magician set himself to procure such for his clients by various devices, such as drawing magical pictures and reciting magical words. The following are examples of spells for procuring a vision and dreams, taken from British Museum Papyrus, No. 122, lines 64 ff. and 359 ff. "To obtain a vision from [the god] Bes. Make a drawing of Besa, as shewn below, on your left hand, and envelope your hand in a strip of black cloth that has been consecrated to Isis (?) and lie down to sleep without speaking a word, even in answer to a question. Wind the remainder of the cloth round your neck. The ink with which you write must be composed of the blood of a cow, the blood of a white dove, fresh (?) frankincense, myrrh, black writing-ink, cinnabar, mulberry juice, rain-water, and the juice of wormwood and vetch. With this write your petition before the setting sun, [saying], 'Send the truthful seer out of the holy shrine, I beseech thee, Lampsuer, Sumarta, Baribas, Dardalam, Iorlex: O Lord send the sacred deity Anuth, Anuth, Salbana, Chambré, Breïth, now, now, quickly, quickly. Come in this very night."

"To procure dreams: Take a clean linen bag and write upon it the names given below. Fold it up and make it into a lamp-wick, and set it alight, pouring pure oil over it. The word to be written is this: 'Armiuth, Lailamchoüch, Arseno-phrephren, Phtha, Archentechtha.' Then in the evening, when you are going to bed, which you must do without touching food [or, pure from all defilement], do thus. Approach the lamp and repeat seven times the formula given below: then extinguish it and lie down to sleep. The formula is this: 'Sachmu . . . epaëma Ligotereënch: the Aeon, the Thunderer, Thou that hast swallowed the snake and dost exhaust the moon, and dost raise up the orb of the sun in his season, Chthetho is thy name; I require, O lords of the gods, Seth, Chreps, give me the information that I desire."

The peculiar ideas which the Egyptians held about the composition of man greatly favoured the belief in appari-tions and ghosts. According to them a man consisted of a physical body, a shadow, a double, a soul, a heart, a spirit called the *khu*, a power, a name, and a spiritual body. When the body died the shadow departed from it, and could only be brought back to it by the performance of a mystical ceremony; the double lived in the tomb with the body, and was there visited by the soul whose habitation was in heaven. The soul was, from one aspect, a material thing, and like the *ka*, or double, was believed to partake of the funeral offerings which were brought to the tomb; one of the chief objects of sepulchral offerings of meat and drink was to keep the double in the tomb and to do away with the necessity of its wandering about outside the tomb in search of food. It is clear from many texts that, unless the double was supplied with sufficient food, it would wander forth from the tomb and eat any kind of offal and drink any kind of dirty water which it might find in its path. But besides the shadow, and the double, and the soul, the spirit of the deceased, which usually had its abode in heaven, was sometimes to be found in the tomb. There is, however, good reason for stating that the immortal part of man which lived in the tomb and had its special abode in the statue of the deceased was the "double". This is proved by the fact that a special part of the tomb was reserved for the *ka*, or double, which was called the "house of the *ka*", and that a priest, called the "priest of the *ka*", was specially appointed to minister therein. The double enjoyed the smell of the incense which was offered at certain times each year in the tomb, as well as the flowers, and herbs, and meat, and drink; and the statue of the deceased in which the double dwelt took pleasure in all the various scenes which were painted or sculptured on the walls of the various chambers of the tomb, and enjoyed again all the delights which his body had enjoyed upon earth. The *ka*, or double, then, in very early times was, to all intents and purposes, the ghost of the Egyptians. In later times the *khu*, or "spirit", seems to have been identified with it, and there are frequent allusions in the texts to the sanctity of the offerings made to the *khu*, and to their territories, i.e., the districts in which their mummified bodies lie.

Whether there was any general belief that the *ka* or *khu* could or did hold intercourse with his relatives or friends whom he left alive upon earth cannot be said, but an instance is known in which a husband complains to his wife, who has been dead for three years, of the troubles which she has brought upon him since her death. He describes his own merits and the good treatment which he had vouchsafed to her when she was alive, and declares that the evil with which she is requiting him is not to be endured. To make his complaint to reach her he first reduced it to writing upon papyrus, then went to her tomb and read it there, and finally tied the papyrus to a statue or figure of his wife which was therein; since her double or spirit lived in the tomb she would, of course, read the writing and understand it. It is a pity that we have no means of knowing what was the result of the husband's complaint. Elsewhere we have a fragment of a conversation which a priest of Amen called Khonsu-em-heb, who was searching for a suitable place in which to build his tomb, holds with the double or spirit of some person whom he has disturbed, and the spirit of the dead tells some details of his life to the living man. The cemeteries were regarded with awe by the ancient Egyptians because of the spirits of the dead who dwelt in them, and even the Arabic-speaking peoples of Egypt and the Sûdân, if we exclude the "antiquity grubber", have them in great respect for the same reason. The modern peoples of the Sûdân firmly believe that the spirits of those slain in battle dwell on the field where they fell, or where their bodies are buried, and the soldiers in the tenth battalion of Lord Kitchener's army declare that the grave of the gallant Major Sidney, who was shot while charging at the head of his regiment, in the battle of Abû Hamed, August 7th, 1897, "is watched regularly every night by the ghosts of the native soldiers who were killed at Abû Hamed, and who mount guard over their dead commander's tomb, challenging, with every military detail, all passers-by. So implicitly is this legend credited by the blacks that none of them will, after dusk, approach the grave. Any one doing so is believed to be promptly halted by a phantom sentry, and even the words (in Arabic), 'Guard, turn out!' are often (so the story goes) plainly heard repeated at some distance off across the desert."

The Egyptians believed that a man's fate or destiny was decided before he was born, and that he had no power whatever to alter it. Their sages, however, professed to be able to declare what the fate might be, provided that they were given certain data, that is to say, if they were told the date of his birth, and if they were able to ascertain the position of the planets and stars at that time. The goddess of fate or destiny was called "Shai", and she is usually accompanied by another goddess called "Renenet", who is commonly regarded as the lady of fortune; they both appear in the Judgment Scene, where they seem to watch the weighing of the heart on behalf of the deceased. But another goddess, Meskhenet, is sometimes present, and she also seems to have had influence over a man's future; in any case she was able to predict what that future was to be. Thus we read that she and Isis, and Nephthys, and Heqet, disguised as women, went to the house of Râ-user, whose wife Râ-Tettet was in travail; when they had been taken into her room they assisted her in giving birth to triplets, and as each child was born Meskhenet declared, "He shall be a king who shall have dominion over the whole land."

And this prophecy was fulfilled, for the three boys became three of the kings of the Fifth Dynasty. The Seven Hathor goddesses also could predict the future of a human being, for in the well-known "Tale of Two Brothers" it is related that, when the god Khnemu, at the request of Râ-Harmachis, had created for Bata a wife "who was more beautiful in her person than any other woman in all the earth, for the essence of every god was contained in her", they came to see her, and that they spake with one voice, saying, "Her death will be caused by the knife." And this came to pass, for, according to the story, when the king whose wife she became heard from her first husband that she had left him and had wrought evil against him, he entered into judgment with her in the presence of his chiefs and nobles, and "one carried out their decree", i.e., they sentenced her to death and she was executed. Similarly, in another story, the Seven Hathors came to see the son who had been born to a certain king in answer to his prayers to the gods, and when they had seen him they said, "He shall die by means of a crocodile, or a serpent, or a dog." The story goes on to say how he escaped from the crocodile and the serpent, and though the end is wanting, it is quite clear that he was wounded by an accidental bite of his dog and so died. The moral of all such stories is that there is no possibility of avoiding fate, and it is most probable that the modern Egyptian has only inherited his ancestors' views as to its immutability. A man's life might, however, be happy or unhappy according as the hour of the day or the day itself was lucky or unlucky, and every day of the Egyptian year was divided into three parts, each of which was lucky or unlucky. When Olympias was about to give birth to Alexander the Great, Nectanebus stood by her making observations of the heavenly bodies, and from time to time he besought her to restrain herself until the auspicious hour had arrived; and it was not until he saw a certain splendour in the sky and knew that all the heavenly bodies were in a favourable position that he permitted her to bring forth her child. And when he had said, "O queen, now thou wilt give birth to a governor of the world," the child fell upon the ground while the earth quaked, and the lightnings flashed, and the thunder roared. Thus it is quite evident that the future of a child depended even upon the hour in which he was born.

In magical papyri we are often told not to perform certain magical ceremonies on such and such days, the idea being that on these days hostile powers will make them to be powerless, and that gods mightier than those to which the petitioner would appeal will be in the ascendant. There have come down to us, fortunately, papyri containing copies of the Egyptian calendar, in which each third of every day for three hundred and sixty days of the year is marked lucky or unlucky, and we know from other papyri why certain days were lucky or unlucky, and why others were only partly so . . . It must be noted that the priests or magicians who drew up the calendar had good reasons for their classification of the days, as we may see from the following example. The 19th day of Thoth is, in the above list, marked wholly lucky, i.e., each third of it is lucky, and the papyrus Sallier IV also marks it wholly lucky, and adds the reason: "It is a day of festival in heaven and upon earth in the presence of Râ. It is the day when flame was hurled upon those who followed the boat containing the shrine of the gods; and on this day the gods gave praises being content," etc. But in both lists the 26th day is marked wholly unlucky, the reason being, "This was the day of the fight between Horus and Set." They first fought in the form of men, then they took the form of bears, and in this state did battle with each other for three days and three nights. Isis aided Set when he was getting the worst in the fight, and Horus thereupon cut off his mother's head, which Thoth transformed by his words of power into that of a cow and put on her body. On this day offerings are to be made to Osiris and Thoth, but work of any kind is absolutely forbidden. The calendars of lucky and unlucky days do not, however, always agree as to a given day. Thus in the list given above the 20th day of Thoth is marked wholly unlucky, but in the papyrus Sallier IV it is wholly lucky, but the reader is told not to do any work in it, nor to slay oxen, nor to receive a stranger; on this day the gods who are in the following of Râ slew the rebels. Concerning the fourth day of the next month, Paophi, the papyrus Sallier IV says, "Go not forth from thy house from any side of it; whosoever is born on this day shall die of the disease *aat*." Concerning the fifth day it says, "Go not forth from thy house from any side of it, and hold no intercourse with women. This is the day wherein all things were performed in the divine presence, and the majesty of the god Menthu was satisfied therein. Whosoever is born on this day shall die of excessive venery." Concerning the ninth day it says, "Whosoever is born on this day shall die of old age," and concerning the fifteenth, "Go not forth from thy dwelling at eventide, for the serpent Uatch, the son of the god, goeth forth at this time, and misfortunes follow him; whosoever shall see him shall lose his eye straightway." Again, the twenty-sixth day of Paophi was a lucky day for making the plan of a house; on the fifth day of Hathor no fire was to be kindled in the house; on the sixteenth day it was forbidden to listen to songs of joy because on this day Isis and Nephthys wept for Osiris at Abydos; a man born on the twenty-third day would die by drowning; and so on. But to the three hundred and sixty days given in the calendars of lucky and unlucky days must be added the five epagomenal days which were considered to be of great importance and had each its peculiar name. On the first Osiris was born, on the second Heru-ur (Aroueris), on the third Set, on the fourth Isis, and on the fifth Nephthys; the first, third, and fifth of these days were unlucky, and no work of any kind was to be undertaken on them. The rubric which refers to these days states that whosoever knoweth their names shall never suffer from thirst, that he shall never be smitten down by disease, and that the goddess Sekhet shall never take possession of him; it also directs that figures of the five gods mentioned above shall be drawn with unguent and *ânti* scent upon a piece of fine linen, evidently to serve as an amulet.

From the life of Alexander the Great by Pseudo-Callisthenes we learn that the Egyptians were skilled in the art of casting nativities, and that knowing the exact moment of the birth of a man they proceeded to construct his horoscope. Nectanebus employed for the purpose a tablet made of gold and silver and acacia wood, to which were fitted three belts. Upon the outer belt was Zeus with the thirty-six *decani* surrounding him; upon the second the twelve signs of the Zodiac were represented; and upon the third the sun and moon. He set the tablet upon a tripod, and then emptied out of a small box upon it models of the seven stars that were in the belts, and put into the middle belt eight precious stones; these he arranged in the places wherein he supposed the planets which they represented would be at the time of the birth of Olympias, and then told her fortune from them. But the use of the horoscope is much older than the time of Alexander the Great, for to a Greek horoscope in the British Museum is attached "an introductory letter from some master of the art of astrology to his pupil, named Hermon, urging him to be very exact and careful in his application of the laws which the ancient Egyptians, with their laborious devotion to the art, had discovered and handed down to posterity." Thus we have good reason for assigning the birthplace of the horoscope to Egypt. In connexion with the horoscope must be mentioned the "sphere" or "table" of Democritus as a means of making predictions as to life and death. In a magical papyrus we are told to "ascertain in what month the sick man took to his bed, and the name he received at his birth. Calculate the [course of] the moon, and see how many periods of thirty days have elapsed; then note in the table the number of days left over, and if the number comes in the upper part of the table, he will live, but if in the lower part, he will die."

Both from the religious and profane literature of Egypt we learn that the gods and man in the future life were able at will to assume the form of any animal, or bird, or plant, or living thing, which they pleased, and one of the greatest delights to which a man looked forward was the possession of that power. This is proved by the fact that no less than twelve of the chapters of the Book of the Dead are devoted to providing the deceased with the words of power, the recital of which was necessary to enable him to transform himself into a "hawk of gold", a "divine hawk", "the governor of the sovereign princes", "the god who giveth light in the darkness", a lotus, the god Ptah, a *bennu* bird (*i.e.*, phoenix), a heron, a "living soul", a swallow, the serpent Sata, and a crocodile; and another chapter enabled him to transform himself into "whatever form he pleaseth". Armed with this power he could live in the water in the form of a crocodile, in the form of a serpent he could glide over the rocks and ground, in the form of the birds mentioned above he could fly through the air, and soar up and perch himself upon the bow of the boat of Râ, in the

form of the lotus he had mastery over the plants of the field,
and in the form of Ptah he became "more powerful than the
lord of time, and shall gain the mastery over millions of
years". The *bennu* bird, it will be remembered, was said to
be the "soul of Râ", and by assuming this form the
deceased identified himself with Khepera, the great god
of creation, and thus acquired the attributes of the soul of
the Sun-god. In the Elysian Fields he was able to assume
any form and to swim and fly to any distance in any
direction. It is noteworthy that no beast of the field or
wild animal is mentioned as a type of his possible transformations into animals.

Now the Egyptians believed that as the souls of the
departed could assume the form of any living thing or
plant, so the "gods", who in many respects closely re-
sembled them, could and did take upon themselves the
forms of birds and beasts; this was the fundamental idea of
the so-called "Egyptian animal worship", which provoked
the merriment of the cultured Greek, and drew down upon
the Egyptians the ridicule and abuse of the early Christian
writers. But if the matter be examined closely its apparent
stupidity disappears. The Egyptians paid honour to certain
birds, and animals, and reptiles, because they considered
that they possessed certain of the characteristics of the gods
to whom they made them sacred. The bull was a type of the
strength and procreative power of the god of reproduction
in nature, and the cow was the type of his female counterpart; every sacred animal and living thing possessed some
quality or attribute which was ascribed to some god, and as
each god was only a form of Râ, the quality or attribute
ascribed to him was that of the Sun-god himself. The
educated Egyptian never worshipped an animal as an
animal, but only as an incarnation of a god, and the

reverence paid to animals in Egypt was in no way different from that paid to the king, who was regarded as "divine" and as an incarnation of Râ the Sun-god, who was the visible symbol of the Creator. The relation of the king to Râ was identical with that of Râ to God. The Hebrews, Greeks, and Romans never understood the logical conception which underlay the reverence with which the Egyptians regarded certain animals, and as a result they grossly misrepresented their religion. The ignorant people, no doubt, often mistook the symbol for what it symbolized, but it is wrong to say that the Egyptians worshipped animals in the ordinary sense of the word, and this fact cannot be too strongly insisted on. Holding the views he did about transformations there was nothing absurd in the reverence which the Egyptian paid to animals. When a sacred animal died the god whom it represented sought out another animal of the same species in which to renew his incarnation, and the dead body of the animal, inasmuch as it had once been the dwelling-place of a god, was mummified and treated in much the same way as a human body after death, in order that it might enjoy immortality. These views seem strange, no doubt, to us when judged by modern ideas, but they formed an integral part of the religious beliefs of the Egyptians, from the earliest to the latest times. What is remarkable, however, is the fact that, in spite of invasions, and foreign wars, and internal dissensions, and external influences of all kinds, the Egyptians clung to their gods and the sometimes childish and illogical methods which they adopted in serving them with a conservatism and zeal which have earned for them the reputation of being at once the most religious and most superstitious nation of antiquity. Whatever literary treasures may be brought to light in the future as the result of excavations in Egypt, it is most improbable that we shall ever receive from that country any ancient Egyptian work which can properly be classed among the literature of atheism or freethought; the Egyptian might be more or less religious according to his nature and temperament, but, judging from the writings of his priests and teachers which are now in our hands, the man who was without religion and God in some form or other was most rare, if not unknown.

GLOSSARY

Abydos. According to legend, the head of Osiris was buried at Abydos. Abydos became a sacred site. A festival was held there. Before the building of the pyramids, it was the burial place (necropolis) of kings and nobles.

Ahmose. Ahmose was a Theban prince, grandson of Queen Tetisheri. He completed the expulsion of the Hyksos begun by his father, Sekenenre Tao II, and re-united Egypt, starting the 18th Dynasty.

Akhenaton. Ahmose was the late 18th Dynasty pharaoh who abandoned the worship of the old gods in favor of Aton, the sun disc, and founded a new capital at El Amarna.

Alexander I of Macedon. Alexander I of Macedon (Alexander the Great) conquered Egypt in 332 BC. This was part of his conquest of the entire Persian Empire. He founded the city of Alexandria. He died in 323 BC. His body was taken to a tomb in Alexandria.

Amen (Amun, Amon). Originally, Amen was an obscure and indistinct god – the Hidden One was one of his epithets – he amalgamated with Re and became Amen-Re, great ruler of Thebes, and just about everyplace else. Lord of the silent, ruler of Karnak. His sacred animals were the goose and the curly-horned ram. He was also depicted as a human figure, sometimes with a ram's head.

Amenemhat. There were four Amenemhats in the 12th Dynasty. The dark-gray mud-brick pyramid of Amenemhat III at Dahshur is known as the Black Pyramid.

Amenhotep. There were three Amenhoteps in the 18th Dynasty. Akhenaton was for a time Amenhotep IV before he changed his name along with his religion. Amenhotep III, his father, is also known as "the Magnificent."

Amnit. Amnit was the Crocodile-headed monster who stood behind the scales in the Hall of Justice and devoured the souls of those who failed the Judgment of Osiris.

Ankhesenamen. Ankhesenamen was the Queen of Tutankhamen, third daughter of Akhenaton and Nefertiti. She had two female children, both of whom were stillborn. She disappeared shortly after the death of her husband, when the throne was taken over by Ay, one of his courtiers. Her ultimate fate is unknown.

Anubis. Anubis was the God of cemeteries and patron of embalming. He escorted the souls of the dead to the Judgment. His sacred animal was the jackal or a wild dog (his representations are not clear).

Apophis. Apophis was the Serpent deity of darkness and enemy of Re. In one version of the tale, Apophis attacked the boat of Re as it passed through the realms of darkness before its journey across the sky and had to be defeated by Set.

Aton. Aton was Akhenaton's "sole god" For a brief period he was identified with Re and shown as human with a falcon's head, but, eventually, all anthropomorphic representations were abandoned in favor of a sun disk with rays ending in human hands that held out the sign of life to his son, Akhenaton, and the latter's family.

Atum. In the Egyptian creation myth. Atum was the first god who stood on the hill Ben-Ben.

Ay (Aye). Ay was Tutankhamen's short-reigned, non-royal successor, who took the throne after the young king died without issue. His unfinished tomb is in the West Valley of the Kings.

Bes

Bastet. Bastet was the Cat goddess of Bubastis. She was shown as a woman with a cat's head An amiable deity who shared many of the attributes of Hathor.

Ben-Ben. Ben-Ben was a hill rose up out of the waters, in the Egyptian creation myth. Obelisks are a representations of Ben-Ben.

Bes. Bes was depicted as a bow-legged dwarf and always full face (This was most unusual in Egyptian art). A jolly god, who looked after women in childbirth and the pleasures of the bedchamber.

Cheops. Cheops was the Greek form of Khufu.

Chephren. Chephren was the Greek form of Khafre.

Djoser (Zoser). Djoser was the 3rd Dynasty Builder of the Step Pyramid at Sakkara. This Pyramid is thought to be the world's first great construction in stone.

Dynasties. Egyptian dating is described in terms of ruling families – dynasties. In 270 BC a historian, Manetho, wrote a history of Egypt giving the number of dynasties, the number of kings, their names and the length

First Intermediate Period. The first Intermediate Period began about the time of the 7th and 8th dynasties, 2181- 2125 BC. The Old Kingdom state collapsed as Egypt simultaneously suffered political failure and environmental disaster. There was famine, civil disorder and a rise in the death rate. The climate of Northeast Africa became dryer, combined with low inundations of the Nile.

God's Wives of Amen. The God's Wives of Amen are also called the Adorers of the God, these women, some of whom were Saite princesses, occupied the position of high priestess of Amen at Thebes during the Late Period dynasties. Their tomb chapels are located within the temple enclosure of Medinet Habu.

Harkhuf. Harkhuf was one of the adventurous princes of Elephantine (Abu) during the 6th Dynasty who led caravans into Africa in search of the exotic treasures the Egyptians enjoyed – including a dancing pygmy. His tomb is at Aswan.

Hapy. Hapy was the god of the innundation, this was the annual flood which made the Nile area fertile. Hapy was shown as a man with a pot belly, shown with water plants.

Hathor. Hathor was the daughter of the sun god, Re. A benevolent goddess, patroness of love and beauty music and pleasure, and one of the guardians of the dead. The cow was her sacred animal and she is sometimes shown as a human female with the ears of a cow at other times as wholly a cow.

Hathor

Hatshepsut. Hatshepsut was the Daughter of Thutmose I of the 18th Dynasty. She was the wife of Thutmose II and she co-ruled as king with her nephew, Thutmose III. Scholars are still arguing about the precise

Isis

relationship between Hatshepsut and Thutmose III. While she lived he was certainly the lesser of the two kings, and at some time after her death he destroyed or usurped many of her monuments; but the virulent hatred he was supposed to have felt for his aunt may be only a romantic theory. The magnificent temple at Deir el Bahari on the west bank at Luxor is her mortuary monument.

Horus. Horus was one of the greatest and most confusing of Egyptian gods. As the son of Osiris and Isis, he fought his murderous uncle, Set, for the kingship. He was also a sun god, known as Horakhte, Horns of the Horizon. He was shown as a falcon or falcon-headed human. The Egyptian king was the "Horns," until he died and became an "Osiris."

Horemheb. Horemheb was the last ruler of the 18th Dynasty. He was the non-royal successor of Ay He was not related to the previous Thutmosid royal house, whose last scion was Tutankhamen.

Hyksos. The Hyksos were the line of western-asiatic rulers of northern Egypt during the 15th and 16th dynasties (c. 1648-1539 BC). They were driven out by Ahmose, king of Thebes. The word means "rulers of foreign countries."

Isis. Isis was the wife of Osiris, mother of Horus. She was the ideal wife, tracking down the body of her murdered husband and restoring it to life; and the ideal mother, often shown nursing the child on her lap. Always one of the great goddesses of Egypt, her cult became very popular in the later period and spread throughout the Roman empire.

Kha. Kha was an architect whose remarkable intact 18th Dynasty tomb was found at Deir el Medina.

Khafre. Khafre was the 4th Dynasty Builder of the Second Pyramid and probably the Sphinx, which is believed to be a portrait of him.

Khepri. Khepri, or 'He Who is Coming into Being', was a god of creation, the movement of the sun, and rebirth. Khepri was shown as a man with the head of a scarab beetle

Khufu. Khufu was the 4th
Dynasty predecessor, probably father, of Khafre;
builder of the Great Pyramid.

Khnum. Khnum was one of
the Creator gods who mod-
eled the ka of the newborn
baby on his potter's wheel.
Khnum's sacred animal
was the ram.

Maat. Maat's name is usually
translated as "truth". She
was the daughter of Re,
and it was against her symbol, a feather, that the
heart of the deceased was
weighed at the Judgment.
Maat is usually depicted as
an attractive lady with a feather on her head.

Kha

Menes. Traditionally, Menes was the the first king of a united
Egypt, who began the 1st Dynasty

Menkaure (Mycerinos). Menkaure was the 4th Dynasty Builder of
the third and smallest pyramid at Giza.

Middle Kingdom. The Middle Kingdom began with the reuni-
fication of the country under Mentuhotep I who defeated the kings
of Herakleopolis. He assumed the title Uniter of the Two Lands.
His mortuary complex at Dayr al-Bahri was the architectural
inspiration for Hatshepsut's temple which was built alongside
some 500 years later. The Middle Kingdom fell because of the
weakness of its later kings, which lead to Egypt being invaded by
an Asiatic, desert people called the Hyksos. These invaders made
themselves kings and held the country for more than two centuries.
The word Hyksos goes back to an Egyptian phrase meaning "ruler
of foreign lands". The Hyksos sacked the old capital of Memphis
and built their capital at Avaris in Lower Egypt. The Jewish
historian, Josephus, depicted the new rulers as sacrilegious invaders who despoiled the land but with the exception of the title
Hyksos they presented themselves as Egyptian kings and appear to
have been accepted as such. They tolerated other lines of kings
within the country, both those of the 17th dynasty and the various
minor Hyksos who made up the 16th dynasty.

Montuhotep (Mentuhotep) There were several Montuhoteps. The greatest was Montuhotep II, who began the 11th Dynasty and reunited the country as the Middle Kingdom after the 1st Intermediate Period. The remains of his remarkable mortuary temple lie next to that of Hatshepsut at Deir el Bahari, Luxor.

Min. Min was a god of fertility Min was shown as a man with a big phallus.

Montu (Mentu). Montu was a war god. Montu's sacred animals were the falcon and the ram.

Nefertari. Nefertari was the chief wife of Ramses II, whose beautifully decorated and recently restored tomb is located in the Valley of the Queens.

Nefertiti. Nefertiti was the Queen of Akhenaton, known to the world from her exquisite painted-limestone portrait head found at El Amarna.

Neith. Neith was a warrior goddess. She was shown in human form. her symbol was a bow and crossed arrows.

Nekhbet. Nekhbet was the Predynastic vulture (and mother) goddess of a portion of Upper Egypt, became the protector of the king in Dynastic Egypt. Nekhbet eventually came to symbolize the White Crown of Upper Egypt.

Nephthys. Nephthys was the sister of Osiris and Isis, wife of her brother, Set. Regardless of her marriage, she took the side of her brother, Osiris, during the conflict between evil Set and good Osiris.

New Kingdom. After the Second Intermediate period, Egypt was unified again under the New Kingdom. This lasted from the 18th dynasty (1550-1295 BC) up to the 20th dynasty (1186 – 1069 BC). The population increased from 1.5 to between 2.5 and 5 million. A third intermediate period followed during which there was dynastic confusion and foreign invasion.

Nubia. Nubia was the land immediately south of Upper Egypt which is Northern Sudan today. In the language of Ancient Egypt, Nubia means 'Land of Gold'. Gold and Amethysts were mined there. Nubia was also called – Upper & Lower Nubia, Kush, Land of Kush, Te-Nehesy, Nubadae, Napata, or the Kingdom of Meroei. The NubiaÕs most prosperous period was that of the kingdom of Kush, which endured from about 800 BC to about 320 AD.

Nun. Nun was the dark waters of chaos, in the Egyptian creation myth. Nun was shown as a man carrying a boat.

Nut. Nut was the Sky goddess. Her body spanned the heavens; she swallowed the sun each night and gave birth to it each morning.

Nut was the younger child of Shu and Tefnut. Nut and Geb had four children: Osiris, Isis, Seth and Nephthys.

Old Kingdom. The Old Kingdom began when Egypt was united. Before the first dynasty Egypt was in fact two lands. Tradition credits the unification to Menes. He was known as the first mortal king of Egypt. The Greek historian Herodotus, records that this king founded the capital, Memphis, by damming the Nile to reclaim land for the city. The period of pyramid building was during the 3rd to the 6th dynasties. the Old Kingdom state collapsed during the 7th and 8th dynasties (2181- 2125 BC).

Osiris. According to legend he was a primeval king of Egypt who brought peace and plenty. Murdered by his jealous brother, Set, he was revived by his sister-wife, Isis, who bore him a (very) posthumous son, Horus. The gods appointed him king of the Afterworld and he presided over the judgment which had to be passed before a dead man or woman could enter into eternal life.

Persian Empire. The Persian Empire conquered Egypt in 525 BC. The Persian Empire was itself conquered by Alexander I of Macedon.

Ptah. Ptah was the Patron of craftsmen and one of several creator gods. He is easy to identify because his body is shrouded like a mummy, he wears a curious sort of skull-cap and carries a combination of sceptres. His home base was Memphis.

Re (Ra). Re was the sun god par excellence who became amalgamated with Amen and, as Amen-Re, was top god of Egypt during and after the 18th Dynasty. He was depicted as a man with a hawk head crowned by a sun disk.

Ramses (Rameses, Ramesses) There were eleven Ramses, but the two who are most interesting are: Ramses II, builder of Abu Simbel and innumerable other temples; and Ramses III, whose mortuary temple is at Medinet Habu.

Ramses

Ramose. Ramose was one of the high officials of Amenhotep III and Akhenaton. His beautifully decorated tomb at Gurneh is a popular tourist attraction.

Saite Princesses. The Saite Princesses were princesses of the Kingdom of Sais. Some of the God's Wives of Amen who are also called
the Adorers of the God, were Saite princesses. The God's Wives of
Amen occupied the position of high priestess of Amen at Thebes
during the Late Period dynasties. Their tomb chapels are located
within the temple enclosure of Medinet Habu. The Saite princess
Shepenwepet was one of the God's Wives of Amen.

Second Intermediate Period. The Second Intermediate Period
followed the Middle Kingdom which fell when Egypt was invaded by an Asiatic, desert people called the Hyksos. These
invaders made themselves kings and held the country for more
than two centuries. The word Hyksos goes back to an Egyptian
phrase meaning "ruler of foreign lands". The Jewish historian
Josephus (1st century AD) depicted the new rulers as sacrilegious
invaders who despoiled the land but with the exception of the title
Hyksos they presented themselves as Egyptian kings and appear
to have been accepted as such. They tolerated other lines of kings
within the country, both those of the 17th dynasty and the various
minor Hyksos who made up the 16th dynasty. One of these was a
new line of native rulers was developed in Thebes. These Theban
rulers controlled the area from Elephantine (Abu) in the south, to
Abydos in the middle of the country. The early rulers made no
attempt to challenge the Hyksos but an uneasy truce existed
between them. However, the later rulers rose against the Hyksos
and a number of battles were fought. King Tao II, also know as
Seqenenre, was probably killed in one of these battles since his
mummy shows evidence of terrible head wounds. It was to be one
of his sons Ahmose, the founder of the 18th dynasty, who was to
expel the Hyksos from Egypt.

Sekenenre Tao II. Sekenenre Tao II was a courageous but
unfortunate ruler of Thebes at
the end of the 17th Dynasty
who began the struggle against
the Hyksos – a people of Asiatic
origin who had occupied Lower
Egypt for over 100 years. His
mummy shows the marks of
horrible wounds, and it is assumed he died in battle. He was
the son of Queen Tetisheri, who
was regarded as the grand
matriarch of the 18th Dynasty

Sekenenre

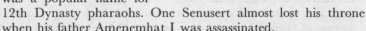

Sekhmet. Sekhmet was the lioness-headed warrior goddess. Many statues of her have been found around the Temple of Mut at Karnak.

Seshat. Seshat was the Goddess of writing.

Senusert (Senwosret, Sesostris, Usertsen). Senusert was a popular name for

Sekhmet

12th Dynasty pharaohs. One Senusert almost lost his throne when his father Amenemhat I was assassinated.

Seti (old form, Sethos). Seti means Man of Set. The name of two pharaohs of the 19th Dynasty the foremost being Seti I, whose temple at Luxor was the scene of one of Ramses and David's more unlucky encounters. His mummy was found in the Deir el Bahari cache. It is relatively well-preserved.

Set. Set was the bitter enemy and murderer of his brother, Osiris. After the child Horus (son of Isis and the temporarily reanimated Osiris) came to manhood, he fought his uncle for the

Senemut

Seti

kingship. It was eventually awarded to Horus, but Set was neither condemned nor punished; Re apparently forgave him and awarded him his own place as a god of storm and chaos. Set is thus, in one sense, a force of evil opposed to the noble Osiris; yet he was the patron of the royal house during the 19th dynasty. Although confusing, it is typical of Egyptian theology.

Senenmut (Senmut). Senenmut was one of the female pharoah Hatshepsut's favored officials, who was responsible for many of her monuments. He may have been her lover.

Seshat. Seshat was the goddess of writing and measurement. Seshat was shown as a woman wearing a panther skin dress and a star headdress.

Shepenwepet. Shepenwepet was one of the God's Wives of Amen, whose reburial with that of three other Saite princesses was found at Deir el Medina.

Shu. Shu was the god of the air. Shu was created when Atum coughed.

Smenkhkare. Smenkhkare was a mysterious, short-lived king, predecessor of Tutankhamen, who was probably his brother or half brother.

Sneferu. Sneferu was the first king of the 4th Dynasty. He built two of the greatest pyramids in Egypt, at Dahshur. His third one at Medum may have been started by his predecessor.

Sobek. Sobek was the crocodile god. His centers of worship were in the Fayum and at Kom Ombo in Upper Egypt.

Sobek

Tausert

Tausert (Taweret, Thoueris). Tausert was the protector of women in childbirth. For some reason she is always shown as a monstrous looking, pregnant hippopotamus. Also the name of the queen of Seti II, who ruled briefly after him as pharaoh.

Tefnut. Tefnut was the goddess of moisture, who was married to Shu. They had two children, Geb, the god of the earth and Nut, the goddess of the sky.

Tetisheri. Tetisheri was the Queen of Senakhtenre Tao I, mother of Sekenenre Tao II, grandmother of Ahmose I. Her hidden tomb at Dra Abu el Naga on the west bank at Luxor was found by Radcliffe Emerson in 1900.

Thoth. Thoth was the God of wisdom and learning, the divine scribe. He sometimes is shown as a man with the head of an ibis, one of his sacred animals. Otherwise depicted as a baboon.

Tiye (Tiyi, Ti). Tiye was the Queen during the later 18th Dynasty and chief wife of Amenhotep III; mother of the heretic pharaoh, Akhenaton.

Thebes. Thebes was the Greek name for the city of Wast

Thutmose. There were four 18th Dynasty pharaohs named Thutmose. The most famous was Thutmose III. He was the warrior king, who extended the boundaries of the Egyptian Empire to the Euphrates.

Thuyu. Thuyu was the non-royal mother of Queen Tiye. See Yuya and Akhenaton.

Tutankhamun. Tutankhamun was a successor of Akhenaton, possibly his son. His name was originally Tutankhaton. He came to the throne at approximately nine years of age and married his (probably) half-sister, Ankhesenpaaton/Ankhesenamen. Shortly thereafter he changed his name, as did his wife, to honor Amen instead of the heretic's god, Aton, and abandoned Akhenaton's religious beliefs. He died at the age of 18, cause unknown (the theory that he may have been murdered is provocative but completely unsubstantiated) and was buried in the Valley of the Kings. The discovery of his tomb in 1922 was the archaeological sensation of the 20th century.

Tutankhamun

Wast. Wast was the ancient name for the city of Thebes

Yuya. Yuya was the non-royal father of Queen Tiye and husband of Thuyu. His and his wife's joint tomb was found virtually intact in the Valley of the Kings in 1905.

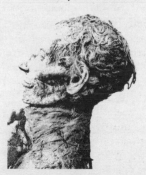

Yuya

SOURCES AND ACKNOWLEDGMENTS

The editor has made every effort to locate all persons having any rights in the selections appearing in this anthology and to secure permission from the holders of these rights. Any queries regarding the use of material should be addressed to the editor c/o the publishers.

Part One: The Age of the Pyramids

Anonymous, "The Life of Methen", adapted from *Ancient Records of Egypt* Vol I, translated and edited by James Henry Breasted, University of Chicago Press, 1906

Anonymous, "The Expeditions of Snefru", adapted from *Ancient Records of Egypt* Vol I, translated and edited by James Henry Breasted, University of Chicago Press, 1906

Anonymous, "The Dead Pharaoh Ascends to Heaven and Other Pyramid Spells": spells 309, 217, 476 extracted from *Development of Religion and Thought in Ancient Egypt*, J.H. Breasted, 1912; spells 220 and 222 extracted from *The Ancient Pyramid Texts*, trans. R.O. Faulkner, Clarendon Press, 1969.

Debhen, "Pharaoh Menkaure Insepcts the Pyramids at Giza", adapted from *Ancient Records of Egypt* Vol I, translated and edited by James Henry Breasted, University of Chicago Press, 1906

Harkhuf, "The Journeys of a Caravan-Conductor", adapted from *Ancient Records of Egypt* Vol I, translated and edited by James Henry Breasted, University of Chicago Press, 1906

Henku, "I Gave Bread to the Hungry . . .", adapted from *Ancient Records of Egypt* Vol I, translated and edited by James Henry Breasted, University of Chicago Press, 1906

Hotep, "Tomb Dedication", extracted from *Ancient Records of Egypt* Vol I, translated and edited by James Henry Breasted, University of Chicago Press, 1906

Hotephiryakhet, "I Will Commend Thee to the God", adapted from *Ancient Records of Egypt* Vol I, translated and edited by James Henry Breasted, University of Chicago Press, 1906

Mernuterseteni, "The Sadness of the Pharaoh Neferikare", adapted from *Ancient Records of Egypt* Vol I, translated and edited by James Henry Breasted, University of Chicago Press, 1906

Pepi II, "Pepi II Demands to See the Dancing Dwarf", adapted from *Ancient Records of Egypt* Vol I, translated and edited by James Henry Breasted, University of Chicago Press, 1906

Ptah-hotep, "The Maxims of Ptah-hotep", extracted fom *The Sacred Books and Early Literature of the East*, Vol II, Charles F. Horne, Parke, Austin & Lipscomb, 1917.

Sebni, "The Recovery of a Father's Body from Negroes", adapted from *Ancient Records of Egypt* Vol I, translated and edited by James Henry Breasted, University of Chicago Press, 1906

Weni, "A Palace Conspiracy", "The War Against the Sand-Dwellers", "Weni Beseeches the King for a Limestone Sarcophagus", "The Building of a Pyramid", adapted from *Ancient Records of Egypt* Vol I, translated and edited by James Henry Breasted, University of Chicago Press, 1906

Zau, "Zau Builds a Tomb for His Beloved Father and Himself", adapted from *Ancient Records of Egypt* Vol I, translated and edited by James Henry Breasted, University of Chicago Press, 1906

Part Two: Chaos and Resurrection

Akhtoy, "The Instruction of the Pharaoh Amenemhet", extracted from *Egyptian Myth and Legend*, Donald A. Mackenzie, Gresham Publishing, 1907

Anonymous, "A Dispute over Suicide", trans. The Old Society for Old Testament Study in Documents from *Old Testament Times*, ed. D. Winton Thomas, Harper & Row, 1961. Copyright © 1958 Thomas Nelson & Sons Ltd.

Anonymous, "The Tale of the Eloquent Peasant", extracted from *Archaeology and The Bible*, George A. Barton, American Sunday School, 1920

Anonymous, "Coffin Texts": spells 33 and 404 adapted from *The Ancient Egyptian Coffin Texts*, Vol 1, trans R.O. Faulkner, 1973; spells 74, 330, 714 extracted from *Myth and Symbol in Ancient Egypt*, R.T. Rundle Clark, 1959

Anonymous, "The Wonders in the Wadi Hammamat", adapted from *Ancient Records of Egypt* Vol II, translated and edited by James Henry Breasted, University of Chicago Press, 1906

Anonymous, "The Prophecies of Nerferti", trans. R.O. Faulkner, in *The Literature of Ancient Egypt*, ed. William Kelly Simpson et al, Yale University Press, 1972. Copyright © 1972 Yale University

Anonymous, "Horus and the Pig", *The Egyptian Coffin texts*, A. de Buck, 1918

Anonymous, "Hymn to the Nile", *The Library of Original Sources*, ed. Oliver Thatcher, University Research Extension Company, 1907

Dua-Khety, "The Trades in Egypt" (originally, "The Satire on the Trades"), trans. W.K. Simpson in *The Literature of Ancient Egypt*, ed. William Kelly Simpson et al, Yale University Press, 1972. Copyright © 1972 Yale University

Anonymous, "Senusret III Conquers Nubia", adapted from *Ancient Records of Egypt* Vol. II, translated and edited by James Henry Breasted, University of Chicago Press, 1906

Harrure, "Mining in Sinai", adapted from *Ancient Records of Egypt* Vol II, translated and edited by James Henry Breasted, University of Chicago Press, 1906

Henu, "Myrrh, Soldiers, Wells", adapted from *Ancient Records of Egypt* Vol. II, translated and edited by James Henry Breasted, University of Chicago Press, 1906

Heqanakhte, "Famine" and "Mistreatment of a Stepmother", adapted from *The Heqanakhte Papers and Other Early Middle Kingdom Documents*, T.G.H James, Metropolitian Museum of Art, 1962

Kheti, "Aristocratic Childhood", adapted from *Ancient Records of Egypt* Vol. II, translated and edited by James Henry Breasted, University of Chicago Press, 1906

Meryibre Khety, "The Instruction for King Merykare", trans. The Old Society for Old Testament Study in Documents from *Old Testament Times*, ed. D. Winton Thomas, Harper & Row, 1961. Copyright © 1958 Thomas Nelson & Sons Ltd.

Sinuhe, "The Flight of the Courtier Sinuhe", adapted from *Ancient Records of Egypt* Vol I, translated and edited by James Henry Breasted, University of Chicago Press, 1906

Sinuhe, "The Return of Sinuhe to Egypt", extracted from "The Story of Sinuhe", trans. W.K. Simpson in *The Literature of Ancient Egypt*, ed. William Kelly Simpson et al, Yale University Press, 1972. Copyright © 1972 Yale University

Thuthotep, "Transport of a Giant Statue", adapted from *Ancient Records of Egypt* Vol. II, translated and edited by James Henry Breasted, University of Chicago Press, 1906

Part III: Empire

Ahmose, son of Ebana, "The Expulsion of the Hyksos", "The Nubian War: Tuthmosis I Casts the First Lance", adapted from *Ancient Records of Egypt* Vol. II, translated and edited by James Henry Breasted, University of Chicago Press, 1906

Ahura, "Brother-Sister Incest", quoted *Internet Ancient History Sourcebook*, http://www.fordham.edu/halsall/ancient/asbook.html

Akhenaten, "The Akhenaten Revolution: The Hymn to Aten", trans. The Old Society for Old Testament Study in *Documents from Old Testament*

Times, ed. D. Winton Thomas, Harper & Row, 1961. Copyright © 1958 Thomas Nelson & Sons Ltd.

Amenemhab, "Tuthmosis III Hunts Elephants", "The Syrian Wars: Amenemhab Breaches the Wall of Kadesh", adapted from *Ancient Records of Egypt* Vol II, translated and edited by James Henry Breasted, University of Chicago Press, 1906.

Amenpanufer, "The Robbing of the Tomb of Sobekemsaf", quoted in *Judgment of the Pharaoh*, Joyce Tyldesley, Weidenfeld & Nicolson, 2000

Anonymous, "Spells for the Afterlife": Hymn to Osiris, spell 125 extracted from The Papyri of Ani, E.A. Wallis Budge, G.P. Putna's Sons, 1913; spells 30B, 1B, 27, 32, 44, 130, extracted from *The Ancient Egyptian Book of the Dead*, trans. Raymond O. Faulkner, British Museum Publications, 1985. Copyright © The Limited Editions Club, New York

Anonymous, "Rebellion in Kush", adapted from *Ancient Records of Egypt* Vol. II, translated and edited by James Henry Breasted, University of Chicago Press, 1906.

Anonymous, "Queen Hatshepsut's Expedition to Punt", adapted from *Ancient Records II*, Breasted

Anonymous, "Hymn of Victory", adapted from *Ancient Records II*, Breasted

Anonymous, "Amenhotep II Sacrifices Captives to Amun", adapted from *Ancient Records II*, Breasted

Anonymous, "The Teaching of Amenemope", trans. The Old Society for Old Testament Study in *Documents from Old Testament Times*, ed. D., Winton Thomas, Harper & Row, 1961. Copyright © 1958 Thomas Nelson & Sons Ltd

Anonymous, "Amenhotep III Builds His Mortuary Temple in Splendour", adapted from *Ancient Records II*, Breasted

Anonymous, "Wild Cattle Hunt", adapted from *Ancient Records II*, Breasted

Anonymous, "Massacre at Ibhet", adapted from *Ancient Records II*, Breasted

Anonymous, "Amenhotep III Constructs a Pleasure Lake for Queen Tiy", adapted from *Ancient Records II*, Breasted

Anonymous, "The Water in the Netherworld Hearkens to Him", adapted from *Ancient Records III*, Breasted

Anonymous, "Kadesh: The Poet's View", adapted from *Ancient Records II*, Breasted

Anonymous, "Great Rejoicing Has Arisen", trans. The Old Society for Old Testament Study in *Documents from Old Testament Times*, ed. D. Winton Thomas, Harper & Row, 1961. Copyright © 1958 Thomas Nelson & Sons Ltd

Anonymous, "Ramses II Finds the Necropolis Buildings in Ruins", adapted from *Ancient Records III*, Breasted

Anonymous, "Love Songs", nos 1–5 extracted from *The Literature of Ancient Egypt*, ed. William Kelly Simpson et al, Yale University Press, 1972. Copyright © 1972 Yale University; nos 6–13 extracted from *The Ancient East, No. V: Popular Literature in Ancient Egypt*, A. Wiedemann, David Hunt, 1902

Anonymous, "The Fate of an Unfaithful Wife" (originally "The Peasant Who Became King", extracted from *Egyptian Myth and Legend*, Donald A. Mackenzie, Gresham Publishing, 1907

Anonymous, "A Soldier's Lot", extracted from *The Literature of Ancient Egypt*, ed. William Kelly Simpson et al, Yale University Press, 1972. Copyright © 1972 Yale University.

Anonymous, "Prayer to Thot for Skill in Writing", extracted from *The Literature of Ancient Egypt*, William Kelly Simpson, Yale University Press, 1972, Copyright © Yale University.

Anonymous, "Prayer to Amun", extracted from *The Literature of Ancient Egypt*, William Kelly Simpson

Anonymous, "Out of Anarchy", adapted from *Ancient Records IV*, Breasted

Anonymous, "The Fight Against the Sea Peoples", adapted from *Ancient Records IV*, Breasted

Anonymous, "No One Can Rival Her", quoted in *Egypt's Golden Empire*, Joyce Tyldesley, Headline, 2001. Copyright © 2001 Lion Television and Joyce Tyldesley.

Anonymous, "Ten Days in the Life of an Egyptian Frontier Official", adapted from *Ancient Records III*, Breasted

Any, "Beware of a Woman Who is a Stranger", extracted from *Ancient Egyptian Literature, I*, Miriam Lichtheim, University of California Press, 1971

Court Recorder, "The Harem Conspiracy: The Plotters Try Magic to Kill Ramses III", "The Harem Conspirators: Their Crimes and Their Fate", "Tomb Robbers' Confession", adapted from *Ancient Records IV*, Breasted

Nebre, "A Prayer of Gratitude" (originally "A Penitential Psalm"), trans. The Old Society for Old Testament Study in *Documents from Old Testament Times*, ed. D. Winton Thomas, Harper & Row, 1961. Copyright © 1958 Thomas Nelson & Sons Ltd.

Horemheb, "Horemheb Delivers the Poor from Oppression", extracted from *Ancient Records of Egypt* Vol III, translated and edited by James Henry Breasted, University of Chicago Press, 1906.

Ramses IV, "The Gifts of Ramses III to the God Amun", adapted from *Ancient Records of Egypt* Vol. IV, translated and edited by James Henry Breasted, University of Chicago Press, 1906

Rekmire, "Duties of the Vizier", adapted from *Ancient Records II*, Breasted

Seti, "Beatings, Impalings and the Cutting Off of Ears", adapted from *Ancient Records III*, Breasted

Thanuny, "Megiddo", adapted from *Ancient Records II*, Breasted

Tuthmosis I, "Coronation Decree", adapted from *Ancient Records II*, Breasted

Various, "Collapse of Empire: Letters from the Syrian Frontier": letters from Officials of the City of Dunip and Rib-Addi nos 1–8 extracted from *Tell el Amarna Letters*, Hugo Winckler, Luzac & Co., 1896; letter from Abdiheba, trans. The Old Society for Old Testament Study in *Documents from Old Testament Times*, ed. D. Winton Thomas, Harper & Row, 1961.

518 SOURCES AND ACKNOWLEDGMENTS

Copyright © 1958 Thomas Nelson & Sons Ltd.; letter no. 9 by Rib-Addi, letters by Abi Milku and Yapahu extracted from *Amarna Letters*, ed. William L Moran, John Hopkins University Press, 1992

Wenamon, "An Egyptian Abroad", adapted from *Ancient Records III*, Breasted

Part IV

Amosis, "Robbery in a Vineyard", extracted from *Select Papyri II*, trans. A. S. Hunt and C.C. Edgar, Loeb Classical Library, Harvard University Press, 1934

Anonymous, "Floods in Thebes", adapted from *Ancient Records of Egypt* Vol IV, translated and edited by James Henry Breasted, University of Chicago Press, 1906

Anonymous, "The Nubian Invasion", adapted from *Ancient Records of Egypt* Vol IV, translated and edited by James Henry Breasted, University of Chicago Press, 1906

Anonymous, "The Battle of Carchemish", trans. The Old Society for Old Testament Study in *Documents from Old Testament Times*, ed. D. Winton Thomas, Harper & Row, 1961. Copyright © 1958 Thomas Nelson & Sons Ltd

Anonymous, "Shall Supply All That is Proper for a Freeborn Wife", extracted from *Select Papyri* I, trans. A.S. Hunt and C.C. Edgar, Loeb Classical Library, Harvard University Press, 1932

Anonymous, "The Sale of a Slave Girl", extracted from *Select Papyri I*, trans. A.S. Hunt and C.C. Edgar, Loeb Classical Library, Harvard University Press, 1932

Anonymous, "Compensations for Crimes", extracted from *Select Papyri II*, trans. A.S. Hunt and C.C. Edgar, Loeb Classical Library, Harvard University Press, 1934

Anonymous, "The Drinks Bill for a Wake", *Select Papyri I*, Hunt & Edgar

Anonymous, "Try Going from Place to Place", extracted from *Select Papyri II*, trans. A.S. Hunt and C.C. Edgar, Loeb Classical Library, Harvard University Press, 1934

Anonymous Police Officer, *Select Papyri II*, Hunt & Edgar

Anonymous, "Reward for Escaped Slave", *Select Papyri I*, Hunt & Edgar

Athanaeus, "The Magnificent Procession of Ptolemy II Philadelphus", quoted in *Readings in Ancient History*, I: Greece and the East, William Stearns Davis, Allyn & Bacon, 1946

Antony, Mark, "On Going to Bed With Cleopatra", quoted in *Treasury of the World's Greatest Letters*, ed. M. Lincoln Schuster, Simon & Schuster, 1948

Cicero, "Cleopatra in Rome", extracted from *Cicero: Selected Works*, trans. Michael Grant, Penguin 1970. Copyright © 1960, 1965, 1971 Michael Grant

Ctesicles, "I Beg You, O King", *Select Papyri II*, Hunt & Edgar.

Demophon, "Send Me Zenobius the Effeminate dancer", *Select Papyri I*, Hunt & Edgar

Dionysius, "Nor to Keep A Concubine or Boy", *Select Papyri I*, Hunt & Edgar

Dryton, "The Will of a Soldier", *Select Papyri I*, Hunt & Edgar

Hermias, "Arrangements for a Roman Tourist", trans. B.P. Grenfell, A.S. Hunt and J.G. Smyly in *Private Letters Pagan and Christian*, ed. Dorothy Brooke, Ernest Benn Ltd, 1929

Herodotus, "General Amasis Usurps the Throne", "The Persian Conquest of Egypt", "A Traveller's Egypt", "Exactly the Reverse of the Common Practice of Mankind", "Animal Sacrifice", "Religious Festivals", "Cats and Dogs", "Hunting Crocodiles on the Nile", "Mummification", extracted from *Histories*, trans. George Rawlinson, Murray, 1862

Isias, "But You Have Not Even Thought of Returning Home", trans G. Milligan in *Private Letters Pagan and Christian*, ed. Dorothy Brooke, Ernest Benn Ltd, 1929

Philista, "A Petition from A Scalded Woman", *Select Papyri II*, Hunt & Edgar

Pisicles, "One Man's Clothing", *Select Papyri I*, Hunt & Edgar

Plutarch, "How Cleopatra Bewitched Antony", *Lives of Illustrious Men*.

Theocritus, "Men, Clothes, Chattering", extracted from *They Saw It Happen in Classical Times*, B.K. Workman, Basic Blackwell & Mott, Ltd, 1964

Strabo, "Envoi", quoted in *Readings in Ancient History*, II: Rome and the West, William Stearns Davis, Allyn & Bacon, 1946

Yedoniah, "The Destruction of the Jewish Temple at Elephantine", trans. The Old Society for Old Testament Study in *Documents from Old Testament Times*, ed. D. Winton Thomas, Harper & Row, 1961. Copyright © 1958 Thomas Nelson & Sons Ltd